In memory of Rita Dillon
Pray for

OCCASIONAL SERMONS OF
RONALD A. KNOX

OCCASIONAL SERMONS

OF
RONALD A. KNOX

Edited, with an Introduction, by

PHILIP CARAMAN, S.J.

SHEED & WARD INC.

NEW YORK

Library of Congress Catalog Number: 60-14646

PRINTED IN GREAT BRITAIN

INTRODUCTION

As Mr Evelyn Waugh points out in his recently published Life,[1] Mgr Knox created a new and entirely original form of sermon. It was not a literary essay; it appealed to the intellect first, and was planned with a mounting force of argument and emphasis. There was only a brief sentence of exhortation, almost diffident but pungent. Both on the scheme and the detail greater labour was spent than on the preparation of his books. Each sentence was written, the emphasis and pauses were marked, any cuts bracketed off, words scored out and others substituted, on the typescript which unfailingly he carried with him into the pulpit. He was never known, at least in his later life, to preach even a short Sunday homily to a country congregation without a typescript. Sometimes he disappointed friends with whom he happened to be staying by his refusal to preach on insufficient notice. The long sermon had been out of vogue for many years before he established himself as the leading preacher for important or significant occasions. He had seldom more than twenty or twenty-five minutes in which to say all that the event required. Therefore he was compelled to prepare every word of a sermon with greater care than an essay which imposed no limitations of space. This is fortunate indeed for the editor, who is able to leave Mgr Knox's text untouched, for there are none of the repetitions of phrasing or ideas that make the sermons of spontaneous orators such tedious reading. While the sermons of an earlier generation of preachers are, in Mgr Knox's own phrase, "dead seaweed" almost before publication, his own are undated in style and, because they touch on personal and perennial problems, have a more enduring value than many of his books.

Rarely is there anything approaching rhetoric in these sermons, for Mgr Knox did not play on the emotions. But there are passages in which his customary restraint is relaxed, when the unfolding of tragedy and doctrine speeded his thought. For instance, in the second of his sermons on Blessed Philip Howard he can write: "When we call, as we called just now, on the names of those others, a Burleigh, a Drake, a Shakespeare, we know that we are only indulging in an exercise of rhetoric; our voices die away upon the faint echoes of the past. But when we call upon Philip Howard, we know that his voice is raised

[1] *The Life of Ronald Knox*, p. 241.

in answer to ours; that he, once so unsuccessful a courtier in the splendid world of Queen Elizabeth, is a courtier now amidst splendours which surpass all our human imagination." It is unusual to find such a peroration. Normally his sermons ended in a calmer phase of self-examination or with a reminder of Christian duty. It is this quality that makes his sermons acceptable to generations other than his own. One of the earliest sermons in this volume is the panegyric preached at the Requiem Mass of Fr Henry Harrington, his contemporary on the teaching staff of St Edmund's. It was spoken nearly thirty years ago, but it is as fresh and stimulating as the latest in this volume.

What is perhaps more remarkable is the uniqueness of each sermon. With the exception of certain sections in two centenary sermons, every sermon in this volume is unlike any other in construction and content. Moreover, I think there are very few allusions—to Blessed John Kemble's last pipe, for example—that occur more than once. While Mgr Knox often read the same essay to different societies on different occasions (he made no secret of this), when he was asked to preach to the same congregation a second or third time his sermon on each occasion was new. This is more noticeably illustrated in his sermons on St Philip Neri, preached at the London and Birmingham Oratories. They form perhaps one of the best portraits of the saint. Each is incomplete without the others and there is no overlapping.

The sermons in this group must have demanded even more exacting preparation than his purely pastoral sermons in the companion volume to this. Frequently his hearers must have been surprised by the precise knowledge he showed of the history of the parish or country-side, of topographical features of the district or of the lives of the priests who had served the church in which he was preaching. His knowledge is always accurate and always has a bearing on his argu-ment; he was never contented with the vague and safe references which an occasional preacher, less ready to spend time in preparation, might make without fear of being caught out. In all cases of centenary or jubilee sermons he worked local history into the larger canvas of the story of the Church in England; and in that story he showed the development of God's Providence.

While I was arranging these sermons for publication, it became clear to me that they form a unique commentary on the Church in England during the last hundred years, a Church "so often nearly retrieving her position but never quite" succeeding. The mystery of failure or half-success haunts him, not only in the story of the Church but in the history of the English martyrs, in the lives of the saints, in the conversion of Newman, in the tragedy of Philip Howard or Henry VI. Indeed there was a mystery to him both in personal failure and in the apparent failure of the Church, which followed the pattern of the Crucifixion and was an extension of it. The theme is most explicitly developed in the sermon on St Edward the Confessor. "When we venerate him", he said, "we venerate a failure"; yet St Edward is the one with whom we would rather be associated today in preference to any other person buried in Westminster Abbey. This was Providence working out the mystery of suffering in the lives of the saints; Providence as he experienced it, not as it was understood by Englishmen to whom it meant God arranging history as they themselves would have arranged it.

With a truthfulness that becomes apparent to readers, Mgr Knox stated that he had more regard for the susceptibilities of Catholic congregations than the newspaper critics of his books. The careful preparation that went into his sermons came from his essential humility of soul which reveals itself also in the perfectly natural manner in which he identifies himself with the people he is addressing. The "we" of his sermons is not the cliché of the orator; it is the unobtrusive link binding priest to people. When he gives an admonition he makes no distinction between himself and his hearers. Their difficulties are also his; anything that might sound unreal to them has some measure of unreality for himself—St Paul's phrase, for instance, about "always carrying around with us the death of our Lord Jesus Christ". That seems, he says, "so highflown and impractical to *us* half-hearted Christians of a later time". Unlike the orator, he was determined to grapple with such phrases until he had reduced them to terms that had meaning for his audience. There is always a sternly practical core in what he says. He was careful that his hearers should not go away saying "all very beautiful, all very edifying". He was a scholar, but far from the scholar who lived solely for his subject. Such a person he would have rejected as a mere fragment of a man dwelling in a shadow world. In his view a priest, who was also a scholar, cannot just love his subject; he must love people and must above all, like St Philip, love souls.

Still it is the scholarly discipline of his mind that makes Mgr Knox's sermons such a lasting joy to read. Only on one occasion, in the sermon preached to celebrate the Golden Jubilee of Campion Hall, does he overstate the terms of a contrast; but he has hardly done so, when he confesses to the fact.

His humility of approach is particularly noticeable in the sermons addressed to audiences of priests and ecclesiastical students. In a panegyric preached at Ware on St Edmund's day, 1956, nine months before his death, he spoke about St Edmund as the saint who, for the greater part of his life, was a "plain priest, *one of ourselves*". While "plain" was the last description any of Mgr Knox's friends would have applied to him, the phrase underlined his wish to be known above all, not as a writer or a prelate, but simply as a priest, for in his eyes all distinctions of ecclesiastical rank and honour were nothing compared with the levelling privilege of sacramental ordination. His uneasiness was clear when he addressed his fellow priests, but it did not make him shirk his duties as a preacher. He spoke strongly on the harm done by the unkindness of priests. "Kindliness, on the part of a parish priest, is or isn't there. He may be a man of ascetic life, regular in his prayers, an admirable diocesan official, but if he doesn't love his people, he isn't loved. . . . Tell yourself you've got to be everybody's friend, even if it's somebody who opposes your influence, somebody you've got to have rows with." Similarly, addressing Benedictine monks on the feast of their founder, he ends: "It will be a hard day for the Church, if the Black Monks, who are meant to hand on a message of peace to us others, lose the spirit of peace which is their inheritance." Another example occurs at the conclusion of his sermon on St Thomas Aquinas, perhaps one of the greatest sermons in this volume.

In the Introduction to the companion volume to this, I have written some paragraphs on Mgr Knox's spiritual teaching. It is perhaps more appropriate there, though this present volume is full of spiritual insight and wisdom. There is no sermon that is purely historical; and there are flashes of spiritual wisdom in the most unexpected places. It would be difficult, for example, to improve on his description of the virtue of simplicity as the "filter through which conflicting influences have to pass if they are to have the right effect on you". Much reflection must have gone into the sermon on St Benedict and into his analysis of the Benedictine *pax*, "an influence, an energy, an atmosphere which laps you round like health"; or into his examination of the role played by Jesuits in the universities of Europe. These are examples of Mgr Knox at his most brilliant; but there is hardly a sermon from which the reader will not be able to extract one or more passages to match them.

It is yet another facet of his humility that there seldom occurs a reference to himself. There is one brief autobiographical passage which describes his boyish enthusiasm when he attended the Aston Villa football ground. Unexpectedly it occurs in a sermon on the English Martyrs, heavenly spectators of our earthly contests, who are as partisan as football enthusiasts. They do not simply look on and wonder

which side will win. "Is that", he asks, "the common attitude of spectators . . .? That is not my memory of the days nearer thirty years ago
than I dare to think, when I used to watch football matches at the
Aston Villa ground. My memory is rather of a small boy, wearing a
claret and light-blue favour, who stood up on his seat and booed the
referee." In the sermon he preached at the enthronement of Archbishop Grimshaw of Birmingham, Mgr Knox could not resist pointing
out that he was born on the day the Archbishop's predecessor, Dr
Ilsley, was enthroned. But the reader will have to look hard for
further biographical material. There are a few suppressed vignettes,
usually in some protracted comparison. Certainly this passage from a
sermon on St Philip Neri evokes a picture of him at the Old Palace,
Oxford, trying to revive the dying embers of his fire in the Chaplain's
Room. "When a fire is in danger of going out, you will do no good
by aiming your bellows now at this point, now at that, blowing furious
blasts at the struggling flames, which only need that to extinguish them.
No, you must find out first of all, by a series of experiments, which is the
real focus that responds to your efforts, and then keep fanning that one
spot, quite gently, quite patiently, till the fire spreads all around. Rome
is the heart and focus of Christendom; and Philip could not have done
better service to his Master, than by fanning the dull embers that
seemed so unresponsive, there in Rome."

It is a rare example, for Mgr Knox was convinced that the preacher
should not obtrude himself into his subject. Those who were close to
Mgr Knox may be able to recognize other passages that are drawn
from his experience of life and persons; but there cannot be many. It is
only in his sermons on St Philip that he comes near to revealing his
inclinations in the spiritual life. It is not far-fetched to seek here his
ideals of the priesthood. As a humanist, with a love of letters, music and
friends, St Philip became his special study. It was the appeal of the saint
that brought him so frequently to the Oratory, not merely his wish to
oblige the Fathers who had given him a home in his first year as a
Catholic. He admired St Philip's simple intimacy with the supernatural,
his love of a jest, people and souls, his largeness of mind, the sharp
tang, as he called it, of his unwonted spirituality that "acted as a seasoning to the Tridentine experiment". While Philip could say with
Chremes in Terence's play, "I am a man, whatever is human is my
business", he would at the same time exploit with untiring zeal all the
possibilities that the world offered to make a man love God more.
It was for this reason that Mgr Knox thought that the saint had a
special message for our times.

When he preached at the Oratory or St Edmund's, Mgr Knox seems
to have felt in closer contact with his hearers than elsewhere. The final
sentences of his last sermon at St Edmund's form perhaps the most
poignant passage in this book. It was spoken shortly before he underwent the operation that failed to arrest the sickness that was shortly to
close his life. It is his adieu to the college and his testament to his priest
friends, his last message and a summary of what he had tried to achieve
since his ordination. "Nobody", he said, "who ever tried to do good
in the world has managed to get through life without experiencing
frustration and disappointment. Least of all a priest, who has to work
on the stubborn soil of men's souls, in a world always ready to criticize,
limited by the authority of human, and not always wise, superiors.
He will find his plans set aside, his advice neglected, cold water poured
on his aspirations. He will take that well, precisely in so far as he has
learned, from the outset, to put God's will in the foreground, not the
background, of his world-picture. Force yourself, in your prayer, to see
his will as the only thing that matters; be prepared to see all the good
you meant and tried to do done by some other man, on the ruins of
your failure. Then, in life and in death, you will be able to call yourself
an Edmundian."

This volume includes all the sermons that can be conveniently
labelled "occasional". They fall into three groups—saints, occasions,
and panegyrics. With the exception of nine sermons selected and
edited by Mr Evelyn Waugh for the limited de luxe edition of Mgr
Knox's sermons,[1] none of the sermons in the third and fourth sections
have hitherto been gathered into books. Twenty of the thirty-one
sermons in the first and second sections have previously been published in book form under the title *Captive Flames* (1940), which has
been unobtainable for many years. In the first and second sections the
chronological order of the saints' lives has been followed; in the third
and fourth sections the sermons are placed in the order in which they
were preached. Two sermons, at the end of the third section, I have
been unable to date.

When an occasional sermon had previously appeared in *The Tablet*
or some other journal I have followed the printed text in preference
to the typescript in all cases. However, where cuts were made in the
printed sermon, I have restored the missing paragraphs from the
typescript.

[1] *Sermons by Monsignor Knox*, selected and edited by Evelyn Waugh (Dropmore Press),
London, 1949.

For the purposes of this volume, I have taken the word "sermon" in the strict sense of a spoken address on a religious subject to a general Catholic congregation. It has been my endeavour to make these volumes a complete collection of sermons in this sense. There is record in his engagement books and elsewhere of certain sermons which it has been impossible to trace. It is likely that in some, though not in all, instances, the sermons preached on these occasions had been given in other places and may well be included in this volume. I have excluded all conferences, published or unpublished, given by Mgr Knox when he was Chaplain to the Catholic undergraduates at Oxford; also all retreat discourses, all notes for sermons published in *The Clergy Review*, some half-dozen unpublished wedding addresses, and the short sermons printed monthly in *The Sunday Times*. In this volume there are a few sermons preached at the University Chaplaincy after Mgr Knox had retired from Oxford, but they fall into the category of sermons rather than conferences; similarly there are certain sermons broadcast direct from the studio, which were given as sermons and not as talks. A second collection of short *Sunday Times* sermons has recently been published under the title *Lightning Meditations*. It is hoped to include the remaining unpublished wedding addresses in a second edition of *The Bridegroom and the Bride*. The greater part of the matter contained in *The Clergy Review* sermon notes was published in a different form in Mgr Knox's books of scriptural exegesis.

By enquiry, by use of his engagement books, by reference to *The Tablet*, *The Edmundian* and other journals, it has been possible to date many, though not all, of his sermons and to give information about the occasion and place of delivery.

I have judged it helpful to add a number of notes explaining references and allusions that might otherwise be missed by readers. I trust that I have not burdened Mgr Knox's text with unnecessary information.

I would like to thank again those who have helped me in the preparation of these volumes. In the Introduction to *Pastoral Sermons* a full list of acknowledgements has been made. There is need only to add the name of Rt Rev. John A. Murphy, Bishop of Shrewsbury, who placed in my hands the sermon entitled "Priesthood".

PHILIP CARAMAN, S.J.

31 Farm Street, W.1.
30th May 1960.

Contents

Page

IV. PANEGYRICS

I

SAINTS

I

SAINTS PETER AND PAUL[1]

WHAT is the nerve of that indissoluble connection which binds St Peter to St Paul in the liturgical thought of Christendom? Our separated brethren know nothing of it; for them, June 29th is St Peter's Day, and St Paul's conversion is celebrated on January 25th; what more could you want? Instead of which, our liturgical tradition can never mention either of the two names without agonies—if I may put it so—of scruple over a point of hagiological etiquette. What will St Paul think (we ask), what will St Peter think if he does not get his mention too? On every feast of either saint, the other must have his commemoration, which takes precedence of all other commemorations; they must always be mentioned in the same breath. And on June 29th they must be celebrated jointly; even so, for fear that St Peter may have had the lion's share of our attention, St Paul on the 30th must have a separate feastlet of his own. The Church, in short, behaves like an anxious mother arranging birthday-parties for a couple of morbidly jealous twins. What is the meaning of it all?

If we are not to regard St Paul as partner, on more or less equal terms, with the chief of the apostles, shall we not be disposed to regard him as St Peter's rival, competing with him for the title? It has been suggested before now by learned and untrustworthy men that the Acts of the Apostles is a composite document, one of its sources exalting Peter at the expense of Paul, and the other vice versa. If Peter is rescued from prison at Jerusalem, Paul must be rescued at Philippi; if Paul raises Eutychus to life, Peter must do as much for Dorcas; and so on throughout. Most of us will find it difficult to believe in this sort of thing; but if the habit of setting off St Paul against St Peter was not invented in the sub-apostolic age, at least it has had a good run since the Reformation. Protestantism, in revolt against the Petrine claims, and basing its most characteristic theology on a false reading of St Paul's epistle to the Romans, could hardly fail to draw invidious comparisons, in which St Paul always came out best. It is rare to come

---

[1] This sermon was preached to the Catholic undergraduates at Oxford and published in *The Tablet*, 28 June 1941.

across a book of non-Catholic theology which mentions the two saints without exalting the latter at the expense of the former.

On one famous occasion (only one) the two apostles are actually found at cross purposes. When St Peter left Jerusalem after his imprisonment, the "other place" to which he removed was naturally Syrian Antioch. It was outside Herod's jurisdiction; it was the obvious port of embarkation for Asia Minor and for the West. He found there a Church in which Jew and Gentile fraternized, even at that early date, to the extent of eating their meals together; he sat down with them—had he not been warned, by a special revelation, that with God nothing is common or unclean? All went well, until some Jews of the stricter school came down on a visit from Jerusalem; for these, a separate table had to be provided. Was Peter to humour the scruples of the new-comers, or to set them an example of broad-mindedness? He decided to eat with the Jews, as the safest course—it is difficult not to add, when you have read Romans 14, the more Pauline course. To Paul, it seemed a betrayal; and the epistle to the Galatians[1] preserves for us his boast that he withstood Peter face to face. We are not told what happened, but two things emerge as plainly implied by the narrative. One is that an open disagreement with St Peter was a thing not to be lightly undertaken; even if you had the boldness of Paul, such an event was rare and noteworthy, and attested a deep conviction. The other thing is, that St Peter was a person you normally counted on to take the less narrow view, to adopt the cause of the Gentile Christians no less readily than St Paul himself; that is why his attitude was so disappointing.

I know it has often been suggested that the two apostles represented two different schools of policy about the inclusion of the Gentiles in the Church; they kept up friendly relations of course, to edify the public, but in fact there was a deep cleavage between them; there was a race, whether the world should be converted to Christianity with or without circumcision, and Paul won. That picture of the situation is based on no kind of historical evidence. The only indication we have that a Petrine faction and a Pauline faction existed in the early Church comes from the introduction to I Corinthians, a passage full of interest and of obscurity. "Every one of you saith, I indeed am of Paul; and I am of Apollo; and I of Cephas; and I of Christ." It seems clear that the visit of Apollo, the eloquent Jew from Alexandria who had been preaching an imperfectly comprehended Christian gospel at Ephesus, had brought confusion into the Church of Corinth. Had he in fact been content to

[1] Gal. 2. 11.

water where Paul planted, or had he oversowed cockle among Paul's wheat? Whatever his intentions may have been, he seems to have left behind him a party of Apollo, distinguished from the party of Paul. Must we suppose, further, that there was a party which disclaimed the authority of both, and would recognize none but that of St Peter; and a fourth party which described itself, still more audaciously, as the party of Christ? Is it not rather probable that the followers of Paul claimed to be followers of Peter, since Peter had given Paul the right hand of fellowship, and the rival school of Apollo, determined to appeal still further back, wrote "Christ" instead of "Peter" on its banners, with the fatal instinct, common at so many periods of history, of monopolizing the Christian title? One belongs to Paul—Peter's candidate; the other can only retort that he belongs to Apollo— Christ's candidate; these are the traditional amenities of sectarianism.

No, you cannot make the two apostles into professional rivals except by inventing a story which is neither in the Acts nor in the Epistles. If, instead, we are to make them into a team, how are we to adjust the relations between them? We are not allowed to think of them as Co-Popes; can we think of them as Co-Bishops of Rome? The outlandish look of the word reminds us that the idea it represents is something unknown to Christendom. Or are we to think of St Paul as a Coadjutor Bishop, a kind of Cardinal Vicar? If anything, the reverse of a Cardinal Vicar, whose business is with the "urbs" rather than the "orbis"; St Paul never seems to have stayed in Rome, except when a dungeon and a military guard made missionary journeys impossible. Could we describe him as Apostolic Delegate to anywhere and everywhere? Or are we to think of him simply as an apostle, with a roving commission like that enjoyed by the other apostles, who happens to have become associated with St Peter because his journeyings led him—*malgré lui*, it must be confessed—to Rome?

I suppose the fact is that the early Church was, before all things, relic-conscious; and that Rome, possessing the bodies of two apostles who were local martyrs, boasted of the two names in one breath without stopping to consider whether both were local bishops, or how it was possible for two bishops to hold the same See at the same time. And this juxtaposition of the two names was no doubt encouraged by the tradition that both suffered on the same day. Monsignor Barnes[1] used to say, "On the same day, but in different years"; I forget which of his theories depended on that point. If so, the coincidence would be

[1] Mgr A. S. Barnes was Mgr Knox's immediate predecessor as chaplain to the Catholic undergraduates at Oxford. He retired in 1926.

all the more remarkable; Peter and Paul, Paul and Peter—like Saul and Jonathan, they were not divided in their deaths; like Romulus and Remus, they must somehow be regarded as joint founders of the Roman Church. Meanwhile, was St Paul a bishop? And if so, of what?[1] They could not waste time over these abstract questions; the point was, both bodies were there. And so both names were rattled off in all the lists, without prejudice to the unique position of that one apostle to whom the keys were given; St Paul must fit in as best he could.

2

ST CECILIA[2]

In like manner also, let wives be subject to their husbands: that, if any believe not the word, they may be won without the word, by the conversation of the wives, considering your chaste conversation with fear.—1 Peter 3. 1.

THE legends of the early Roman saints, among whom your holy patroness St Cecilia is numbered, do not always command great attention from the critically minded historian. The records, he will tell you, were compiled at an uncertain date, but a date very much later than the events they deal with; the miracles in them are purposelessly elaborate; the tone of them rather suggests that they have been written up for the edification of pious readers. That is all very well, but every now and again you meet with curious evidences of the accuracy of these Roman traditions, and not least in the case of St Cecilia herself. A little time ago they dug underneath the Church of St Cecilia across the Tiber, to find out whether there was any justification for the tradition that that church was built on the site of St Cecilia's house. And sure enough it proved that St Cecilia's, like St Clement's, was built over an old Roman house. But there was more than that—there is one chapel in the church which was always supposed to be the exact site of St Cecilia's martyrdom. In the story, you will remember, St Cecilia was finally put to death in a bath. And just underneath the chapel of the martyrdom, so I am told, in the structure of the old Roman house, they found the traces of the old Roman apparatus for

[1] It is clear from the previous paragraph that Mgr Knox is not questioning St Paul's episcopal character; he is merely asking: was he ever a *diocesan* bishop?

[2] This sermon was preached at the Church of St Anselm and St Cecilia, Kingsway, London.

heating the bath water. Which shows that we ought to be very careful
about how we disbelieve the Roman legends.

But whether the story of St Cecilia as it is told in her acts is all true
or only partly true, there is a simplicity about the whole story and a
simplicity about St Cecilia's character in the story which demands that
anyone who stands in the pulpit on an occasion like this should preach
a simple sermon about her. She is not like that other great Virgin
Martyr, St Catherine of Alexandria. St Catherine of Alexandria was a
great philosopher, according to the story, who confounded all the
thinkers of Alexandria by the acuteness of her apologetics. And,
though I have every respect for St Catherine as the patroness of my own
College, I do imagine St Catherine as a rather formidable person to
meet; she would, I fancy, lecture on Catholic Evidence platforms. But
there is nothing of that about St Cecilia, although she is full of zeal for her
religion; her public is the home, her platform the breakfast table. I hope it
is not necessary to remind you, except in the most general way, of her
story—how she was married to a young pagan called Valerian, but persuaded him to respect her vow of virginity, because her guardian
angel would make him sorry for it if he did otherwise: how Valerian
wanted to see this guardian angel, but Cecilia, with her innocent
craft, said he could not do that unless he was baptized first; how he was
baptized, and saw the angel at her side as she prayed; how he made
a convert of his brother Tiburtius, and how first the two brothers, and
then Cecilia herself, were punished with death for professing the
Christian religion. It is an old story, and a familiar one: and while we
do all homage to St Catherine for her courage in lecturing in the
parks, we shall always need St Cecilia as well, quietly working at home
for the conversion of her own husband and his family.

Not that St Cecilia herself was in the position of a modern wife. Like
so many Christian ladies of her time, she had taken, in imitation of our
blessed Lady, a vow of perpetual virginity. When you read of the
virgin martyrs you must not think of that connection of titles as an
accidental one; that certain martyrs happened to be virgins or certain
virgins happened to be martyrs. They were martyrs because they were
virgins: it was because they insisted on keeping their vow when their
parents wished them to marry that the secret of their attachment to the
Christian faith was discovered; and it was their persistency in maintaining it that led to their martyrdom. It would be hard to estimate, I
think, how much of its unpopularity in Roman society the Christian
faith owed to its tradition of virginity. You know the horror the world
feels when somebody becomes a Catholic; you know the horror the

world feels when somebody goes into a convent: combine those two, and transplant them into a society which is heathen and regards the Christian religion as a dangerous and debased cult and you will realize what the pagans thought of a resolution like St Cecilia's.

Virginity is an ideal which the pagans had no right to misunderstand. For, in theory, they, too, honoured it; and it should have commended itself to their heathen instinct for sacrifice. For the point of a sacrifice is that the victim should be spotless, the best of its kind. You must offer not what you can well afford to spare, but what will cost you something. The victim must be young, not old; perfect, not mutilated; pure bred, not of inferior stock: it is the fairest flower that must wither in front of the statue. That is the pagan idea of sacrifice; and the Christian idea of sacrifice is based on the same principle. In order to give up something to God, we forgo, not the sinful pleasures which we have no right to in any case, but the lawful pleasures which he has given us to enjoy if we will. And it is not broken hearts or wasted careers that produce vocations to the religious life. It is the young, the attractive, the brilliant, those who have the fullest life and the highest hopes before them, who make the perfect sacrifice when they devote themselves to almighty God in holy religion.

The pagans ought to have understood that; our modern world does not; it simply talks about waste. Well, I am not going to argue that now: I am only pointing out that Catholics, in whatever age of the world, must think of the life of virginity as the highest vocation of all. But for this morning, let us think of St Cecilia rather as an example to people living in the world, a patroness of the home. Hers was a mixed marriage; of course, she could not help herself; parents in her day had all the arrangement of such matters in their hands, and presumably her parents were not Christians. Do not let us run away with the impression that all Catholics ought to make mixed marriages, in order to bring fresh families into the Church. There is at least as much harm done to the Church by mixed marriages as good; at least as much harm. And there is no doubt that, in the eyes of the Church, such marriages are an unfortunate necessity that you cannot avoid, not an ideal to be aimed at. A Catholic who means to marry, but has not (so to speak) filled in the name yet, ought to mean, God willing, to marry a Catholic. But mixed marriages, I suppose, will always go on; and at any rate we have to allow for the case where, after marriage, the husband or the wife becomes a convert, but not both. The same situation arises—a difference of creed within the four walls of the same house. And it is there that St Cecilia ought to help us.

What won her husband to the faith, in spite of his passion, in spite (you might almost say) of his love for her, was the purity of her nature which, though a heathen, he could already discern. His eyes were not yet open to the supernatural world that rules and interpenetrates ours; he could not see the angel until he was baptized. But he could see, in his Christian bride, a new experience in his life—a blinding flash of purity. And the first duty of a Catholic wife or a Catholic husband, if they would redeem the promise they made to labour for husband's or for wife's conversion, is to be a model of Christian purity. The religious life, the life of virginity, is not for them; they have made their choice. But within the holy bond of matrimony, the Catholic has to hold up the highest possible standard of faithfulness—faithfulness both to the person of the other partner in the marriage, and to the will of God in designing matrimony for the procreation of children. Let husband or wife be won to the faith by the behaviour of wife or husband, by considering the chasteness of that behaviour with fear. The world knows that Catholics have a high standard of purity. But the world is not going to be impressed unless it is assured that Catholics keep it.

And that is not only a lesson for wives and husbands; it is a lesson for all of us. The purity which is our traditional inheritance as Catholics has a message and a charm for the world about us. Each of us, whether he likes it or not, is an advertisement of the Catholic faith to the little circle of his neighbours—a good advertisement, or a bad advertisement. And it is such a mistake to think that we ought to try and impress our neighbours by making it clear to them that Catholics are not Puritans, are not strait-laced, are sportsmen like anybody else. The world is very ready to say that of us, but it does not really respect us for it. It does not respect us for being ready to join in rather risky conversation, and enjoy rather doubtful jokes; it does not respect us for being careless about what company we keep and what places of amusement we go to. It respects us, if it sees that we shrink from the touch of anything that may defile us; if it sees that the virginity which is practised in the cloister has its complement and its fruit in the chaste conversation of Catholics who are living in the world.

So, while St Anselm's feast reminds us to be loyal sons of the Church, ready to hold the faith and to defend the faith in life and in death, let St Cecilia's feast remind us to take our Christian vocation seriously, to follow out in our lives the words we profess with our lips. And may both, English bishop and Roman maiden, pray for you who worship here and for those who minister to you, that when Christ, the

BX

Master they served, comes again in judgment, you may be found
blameless before almighty God.

3

ST GEORGE

All mirth is forsaken; the joy of the land is gone away.—Isaias 24. 11.

WE are celebrating tonight the Feast of St George, the heavenly
patron of England. I do not mean to derive any lesson from the
life or from the martyrdom of St George, because it appears that
nothing whatever is known about either. We were all brought up on
the story of St George and the Dragon, but these historians who spoil
all our nursery romances tell us that this is quite untrue: indeed, the
Church has very prudently refrained from giving any sanction to the
legend of the saint, and has officially declared him to be one of those
holy men whose actions are known only to God. Instead, we will
occupy ourselves this evening in thinking about England. I say England,
not the United Kingdom, or the British Empire. St George is not the
patron of the United Kingdom, or of the British Empire. He is the
patron of these strange folk that live between the Severn and the
Wash, between the Tweed and the English Channel; a folk honest, on
the whole, kindly, on the whole, shy, a little surly, law-abiding, but
doggedly tenacious of their rights, rather too self-satisfied, incurably
sentimental, dreadfully muddle-headed. He is the patron of that
country of chalk downs, of little fields bordered by green hedges, of
wandering lanes, of hills scarcely rising above the level of cultivation, of
old trees and of long manorial tenure, which we call England. I do not
flatter myself by supposing that this congregation consists of entirely
English stock; I conceive it to be probable that there are one or two of
you, scattered about here and there, whose blood thrills to a different
music, whose loyalties have their focus on the other side of that channel
which we have so strangely dedicated to St George. I cannot help that;
you are a month late for St Patrick's Day. You will have to be honorary
Englishmen for this evening.

It is a peculiarity of the English that they do most things in a vague,
haphazard, untidy sort of way, without being able to give any particular reasons for doing it. And nothing is more characteristic of them

than their choice of a patron saint. There was no conceivable reason why it should have been St George more than anybody else. There is no ground for thinking that St George had ever been in England; it is not even certain, I suppose, that he had ever heard of England. He was represented in popular legend as being a soldier, but England is not, and never was, a military nation by choice. We just picked him up, somehow, in the Crusades, and that was all there was to it. I doubt, even, whether there was a great popular devotion to the saint in the Middle Ages. A fairly large number of parish churches are dedicated to him, but not many, I think, date beyond the Reformation. And I could show you a list of one hundred and fifty country people in the later Middle Ages out of whom only three bear George as their baptismal name. Its real popularity, I fancy, dates from those one hundred and seventeen continuous years of English history during which George was the King's name.

But there is one phrase we all of us know which does, in a curious way, identify our national saint with the memory of our remote fore-fathers, I mean the war cry, the slogan we should call it: "Saint George for merry England!" For *merry* England—when I say that there is no trace of a popular medieval devotion to the saint, I must admit on the other side the great popularity of The George and Dragon as a sign over inn doors. In that most essentially English of our institutions, the country inn, our national saint does seem to have come to his own. He has passed, somehow, into that tradition of hearty good-fellowship, of beef-eating and beer-drinking jollity, of which Chaucer first hymned the praises, and Charles Dickens wrote the epitaph. Merry England— it is hard to see why they should have been so merry. The country was devastated by wars, civil wars mostly; the great plague of the Black Death made whole tracts of the countryside into a wilderness; there were cruel landlords, there were worldly priests, there was poverty, and loose living, and crime. But, somehow, to these forefathers of ours, the England for which they fought was a merry England; it smiled to them across the seas, as they fell at Crécy and Agincourt, in a haze of fun and good comradeship.

Merry England—do we talk much about "merry England" now? If you open your morning paper, and cast your eye down the news— strikes, divorce actions, murders, unemployment statistics, grave warnings to the public, and similar matter that chiefly occupy its pages —is merry the first word that rises to your lips? Oh, I know, we are gay, we are frivolous, we hurl ourselves into our pleasures. No expense can be too heavy for producing a film, for putting on a revue, for hiring a football professional. We dance all night, and play tennis all day—those of us who have the leisure. But is there not something suspicious about this feverish gaiety of ours, about these demands for a brighter London, this dreary cry for the unsexing of women, these lurid posters that herald our public amusements? Does not our laughter ring rather hollow, as if we were making merry not because we feel light-hearted, but because we want to forget the anxieties that are weighing us down? Our industries, our trade, our empire, our birth-rate, our morals—do they encourage merriment? Our poetry, our clever novels, our art—do they reflect a mood of happiness? Our expert critics, do they bid us believe that all is well with England? Is our gaiety real, or is it a smile painted on the face of a corpse?

Oh, I am not going to talk politics. I am not going to discuss how much of our present difficulties we owe to our ancestors, how much to ourselves, how much to circumstances that we could not have avoided. Even at this moment it is doubtful whether our merry England will have a merry month of May. It is no place of mine, here, to discuss such issues, unless perhaps to implore your prayers for the divine guidance of our rulers. I will not even remind you—the theme has become almost a trite one—how the landlordism that was born with the Reformation prepared the way for that terrible division of class interests which has been with us since the industrial revolution. I do not believe that in the last resort the moods of a country, its moods of depression, or of elation, of hope, or of despair, arise from economic causes or can be altered by material changes. Outward conditions do affect us, of course—a little at all times, violently at some times. But in the long run England will not be merry or sad because there is more coal or less coal, because there is more trade or less trade. Ultimately the spirit of man is the arbiter of his happiness; men will be merry or sad according as they have found their right place or their wrong place in the scheme of things; and peace between nations, peace between classes, will come only when man is at peace with himself, and at peace with God.

And England will not be merry until England is Catholic. That word "merry" is not so simple as it sounds. It is a difficult word, for example, to translate into any foreign language. It is typical of our modern conditions that we hardly ever use it nowadays, except when we call a person "merry", meaning that he was slightly drunk. It survives, chiefly, in old-fashioned formulas such as Merry England, or a Merry Christmas. Merry does not mean drunk, or uproarious, or frivolous. It means that a man is light-hearted, that his mind is at ease, that he is in a good humour, that he is ready to share a bit of fun with his neighbours. There is humility in the word, and innocence, and comradeship. And such a frame of mind as that is not to be secured, by grown-up people, through a continuous whirl of excitements, or a long course of dissipations. It comes from within.

A country cannot be merry while it forgets God. And a country cannot be merry for long, or with safety, if it tries to be Christian without being Catholic. England is not, of course, even today, a country of atheists. But there is a very large fraction of our fellow countrymen—I do not think you can put it much lower than four-fifths —which does not go to church. And most of these people do not think about God if they can help it—that is what I call "forgetting God". They try to satisfy themselves with this world; and that is a thing which you cannot do; almighty God does not mean us to do it; he wants to draw us back to himself. The man who confines his outlook to this world is worried all the time, at the back of his mind, by the old riddle of existence; the troubles, the sufferings, the tragedies of the world keep flicking him like briers as he goes along: problems of conduct—which is the right thing to do, and why should I do it? —stick to him like burrs and force themselves upon his notice. You may forget your cares for a time, you may drown them occasionally with your pleasures, but you can never banish them. A man will never be light-hearted in this world unless he is thinking of the next world; this world is too chequered an affair for that.

And in the long run, even a Christian nation cannot be merry unless it is a Catholic nation. For these non-Catholic Christianities—why, I do not know, but as a matter of observation it is true—always go hand-in-hand with some kind of Puritanism that interferes with man's innocent enjoyments. Sometimes they want to make us all into teetotallers, sometimes they are out against boxing, or racing, or the stage; sometimes they insist that we shall sit indoors all Sunday afternoon and go to sleep. Wherever Protestant opinion really rules a country, you always find legislation of one sort or another which is designed to stop people being merry. It sounds distant and old-fashioned to us, but that is because Protestantism has lost its grip on the country. In the United States, where the Protestants, though few in number, are rich and powerful, the thing goes on to this day. And when Protestantism does lose its grip, a reaction sets in, a reaction against Puritanism, which instead of making people merry makes them dissolute. A false religion, no less than lack of religion, will destroy, in the end, a nation's peace of mind.

Let us comfort ourselves, then, those of us who love England, with the thought that in trying to convert England we are not trying to alter her into something that is strange and foreign: we are trying to make her once more merry England—that which she was and that which traditionally she ought to be. Those who hate our religion are fond of pointing us to the example of Catholic nations abroad, of which they draw a very unfair picture, and then say: "Look at Belgium —do you want England to be like that? Look at Spain—do you want England to be like that?" But the truth is that, for better or worse, England will never be quite like any other country. You may love her, you may hate her, but you must take her as she stands. Those native virtues that now grow wild in her hedgerows will only bloom the stronger and the fairer when the faith cultivates them. The more England becomes Catholic, the more English she will become.

Let us, then, on this feast of our patron, pray earnestly and resolve always to pray earnestly for the conversion of the country we love. Let us ask his prayers, and the prayers of our blessed Lady and the English martyrs, that the tide of conversions we see chronicled year by year may flow still more strong, and still more deep, till at last the heart of the country reawakes, and remembers, and returns to her ancient love. It will hardly be in our time, I suppose, that the change comes; but even now we can stand, like Moses on Mount Nebo, and see beneath us the promised land that is one day to be our Catholic heritage. Let us stand together, strong in the faith of that vision, and resolve that through no fault of ours, no lapse of ours, no neglect of ours, that high endeavour to which we are pledged shall fall short of a swift and a lasting achievement. May the prayers of St George protect this country that is dedicated to his honour, and bring all those who do him honour to that true country of ours which is in heaven.

4

ST BENEDICT[1]

Peace be unto you.—John 20. 19.

THE Jews under the old dispensation were ordered to keep the seventh day of the week as a day of rest; and the reason given for this was one which went deep into the very origin of things. In six

---

[1] A sermon preached at St Benedict's Priory (now St Benedict's Abbey), Ealing, on the ansferred feast of St Benedict, April 1937.

days the Lord made the heavens and the earth, and on the seventh day he rested. God rested—what does that mean? Obviously it can only be a metaphorical, not a literal truth. The theologians tell us that God is *semper agens, semper quietus*, always active, and always at rest; there is no alternation, in his changeless and timeless being, of activity and repose. It is only by a metaphor, then, that the Bible speaks of him as first busy with his work of creation, and then resting, as if his tireless energies could need to be replaced or restored. What was important, I suppose, was to persuade the Jews, with their instinct for restless endeavour, that repose, no less than activity, was one of the perfections which exist in the nature of God. And there was, perhaps, a further reason why they were bidden to keep the sabbath holy and do no work on it. The ordinance looked forward into the future, as well as back into the remote past. A day was to come, a sabbath day, on which God would rest from his labours, in real literal truth.

Imagine yourself standing and looking into the tomb of our Lord Jesus Christ, just before Nicodemus and Joseph rolled the stone into its place at the entrance to it. The sacred body is swathed in cerecloths; but you can see the outlines of it, and remember what it was this morning. Those feet, which now lie so still, were treading only this morning the painful road to Calvary; these three years past, they have worn themselves out on the roads of Judea and Galilee, as he went about doing good. Those hands, now spread out motionless, were quick with life; nay, imparted life, radiated it, as Jairus' daughter and the young man at Nain and Lazarus could tell you. In the lines about the mouth, you can trace where he smiled in pardoning the penitent sinner; the brow was furrowed with anxious bewilderment over Jewish unbelief. All that frame, till this morning, was full of vitality; it belonged to one who never seemed to give himself any rest, who prayed at night on lonely hill-sides, and slept from sheer exhaustion amid the perils of a storm-swept lake. And now it lies quite still; God has finished his redemptive work, as he finished his creative work centuries ago, and he is hallowing the sabbath day afresh; God rests, with the most perfect repose of all—the repose of death.

Now imagine that you are standing in the upper room with the ten apostles, exactly two days afterwards. The doors are shut and locked, as if to keep out the turmoil and the distractions of the world outside. Yes, those noises of the world outside only come through to you faint and muffled, but within this holy conclave there is no recollection and no peace. All is eager speculation, excitement, alarm. Can it really be true, the story those women told; was it really a living Christ or only a vision that Peter saw? If it is true, what then? They are to return to Galilee, but what are they to do there? Go back to their old trade, their old pursuits, or begin preaching, there and then, the gospel of a living Christ? Meanwhile what of their enemies, the rulers of the Jews? Will they, who have succeeded in hurrying the Master to a cross, be content with that? Have they not been warned that the fate of the Master will be the fate of the disciple also? Look, what is that? Somebody standing by the door—somebody who has effected an entrance, in spite of locks and bars! Who is it, what is it? Surely it can be no earthly visitant, who comes and goes like this?

Jesus stood in the midst, and said "Peace be unto you". He who is resting now from that life of incessant activity brings with him, to the cenacle, the peace of the grave. He, who three nights ago rebuked them for sleeping while he agonized, seems now to rebuke them for agonizing while he sleeps. They should be enjoying the peace of his sabbath, instead of giving way to the agitation of these unquiet alarms. And then he goes on: "As the Father hath sent me, even so send I you". His Father sent him to be nailed to a cross, to die, to be buried, and so to enter into his rest. They, his followers, have been mystically associated with him in that experience; have been nailed with him to his cross, died with him, been buried in his sepulchre, risen again with him to a life which looks beyond and above all the petty accidents of mortality; a life so mortified that it can enjoy the peace of the grave.

The founders of the great religious orders have picked up, each in his own characteristic way, that one life-giving message which our Lord Jesus Christ brought to earth. St Francis seized upon his poverty, St Philip Neri on his simplicity, St Paul of the Cross on his love of suffering, St Ignatius on his untiring zeal to do the will of his heavenly Father. But the great saint whose memory we are celebrating today, the founder, directly or indirectly, of all our Western monastic institutions, caught up and preserved for ever as the watchword of his order a single word from that interview in the cenacle; the word "peace". In a world so full of unruly agitations and turbulent emotions there should be cells—tombs, if you will—where men should live consciously striving to attain the peace of Christ.

The black monks—they must dress all the time in funeral clothes, to remind us and themselves that they are dead and buried with Christ. They must live, except when obedience calls them outside it, within the limits of an enclosure, narrow limits, as of a grave. And they must observe, in a more or less degree according to the rules of their foundation and the necessities of their way of life, that gracious habit of silence which reproduces for us, in salutary intervals of recollection, the silence of the grave. "We are a good odour of death unto life", "always carrying about with us the putting to death of our Lord Jesus", "ye are dead, and your life is hidden with Christ in God"—all those phrases of St Paul, which sound so highly-flown and unpractical to us half-hearted Christians of a later time, begin to be intelligible to us when we see the black monks going about their daily work, which is the work of prayer. That motto, *Pax*, which you see written up every-where in Benedictine monasteries, is the same motto you see written up in graveyards, and for the same reason. They have inherited the peace of the first Easter Day, the peace which came from a tomb.

It was one of our Lord's last promises, wasn't it, before his cruci-fixion, that he would send peace on his apostles. "Peace I leave with you, my peace I give unto you." Only, if you remember, he went on to qualify that, by saying, "Not as the world giveth, give I unto you". Don't let us make any mistake about it, the world does want peace, wants it desperately. It's true that there can be the widest differences between different people's ideas of how this peace, the peace which the world gives, is to be attained. Some people think we shall achieve it by disarming, some by rearming as quickly as possible; some think we ought to make all the alliances we can, some that we ought to give up foreign alliances altogether. But we all want peace, if we only knew where to get it. The trouble is, that even if we do get the kind of peace we are asking for, it will be a very second-rate sort of article. It will be the peace of Geneva, not the peace of Subiaco.

When we talk about peace nowadays, we mean, in the first place, something merely negative; an absence of fighting, the opportunity to sleep safe in our beds. But peace isn't something merely negative; it's an influence, an energy, an atmosphere which laps you round, like health—healthy doesn't mean simply not suffering from any particular disease. And again, if we do remain at peace with our neighbours, that doesn't do much good, so long as we remain quarrelling with one another inside the nation. And if we could achieve external as well as internal peace, that's only a third, isn't it, of the peace we are encouraged to pray for. We are told to ask God for peace which really deserves that name—peace with him, peace within ourselves, and peace with one another. Where are we going to get peace within ourselves; where are we going to get peace with God? Geneva isn't going to do that for us; round-table conferences aren't going to do that for us. No, we've got to go to the black monks of St Benedict and ask them to tell us their recipe, ask them to let us know where they get their peace from.

That's what they are there for. Oh, I know, the Benedictine Fathers
can and do engage in external work, teaching schools for example or
even running parishes; but that isn't what they are there for. Their work
is prayer; their function in the Christian commonwealth is first of all
to pray for us, a thing we need very badly, and then to be a perpetual
example and a visible advertisement to us of how we ought to live, of
how we ought to die in order that we may live; in a word, of where
our true peace lies.

I think anybody who has spent a few days in a Benedictine monastery
will have been bound to notice certain marks, even in the external
behaviour of the monks, which will have enabled him to catch something of their secret. For instance, their conviction that prayer is the
really essential thing, the real work of God, shows itself in the leisurely
way in which everything is done in Benedictine churches; none of
that breathless hurry you find elsewhere. I remember a man once
saying to me what an extraordinary thing it is that nobody minds
waiting five minutes for a train, but if you wait five minutes in church
for a service to start it always feels like hours. If we could only learn
from the Benedictine Fathers not to be in such a hurry over our prayers,
it would be something. And it isn't only in church that you will notice
this leisurely habit of doing things; there is a general air in Benedictine
monasteries of slow movement, of downcast eyes, of people not
minding waiting, which would be very good for all of us if we could
catch it. For it means recollection; a habit of resting content with the
company of your own thoughts, and so falling back easily on the
thought of God; that is an opportunity which we miss, we others,
because we are always so anxious to distract our minds, to crowd our
leisure with dissipations and amusements, that we seldom or never
give God a chance of speaking to us. And then there is the great
courtesy of the Benedictine family; "in honour preferring one
another", says St Paul—it's so refreshing to move in a society where
everybody has his place and knows it. But all these things are only
outward indications of that inward spirit which the black monks
cultivate; and we have got to live close to them if we want to find out
about that. So that you, in this congregation, are greatly privileged to
have your church served by the Benedictine Fathers; that "good odour
of death unto life" of which St Paul speaks is part of the air you
breathe, preserving you from the pestilent influences of the world you
live in.

Only you must pray for your priests. The spirit of a great institute
like the Benedictine congregation does not survive automatically

through the centuries; there is always danger, as time goes on, that such an institute, depending for its life not so much on any principles of organization as upon the influence of a subtle spirit which animates it, will lose the freshness and the purity of its character; will make terms with the world and forget its secret. "If the salt loses its savour", our Lord asks, "wherewith shall it be salted?" It will be a bad day for the Church if the black monks, who are meant to hand on a message of peace to us others, lose the spirit of peace which is their inheritance. So let us ask our blessed Lady (the Queen of Peace), and St Benedict and all the many great saints of his order, to have the Abbey of Downside and the Priory of Ealing in their keeping; that the monks may live as befits their vocation, men dead with Christ, buried with Christ, risen with Christ, by their prayers and their example giving to the world that peace which, now more obviously than ever, the world cannot give—the peace of God.

5

ST GREGORY THE GREAT[1]

Now therefore you are no more strangers and foreigners, but you are fellow citizens with the saints.—Ephesians 2. 19.

I DO not know if we always pay quite enough attention, except, of course, for the really big days, to the saints whose feasts come round year by year. The smaller ones are apt to pass altogether unnoticed, and even the bigger ones come suddenly and take us by surprise. The saint I want to speak of now is today's saint, whose name, in case you did not catch it when the Collect was sung, is St Gregory—St Gregory the Great.

His name is derived from *egregora*, which, as the prefects would tell you, is the strong perfect (with Attic reduplication) of the Greek verb *egeiro*, to wake up. So St Gregory is the wide-awake man, the man who is always on the spot; there are no flies on him, as the Americans say. I suppose the Church has seldom had a ruler who got through more business. He wrote enormous quantities of theology, and is counted as one of the four great Latin doctors—you will see him pushing our Lord's chariot in the picture in the *ambulacrum*. He was one of the great

[1] This sermon was preached to the schoolboys of St Edmund's, Ware, on the Feast of St Gregory, between the years 1920-22.

early legislators of the Church, especially in matters of liturgy. And all the time, a profound statesman, he was guiding the destinies of the Church through a most difficult period of history, thinking nothing too insignificant or too remote for his personal attention. And one of the very remote and insignificant things he organized was the conversion of an island somewhere off the coast of France, called Britain. The Britons, in the classical authors, are always used as a synonym for the extreme limit, the outside edge of mankind—those Britons, tucked away right at the end of the world, much as we should say "Borneo" or "Patagonia". And I should think in St Gregory's time, owing to the invasion of the Angles and Saxons, England was a still more inaccessible and unheard-of region. And that is where St Gregory sent St Augustine to convert you and me when we were little heathens.

Let us tell ourselves the story again, as the Venerable Bede tells it us, and all the history books tell it in imitation of him. Just imagine that you are an English boy, who went to the seaside and stayed on paddling when his mother told him not to, and a lot of disreputable Danes, coming back from a marauding expedition, bundled you, a whole lot of you, on board their ship and sold you at the nearest French port for the price of a drink. And then you have drifted about from one slave-dealer to another all over Europe, and finally you are standing about in a large market-place at Rome, in the very centre of the world. You are looking bored and sulky, and there is a placard over your head to say: "This size £12". And then a stranger comes up, and says something to the slave-dealer, obviously something like: "Poor kids!" A very kind-looking gentleman, this, all dressed in a long black gown. And he asks who you are, and the man says: "Angles", and you expect the same old joke you've heard all over Europe, about your looking rather obtuse Angles, but no! it doesn't come. It's quite a new one this time. "Angles! You mean Angels? That's the right name for them; at least, they look like Angels, and it's a pity they are not fellow citizens of the Angels in heaven. What part of Anglia do they come from?" "Oh, from Deiri." "Well, they ought to be saved *de ira Dei*"—you probably will not understand that joke, since it is in Latin, but the bystanders seem to find it very funny. "And what is their king called?" The kind gentleman does not have quite such luck this time; their king is called Aella. However, he does his best, and says something about what a good thing it would be if Aella's subjects learned to sing Alleluia. And they all laugh again; only the kind gentleman goes on his way looking rather serious.

Well, of course, the kind gentleman was St Gregory. He was a very holy man, but he did not mind making jokes; there is hope in that for all of us. And he was a very clever man, but he did not mind making rather bad jokes; there is hope in that for some of us. I am afraid, though, that the details of that story are not quite certain. St Bede simply hands it on as a tradition he has heard; and the earliest form of the story does not make the Angles slaves or boys at all; just grown-up Angles who happened to be visiting Rome. And with that, of course, all the point of their looking like Angels is lost. We think of the slave-boys looking very good and clean, like those cherubs with red cheeks and tow-coloured hair on the Christmas cards. I daresay really English boys, even then, would have looked rather grubby little brutes, and no one would have mistaken them for Angels. But the real point, you know, is quite unaffected by what they looked like. The real point is that they were citizens of Anglia, and St Gregory said they ought to be fellow citizens of the Angels. That was just like St Gregory, and the age of St Gregory. He objected to their Angularity. The Church had just begun to realize that she was outliving the Roman Empire, and saw in the spreading of the faith not a philosophy to be preached to the world, but a citizenship to be extended to it. It had been the boast of the Roman Empire that it made the most distant and most barbarous tribes into citizens of a single world-state:

> She (prouder boast than other conquerors knew)
> Gently the captives to her bosom drew;
> Mother, not mistress, made the thrall her kin,
> And 'neath her wing drew all the nations in.
> Orontes knows in Syria, Rhone in Gaul,
> One speech, one race, one governance for all:
> Whate'er is Earth, is Rome; Rome stands till Earth shall fall.

St Gregory, then, like the statesman he was, thinks of these Anglians not as ignorant people who need to be instructed, but as unhappy barbarians whose hearts must be conquered in order that a citizenship may be extended to them—the citizenship of the Angelic kingdom.

When we received the faith, we received it not (as other nations) like a microbe which we caught from our neighbours, nor as a bargain which we picked up from travelling pedlars, we were simply annexed to Rome by a single act of spiritual conquest. I do not say that there were not Christians wandering about in England before St Augustine came. I do not say that the Irish would not have converted us sooner or later even if the Italians had not been first. All I say is that as a matter of fact our conversion was a purely Roman affair. You will still, occasionally, read of Protestant fellow countrymen of ours referring to the Catholic Church in England under the contemptuous title of "the Italian Mission". The name is meant, of course, to twit us with being foreigners, because during the penal times our priests were educated abroad. It is a delightful idea: you make the Mass high treason, and put a price on every priest's head, and so seminaries have to be built abroad, and priests have to come back from foreign centres if they want to preserve the old faith. And when they do come back, you greet them with shouts of: "Oh, you beastly Italian". Well, I am not considering here whether that is a very generous taunt, or a very intelligent one: the interesting point about it is, Who was the first to make it? It was made first by Archbishop Benson, father of Mgr Hugh Benson. And what was he? Archbishop of Canterbury. And why Canterbury? Why that very one-horse, dead-and-alive place on the South-Eastern? Simply because St Augustine, not being able to go on as far as London, had to wait about there for a time and so set up his See there. St Augustine, a Roman envoy sent by the Pope to convert our country to the religion of the Church of Rome. And then an Archbishop of Canterbury describes the diocese of Westminster as an Italian Mission!

Well, we were founded from Rome; and all through the Middle Ages, in spite of the nuisance of living so far away from it, we were known for our loyalty to the Roman See. In St Gregory's time men were looking to the Church as the one abiding institution; it seemed to them that the break-up of earthly dominions and the shifting of nations which was taking place throughout Europe pointed to mere chaos ahead, unless hope lay in the Papacy. Today there is the same break-up of great dominions; the same shifting of the limits of nationality. The world has altered its look since we learned our geography, and it has not got to the end of its alteration yet. In this new world men still look to the Catholic Church, and to Rome as the divinely-appointed centre of the Catholic Church, as the one abiding institution which will survive the new chaos. And we, without ceasing to be Angles (those of us who are Angles), will have to rally more than ever round the Holy See as the centre of our true citizenship, that Angelic citizenship which was St Gregory's gift to us. We ought to be praying earnestly for the Holy Father. We ought to be praying for the conversion of those who, disheartened by the failure of civilization, are turning to the Church for guidance.

May the King of Angels bring us all to the fellowship of the heavenly citizens; to him be glory for ever and ever. Amen.

6

ST EDWARD THE CONFESSOR[1]

For the hope of the wicked is as dust which is blown away with the wind, and as a thin froth which is dispersed by the storm, and a smoke that is scattered abroad by the wind, and as the remembrance of a guest of one day that passeth by. But the just shall live for evermore, and their reward is with the Lord, and the care of them with the most High.—Wisdom 5. 15.

SOMETHING like two months back there died, with the greatest publicity that can attend a death-bed, one of the most characteristic and one of the most successful figures of our time.[2] A man of business, he had restricted himself to a single form of business—that journalism which sells to the public the news it wants to hear told, and the views it wants to hear expressed. A man of political ambition, he contented himself with a single form of political activity—that journalism which praises or blames, and to the best of its power appoints or dismisses, parliaments and ministers of the Crown. Hewing his own way up the difficult path of public fame by the force of his native energy, he achieved a position of prominence almost unrivalled in our memory. True, it was not one of personal prominence; we did not often see his portrait or hear what manner of man he was: many whose thought he influenced from day to day did not even know his title. True again, it was a precarious power he exercised; for the newspaper proprietor, while he aspires to be the tyrant of public opinion, must in many ways stoop to be its slave. Yet within those limits he stood before the world a titanic figure; and when a banquet was given in his honour, a clergyman of the Established Church tactfully included his name among the blessings which he commemorated at grace. Did he do good in the world, or evil? Probably a great deal of both, and both alike accidentally, for he had no mission to preach, and no selfish cupidity to satisfy. Only one thing he asked, the power of an enormous publicity, and that wish was granted him; never, probably, has a man succeeded so utterly in what he set himself to accomplish. And then God required his soul of him, and he died.

He died, and they held a memorial service for him. They held a

---

[1] This sermon was preached at the Church of St Edward the Confessor, Golders Green, London, on the Feast of St Edward the Confessor, 13 October 1922, and was first published in *Captive Flames* (1940).
[2] Alfred Harmsworth, Viscount Northcliffe.

memorial service for him in Westminster Abbey, that strange mausoleum of nine hundred years of English history which is neither church
nor cathedral, because it is too proud to be either. And as the great
congregation that celebrated his obsequies reminded one another, to
the plaintive pealing of the organ, that

> Time like an ever-rolling stream bears all its sons away;
> They fly forgotten, as a dream dies at the opening day,

how many of them gave a thought to the poignantly contrasted
character of that English king who built the Abbey, and who still
keeps in the Abbey his unhonoured shrine? That king, whose more
than royal memory the universal Church celebrates at this time?

Let me give you in brief *his* biography. Born to a throne bequeathed
him by a line of strong men, whose vigorous qualities he was little
likely to emulate, he was driven into exile at the age of ten years; it
seemed that a fortunate catastrophe had robbed him of the terrors of
royalty. Himself patient under that exile, he declared that he would
rather remain uncrowned than win a kingdom at the cost of blood.
That hope was unrealized; he was restored with the goodwill of the
Norman Duke, already England's rival and soon to be her invader.
Very naturally, he took for his advisers and administrators men of
the race that had befriended his exile. Insignificant in person (he was
probably an albino) and lacking at least in his public policy the sterner
qualities of mind, he became a puppet king in the hands of an unpopular
clique, his mother's kinsmen. There was a revolt, and his Norman
advisers fled the country; he became a puppet king once more, overshadowed this time by the figure of the great Saxon earl whose
daughter he had taken to wife. Taken, rather, for his spouse; for they
had no children, and it is constantly asserted that they never lived as
man and wife. The one benefit he might have conferred upon his
country, by leaving an heir in whose veins Norman and Saxon blood
would mingle, he refused of his own choice. His kingdom, already
pledged to the Normans, he now had to bequeath to a Saxon champion.
Foreseeing clearly in his last moments the harvest of slaughter which
was to be the reaping of his own peaceful reign, he died. He died, and
thirty-six years later they found his body uncorrupted, and breathing
the odour of sanctity.

What a record of failure! What a negation of all that the politicians
value, and all that the historians revere! Other saints, other kings whose
memory is venerated, have been no less ineffective in their lives, yet

---

[1] Isaac Watts, "O God, our help in ages past".

breathe some atmosphere of tragedy which endeared them to posterity. St Peter Celestine was unequal to the task of government, but he signalized himself in history by abdicating the triple tiara. Henry of Windsor was a weak man born in a distracted age, but the story of his murder rallied to him the sympathies of his people. Edward, no less incompetent in his lifetime than St Peter Celestine or the sixth Henry, died crowned and died a natural death. One great thing he gave to his country, the Abbey Church of Westminster. And that church, with an absence of humour singular even among our fellow countrymen, they have chosen to be the burial-place of England's great national heroes—not asking what creed they held or what life they lived, but only whether they achieved fame.

> Mortality, behold and Fear!
> What a change of flesh is here! . . .
> Here they lie had realms and lands,
> Who now want strength to stir their hands:
> Where, from their pulpits seal'd with dust,
> They preach, "In greatness is no trust."
> Here's an acre sown indeed
> With the richest, royall'st seed
> That the earth did e'er suck in
> Since the first man died for sin.[1]

Soldier, and statesman, and lawyer, they wait for the last trumpet, and the world's dissolution, and the great Assize. And amidst them all sleeps the poor weakling who graced so ill the throne of England, and they are stared at by visitors, while he, the builder of the Abbey, is forgotten.

We know that there is another side to the picture, a side to which historians, full of great world movements and the fortunes of dynasties, pay scant attention. We know that if he abstained from the use of marriage it was because he hoped to win the palm of virginity. We know that while Norman duke and Saxon earl forgot the pale puppet who had served their turn and slipped through their hands, the poor, better canonizers than earl or duke, remembered the good king Edward as the man who had remitted their taxes and lavished his own fortune upon their needs. We know that in his lifetime men loved him for his gentleness and kindness of heart, and that both in life and death almighty God ratified their judgment by granting him miraculous favours. But for all his practical effect upon our history he might as

---

[1] Francis Beaumont: *On the Tombs in Westminster Abbey.*

well never have lived; had better, perhaps, never have reigned. When
we venerate St Edward, we venerate a failure.

We do so advisedly. Not because success in life necessarily falls to
the grasping and the unscrupulous, so that success itself should be
mistrusted by Christians as a sign of rascality. Not that there have not
been great saints who were also great kings, great statesmen, great
warriors—St Oswald, St Dunstan, St Joan of Arc. But because we will
not let ourselves be blinded by the lure of worldly success so as to
forget that the true statesmanship is exercised in the council chamber,
and the true warfare fought on the battlefield of the human soul. Ask
yourself which you would rather have been, in life, of all those great
dead who lie in Westminster Abbey, and you will find it a difficult
question to answer: there is so much that dazzles, so much that cap-
tivates the imagination. Would you rather have written this, have
painted that, have built that, have discovered that, have won this
triumph or have carried that enactment?—You can hardly say. But
ask yourself which of those great dead you would rather be now, your
body there, your soul far away—is there any Christian who would not
ask to change places with the Confessor; who would not choose his
resting-place, there to wait for the opening of the great Doomsday
Book, in which nothing is recorded of men but whether they meant
good or evil, whether they loved or neglected God?

"The hope of the wicked is as dust which is blown away . . . but
the reward of the just is for evermore." All through this very beautiful
passage in the Book of Wisdom the just man is the simpleton, the
natural prey of designing enemies. They deride him, they make him a
parable of reproach; they esteem his life madness and his end without
honour. All the maxims of worldly prudence, all the sensible considerations, seem to be on their side. The best that can happen to him,
the just man, is that he should be taken away, lest wickedness should
alter his understanding, or deceit beguile his soul. He is not fit to fight
the cunning of his age with its own weapons. And, by a defiant paradox, the book is called the Book of Wisdom! It is a deliberate paradox,
for the word "wise" in Scriptural language has often the sense of crafty;
the unjust steward is commended because he acted wisely, and the children of this world in their generation are wiser than the children of light.
But there is a wisdom which somehow these innocent, gullible, ineffective, open-handed simpletons have got hold of, while these smart, up-to-
date, very much alive men of business have missed it. Now, which is right?

Our divine Lord, quoting from the Psalms of David, has assured us
that the meek shall possess the earth. Does that mean that meekness

is one of those qualities which will gain men a brighter crown in the heavenly kingdom that is to come? It does, of course, but does it mean nothing more? Certainly in this, as in any other age of history, it does not seem as if it is the meek who carry off the world's prizes; go where you will, the advertisements of the mind-training systems and the correspondence colleges will cry out to you that life is a stern battle, that success is for the ambitious, and that the weakest goes to the wall. There is no room, it would seem, for the saintly albinos. Does Christianity, then, simply preach the survival of the unfittest, by promising us in heaven a reversal of all human values and a revision of all human judgments? And must it always be, in this world, the Godwins and the Harolds and the Williams who have the best time, make the best use of their opportunities?

The land of a certain rich man brought forth plenty of fruits. And he thought within himself, saying: "What shall I do, because I have no room here to bestow my fruits?" And he said: "This will I do; I will pull down my barns, and will build greater and into them I will gather all things that are grown to me and my goods. And I will say to my soul: 'Soul, thou hast much goods laid up for many years: take thy rest, eat, drink, make good cheer'." But God said to him: "Thou fool, this night do they require thy soul of thee. And whose shall those things be which thou hast provided?" So is he that layeth up treasure for himself and is not rich towards God. In that telling, almost bitter parable, our divine Lord has shown us the fallacy of the successful life, not only from the point of view of the next world, but even in this. If the rich fool had not died then, do you think he would really have carried out his resolution of retiring from business? Not he. He would have gone on, as he had already gone on all those years, wearing himself out in the pursuit of a visionary contentment which he continually promised himself, yet could never rest to enjoy. A record harvest? Why, then, he must build yet greater barns. And when the barns were built, he would have extended his farming operations so as to have more fruits to fill them with. He was a fool, because he became the slave of his own ambitions. Mind you, we are not told that he was wicked. We are not told that, like Dives, he neglected the poor, and went like Dives into the place of torment. No, we are only told that he was a fool; that his life was a wasted one. No doubt but his funeral sermon and his obituary notices called him a successful man; a pioneer of agriculture, and one who had revolutionized the old type of barn. But in the stillness of the night in which God spoke to him, he knew that he was a failure.

His was a selfish life; not all the lives the world calls successful are selfish lives. Many of those who sleep in King Edward's Abbey were devoted servants of their kind, who left the world better for their passing. But this is certain, that true satisfaction came to them and true success crowned them only so far as their ambitions were for a cause, not for a party; for others, not for themselves. Man's happiness lies in devoting himself; his success in the offering he can make. And our Confessor was a successful man, yes, even in this world, because in his simple piety, in the unaffected generosity of his nature, he set himself to serve the men about him by easing their burdens, by relieving their necessities, by confirming them in their allegiance to the faith. Great opportunities passed him by, and he never marked them; he might have altered the dynastic history of England, have left us different manners and a different political constitution, if he had been other than he was. Instead, he left all these things to God's Providence; and God's Providence, using the ambitions of human agents as its puppets, moulded our history beyond man's expectation. And what do they mean to us now, those human agents? Mere names in the history book, mere stiff, attitudinizing figures on the Bayeux Tapestry, they have become part of a past hardly less remote to us than legend. As dust which is blown away with the wind, and as a thin froth that is dispersed by the storm, and a smoke that is scattered abroad by the wind, and as the remembrance of a guest of one day that passeth by. The Conqueror, who diverted the stream of history, went to his grave disappointed and lies there a historical memory. The Confessor, whose ambitions could be satisfied by finding a poor man his dinner, saw no corruption in death, and lives the patron of his fellow countrymen.

One only task he set before himself that had any external magnificence about it, and that was characteristic of him. It was no fortress, no royal palace, no court of justice that he planned: the House of God lay waste, and he must rebuild it. And, as if it were a symbol of the life he lived, built together from little acts of kindness and little sacrifices of self, stone by stone and arch by arch rose the Abbey Church of Westminster, which for all the additions and the restorations that have altered it in the course of the centuries, we still call his church. The building was actually completed about a week before his death; and, if pride held any place in his gentle character, he must have felt proud to think that he had left one lasting memorial that while his monks continued their daily round of prayer, the last of the dynasty of Egbert would not be forgotten.

And yet, though his Abbey still stands, and even his shrine was

protected—ironically enough, by the shadow of royalty—from dese-
cration, the liturgy of the Church he loved so well is no more celebrated
in the house he built for it. Westminster, with all the other monuments
of our Catholic antiquity, has passed into other hands and hears strange
doctrines preached. It has remained for devoted men in the last two
generations to replace, as best they could with the resources they had
at their disposal, that loss suffered by religion. And among the churches
that have thus been raised, not the least remarkable for its splendid
proportions and its commanding site is this church in which we claim
his patronage today. And this church, too, will perpetuate the memory
of a founder, in whom those who knew him at all could not but discern
the signs of a saintly character. Here was another unsuccessful life, as
the world judges success—a life in which a spirit of indomitable energy
was long thwarted in its activities and too soon cut off by a discipline
of terrible and (the world would say) meaningless suffering. You have
done well to commemorate him at its high altar; for its history is
bound up with his; and so long as the Holy Sacrifice is offered in this
place, it should be offered with grateful memory of the prayers and the
cruel mortifications which Father Bendon[1] used to offer for his parish
and his people.

Their reward is with the Lord, and the care of them with the most
High. May the prayers of our blessed Lady, and St Edward our patron,
and all the saints of God bring us safely from this world of humiliation
and of suffering into the kingdom of the just.

7

ST ANSELM[2]

*And I said: Woe is me, because I have held my peace, because I am a man
of unclean lips, and I dwell in the midst of a people that hath unclean lips,
and I have seen with my eyes the King, the Lord of hosts.*—Isaias 6. 5.

IT is a curious thing what a lot of coincidences there are in history.
Three Archbishops of Canterbury, and only three, between the
Norman Conquest and the time of England's apostasy, have been raised

---

[1] Father Bendon was Rector of St Edward the Confessor, Golders Green, from 1908
to 1920. The church was built under his care and the high altar dedicated to his memory.
He died after a very long and painful illness.
[2] This sermon was preached at the Church of St Anselm and St Cecilia, Kingsway,
London.

to the altars of the Church; St Thomas, the patron of all our secular clergy, your patron St Anselm, and my patron St Edmund. Each of those three men spent a significant part of his time of office in exile overseas. They belonged, respectively, to the reigns of Henry I, Henry II, and Henry III. The attitude of the reigning sovereign was, in each case, the cause of the saint's difficulties and of his consequent merits—a gloomy omen for the day when an eighth Henry should arise, and a time-server be found enthroned at Lambeth.

And there is a singular sort of mathematical progression, I think, about the three characters if you consider them side by side. St Edmund was made archbishop because he was a saint and everybody knew it. St Thomas was made archbishop because he was the last person you would have expected to become a saint—you might almost as well have expected it of Thomas Cromwell, or of Thomas Cranmer. St Edmund's temperament produces few archbishops but many saints, St Thomas's few saints but many archbishops. St Edmund would have been a far happier man if he had never worn a mitre; his archbishopric was only an addition to his long series of mortifications. St Thomas, humanly speaking, only learned to develop his sainthood as the result of being made archbishop; his archbishopric was the occasion of his self-realization. St Edmund was a saint first and an archbishop afterwards; he learned to be great in spite of being good. With St Thomas, in order of time, the process was reversed; he learned to be good in spite of being great. To put it roughly, and merely from the human point of view, you may say that St Edmund probably would not have become archbishop if he had not been a saint, and St Thomas would not have become a saint if he had not been archbishop.

In your holy patron St Anselm these opposing characteristics are curiously reconciled. When he first set foot in our country you may say that he already had all St Edmund's qualifications for heaven, and all St Thomas's qualifications for Lambeth. Take away his prelacy, and you still leave a character comparable with that of St Edward the Confessor. Take away his saintliness, and you still leave a career that rivals the career of Lanfranc. This was the man who, with some misgiving, came over to visit a sick friend in England at a time when the archbishopric of Canterbury had long been left vacant, so that King William Rufus and his creatures might enjoy the sequestrated revenues of the See. You will read in Dean Church's life of St Anselm how at Christmas, 1092, the clergy were allowed to pray for a remedy for the misfortunes of the Church. You will read on the next page how, early in 1093 (which means, if you come to think of it, about a fortnight later), King William fell sick and was evidently at the point of death. The Anglican biographer does not seem to connect the two events even by way of coincidence: fortunately for himself, the Norman king was more prompt in seeing the point of the situation. He promised amendment and restitution of every possible kind, and sent for Anselm at once as the obvious person to be elected archbishop.

And then began a scene which has been enacted with various results a thousand times in the history of sanctity, but seldom with so much publicity or so much dramatic interest as in St Anselm's case. When you try to make a saint accept a bishopric, it is like trying to make a child take medicine: the result is a perfect fury of dissent. Calculation, argument, even personal dignity are thrown to the winds; the saint like the child simply sticks to his point and says: "I won't, I won't, I WON'T". In this case not merely the ordinary considerations but the whole welfare of a long-widowed Church and, as seemed probable, the life of a notorious sinner were depending upon St Anselm's acceptance, and he simply refused. "A great post like the archbishopric", writes Dean Church, "may have had irresistible terrors, overwhelming all its attractions or temptations, to a religious mind and conscience in the eleventh century"—a comment that speaks better for the courage of eleventh-century bishops than for the sense of humour of nineteenth-century deans. Anyhow, it was only by the use of physical force that they dragged the saint to the King's bedside; and there, pressing the crozier against the knuckles that would not open so as to hold it, they elected the Archbishop of Canterbury.

St Anselm is, from many points of view, a famous man, and stood out like a giant among his contemporaries. Yet the work he did was not final, for no human work is final. He was a monastic reformer, but others carried monastic reform further after his death. He was an intrepid champion of the Church against the Crown; and that is the same thing as to say that he defended the prerogatives of St Peter with a firmness which no glosses of the historian can conceal: but even here his work had to be done over again by St Thomas à Becket. He was a philosopher and a theologian, yet today his theological views are generally quoted in order to be refuted, and his most famous exploit in philosophy, the ontological proof of the existence of God, is not only discredited but has, according to some, the dubious credit of being the parent of modern idealism. So I will not apologize for leaving out these considerations—the sort of considerations you get in an obituary notice—and asking you to concentrate your attention on the scene I was describing just now, and to consider with me why it was that the saints, why it was that St Anselm, always began by refusing, and sometimes succeeded in refusing altogether, the offer of ecclesiastical preferment.

Was it because the saints were incompetent in the managing of affairs, and knew it? That might have been true in some cases, but it certainly was not in St Anselm's; he had already given good proof of his competency by being abbot of a large monastery—running a monastery is not always a sinecure. Or was it that they thought they were incompetent although they were not? Surely, if that had been all, obedience should have triumphed over humility, and they should have been content to acquiesce in the estimate others had formed of their worth. Or were they simply afraid that they would not get enough time to say their prayers? But St Anselm was a very busy man already. Or were they afraid of the temptation to worldliness, to love of money, to subservience which high office brings with it? But they must have known that other candidates were, humanly speaking, much more likely to succumb to those temptations than themselves: the good man, Plato tells us, accepts office in the State not for any advantage he gets from it, but because he fears the possibility of worse men than himself attaining to office instead. Or was it that they disliked all the pomp and fuss of it? But they could keep their secret intention pure. All those ordinary reasons which would make it very bad for you or me to be made a bishop were alleged by the saints as excuses, but surely only as excuses. There must be some deeper reason to explain this phenomenon that is always meeting us in hagiography, from St Celestine resigning the triple tiara to the Curé d'Ars running away like a schoolboy from the little French parish where everybody idolized him.

It is not that the saint has become unpractical, like the philosopher: the philosopher blinks because he has come out of the darkness of his study into the light of common things; the saint blinks because he has come out of the light of his oratory into the darkness of the world. He has been with God; and in seeing, as we do not see, the greatness of God, he has seen, as we do not see, his own smallness. It is not that he exaggerates his smallness; he is not like the horse, which shies (so clever people tell us) because its eyes are focused wrong and it sees everything around it twice as big as it really is. No, the saint has got the true perspective, and we the false. Woe is me, because I have held my peace —in the solitude of prayer he has learned his own miserable helplessness. I am a man of unclean lips, and dwell in the midst of a people of unclean lips—he has no illusion, you see, about his neighbours being to

any great extent better than himself. And I have seen with my eyes the
King, the Lord of Hosts—that is it. To the man who has once seen
himself as he looks in comparison with God, all worldly preferment,
not because it is too high or because it is too low a sphere for his
attainments, not because others seem more competent to fill the
post, not because it entails labour or responsibility, but simply because
it must in some measure make him the recipient of worldly homage
and give him honour in the sight of men, is an anomaly not to be
thought of, a miscarriage of justice to be avoided at all costs.

It is not a question of one man being more or being less worthy
than another, the plain fact is, if you have only got your eyes focused
right, that any job is too big for any of us, because all worldly station
involves the bestowing of some credit, and bestowing it where in truth
credit is not due. Modesty is quite a different thing from humility. It
is a very attractive thing, modesty, even where it is something of an
affectation. The boy, for example, who got the D.S.O. almost
immediately after leaving school, and when we asked him what he
was doing when he got it could only reply: "Oh, I don't know, fooling
round somewhere, I suppose"—that is modesty. There is a great deal of
modesty going about; it is fashionable, and the lack of it stamps you
with vulgarity—a lot of modesty, but very little humility. For modesty
is only the disinclination to hear our own praises sounded above those
of other men; by humility man learns that simply because he is man
he is nothing. Of such humility the Queen of Heaven herself could
leave us an example; let us make it the subject of our prayer on St
Anselm's festival. We can find excuses for ourselves when we do not
rival the saints in their heroic exercise of other virtues, but it is not so
with their humility. For in proportion as we are less than they, with
all the more justice can it be claimed of us that we should be humble.

And remember, this Christian humility does not unfit a man for
great deeds. A critic of St Edmund might say of his *Nolo episcopari*:
"Well, perhaps after all he was right; perhaps a more unscrupulous
man would have made a more successful job of the archbishopric in
his day." But St Anselm does not even leave room for the worldly
point of view. He knew, in his humility, that neither he nor any other
man living was worthy of the crozier that was pressed against his
clenched fingers, but, once clasped, it was clasped in a grip of iron.
We must not be afraid, then, of the meditation of our own littleness:
it could not dim the lustre of Anselm's earthly fame, yet made his
coronal in heaven shine, who knows how much brighter? May his
prayers protect the Church he laboured in life to defend, still bringing

C

back stubborn hearts to the allegiance of the Holy See: his prayers win for each one of us the grace he most needs, to God's glory and our eternal salvation.

8

ST DOMINIC[1]

Ye are the salt of the earth. But if the salt lose its savour, wherewith shall it be salted?—Matthew 5. 13.

Two men, at the beginning of the thirteenth century, were raised up by God to season his Church, that seemed in danger of perishing through its own corruption. They were both comparatively short-lived. God will be glorified, now in a short lifetime, now in the fullness of years; St John Vianney, whom we celebrate on Thursday, died worn out with his labours at the age of seventy-three; St Laurence, whom we celebrate on Friday, was cut down by persecution during his diaconate. If you add the ages of St Francis and St Dominic together, they do not cover a full century. And the career of St Dominic is particularly remarkable, because he did not find out what his life's work was to be until he was thirty-five years old, with only sixteen more years to live. That short time sufficed for doing the special thing God had called him to do; for meeting a particular situation, and warding off a particular danger from the gates of Christendom. If you will bear with me, I will sketch very briefly—at the risk of repeating things you may have heard yesterday and the day before—what that situation, what that danger was.

Two important heresies at that time threatened the peace, and perhaps the life of the Church; the Waldensian and the Albigensian heresies. The Waldenses, of whom a remnant still remains in Italy, seem to have been among the most harmless of the sects; erring through their simpleness rather than through any constructive malice. Scandalized by the riches of the higher clergy, by the sight of so many priests living unpriestly lives, they formed themselves into a little Protestant community before the time of Protestantism was yet come. They

[1] This sermon was preached at St Dominic's Priory, Haverstock Hill, London, on 6 August 1934, during a solemn triduum to celebrate the seventh centenary of the canonization of St Dominic.

lived in poverty, they studied and translated the Bible, they refused, like the Anabaptists and the Quakers after them, to bind themselves by any form of oath. Their main false doctrine was that a priest living in mortal sin was no priest at all; and they thought to replace the ministry of the ordained clergy by a kind of lay ministry of their own. They were, if such a phrase may be used, Nonconformists rather than heretics; and it is possible that, if they had not been involved in the fate of less worthy neighbours, they would have been treated by the Church with leniency, and returned gradually to her communion.

But the Albigenses, who resembled them outwardly, because they too made a parade of great simplicity and innocence, were the revival or the continuation of a very old and very dangerous heresy; that Manichean heresy which attracted, for a time, the restless genius of St Augustine. In order to account for the existence of the evil in the world, the Manichean maintains a total divorce between matter and spirit, believing that matter is of its nature evil, and owes its existence not to the Providence of God but to the interference of a malign spirit. Accordingly, he rejects the doctrine of the Incarnation, which degrades, to his mind, the spiritual nature of the Godhead. The more fully initiated of the sect, who called themselves the Perfect, repudiated altogether the use of marriage, and abstained, in their diet, from all animal life and whatever owed its origin to animal life. They were the declared enemies of Christendom, and, patronized as they were by the Count of Toulouse, threatened to supersede it altogether in the southern districts of France.

We remember St Dominic and his order, in the first instance, for the intellectual protest which they opposed to that sinister outbreak of Oriental philosophy in the heart of Western Christendom. Heresies, after all, have their place in the elucidation of religious truth. The fine flower of Christian scholarship is fertilized, you may say, by the decaying corpse of false doctrine. Or perhaps you may say with greater accuracy that Christian theology has at all times been a reaction to the assaults of heresy, just as a living organism will develop a protective shell there, where a hostile stimulus from without has made itself felt. When the germs of the Manichean heresy sought to find a lodgement in the healthy body of Christendom, the reaction of that healthy body was the great Dominican tradition of learning. It developed, we may well believe, beyond the saint's own hopes. Almost at the moment of his death another saint was being born to carry on his work: St Thomas, destined like Eliseus to have a double portion of his Master's spirit. Who shall say what we owe to that providential impetus which the

Manichean peril gave to Christian thought? Just as a healthy body may
gain immunity from a disease by being inoculated with a mild form of
it, so Christian thought was immunized against the false doctrines
which threatened to destroy it, three centuries later, by its inoculation
with the dying germs of Orientalism which it had encountered, and
triumphed over, at Toulouse.

That intellectual protest we associate especially with the Dominican
order, because it is more individually, more characteristically theirs.
The sons of St Francis only entered the vineyard of scholarship as late-
comers, by a happy deflection from their original design. But meanwhile, let us not forget that the coming of the Friars was a moral
protest too; and in that moral protest the sons of St Dominic from the
first took, and were meant to take, their full part; Cherubim and
Seraphim must hymn together the dazzling holiness of God. Those
were times, it is sad to say it, in which the Church seemed to have lost
the salt wherewith Christ had commissioned it to season the world.
The great St Bernard was dead; and the monastic orders, even at their
best, were too remote from the world to affect powerfully the standard
of Christian living. There were crying abuses; and, whereas the
Albigenses, a purely destructive movement, deserve little of our
sympathy, the poor Waldenses could at least claim that they had reason
for the disaffection which made them the antagonists of the Church.
An intellectual heresy can be met by the weapons of the intellect; a
moral protest, such as that of the Waldenses, can only be met by a rival
moral protest within the Church itself. Just as the tide of the Reformation was stemmed, not merely by polemical writing and preaching,
but by the great spiritual renewal which was accomplished throughout
Europe by the saints of the sixteenth century, so three hundred years
earlier it was not only the learning of the Friars, but their poverty, their
chastity, the simplicity of their lives and manners, that saved Europe
for the faith.

Reverend Fathers, the times in which we live, seven hundred years
removed from those days of persecution and terror, still need the
intellectual protest, still need the moral. The old difficulty of reconciling
God's omnipotence with his benevolence still presses upon us; and
today, instead of trying to save the one at the expense of the other, like
the medieval heretics, men are driven, by that apparent inconsistency,
to deny his very existence. It is to you, with the old weapons in your
hands, that we look for the solving of these difficulties as of those;
like King David, when he found once more the sword with which he
slew the giant in the valley of the terebinth, "there is none like that",

we say, "give it me". But while we call upon you as scholars for an intellectual protest against the tendencies of the age, we call upon you as Friars for a moral protest as well. For the times are evil; and the world's mind would not have travelled so far from God if its heart had not travelled far from God first.

We heard much lately in the newspapers—not so much quite lately, for the newspapers tire of their fancies quickly—about a new religious movement in the Protestant world around us which was to have prodigious effects in bringing men back to the service of God. It has much in common with earlier revivalist movements; and in one point at least it may well remind us of the Waldenses, about whom we were speaking just now. The Waldenses, as I was saying, distrusted the ministrations of an ordained clergy; every good man, they held, in so far as he is a good man, is a priest. Just so these new teachers have revived the idea of confession; but their confessions are made, not to an ordained minister of whatever denomination, but to one another —to the friends in whose goodwill and spiritual insight they can trust. I do not know whether this particular movement is destined to fulfil the hopes of its promoters; but of this at least I feel certain, that either this or some similar reaction will begin, before long, to stem the tide of demoralization which has so long closed in upon our society. Grace, like nature, abhors a vacuum; and any public neglect of God and of the soul's needs will be followed, before long, by a return. Are we to suffer our fellow countrymen to take refuge once more in the half-truths of a revived Protestantism, instead of learning to find peace where true peace can alone be found, in the bosom of the Catholic Church?

We shall suffer them to do that, unless we can oppose to the revived spirit of Protestantism a revived spirit of Catholicism. We Catholics want more simplicity, more contentment with plain living and with common things, more unworldliness about money and social position, more daily trust in Providence, more honesty of speech, more kindliness towards our fellow men; we want to get away from a great deal of that complexity, that sophistication, that worship of good form, into which the influence of our modern surroundings has led us. We want to restore, somehow, not the outward conditions, but the moral attitude which belonged to the medieval world. It is to the mendicant orders, to you not less than to the Franciscans, that we must look if if we are to revive that spirit of gaiety which goes with poverty, that open-hearted acceptance of the world which belongs only to those who have learned to despise it. Your continuous tradition must link us with our past, if we are to find refuge from this over-mechanized, over-commercialized age; like a shaft bringing the fresh airs of the sea into a Tube station. Persuade us that the Catholic religion is something more than a mere label, a mere favour that a man can wear on his sleeve; that it is a life, and an interpretation of life; an attitude towards our daily tasks, as well as an attitude towards God.

We expect of you that today, as seven hundred years ago, you should leaven human thought, by justifying the ways of God to men; by asserting the truth of our Lord's Incarnation, and vindicating the honour of his blessed Mother. We expect of you also that today, as seven hundred years ago, you should leaven human society, by showing us in your own lives, and in the lives of that great Third Order which derives its inspiration from you, the grand simplicity of former times. So will men learn to find, in the Catholic Church, the key to their disillusionment, and the remedy for their despairs; learning will not do that, argument will not do that. May the prayers of your holy patron, raised so long ago by an infallible oracle to the altars of the Church, win such grace for you and for us; may the bewildered minds of our non-Catholic fellow countrymen be led back, more and more, through the Dominicans to Dominic, and through Dominic to Christ.

9

ST EDMUND OF ABINGDON: I[1]

And the priest said: Lo, here is the sword of Goliath the Philistine, whom thou slewest in the valley of the terebinth. If thou wilt take this, take it, for there is no other but this. And David said: There is none like that; give it me. —1 Kings 21. 9.

WE have no means of knowing what was the age of David when this interview took place. Certainly he was married, and had occupied an important military position; we may imagine him, perhaps, as nearing thirty. The bitter jealousy of King Saul, the master whom he had served so faithfully, had driven him to take refuge as an

---

[1] This sermon was preached at St Edmund's College, Ware, on St Edmund's Day, 16 November 1925.

outlaw among the hills. On his way he visits the priests at Nobe, who supply him and his followers with bread for their journey. Then—it seems a poor chance, but he asks if they have a sword there; he has come out unarmed. And they tell him: Yes, there is one sword, the sword of Goliath the Philistine, the giant whom David himself slew, and dedicated the sword he had plundered from his body in the tabernacle of God.

As the priest is talking, David's mind travels back over the years, ten years perhaps, and he sees the valley of the terebinth as if it were yesterday. He sees himself as a boy, rather tired and hot after his journey from Bethlehem—he had been bringing presents from his father to his three soldier brothers, a bushel of corn, and ten loaves of bread, and ten small cheeses for their commanding officer, with father's compliments. To and fro along the valley strides the gigantic figure of the Philistine, taunting the armies of Israel and challenging them to provide a champion who will meet him in single combat. David remembers how he expected his brothers to be pleased with their hamper from home, and how disappointed he was at the very elder-brotherly greeting of the eldest, Eliab: "Why camest thou hither? And why didst thou leave those few sheep in the desert? I know thy pride, and the wickedness of thy heart, that thou art come down to see the battle." So unfair of him—and besides, David *had* wanted to see the battle rather. And then the sudden resolve, to ask if he might accept the giant's challenge—that heroic resolution, with just a faint tinge of anxiety to get even with Eliab. It felt rather frightening at first, walking down the valley to meet the boaster—and then he was kneeling down by the brook side, while he picked up five pebbles just the shape he wanted; and then the confidence he felt as the sling whirled round his head, and the stone flew dead straight, and hit his enemy full in the forehead, so that he lay there stunned. Quick! no time to be lost; weaponless himself, he takes out the giant's sword and cuts off the monstrous head with it. And then, a confused memory, the stir and the cry as the men of Israel went out to battle. Yes, he has seen many engagements since then; many a sword has broken in his victorious hand, but . . . the sword he took from Goliath, what could bring better omens for his present journey? There is none like that; give it me!

Let me give you another picture for comparison—one, perhaps, with which you are more familiar; St Edmund on board ship, looking back at the cliffs of Dover for the last time. He, too, is going into exile, though it be voluntary exile; he, too, is hated and thwarted by the

king for whom he has done so much, for whom he would have done
so much more. And to him too, surely, comes a picture of the past;
only he needs a longer retrospect; it is nearly fifty years now since he
first made that Channel crossing. He sees himself as a boy of fifteen
or thereabouts, tremendously excited at the prospect of going to study
at Paris. The sea itself was a stranger to him: he knew the Thames
where it sweeps down nobly from Oxford to Abingdon, or where it
hastens past the ferry at Bablockhythe; but the beauty and mystery of
the ships and the magic of the sea—that was all a new experience. And
probably, so wayward is memory in the associations she brings
together, he connects that experience with the first time he wore a
hair-shirt, his mother's parting gift. Smile at the picture if you will,
but do not laugh at the symbol; he was going to the worldliest city of
all time, and he was to keep himself unspotted from the world. That
love of Christ and his blessed Mother which he had learned at Oxford
was to be put to a severer test now. Since then, St Edmund has met
the world at a hundred different angles in the course of his busy life,
has done heroic penance, has inflicted cruel mortification on himself.
But those first impressions of his boyhood, which the hair-shirt
symbolizes, are still his formative impressions; the religion of his boyhood is still, to him, the giant's sword—there is none like that, give it
me.

Will you place yourself, you who are an Old Edmundian, in some
such position of retrospect, and let your mind focus itself upon some
incident, some impression, some crisis of your school time? Not on
the common memories which you will be talking over later in the
day, about the rules which you broke, and the professors whose lives
you made uncomfortable: dig deeper, and bring to light some aspect
of your boyhood which you have never discussed, except perhaps in
the confessional. The moment, it may be, or the period at which you
realized and accepted your vocation to the priesthood. Hitherto, you
had taken it for granted you were to be a priest; then the awkward
age came, and with it difficulties, temptations; you had to fight your
way through, perhaps with the advice of others, perhaps with the
light God gave in answer to your prayer. Or, not aspiring to the priesthood, you nevertheless met on this field the first onslaught of spiritual
difficulties; doubts, temptations, falls into sin, what you will. Hitherto,
confessions and communions had been scarcely more than a matter of
routine; now you had an enemy to face, perhaps to dislodge, and you
paused a little longer over your prayers in front of the statue or the
shrine. Try to recapture some such experience, and from it take heart

for whatever needs, whatever dangers you experience now. The love of Christ and of his blessed Mother you learned here; the sword you killed the giant with. Say to yourself: There is none like that; give it me.

Meanwhile, may I address myself to present Edmundians, in so far as I still claim their attention? You have been born into an age of decision for the world and for the Catholic Church. Before our very eyes the half-faiths and the false Christianities which the Reformation brought with it are crumbling away. The number of their adherents is steadily diminishing, and even those who do profess to adhere to them are more and more abandoning belief in the Bible, belief in revelation, belief in the sacraments, belief in a world of rewards and punishments hereafter. And it is not only their beliefs but their moral standards that are disappearing. Especially the sanctity of marriage is being profaned; divorce is treated as a natural occurrence; no age before ours has so openly and so flagrantly set at naught the ordinance of God. And, while Protestantism crumbles away, the Catholic Church is winning back lost ground. We Catholics, in our effort to convert England, are not like furniture removers, paid by the hour, slowly and gingerly piling things on to a van. We are like men fighting a fire, desperately keeping at bay, here and there, the flames of unbelief and of social disorder, while we hurriedly rescue all that we have time to rescue. The fire will get ahead of us if we stop to contemplate our work.

In such an age, to aspire to the priesthood is not to aspire to comforts or to earthly rewards. You do not want to be a priest who simply does his job and knows his rubrics and hopes to pay off a bit of the parish debt. You want to be an ambassador from God to men, ready to take every opening, to follow up every trail, where there is a human conscience to be enlightened or a lost soul to be won back. You want to love souls; if you do not love souls, you will be hard put to it, in a world of so many temptations, to save your own.

And even if the priesthood has no place in your ambitions, you must still want to leave St Edmund's not as a Catholic merely, but as a fighting Catholic and a working Catholic. It is possible nowadays, thank God, for laymen to take a direct and public part in spreading the faith. But even apart from that, we Catholics do not live, as our grandfathers used to live, in a sort of water-tight compartment, separated from the world around us. We mix freely with Protestant neighbours, and either we shall influence them or they us. If we are not strongly fortified in the practice of religion, their unbelief will tell upon our faith, their low standard of morality will infect and degrade our consciences. It is becoming a clear issue in our day, the Church or nothing. Do you remember what the priest said to David about the giant's sword? "If thou wilt take this, take it; for there is none other but this." So it is with the religion you are taught here: there is none other but this. The doctrines which you are taught in apologetics or Christian doctrine class are not a sort of continuation of the gender rhymes; the practices of piety in which you are encouraged are not a tiresome regulation made for you by house masters. They are the world's last hope, which is committed to your keeping. They are the giant's sword, with which you now face the temptations of boyhood, with which you will face later the temptations of manhood. If thou wilt take this, take it, for there is none other than this.

David was an outlaw in his own country; you, too, if you are faithful Catholics, still more if you are preaching the Catholic religion, will be outlaws to some extent in the world of today, a world which tends more and more to banish religion from its speech and its thought. Other schools have other traditions—this one has bred great soldiers, this has been a nursery of poets, there the civic virtues are practised and extolled. Our tradition is a different one, and in these days, I think, a more important one. We are a college of outlaws; those who have gone out from us were men who could set their face against the false standards of the world they lived in, who could stem the current of their times instead of being carried away with it. The names which we record here, with honour and with gratitude, are not those of men whom the world recognized, men who ruled empires or moulded the thought of their day, but those of exiles condemned as traitors, men who loved England too well to leave England what it was. The College has seen many changes, and may see more, but one thing remains constant about our tradition, that the man who is ready to let the world dictate its beliefs to him is a bad Edmundian.

He at least would tell us so, whose festival we keep, whose relics we venerate here. He would tell us that even in a world avowedly Catholic, a world obedient in every outward observance to the discipline of our holy faith, the widest learning, the most cloistered humility, the most single-hearted sincerity of purpose are no protection against hatred, and calumny, and misunderstanding. He has loved justice and hated iniquity, *therefore* he dies in exile—the grim irony of that word "therefore" should be the Edmundian's armour against the world. He lives and dies an exile who will not take the world at its own valuation, who despises its folly and protests against its wrongs. Even if there were no hereafter to reward us, could we doubt where the man's part lies, which standard beckons us to more adventure, the world's standard or

Christ's? But we must not face that battle in blind confidence; we must learn to hold and to wield our boyhood's sword, the religion of the Catholic Church. If thou wilt take this, take it, for there is none other than this. And he said: There is none like that; give it me.

IO

ST EDMUND OF ABINGDON: II[1]

As for Moses, whom they attacked, never was a man more patient on the whole face of the earth.—Numbers 12. 3.

THERE is a phrase in our language, "As meek as Moses". When we first come across it, it takes us by surprise. Surely, we say to ourselves, if ever a man had a tough job to do, and a tough crowd to deal with, it was Moses; and on a variety of occasions he seems to have stood up to them very successfully. Competent, if you like, impressive, if you like; but why meek? Well, it comes from that verse I have just quoted; a sudden floodlight is cast by divine revelation on the character of a man we had all been accustomed to read quite differently. Moses could be stern enough, ruthless enough, where God's honour was concerned. But attack him personally, express a doubt whether he personally was up to his job, and there was no man more patient on the whole face of the earth.

Those of us who have been privileged to listen to a good many St Edmund's Day sermons in our time expect the preacher to produce reasons—sometimes rather far-fetched reasons—for regarding St Edmund as a great figure in English history, or in the history of thought, or in the history of devotion. My mind goes back to a sermon, fifty minutes in length, which proposed the saint to our admiration as the man who really introduced into England the study of Greek. That one didn't go down very well. As a matter of fact, in a curious way, our saint stood outside all the movements of his time. His date is more easily remembered than any other date in history—he became Archbishop of Canterbury in A.D. 1234. He was too young to figure, as Stephen Langton did, in the agitation which gave us Magna Charta.

---

[1] This sermon was preached at St Edmund's College, Ware, on St Edmund's Day, 16 November 1956.

He did not live long enough to take part, as St Thomas of Hereford did, in the Barons' War which saw the birth of Parliament. His lifetime over-lapped with that of St Thomas Aquinas, with that of St Bonaventure; but (although he was a man of the schools) you will never see his authority quoted for any theological opinion. He was the contem-porary of St Francis and St Dominic, yet he took no part in that great spiritual adventure by which the friars conquered Europe. He does not dominate the scene.

For six years, only six years, full of trouble but devoid of glory, he was Archbishop of Canterbury. Till then, he was a plain priest, one of ourselves. The best years of his life were spent in lecturing on theo-logy, and acting as treasurer to the cathedral of Salisbury. A professor, a diocesan official; put him into modern dress, and you can imagine him walking, day after day, round the four roads, taking the bus, day after day, to Westminster. A plain secular priest, like so many of us here; why was he so different from the rest of us? Why did the Church declare that he was in heaven before he had been six years in his coffin? Let's seize upon one or two points in his character, and ask him to tell us how an ordinary secular priest can be a good priest.

First, let's take one rather unpopular point, and get over it; let's admit that St Edmund went in, in a big way, for mortification. We all know the stories about his mother making sure that he packed his hair-shirt when he went off to school at Paris; how, in boyhood, he made his vow of chastity to our Lady and how, even at the busiest time of his life, he didn't go to bed; he just got what sleep he could leaning up against the wall. Well, I'm not going to try and rub that in, because I'm speaking largely to people who haven't yet finished their education; and as long as you're at school or even in the seminary, you're apt to feel that the mortification is mostly being done for you. And I know that modern lives of the saints are inclined to soft-pedal all this business about bodily mortifications; it may be true that we're not as tough as the medieval people were, and we need a different kind of asceticism. But the fact remains, and it's true although you have heard it so often, that a life which leaves no room in its programme for deliberate self-discipline can hardly be a Christian, let alone a priestly life. Don't go out of your way to multiply the things you can't do without. Even a particular armchair or a particular wireless programme can be the enemy of sanctification. Make sure that there is, at fairly frequent intervals in your life, a head-on conflict between your will and your inclinations—I mean, of course, in matters where no actual sin is concerned. The last five minutes out of bed can be a decisive battle-ground. No matter how often you lose, the conflict must go on. And then you will be able to call yourself an Edmundian.

But that isn't everything. To be strict with yourself isn't everything. You have to share the world with your fellow men, and if you are a priest working in a parish your chief concern is with the souls of your fellow men. And it does sometimes happen that a priest who, for the love of God, treats himself harshly, is led into the temptation of treating other men harshly too. When they won't toe the line, when they are slack about their duties as Christians, he shrugs his shoulders and writes them off as people not worth taking trouble about. He doesn't try to understand their difficulties, or to win them by gentleness. And here St Edmund may serve us once more as a model, because although his biographers, like most biographers of the saints, fail completely to give us a picture of what he was really like, one thing does emerge from the story—he was a man of great kindliness. He just couldn't quarrel with anybody. Mark you, he had plenty of opportunity for quarrelling; he was trying to reform some of the more obvious abuses of his time, and when he wasn't being thwarted by the King, he was being thwarted by the Papal legate, and when he wasn't being thwarted by the Papal legate he was being thwarted by his own monks at Canterbury. I remember a friend of mine, who was teaching with me here, making a rather curious comment when I told him about a new bishop who'd just been appointed; "Father So-and-so?" he said. "I shouldn't have thought he was vindictive enough for a bishop." Well, St Edmund wasn't vindictive at all; he stood up like a rock for his principles, but nobody ever suspected him of working off a grudge, or of bearing malice. He was such a kind man.

May I make, just there, a digression? There are many of us priests who cannot return to Old Hall on an occasion like this without being reminded, at every turn and at every moment, of the President we knew, Archbishop Myers.[1] Let me say of him, for the sake of those who knew him less well, what seems a platitude to us who worked under him, that he was a man compact of kindness. Behind all that learning we admired, behind all those tricks of manner and speech which we parodied, we knew him for a man always approachable; who never dreaded an interruption, always gave you the best of his advice, was ready to listen to any request, and meet it with sympathy. To call him genial would be to miss the point of him; it costs so little effort to be genial—on the surface. But this man had a kindly heart.

---

[1] Archbishop Myers was President of St Edmund's College from 1918 to 1932, when he was appointed Auxiliary to the Archbishop of Westminster.

And, believe me, this is what really makes the difference in a parish; kindliness, on the part of the parish priest, is or isn't there. He may be a man of ascetic life, regular in his prayers, an admirable diocesan official, but if he doesn't love his people, he isn't loved. Oh, I know some of us are more forthcoming, more generous by temperament, and find it easier to make our neighbours feel at home than others do. But it's something deeper than that you want; it's a love of Jesus Christ which sees his image in every soul and comes out to meet it. A shy man and a blunderer, if he has that quality, will be a good parish priest, and nothing you learn here, none of the drill you get here, will make up for the lack of it. Tell yourself that you've got to be everybody's friend, even if it's somebody who opposes your influence, somebody you've got to have rows with. Then you will be able to call yourself an Edmundian.

And finally, St Edmund was utterly resigned to the will of God. He didn't want to be made an archbishop, he protested and struggled, but gave way in the end because if seemed as if this was God's will for him. He stood out against the abuses of his time, not because he enjoyed being in opposition to everybody else, but because he knew that it was his job to stand out against them, even if nobody, not even the Papal legate, would support him. And when he found that all his remonstrances were useless, he couldn't associate himself any longer with policies which, to his mind at least, were not God's will, so he went into exile. Historians have criticized him as ineffective; and perhaps if he had been a born fighter he would have held out longer, perhaps if he had been a practised intriguer he would have got his way. But he followed God's will as he saw it, and it was with no tinge of bitterness or regret, but full of comfort and resignation, that he gave up his soul in death. "In thee, Lord, I have believed"—such was his last testament —"thee I have preached and taught. Thou art my witness that I have desired nothing on earth but thee alone. As thou seest that my heart desires only thy holy will, let it be accomplished in me."

Nobody who ever tried to do good in the world has managed to get through life without experiencing frustration and disappointment. Least of all a priest, who has to work on the stubborn soil of men's souls, in a world always ready to criticize, limited by the authority of human, and not always wise, superiors. He will find his plans set aside, his advice neglected, cold water poured on his aspirations. He will take that well, precisely in so far as he has learned, from the outset, to put God's will in the foreground, not the background, of his world-picture. Force yourself, in your prayer, to see his will as the only thing that matters; be prepared to see all the good you meant and tried to do done by some other man, on the ruins of your failure. Then, in life and in death, you will be able to call yourself an Edmundian.

II

ST ALBERT THE GREAT[1]

Every scribe instructed in the kingdom of heaven is like to a man that is a householder, who bringeth forth out of his treasure new things and old.— Matthew 13. 52.

My text is one of those which we are accustomed to carry in our heads without remembering the occasion upon which the utterance was made, and, partly for that reason, to hesitate about the precise meaning we should attach to it. It comes, actually, at the end of that great chapter, his thirteenth, in which St Matthew has collected for us seven of our Lord's parables, six of which, if not all seven, deal with the growth of his kingdom, the Church; the sower, the cockle among the wheat, the mustard seed, the leaven, the hidden treasure, the merchant seeking pearls, the net cast into the sea. And four are particularly concerned to point out to our Lord's hearers that his kingdom was not, as some of them imagined, to be a clean sweep of all that went before it, a complete break-away from all human experience. It was not to be a millennium, in which all sin and suffering would have disappeared; those who were partakers of it would not be all perfect souls, already confirmed in goodness and destined for eternal life. No, the new kingdom or *ecclesia* of Christ was to be in some ways like the old *ecclesia*, the old congregation of the Jews. There would still be tares among the wheat, worthless fish amongst the catch, side by side with the others. Our Lord, therefore, is not exactly creating a new thing in the world when he lays the foundations of his Church; in a sense he is only reconstituting, on a new basis and with more extended possibilities, the old *ecclesia* of the Jews which he called to himself so long ago. Do the apostles understand that? They do? Good, then they are scribes instructed in the kingdom of heaven; they see that every

---

[1] This sermon was preached at Blackfriars, Oxford, on 16 May 1932, at the opening of a solemn triduum in honour of St Albert.

new thing in human history is built against the background of some
older thing which went before it. As the picture gallery of some great
house preserves the memory of its ancestry, tracing down to the latest
instance the persistence of the same characteristics, and linking up the
present with the past; so the greatest institutions of the world are
those which combine something ancient with something new. And
among these, even the Catholic Church.

It is a human weakness of ours to be always crying out for complete
novelty, an entire disseverance from our past. Our old traditions have
become so dusty with neglect, so rusted with abuse, that we are for
casting them on the scrap-heap and forgetting that they ever existed.
The Church conserves; she bears traces still of the Jewish atmosphere
in which she was cradled; traces, too, of the old heathen civilization
which she conquered. And in her own history it is the same; nothing
is altogether forgotten; every age of Christianity recalls the lineaments
of an earlier time. People think of her as if she kept a lumber-room; it
is not so; hers is a treasure-house from which she can bring forth when
they are needed things old as well as new.

It is not difficult to see how all this applies to the history of the
thirteenth century, and the reinstatement of Aristotle's philosophy
by St Albert and St Thomas. The first instinct of Christendom had
been to neglect and to disparage the pagan authors, whose works were
so saturated with allusions to an idolatrous worship. St Jerome was
afraid of being too good a Ciceronian to be a Christian; and St
Augustine was ashamed of having been moved to tears by the story
of the Aeneid. Buried away in libraries, the works of the ancients
slept on; there is no clear proof that the great library of Alexandria,
for instance, suffered much from Christian hands. But the libraries
had been collected in the East, and when the East passed under the
dominion of Islam, Islam became, for better or worse, the world's
librarian. So it was that when Aristotle returned to Europe he returned
in Oriental guise, translated and interpreted by the sectaries of the False
Prophet. His works were not only dusty with the neglect of centuries,
they were corroded with the rust of heretical contamination. Is it
wonderful that the Christian world mistrusted their influence? You
have to imagine, if you seek for a modern parallel, a situation in
which all the available scientific literature of the world should be in
the hands of Soviet Russia, and accessible only in the form of editions
scrawled over with Bolshevist comment. It was a heroic adventure,
only made possible through the guidance of the Holy Spirit, when the
theologians of a new order, which still had its reputation for orthodoxy

to establish, took upon themselves to make a niche for Aristotle in the ante-chambers of Christian thought. The old weapon, soiled and rusty, useless, you would have thought—but there were men ready to scour and polish it, and make use of it, an instrument as keen as ever, for the confuting of false doctrine and the systematization of knowledge.

New things and old—St Albert, as a scribe instructed in the kingdom of heaven, realized perhaps more than most men of his day that the secular sciences had great advances still to make, and that there must be room for new discoveries in any philosophy which was to express fully the thought of mankind. It was an age unfriendly to research for many reasons. The best brains were either devoted to practical administration in the world, or to theological studies in the cloister; the tools of science, though they had already been dreamt of, had not yet been forged; above all, printing had not yet appeared, with all its opportunities for garnering the fruit of human speculation. And the men of today will speak in contemptuous terms of the medieval world, as one in which research made no progress; they forget the difficulties which I have just mentioned; they forget also that St Albert was characteristic of his period no less than St Thomas. And St Albert certainly had the build of mind which goes to make the research worker. If he had enjoyed more leisure from controversy and from the cares of administration, he would be remembered, as Roger Bacon is remembered, as part of that false dawn of science which went before the Renaissance; and he would be honoured today for activities which he himself would have been the last to think important. But they are important, for this reason if for no other—they prove that the Middle Ages, in taking over Aristotle as their master, did not suppose he had said the last word on every possible subject of discussion. St Albert was too good an Aristotelian to think that Aristotle must be always right; he would imitate his master, not merely by borrowing opinions from him, but by instituting original research as he did.

Today, perhaps more than ever before, the world is eager to make a clean sweep of its past. The war has driven a deep furrow across human experience, separating all that went before it from all that has come and that is to come after it, hardly with less of decisiveness than the Flood in earlier civilizations, than the Christian era in later times. Because we are in a mess with our economics, because Russia has shown the way to infidelity, because Europe is feeling after a new solidarity, this post-war world feels a different world to us elder people, and our juniors are not slow to rub it in. They talk, they write, as if the world of Einstein and Jeans and Rutherford and Eddington were a world re-born; as if every earlier guess after the truth were now superseded or exploded; as if, for the first time, we had begun to know. In such ears, what use to celebrate the praises of St Albert? The very name sounds worse than medieval; it sounds Victorian.

That is the secret of the modern world's antipathy towards the Christian religion, and towards the Catholic Church in particular. They hate it not because it is something arrogant, not because it is something uncomfortable, not because it is something foreign, but because it is something out of date. They know that it will always bring new things and old out of its treasure-house, will not consent to the modern worship of the modern. And they know that there is strength in this deeply rooted tradition which can yet absorb, as it has absorbed all through the ages, lessons that are new. *Stat magni nominis umbra*: they feel, when they meet us, that though they may have heard the last of Albert the Good, they have not heard the last of Albert the Great. A hundred years back they hoped to dispose of the Church by disposing of the Bible; now their tactics have grown more subtle. They hope to dispose of the Church by disposing of Aristotle. It has become the fashion to gird at us because our whole thought is built up round a philosophical system which was fifteen hundred years old when we assimilated it, and has now ceased to hold the speculative allegiance of mankind. Only the other day I read a book by a popularizer of science, well known in the broadcasting world, whose whole thesis was that Einstein has shown up Euclid, and if we are not going to believe in Euclid it would be absurd to believe in Aristotle, and if we no longer believe in Aristotle, then Christianity has ceased to count.

It is with happy omen, then, if we may dare to criticize the solemn actions of the Church in terms of human congruity, that the Holy Father has just raised St Albert to the altars of the Church, and numbered him among her doctors. Not in the sense that the Church is concerned to applaud the physical speculations of the great philosopher, or to regard them as final, when St Albert himself was not content to regard them as final. Nor even in the sense that Aristotle's metaphysics are the only possible framework of thought in which the Christian world-idea can be stated. Rather because, in the speculative confusion of our time, when men talk as if the theories advanced by natural science were inconsistent with the doctrines of our faith, it is good to look back on a time when Aristotle himself seemed to be an anti-Christian writer, and the attempt to rehabilitate him was regarded with deep suspicion by the old-fashioned. Rather because, when the cry is all for novelty, for further discoveries which shall sweep us away,

more and more, from our intellectual bearings, it is well to be reminded
that sooner or later human thought always turns back on itself, and the
system which was once discredited creeps back into favour again. The
modern world lives on its intellectual capital, exploits the prevalent
doctrine of the moment in the interest of its heresies; floodlights the
universe with a gleam of partial illumination, or darkens the skies with
doubt; the Church, who is wiser and older, stores new things and
old alike in her treasure-house, and brings them out in their due relation
to enrich, permanently, the experience of mankind.

May we go further, and admire the Providence which has left it
for a pope, pre-eminently a man of thought as well as a man of action,
to canonize a saint who was pre-eminently a man of action as well as a
man of thought? For, after all, the really surprising thing about St
Albert is not so much the enormous range of learning which won him
his title of the Universal Doctor, as the fact that the life which included
so much reading and writing, in days when reading and writing were
difficult, included also a vast amount of administrative activity; he
was not a mere lecturer or regent of studies; he was Provincial of his
order in Germany, and for three years a bishop. Well might a contemporary describe him as "the astonishment and miracle of our times".
How did he manage it all? The secret is out at last; he was a saint. The
tradition of him preserved in his own order and in his own country
has been ratified by the solemn judgment of the Church. Too long we
have thought of him as merely reflecting the rays of St Thomas's
beatitude; we know now that those who were so intimately associated
in their lives, and not divided in their loyalty by death, were not
divided, save by a few years, in their entry into a blessed eternity.
Master and pupil, they could share with our blessed Lord and our
blessed Lady the joys of an everlasting reunion.

May St Albert's prayers bring peace to a distracted Europe; may
they enlighten, as he himself enlightened in his time, the darkness of
human thought. And may your own order, Reverend Fathers, be
worthy of its saintly heritage, and prove ever fertile of scribes instructed
in the kingdom of heaven, to bring out of your treasure-house new
things and old.

12

ST THOMAS AQUINAS[1]

The lessons she taught me are lessons honestly won, shared without stint, openly proclaimed; a treasure men will find inexhaustible.—Wisdom 7. 13.

AT any time during the early years of this century, if you consulted Brewer's *Dictionary of Phrase and Fable*, and turned up the reference under "Angelic Doctor", you would read this: "Angelic Doctor, The, Thomas of Aquino, so called because he discussed how many angels could dance on the point of a pin". Whether, in fact, any schoolmen did devote attention to this rather specialized subject, I have often tried to discover, but have never managed to trace the legend further back than Tristram Shandy, where I strongly suspect that it originated. I only use that quotation here to draw your attention to a singular fact; namley that in the last twenty-five years or so the great saint whom we commemorate today has, in a way, come into his own—even in these days of loose thought, and of unlaborious reading. Today, even Brewer's *Dictionary of Phrase and Fable* has been corrected, and wherever you meet a man who professes interest in things of the mind, you will find that St Thomas means something to him. Possibly he will use the name "Aquinas" to indicate that this is not an author with whom he is on friendly terms; almost certainly he will admit that he has never tried to read "Aquinas". But there will be respect in his voice; he will know that he is referring, not to a medieval quibbler, but to an author whose works are one of the milestones in the history of human thought.

St Thomas was a great saint; and what we properly celebrate on the feast of a great saint are his virtues; his purity of soul, his humility, his easy converse with the other world. If he happened to be a philosopher as well, that does not really concern us; it was part of God's Providence that he should realize his sanctity in the life of a philosopher, just as it was part of God's Providence that St Benedict Joseph Labre should realize his sanctity in the life of a tramp covered with vermin. There is no more reason to talk about philosophy when you are celebrating the virtues of St Thomas than there is to talk about entomology when you are discussing the virtues of St Benedict Joseph

[1] This sermon was preached at Hawkesyard Priory, Rugeley, on the Feast of St Thomas Aquinas, 7 March 1945.

Labre. We know, indeed, that God does sometimes give supernatural illumination to the minds of his saints; we know that St Thomas himself had an ecstasy at Mass in which he saw enough of divine truth, as it really is, to make all his own writings seem poor stuff by comparison. But those glimpses are incommunicable, alas, to us others. No, the theology of St Thomas is not an esoteric mystery, it is based on hard facts and mathematical reasonings; "honestly won", as my text says, not smuggled in from some celestial black market; "shared without stint, openly proclaimed"—there is no incommunicable quality about it. Penetrated, doubtless, like all the relics which the saints leave behind them, with a virtue not of the world, but not part of the stuff of his sanctity. The *Summa* is only a by-product of his true genius; the composition of it whiled away the leisure hours of a man whose business was prayer. Sanctity is not a work done, it is a life lived.

Yet, in a house dedicated to study under his auspices, it would be out of place to commemorate the thing that happened on 7 March 1274 without reminding ourselves, in brief and perhaps commonplace outline, of the work St Thomas did in his day, the work that remains to be done in ours, not least by the children of St Dominic. I would simply point to two principles, which jut out like buttresses from the great edifice he has left behind him, lucidly evident, yet in danger of being forgotten in our day no less than in his. One is, that you must have a philosophy which covers the whole of your experience, which faces all the facts; not a philosophy which explains half your experience and explains away the other half. And the second principle is, that truth is all one; that you must have a system which dovetails together the results of all your knowledge; not one kind of truth for the physicist and another for the philosopher, or one kind of truth for the philosopher and another for the theologian.

There is a constant tendency for the human mind, when it philosophizes, to cut the knots instead of untying them; to isolate one part of your experience and thrust away the other half into a corner as something that cannot be explained, or is unworthy of explanation. There is no more puzzling riddle for a philosopher to solve than the relation between matter and spirit, between the world which meets our eyes and the eyes with which we look out on it. In the thirteenth century the Church was still grappling with that curious outbreak of heresy in Europe which produced the crusade against the Albigenses. Somehow, nobody quite knows how, the South of France had been invaded by a set of ideas, reintroduced from the East, which Christian people thought had been killed once for all by St Augustine eight hundred years earlier. It was not a philosophical system which denied the existence of matter, it was a religious system which held that matter was wholly evil. Marriage was wrong, taking life was wrong, eating animal food was wrong, sacraments were valueless—everything that concerned the material side of man's nature must be thrust away, hidden in a corner. The Catholic religion, these heretics maintained, was something carnal, material, false to its mission.

Against that background of error St Thomas built up his Aristotelian philosophy, his theology of the Incarnation. Matter was not something which human thought could thrust away out of sight, the sensible world was not something that could be despised utterly; on the contrary, it was from our sensible experience that all our knowledge ultimately came. Matter was not something evil; God himself had become flesh, had sanctified a fallen earth with his tread, had bound up some of his chief graces with the sacramental use of material things. "God and his creatures"—what a world of comfort there is in the very formula which, instinctively, the name of St Thomas conjures up to us; God's creatures, not the work of some jealous demiurge, acting in defiance of his will; creatures representing God and conveying good to man; the cosy furniture of this, our temporary home!

In our day, the chief danger lies in the opposite direction. Our minds are ruled, more than we know, by suggestion and association. And the mechanized world in which we live, eating eggs that come out of a tin, with unpiloted aeroplanes droning overhead, seems to have put us at the mercy of our own inventions; the machinery we created to be a useful servant has become a pitiless master. And it is not wonderful if the bent of the human mind is towards a mechanical explanation of things; if a popular philosophy traces every act of the mind, every development in history, to blind, irresistible forces that have no human will directing them. And still we need the splendid sanity of St Thomas to convince ourselves and to persuade others that such a view, once again, is only looking at one side of the picture. Sense experience is not knowledge, does not account for knowledge, could not by itself develop into knowledge; there must be a spiritual principle at work. Trained instinct does not account for all our behaviour; a place must be left in your scheme for purposive will. God and his creatures; those creatures dazzle us by their complexity, daunt us by their persistent presence at our elbows; but they are his.

And the other great buttress which seems to stand out from St Thomas's thought is the unity of the sciences. It was a decisive moment in the world's history when St Albert and St Thomas, in defiance of so much nervous opposition, determined to make a Christian of Aristotle; Aristotle, the master-knower, the flower of pagan enlightenment. The Arabs had already adopted him, but they never made a Mohammedan of him. It is one of the most striking proofs of the superiority of Christianity to Islam, that when both tried the same philosophical diet we could digest it and they couldn't. In the Mohammedan world, the result was a struggle between the theologians and the philosophers, and the theologians won. They buried Aristotle away, like a dangerous explosive; and the Mohammedan culture, till then a dangerous rival to our own, became sterile. The Crusades were not yet over; we had not yet fought them to a standstill; but we had thought them to a standstill; nay, we had thought them back into the desert.

And if we did that, if the Christian world did that, the praise is due, under God, to St Thomas's fearless instinct that you must not be afraid of knowledge; that truth could not contradict truth, and whatever in Greek philosophy was true would harmonize with the Christian tradition; they would link together automatically, like St Peter's chains. He had to fight an ultra-orthodox party, which dreaded Aristotle as a materialist. He had to fight another set of thinkers, who accepted Aristotle as philosophical truth, and, because they could not fit the Christian tradition into his system, invented a distinction between two kinds of truth, philosophical and theological. No, truth was and ever must be one; philosophy was the handmaid of theology, and where you could bring them to an understanding, there you had the perfect *ménage*.

Today, for a multitude of reasons, we have far less apparatus than St Thomas's contemporaries ever had for integrating our thought. Learning and speculation have so multiplied that it is hard, even within the sphere of theology itself, for one man to be more than a specialist; and you will find a dogmatic theologian attaching importance, perhaps, to some isolated text which the Scripture professors have decided to interpret in quite another sense. And when you survey the field of the sciences generally, the psychologists interpreting everything in terms of mental aberration, the economists interpreting everything in terms of bread and butter, the physicists annihilating matter, limiting space, and snapping their fingers at law—what synthesis is possible in such a rough and tumble as that? Once more men's minds are tempted to wonder whether religious truth isn't perhaps an altogether different kind of truth, valid in its own sphere just as the economist's truth or the physicist's truth are valid in theirs. Philosophy, even, that was once the handmaid of theology, seems to have given notice, and the most theology can hope for is a little occasional help. Is it not time, perhaps, that religion should shut itself up in its own precincts, and live its own life in isolation from the debates of the world around it?

Once more, against this subtler peril, we have to arm ourselves with the thought of St Thomas. Somehow, sooner or later, the multitudinous opinions of our time have got to be integrated, unless we are all to end in the mad-house. And we know that because our religion is true the Christian theology must inevitably fit in with the rest, and fit in as the key-piece of the whole structure. It is, I think, to the sons of St Dominic, with their roots so firmly fixed in the past, their minds so keenly alive to the atmosphere of the present, that we look most confidently to achieve that vast synthesis in its time.

"A treasure men will find inexhaustible"; those were the concluding words of my text—are the works of St Thomas inexhaustible? Not, evidently, in the sense that he could foresee all the discoveries which would be made, all the theories which would be propounded, by the scientists of later ages, and frame his speech to allow for them. Not even in the sense that he could foresee, in their precise form, all the hesitations of the philosophers who would come after him, the subtle distinctions they would draw, the analogies by which they would illustrate their thought. But the channel has been buoyed now; and the modern explorer, be he as adventurous as he will, marks, and will ever mark, the indelible traces of the Master Mariner's passage.

Meanwhile, Reverend Fathers, let us remind ourselves again that we did not come here to admire the profundity of a great human genius, and the record of his achievement. We are here to thank God for the life of a poor friar, who kept the rule and scrubbed his cell and said his office and loved our blessed Lady like the rest of us. If he had never put pen to paper, earth would be the poorer for it, but heaven would not have missed a citizen. He had that holiness, that setapartness, which would have supernaturalized his life's work, whatever his life's work had been. He entered the kingdom of heaven as a little child; it is the only entrance. Let us ask him to win us his purity, his humility, his love of obedience, before we ask for any tincture of his learning.

13

ST JOAN OF ARC[1]

All these died according to faith, not having received the promises, but beholding them afar off and saluting them, and confessing that they are pilgrims and strangers on the earth. . . . Who by faith conquered kingdoms, wrought justice, obtained promises, stopped the mouths of lions, quenched the violence of fire, escaped the edge of the sword, recovered strength from weakness, became valiant in battle, put to flight the armies of foreigners.—
Hebrews 11. 13, 33, 34.

I DO not know how it is with you, but, for me, almost ever since I can remember hearing it read, this chapter of the Hebrews has exercised a special fascination, has enabled me to follow the story of the Old Testament in a new attitude and with a new interest. The patriarchs as you knew them when you were quite small, whether from picture-books or from the confirmatory evidence supplied by stained-glass windows, were old gentlemen with beards who had their clothes, mostly in rather dowdy purples and browns, hitched up round them in an inconvenient sort of way, and always carried a large stick in one hand and a thurible in the other when, apparently, they were just going out for a walk. Heavy, lifeless figures they seemed, against a flat, conventional background of palm-trees, and you felt it was impossible that they should ever mean anything to you or carry any living message. And then came this chapter of the Hebrews and filled the whole scene with life, set the cardboard palm-trees waving and the long skirts rustling, and everything was astir. It was not simply that they went to the same tailor, they had something in common; there was a secret behind their dignified silence. They died according to faith, not having received the promises, but beholding them afar off and saluting them; God providing some better thing for us, that without us they should not be perfected.

By faith he—that is, Abraham—abode in the land, dwelling in tents with Isaac and Jacob, the co-heirs of the same promise; for he looked for a city that hath foundations, whose builder and maker is God. He managed to live in tents, to endure that uncomfortable, makeshift, draughty sort of existence—how? Because he looked for a city that hath foundations, whose builder and maker is God. That is the

[1] This sermon was preached to the schoolboys at St Edmund's College, Ware, on Dedication Sunday, 16 May 1920.

faith of the Old Testament saints, to live as strangers in a transitory world on the strength of a promise—a promise they knew they would not live to see fulfilled. Faith is the substance of things hoped for, the evidence of things that appear not. And you will find that same common quality among the saints of the Christian dispensation. They lived in very different ages and very different countries; their circumstances differed widely, and their manner of life. Yesterday we had the office of St John Baptist de La Salle, who rose to sanctity in the exercise of a very humble and a very humdrum occupation, and one that does not often produce saints: he was a schoolmaster. And today the infallible Voice of Christendom is raising to the altars of the Church, as she was long since raised to the glories of heaven, the heroine of a very different career: a village girl who really did conquer kingdoms, really did recover strength from weakness, became valiant in battle, put to flight the armies of foreigners—yes, St Joan of Arc. How nice it sounds, "St Joan of Arc". But through all the history of sanctity you will find this same quality persisting—the quality of realizing that what we see and touch and feel are transitory things and unreal, and that the solid things, the substantial things, are the things that appear not, the world we only grasp by faith.

And I am insisting on that particular quality this morning because I think it is one that stands out with quite extraordinary clearness in St Joan's life: she did really live for a promise, and we know that the promise came true, but she did not—not in this life. She was very young, you know. Did you realize that she was less than twenty years old when she was burnt at the stake? It is not true that she dressed as a man; she dressed as a boy. When she was only thirteen years old, at the age when the other boys and girls were fidgeting and playing the fool during Mass, as people did in those days, she could hardly go out of doors without hearing the voices of saints and angels talking to her. And those voices dominated her life; they echoed so loudly in her ears that all the world's noises were drowned for her. People said: "It is very silly of a small girl like you to think she can go and see the King"— she did not hear them. And the King, as you know, disguised himself and hid among his courtiers, and she went straight up to him: "But I am not the King", he said; "that is the King over there." "Oh, yes, you are; I have come to raise the siege of Orleans and crown you King at Rheims." It was no good; the voices had told her about it. And I suppose when she had been appointed Chief of the Army the General Staff would always be raising military difficulties about re-entrant angles and being enfiladed by arquebus-fire, and so on, but it did not

make a bit of difference to her, she always did what the voices told her
—they were close to her ear, you see, and the criticisms of the General
Staff were only a distant echo. She went out, not knowing whither she
went.

And of course she had disappointments. After the first few victories,
after the crowning of the King, the people she had come to save
contented themselves with a partial conquest, and hung about making
treaties and demobilizing troops. And truly, if she had been mindful
of that from whence she came out, she had doubtless time to return;
she could have gone back to Domrémy and rested on her laurels. But
the ingratitude and apathy of the court affected her no more than its
honours had done; she simply went on obeying the voices. And the
French lords played her false, and she was taken prisoner. But she
endured, as seeing him who is invisible.

And then came the hardest time of all. I do not think she minded
being in prison; I do not think she minded the threat of execution; that
was not why she tried to escape. No, it was simply that it seemed quite
obvious to her she was to deliver France—the voices had told her so—
and France was not yet delivered. And so she went to the stake, her
hopes still unfulfilled, but never doubting for an instant that the voices
were true. Five years later the King entered Paris; twenty-two years
later, England had no possessions left on French soil. She believed that
he was faithful who had promised, not having received the promises,
but beholding them afar off and saluting them. She could not foresee
that her unjust condemnation would be reversed, point by point,
twenty-five years after her death: she could not foresee that, nearly five
hundred years after her death, France, once more liberated, would
receive the tidings of her canonization by the tribunal to which, in
life, she never ceased to appeal, the tribunal of the Holy See. But she
believed that he was faithful who had promised.

That, then, is her great witness, as it is the witness of all the saints:
that is her capital contribution to our Christian hope—we know,
because the saints have told us so, that it is the things of this world that
are shams and shadows, and the real things and the solid things are the
things we cannot see. Our Saviour Christ has ascended up into heaven,
and a cloud received him from our sight, but we are not therefore to
think of the spiritual world as something far removed from us, only
to be reached by a supreme effort of thought. On the contrary, the
spiritual world is all about us: the voices are still there, only St Joan
could hear them and we cannot. I wonder whose fault that is? Blessed
are the pure in heart, for they shall see God.

The Angels keep their ancient places;
   Turn but a stone, and start a wing:
'Tis ye, 'tis your estrangèd faces
   That miss the many-splendoured thing.
But, when so sad thou canst not sadder,
   Cry, and upon thy so sore loss
Shall shine the traffic of Jacob's ladder
   Pitched between Heaven and Charing Cross.[1]

This is no other but the house of God, and the gate of heaven. When
we keep, as today, the festival of the Dedication of a Church, this
earthly edifice is a sort of sacrament to us, a type of the true city which
hath foundations, whose builder and maker is God: of the temple that
is built in a world beyond the reach of our sense, by a heavenly Architect, the blows of whose mallet, the polishing strokes of whose chisel,
we call pain in this world, and defeat, and loss. Whither may God of
his great mercy bring us, that we may see with open vision, among the
choir of virgins that are our Lady's handmaids, the saint whose glorious
merits the Church commemorates today.

14

ST IGNATIUS LOYOLA[2]

Then his son Judas, called Machabeus, rose up in his stead; and all his
brethren helped him, and all they that had joined themselves to his father,
and they fought with cheerfulness the battle of Israel.—1 Machabees 3. 1.

THERE are few stories, I suppose, in history, so epical as that of the
resistance made by Juda under the Machabees to the power of
Syrian tyrants; there have been few movements which combined, so
perfectly as theirs did, the twin aspirations of religion and patriotism.
That the Church holds them in special honour is witnessed by the
curious fact that they, almost alone among all the heroes of the Old
Testament, have a feast and a Mass and an Office dedicated yearly to
their honour. We Catholics are not always very well read in the Old

---

[1] Francis Thompson, "The Kingdom of God is within You".
[2] This sermon was preached at the Church of the Immaculate Conception, Farm Street,
London, on the Feast of St Ignatius, 31 July 1930.

Testament; let me just remind you briefly, then, of what it was these men did, and what was the quarrel in which they fought.

The conquests of Alexander the Great at the end of the third century before Christ had let loose all over the East, as far as the borders of India, a flood of Greek influence and rather superficial Greek civilization. At his death, his chief captains, like the marshals of Napoleon, ascended royal thrones; in Egypt, the Ptolemies, in Syria, the Seleuci. When war arose between these two dynasties, as it did a generation later, it was inevitable that the little people of Juda, with their territory lying on the high road from Syria to Egypt, should be swept into the current of world politics once more. And that meant grave peril to their national faith, and to their mission as the one people in the world which maintained, in its integrity, the worship of the one true God. Gentile influences began to creep in—the Greek tolerance of false worship and of superstition, the Greek cult of beauty, the Greek contempt for morals. There was a party in Judaea itself favourable to this foreign culture. And when Antiochus Epiphanes came up with an army to Jerusalem, and sacked it, and robbed the temple treasures, and set up heathen worship in the holy places, it was not the whole nation that protested and suffered. Some Jews, in that degenerate age, were ready to conform to the new order of things; they consented to eat the flesh of swine, forbidden to them by the Mosaic law, in witness of their apostasy. But there was a remnant which remained faithful; and it was these who, under the leadership of the Machabean brethren, won back the holy city, and defeated army after army sent against them by their oppressors, and re-established the independence of their country until it was finally lost through the conquests of the Romans a century later.

I would like you to notice three points especially about the triumphant career of these patriots. The first is this—that we are dealing with a succession of men, all of the same family, who all showed the same spirit and maintained the same policy with equal fearlessness. You do not often find that in history; you find it very seldom in the history of the Jews. Now and again, by the special decrees of Providence, some great prophet appoints, before his death, another great prophet to succeed him; so Moses appoints Josue, and Elias appoints Eliseus. But as a rule the great figures of Old Testament history are solitary figures, and when they disappear there is nobody, or worse than nobody, to succeed them. The sons of Gedeon, one of the greatest of the Judges, the sons of the high priest Eli, the sons of the prophet Samuel, how soon they degenerated, and disgraced the traditions of their family!

But Mathathias, dying at the very outset of the campaign, leaves five sons. Of these, Eleazar is killed in the first important battle, but Judas is left in command; only for a year or two, then he is killed in battle, and his brother John treacherously slain. Jonathan succeeds, and for eight years keeps the enemies of religion at bay. At last he is caught in an ambush; but there is still one left; Simon, the last of the brothers, eclipses the triumphs of his predecessors, and during the eight years of his leadership the nation flourishes as it has never flourished since, I suppose, the time of King Solomon. One patriot with five sons to succeed him, and not a single weak link in the chain; here is a rare accident of history.

And the next point is this, that before they could muster their forces, and dispute with the heathen the mastery of their native soil, it was necessary for them to take refuge in the hill country, in their native city of Modin. Mathathias cried with a loud voice, "Everyone that hath zeal for the law and maintaineth the testament, let him follow me", and he and his sons fled into the mountains, and left all that they had in the city. It was in those same mountains that David had taken refuge, when he fled from the persecution of King Saul; and he has sung of those outlaw strongholds of his in words that still echo through the sanctuaries of Christendom; "I will lift up mine eyes to the hills, whence cometh my help", "the Lord hath brought me out, and set me upon a rock of stone"—the Machabees took him for their model, and retired to the hill fastnesses till they had gathered the strength needed for their effort.

And the third point is this; that the Machabees did resolve to defeat the heathen with their own weapons. There was always a party among the Jews, at any moment of national crisis, which was for a non-resistance policy, what they called "waiting on the Lord"; if God saw fit to deliver them, he would do so by a miracle; no need, then, to oppose force with force. There were such men in the time of the Machabees; and in particular there was a party of refugees which refused to fight on the sabbath day, and was exterminated by massacre rather than break the letter of the Mosaic law by fighting on the day of rest. And we are told that the Machabees took, in view of that incident, a remarkable decision. "Whosoever shall come against us to fight on the sabbath day, we will fight against him, and we will not all die, as our brethren that were slain in the secret places." If they were to do battle for the law of Moses, they must not press the letter of that law so as to imperil the whole success of their enterprise.

It is difficult for any English Catholic to read the two books of

Machabees without being reminded of the situation in Europe four hundred years ago. It was, after all, the Renaissance, the rediscovery of the classical authors, and the return to classical models, which paved the way for the Continental Reformation; it was the scepticism of the Greeks that infected the pure atmosphere of the Middle Ages, as it had infected, long before, the pure atmosphere of Jewish life. And the result, in our own country as in many others, was a profanation of holy places, a breaking down of altars, and carrying away of consecrated things; so that the very words of Scripture seem as if they had been written for our use. "The holy places are come into the hands of strangers, her temple is become as a man without honour; the vessels of her glory are carried away captive.... Our sanctuary and our beauty and our glory is laid waste, and the Gentiles have defiled them."

As the invasion of Antiochus had the effect of producing a reaction among the Jews, a return to stricter observance of the law and greater jealousy for the honour of the true God, so under the hand of Providence the apostasy of the sixteenth century produced, in Europe, that return to loyalty and that increase of Catholic zeal which we call the Counter-Reformation. And although St Ignatius, when he founded the Company of Jesus, was not specially concerned to combat the errors of Luther, and turned his eyes rather to the Mohammedan world, at first, in his dreams of spiritual conquest, it is clear to us now that his Institute came just in time to put itself at the head of the Counter-Reformation movement, and save Europe for the faith. I hope you will not think me fanciful, then, Reverend Fathers, if I see in the Machabean brethren a type of that little Company of free-lances with which your holy founder defied the forces of his age, and fought with cheerfulness the battle of Israel.

I said that the Machabees, unlike other Jewish patriots, had the advantage of being a series; their greatness did not die with Mathathias, or with Judas, or with Jonathan. So your Order is distinguished, I think, among the religious orders by the permanence of its tradition and its unfailing output of sanctity. From the year 1491 to the year 1716 there was never a moment at which there was not a Jesuit saint alive on earth. I mean by saints only such as have, by now, been canonized by the Church; is there any other order, I wonder, that could make a similar boast? And what you can say of actual sanctity, you can say also of the spirit of the Order. The Society of Jesus has not, like other institutes, its periods of revival and its periods of decay; it retains, beyond precedent, the memory of its first fervour. Where men complain of it, they complain not of its relaxation, but of its activity;

it has been suppressed, but it has never been reformed. Let us thank God for that first, this unintermittent spiritual energy which has marked the history of the Society for four hundred years.

I said that the Machabees, as the condition of their successful resistance, had first of all to withdraw into the mountains and rally their forces there. "He and his sons fled into the mountains, and left all that they had in the city"—it is surely, under Providence, the long and careful novitiate of the Order, with the spirit of detachment it produces, that has kept the spirit of St Ignatius alive. Other institutes have encouraged retirement from the world, and access to the mountain-life of contemplation, as an end in itself; they have exiled themselves from the corruptions of the world. With the sons of St Ignatius it is otherwise; they have retired to those mountains that they might swoop down all the more successfully on the world they seemed to have abandoned, and conquer it with the impetus of their descent. Men have talked and written foolishly as if the strength of the Society lay in its guardianship of a secret, a secret oath, or a code of secret instructions, or something of that kind. But it is not so; the path by which it guards its mountain stronghold is not a secret path, but one plain to view, discouraging access only by its steepness and ruggedness; it is called "The Spiritual Exercises". The secret of the Order is a secret which it has been giving away, century after century, to anyone who will try its efficacy for himself.

I said that the Machabees determined to meet the world with its own weapons; that they abandoned the policy of non-resistance which some of their partisans would have maintained, would not even be bound, in case of hostile attack, by the prescriptions of the Mosaic law which defined the sabbath rest. They realized that armies trained under the Macedonian discipline could not be kept at bay by the same methods which had repelled, in time gone by, attack from the barbarians of the desert. And that, surely, is the astounding thing about St Ignatius, if you view his influence on history merely from its human side. Long ago, when I was a Protestant, I remember playing some after-dinner game in which you were expected to write down the names of the six greatest men—I think it was—in history, and surprising my company by including St Ignatius's name among the list. When you read the beginning of his story, you are impressed with the feeling that you have here a thoroughly unpractical man; the last, you might say, of the knights-errant. He was saturated himself, like Don Quixote, in the adventurous romances of his period, and he has developed, as the result, a Quixotic habit of mind. He will pursue and kill the Moor who has blasphemed our Lady—no, on second thoughts, he will give his horse its reins and see which path it takes. He will go out to the Holy Land and convert the Turks; he will dress oddly to make the street-boys laugh at him—oh, a generous character, a lovable character, who will possibly do great things, but will he leave behind him any permanent legacy to be remembered by? And then, all of a sudden, you find that this last of the knights-errant has turned into the first of the great business men. He has developed, heaven only knows how, capacities for organization which might have enabled him to name his own salary as the director of any modern enterprise; he can make the world his chess-board.

He saw—not, surely, by any natural light—that the old fabric of Christendom was breaking up around him; and that, in the troublous days which followed, the Church would need a body of free-lances, not specializing in one department or following one way of life, but ready to adapt themselves to any environment, to take up any form of legitimate activity, to go anywhere and do anything for the greater glory of God. And all that would need a spirit of obedience for which the existing religious orders, with their carefully defined spheres of activity, were unsuited. A flying column of picked troops, throwing themselves into all the multifarious life of the modern world, yet always with the glory of God before their eyes. All the world's caricatures of Jesuit aims and Jesuit methods, all its cant use of the very word Jesuit, are a kind of distorted compliment. The modern world knows that the Society is a match for it, and takes its revenge in abuse.

I have left myself little time to draw a moral from all this for us others. Let us propose to ourselves a lesson of warning. When the Machabean brethren were at the height of their success, Joseph the son of Zacharias, and Azarias captain of the soldiers, said, "Let us also get us a name, and let us fight with the Gentiles that are round about us"; they were routed and put to flight, because, says the sacred author, "they did not hearken to Judas and his brethren, thinking that they should do manfully; but they were not of the seed of those men by whom salvation was brought to Israel". How easy it is to excuse ourselves for mingling freely in all society and in all pursuits of the world around us, thinking that we will be all the more effective Christians for being thorough men of the world; how easy it is for us to get the worst of that encounter, and lose our standards, and be dragged down to the world's own level, if we are not of the seed of those men by whom salvation is to be brought to the Church! Before we can do any good in the world or to the world, we must go up to the mountains

D

and learn to separate ourselves from the world; for us, as for the sons of St Ignatius, the preface to any victory must be a retreat. The saint whom we celebrate today bequeathed, not only to his own institute but to Christendom in general, one legacy for which, even if he had left no Order behind him, Christendom would owe him eternal gratitude—the Spiritual Exercises. It is generally so hard to imagine, "What advice would such and such a saint give to me, if I could meet him nowadays in the flesh?"; and, if our imagination can supply us with the answer, so hard to find how we, in our circumstances, can apply just that advice to ourselves. But with St Ignatius it is quite simple. Roughly speaking, you may say there was only one piece of advice he ever gave to anybody, and that was, "Go into retreat". He cries to us still, like Mathathias of old, "Everyone that hath a zeal for the law, and maintaineth the Testament, let him follow me"; for our age, more than ever, that message holds good, if we are to save the world, if we are to save our souls.

15

ST PHILIP NERI: I[1]

We are fools for Christ's sake.—1 Corinthians 4. 10.

IN uttering the praises of the saints, it is possible to concentrate your whole attention on the few features of character that seem to be dominating, essential features, and rule out of your considerations all that is second and subsidiary to these as of no real importance. In doing so, you assure yourself of an excellent moral; the only thing is that the farther you proceed the more conscious you become that your saint is beginning to look exactly like everybody else's saint— the same mortifications, the same abandonment of love, the same gifts in prayer. And at the end of your task you have little left but a panegyric of St N., which you can easily use for St Gregory the Great one week and St Margaret Mary the next. Now, if such a study be your aim, there could be no saint who satisfied more minutely all the tests of holiness than St Philip. If an outside enquirer wanted a book which

---

[1] This sermon was preached at the Oratory School, Birmingham.

would explain to him what sort of person you meant by a saint, you certainly could not do better than refer him to Father Bacci. But there is about St Philip something so personal, so intimate, so encouraging of familiarity, that devotion in his case runs away from common themes and edifying generalizations, and claims the right to busy itself rather with what was singular and characteristic about him than with the vital secret of his sanctity.

I do not mean simply his extraordinary humanness. It is quite true; his figure stands out to us, after all these centuries, as something very near and very natural to us. He is "the saint of gentleness and kindness"; "love is his bond, he knows no other fetter, asks not our all, but takes whate'er we spare him"; whatever difference of temperament there might be, the greatest of his English sons has not misinterpreted him. He is fond of animals. He likes to have boys around him, and does not mind how much noise they make if he can keep them from sin—a mortification which, perhaps, it takes a schoolmaster to appreciate. He fishes for souls with the line, not merely with the net; each penitent is, to him, an individual soul to be wooed and won, not a fresh case to be pigeon-holed. His portraits let you see him; nay, you can almost hear the cheerful "What's up? What's up?" with which he greets his company. I suppose the simplest way of putting it into a phrase is to say that if you were alone in your room and the door opened and one of the saints walked in, if it were almost any other you would fall on your knees, but if it were St Philip you would run to his heart.

But there is one special element in that humanness which marks out Philip still more clearly from his heavenly compatriots: I mean his fun. You hear in the Middle Ages of God's minstrels or our Lady's troubadours, but I think it was left for the Counter-Reformation to produce that still more startling combination, God's jesters. We have one of them, thank God, in England, St Thomas More. There was nothing pleased him so much as the reflection that if you put his name into Greek it meant a fool. He was, perhaps, the only saint who kept a private jester as an honoured, almost a reverenced member of his household. He carried off his sanctity (which, surely, was there long before he won his crown by martyrdom) in a cloud of raillery, and went to the scaffold joking, not like a man who has screwed himself up to it, but like a man bubbling over with irrepressible amusement. And St Philip has, as we all know, something of this same character. I do not mean his delightful habit of self-depreciation, in which he has few parallels except, perhaps, the Curé d'Ars. No, I mean that real, rollicking fun of St Thomas More, effervescing, in our saint, in the form of the most reckless practical jokes, played, now on himself, now on his spiritual children. There is no denying it, is there? Why, one of the first fathers of the Oratory confessed to having wondered whether St Philip were not touched in the head, and St Philip, in one of his most glorious flights of holy fooling, made the poor man confess it in refectory. No, we cannot get out of it, it is certainly there; St Philip is always dancing in public, or changing hats with somebody, or making his penitents put their coats on inside out; the fact cannot be disputed.

And of course we all know—our aunts, I suppose, did not let us forget it when we were small—that the laughter of fools is like the crackling of thorns under a pot, and a loud laugh betrays an empty mind. Laughter, it is quite true, is a difficult thing to find a warrant for in Scripture. It is quite true that St Philip always joked in public and because he was in public; quite true that his jokes always produced a holy fruit of mortification. In a full church, he went up to the Suisse or beadle at the church door and pulled his beard. I suppose none of us, in entering a foreign cathedral, can fail to be conscious of a temptation to do that: the point is that we are restrained by the fear of looking fools and the fear of hurting the beadle's feelings—precisely the two reasons why St Philip did it. He succeeded in making the bystanders think the worse of him, and I suppose he succeeded in inflicting a salutary mortification on the beadle, though Father Bacci, to the annoyance of his readers, does not say what followed. But the laughter was there, and if it had not been there would have been no mortification; if everybody had kept his face who would have minded? I do not suppose St Philip pulled the beard really hard. No, St Philip really believed in ragging, and believed in it as a means to attaining the salvation of souls.

And I do not think it is any good saying that this was part of Philip's natural temperament, which came out in spite of his sanctity. I find no evidence for that; his early years are much like those of other saints. No, it is a part of his sanctity; somehow, in those long vigils at the catacombs, he had found out a secret; and that secret, for all his wonderful gift of tears, for all the miraculous palpitation of a heart love-sick for God, was one that could at times be communicated, could at times best be communicated to others, as a kind of celestial joke. The Holy Innocents, you would think, had been whispering in his ear. And he proceeded, not with a deep, artificial design, but, as St Philip did everything, with complete naturalness and spontaneity, to make a fool of himself for Christ's sake.

Of course, if you were to ask which was nearer to the saint's real interior life, his gift of tears or his gift of laughter, no one could hesitate in answering that it was his gift of tears. But the gift of tears is one which God, in his mercy, has granted to many others; the laughter is a more special feature, a more isolated characteristic. Will it, then, be a waste of time to try and see what it was that gave the edge to Philip's sense of merriment as he moved about in this valley of divine chastisement and of human tears? I do not say that we shall be able to see the joke, if I may put it in that way; but it might be good for us even to understand what it was.

I say it may be hard for us to see it, because after all it is a joke against you and me and the world in general, and it is not always easy to see a joke when it is against yourself. There is, I suppose, no form of the ridiculous which has such a direct appeal as a situation in which somebody is putting on dignified airs, and all the time there is some circumstance, unknown to him but clearly seen by his audience, which makes that dignity absurd. You have come down without a tie, or somebody has written DONKEY on your back; and not only is your dignity unavailing but actually, the more dignity you assume, the more irresistibly funny you look—to those who can see. Now, the saint who has been with God, who has familiarized himself with the thought of God's greatness and the heavenly scale of values—what must he think when he comes back to the unreal pomps, the sordid competition, the pretentious would-be wisdom of the world's citizens? Must not he see man as a coxcomb, strutting about in borrowed plumes, and making himself ridiculous afresh with every fresh air he puts on of proprietorship or of self-assertion? Must not he see the world's mad competition as a fond striving for prizes not worth the dust of conflict, and only capable of deluding us because we never rest satisfied with their attainment, but press on at once after others no less transitory? Oh, yes, I grant you, the cynic equally gets that point of view, but the cynic has only found the moral from the record of his own disappointments, and his heart is soured and warped, so that he may scourge the world with satire, but cannot save it from itself. But the saint, the man whose heart is all on fire with desire for the salvation of his fellow men, yet reads in the world about him the pathetic story of their misdirected effort: who sees the mockery of man's boasting, the futility of his striving, yet knows that man, so ridiculous in his parade of earthly circumstance, is really a prince, if he but knew it, only not here—will not he be privileged to greet man's follies with the kindly laughter which has in it an echo of heaven and, with the infectiousness of that laughter, teach

man to know his present littleness, and through his littleness the greatness that might be his?

Sanctity, St Philip used to say, rests within the compass of three
inches; and he would point to his forehead to show that what he meant
was the mortification of the *razionale*, the proper pride that is perfection's most fatal enemy. And he knew that if he could get a penitent
to laugh at himself—especially if worldly circumstances made it
natural for him to think too highly of himself—that laugh, under God's
providence, would be the salvation of his soul. And he knew that
there was one man who, but for God's grace, was in hourly danger of
falling into a fatal self-satisfaction over the greatness of the revelations
vouchsafed to him, and that man was Philip Neri—very well, then,
Philip Neri must be relentlessly pursued with ridicule, must not pass a
day without being made to look silly. Yes, of course there was the
need of edifying others, but . . . of the people that come to be edified,
how large a proportion are really in earnest, how many are merely
sightseeing? Some Polish nobles to see him? No, they are not really
wanting to be edified; come on, down with the detective-stories, and
let us be found reading them to one another. . . . How like St Philip!
And, if I may be pardoned for saying so, how Oratorian!

But, you will say, you have not recommended any of his virtues
to our imitation, for surely this playfulness of his is the last thing we can
afford to copy. No, I am not suggesting ways in which we could
imitate St Philip, but I think there is a quite practical lesson for our
own advancement. Suppose you went into one of these confessionals,
and found the saint himself sitting there; suppose that, won over by
that invitation so few could resist, you opened to him (if he had not
opened it already to you) your whole heart—try to think what advice
he would give. What humiliating penance would he impose? In what
strange garb would he make you walk through the streets of Birmingham? What cherished calculations of self-interest would he dispel with
that patient, insistent question: "Yes, and then . . .?" "Yes, and
then . . .?" They are not distant historical figures, these Massimis and
Tarugis you read of in the life; they are men of the same fashion with
us, with our temptations, our difficulties. Can we not learn to read in
their story the needs of our own souls?

Reverend Fathers, you cannot keep St Philip to yourselves. The
plant of devotion which seemed so exotic when first you imported it
into England from beneath Italian skies, has become acclimatized to
our northern region, and springs self-sown in our hedgerows. He sees,
I do not doubt, other temptations in our hearts beyond what he read

in the hearts of his own penitents, but surely none that his example cannot arm us against, or his prayers cannot remedy. May those prayers bring health to us who here celebrate his memory, and to all our countrymen, however little they have felt that influence till now, the graces they need for their eternal salvation.

16

ST PHILIP NERI: II[1]

If salt loses its taste, what is there left to give taste to it?—Matthew 5. 13.

L ast Wednesday was a centenary; unmarked by the world, but in the world's history, if we could read the world's history from the inside, one of high significance. On 23 May 1551, Giovanni Lunelli, Bishop of Sebaste, conferred the sacred order of the priesthood on a young Florentine living in Rome, whose name was Philip Neri. To you, Reverend Fathers, to you, his own parishioners, the fame of him stands in little need of commendation. And we, who have come from a distance to share your happiness, attest by our very presence the fact that he is still, as he was ever, a magnet to attract souls. Let us be content to say only a little about graces so abundant, about a personality so many-sided as his; to concentrate our attention upon one facet of his heavenly crown as it shines in human memory. He is the saint of freedom.

When I say that, I am not thinking of political liberty, and the world-problems which exercise us today. Yet it is perhaps worth-while to remember that his later boyhood was spent in Florence, just when Florence had driven out the Medici family, and was making its last, vain bid for self-government. If we find him something of an original, somewhat unrepresentative of the age he lived in, let us remember that for him the splendours of the Renaissance were only the trappings of tyranny. Such a man, even on his human side, is a little contemptuous of those worldly estimates, those fashionable conventions, which we others take for granted. He had, perhaps, the makings of a rebel in him. But the thing he stood for and stands for

[1] This sermon was preached at the London Oratory on the Feast of St Philip Neri, 26 May 1951.

has nothing whatever to do with political considerations; it is something subtler, more intimate, more delicately balanced. It is what devotional authors have called the liberty of the spirit.

If he was not a rebel, Philip was nevertheless a reformer. So were all the saints of his age. The sixteenth century was such a crisis in the history of religion that you could not be sensitized to its atmosphere without becoming either a rebel or a reformer, or both at once. And because Rome was, then as always, the capital of our fortunes, the cleaning-up process must needs begin at Rome. Even in the Middle Ages, they told the cynical story of a Jew who had been converted to Rome, and explained, in answer to his questioners, that the Catholic religion must be true if it could survive so much of corruption in high places as this. And the Renaissance, that splendid rediscovery of the classical tradition, that splendid flowering of scholarship and of the arts, only served to debase the lives and the thoughts of many among those who were influenced by it. A city that is built on a mountain-top, our Lord warns us, cannot be hidden; and it is in the same context that he uses the words of my text, "If salt loses its taste, what is there left to give taste to it?" Salt of the earth, it was for Rome to save the world from corruption; when Rome itself was corrupt, what was to be done with it? That was the problem which faced the saints of the Counter-Reformation, and St Philip in particular.

I say, St Philip in particular, because God raised him up to be, in a special sense, the Apostle of Rome. All the great founders of religious institutes have made their way to Rome, as St Ignatius did, because it would give them the necessary leverage for doing good in other parts of Christendom. St Philip made no calculations of that kind; he made no calculations of any kind. He drifted to Rome because that was God's will for him; and he set about spreading abroad the love of God there, not because he thought it was a very wicked place; he would have done the same anywhere else. Only, that was just what was wanted. When a fire is in danger of going out, you will do no good by aiming your bellows now at this point, now at that, blowing furious blasts at the struggling flames which only need that to extinguish them. No, you must find out first of all, by a series of experiments, which is the real focus which responds to your efforts, and then keep on fanning that one spot, always the same spot quite gently, quite patiently, till the fire spreads all round. Rome is the heart and focus of Christendom; and Philip could not have done better service to his Master than by fanning the dull embers that seemed so un-responsive, there in Rome.

But it would be grossly unhistorical to suggest that his was a lonely protest. On the contrary, he lived under a series of reforming popes; he was the contemporary and the friend of St Charles Borromeo, who did more than any other man to restore Church discipline in accordance with the canons of Trent. Everywhere bishops were being told to put their sees in order; the luxury of the Papal court was being repressed, the Holy Office was bringing to light those strange aberrations of doctrine which an age of restless intellectual activity had allowed to creep in. Meanwhile, St Ignatius and his companions were holding up to the world an incomparable example of organization and discipline. What need, we are tempted to ask, for a Philip as well?

I have tried to suggest the answer when I spoke of St Philip as the saint of freedom. Reforms brought in from above may change the habits of society without changing its heart. You may repress luxury without repressing the love of luxury; you may drive paganism into the catacombs, but it is paganism still. Organization and discipline, the multiplying of rules and methods whether for clergy or laity, produce little effect unless they are freely accepted by the will; they develop scruples in the timorous, command but a lifeless acquiescence from the indifferent. All the salutary reforms which the Council of Trent initiated might have succeeded in their measure, and yet left us with a dull, flat, uninspired level of performance. That they produce more than that, we owe in great part to St Philip. It was the sharp tang of his unwonted spirituality that acted as seasoning to the Tridentine experiment. The little world of Rome, from cardinals in curia to loungers in the street, felt his influence, and came hurrying back to God.

But it was an influence freely exercised, and one which made for freedom. And, partly because it was an influence of freedom, not depending on regulations or formulas, it remains the same influence today, reasserted in his children. Wherever the Congregation of the Oratory flourishes, there you will find an atmosphere that breathes liberty; an atmosphere which is at once spacious, and completely natural, and intensely personal.

Spacious—St Philip, I think, liked space; liked to say his prayers on the roof, liked to go out for a walk in the country round Rome, with a party picked up anyhow, that attached itself to him at the last moment, without any plan, visiting a church here and there when the mood took him. It was characteristic of him that when they built the Chiesa Nuova he should have kept on altering the architect's plan so as to make a wider nave for our Lady's church; "More elbow-room", he seems to say; "don't let us make anybody feel cramped." And wherever the Oratorians go they built large; a big church, a roomy house next door; not out of ostentation, but so as to get the sense of freedom. You shall be able to wander about in their churches, and say your prayers in this chapel or that as the mood takes you, without attracting attention. And this largeness is only the symbol of something more interior and more intimate; you are to come to God at your ease, not cramped by any system or method, your heart, like the saint's own heart, enlarged.

Natural—of all the saints, none is so full of nature as St Philip; that is why he shocks some people, that is why he attracted Goethe. He remained, all his life, very much of a schoolboy; loved to make himself look ridiculous by pulling the beard of the beadle in church, loved to make his fashionable penitents look ridiculous by carrying his cat through the streets. How much was it a calculated effect? Did he sometimes go out of his way to play the fool, force himself to be natural? It is hard to say; but, whatever the secret of it, he was always himself; never for a moment were you tempted to say "There goes Ignatius", or "There goes Charles Borromeo". And he wanted all his disciples to be themselves, once they had overcome that *razionale*, that spirit of pride, which is the enemy of all holiness. He would not mould them into a type; they should live by a tradition, not by a rule. In this, as Newman wisely saw, his spirit accommodated itself to the English genius. I have been privileged to know many Oratorians, but never one of whom I felt inclined to say, "He is typical".

And—personal; with the saint himself, that is a point hardly worth proving. His apostolate was neither of the pen nor, chiefly at any rate, of the pulpit; if you came under his influence, it was because he plucked you by the sleeve, folded you to his heart. And he was always there; as well expect to find Ars without St John Vianney, as Rome without St Philip. In this, above all, he has bequeathed his own spirit to his children. The sons of St Ignatius are ready to be sent off, at a moment's notice, on some perilous mission; the sons of St Philip, called to a different form of self-sacrifice, are always at home. Nor is their love of room like the Benedictine's love of his cell; the Benedictine's abbey is his fortress, the Oratorian's house is an open town, where all the world may pass through. He gives you that freedom which of all others is today most lacking: freedom of access.

Reverend Fathers, you do not keep St Philip to yourselves; you share him with the world. Pray for us others, that we too may learn something of his spirit.

17

ST PHILIP NERI: III[1]

IF you or I had been called into consultation by Mr Newman in the
year 1846, and asked what was the best kind of religious foundation
to canalize the energies and perpetuate the memory of the Oxford
conversions, what should we have said? We should have said, I think,
in our wisdom, "It doesn't matter which religious institute you choose,
as long as it is something medieval, and something English. Why not,
for example, revive the Gilbertine order, which never went outside
these islands, and perished at the Reformation?" We should have
pointed out to him that the whole swing of public taste was away from
the classical and the baroque; that the Romantic Movement, with the
novels of Sir Walter Scott as its spearhead, had carried men's minds
back to the Middle Ages, and thrown a kind of wistful glamour over
the days of chivalry. We should have called his attention to the
Gothic revival, to the triumphant career of Pugin, and the widespread
impression that the conversion of England could be effected overnight
if only we put up a few more rood-screens. We should have reminded
him, too, that Emancipation was only a recent affair; above all things,
English Catholics should take great pains to be English. . . . In point of
fact, Newman consulted Pope Pius IX, and was told to found an
Oratory of St Philip Neri. We, in our wisdom, should have said,
"How typical! A little piece of Italy in Edgbaston, smelling of the
Renaissance! That just shows how little Rome understands England."
And we should have been wrong, quite wrong.

There are those who are much concerned to recall us to the primitive;
who are impatient of all forms of prayer, all adjuncts of worship,
which do not date back behind the Counter-Reformation—indeed,
which do not go back to the Dark Ages. Our music must be plain
chant of the strictest, our vestments must be copied from a medieval
brass, or, better still, from an early mosaic; or they are (for such
people) decadent, debased, unliturgical. Well, God forbid that we
should forget our remote past, that our memories should not be as
old as the catacombs. At certain solemn times of the year, we are
careful to go back to our origins; most of all in Holy Week. And
because the old Holy Week services, primitive as they were, had

---

[1] This sermon was preached at the Birmingham Oratory on the Feast of St Philip Neri,
6 May 1956.

altered somewhat, as old customs will, in the course of the centuries, it was fitting that we should have them purged for us, only the other day, by an act of the Supreme Pontiff. But a wholesale return to antiquity would be an impoverishment of our heritage. The Church, as the Gospel tells us, is like a man of riches and of taste, who brings both new and old things out of his treasure-house. And the liturgy reminds us of some great cathedral which has been added to by successive generations, all the more beautiful because it retains the tally of the centuries. It brings back memories not only of the catacombs, but of the Crusades and of the Counter-Reformation, and of more recent perils still. Our traditions have mellowed and matured; and the spell which the Church exercises over men's hearts depends, not a little, upon her variety.

Ever old, ever young, she encourages her children to sow beside all waters. Only this year, the Holy Father issued an encyclical about Church music, which has not been translated over here.[1] He dwells, as you would expect, on the unique position of the Gregorian chant, so felicitously wedded to the cadences of the Latin liturgy. But he adds that it is not in any way his intention to banish polyphonic music from the rites of the Church. And he singles out for special praise the music of the sixteenth century, which owes its origin so largely to St Philip. Did we think that no accompaniment except that of the organ was suited to the solemnity of divine worship? We were wrong; he recommends other instrumental music, especially that of a string orchestra, as having "an unutterable power to express our sentiments of joy and grief". He goes on to encourage the singing of popular, vernacular hymns during Mass, except where the Mass is solemnly celebrated. The faithful are not to be like children of the Victorian age, having to put away their toys when Sunday comes round. As far as reverence permits, all our various moods and contrivances are to be pressed into the service of the God who gives us his gifts so abundantly.

And St Philip is typical of that splendid resourcefulness with which, from century to century, the Church finds new ways of meeting new needs. If the Institute which he so absent-mindedly founded had perished within a century of his death, musicians would still be talking about "Oratorios"; and if we asked what that word meant we should be referred back, as a mere matter of history, to St Philip and the Chiesa Nuova. But that idea of his, the idea that you could get people to stop sinning for a bit if you invited them to listen to some music

---

[1] *Musicae Sacrae Disciplina*, issued on 25 December 1955. After the date of this sermon the translation of the Encyclical was published in *Catholic Documents*, No. XXI.

which wasn't quite a concert and wasn't quite a religious service, was only one of innumerable ideas which occurred to him for making the best use of the world as he found it. Never tell us that the saint was deaf to the charm of antiquity; he loved the catacombs, he was for ever leading pilgrimages to the Seven Churches. But he lived in the great age of humanism, and his apostolate was to Rome, the centre of humanism; the pulsing life of that strange period was all around him, and he was not content to register a Puritan protest, and leave the world to its sins. He would say, with Chremes in Terence's play, "I am a man, and whatever is human is my business". Only, with untiring inventiveness, he would exploit all the possibilities which that world offered to make men love God more.

He had no theories, no plan of campaign. His mission was not specially to the sick, or specially to children, like that of so many other saints; for him, we were all sick men, languishing for the air of the supernatural; we were all children, exciting ourselves over toys— himself included. He didn't shut himself away behind the bars of a cloister, in the silence of his own thoughts. The shouting of boys at play should be his welcome distraction; and still he would hobble about Rome, buttonholing people as he went, like a bee that flits from one flower to the next and dives deep to bring up the honey that lurks there, still hoping for some reaction to his embarrassing question, "When are we going to start loving God?" He didn't write books; his message was written in the hearts of those innumerable penitents who lived by his counsels, and could not die without the comfort of his presence. It was an intensive apostolate, and the obvious danger was that it would die with St Philip himself; gifts like his, you felt, could hardly be put in commission. There were, to be sure, a few disciples of his, "the people up at San Giovanni"—he did not even live under the same roof with them. Later, the thing took shape; he was able to accept the headship of the community at the Vallicella, and (an even greater sign of progress) to relinquish it. But could this very individual thing last?

It did last, and spread. But the spell of it, the secret of it, is something that has always defied analysis. A set of secular priests, living together with no vow of stability, with a minimum of rule, under a superior who must be called "the Father" and no more—how should they develop a spirit, a tradition of their own? Yet, of all the religious institutes, I know none that possesses a spirit so unmistakable, a tradition so vital. A rule may be interpreted; a tradition must be preserved, or perish.

And somehow Pio Nono had been right. It must have seemed a venture of faith—but men had faith, in those days—to bring the Oratory to England; the Oratory, recalling by every detail of dress and furniture a period of history which did not belong to England's Catholic past; the Oratory, with its preference for the polyphonic and the baroque, its dressed-up Madonnas, its gesticulating cherubs, its faint smell of bay-leaves; so foreign, so Roman. And yet from the first this exotic plant took root as effortlessly as if it had been native to these Midland hedgerows. What was it, under Providence, that made, that makes the institute of St Philip so congenial to our English way of life?

Something, perhaps, there is about it of spaciousness, of leisureliness, which recalls a more dignified age; things done on the grand scale, correctness of procedure—an atmosphere which we took for granted a hundred years ago, which lives today in our regrets. And we are lovers of continuity; in an Oratorian parish, as nowhere else, you have a reasonable chance of being married by the priest who baptized you, or alternatively of the priest who married you seeing your body to the grave. Or you may lay your finger upon this or that characteristic of an institute which abounds in gracious idiosyncrasies, and suggest that the spell of the Oratory lay there. But I suspect that the explanation is much simpler. I think the fact was that St Philip had, in an unusual degree, and passed on to his children, an individual love of souls.

A love of souls; he didn't just love people, with a fond love that made him blind to their shortcomings; he loved their souls; loved, with a fierce, supernatural jealousy, the image of Christ in them. And at the same time it was an individual love of souls; there was nothing in him of the ecclesiastical recruiting sergeant who tries to send people to heaven by numbers. And that is the meaning of the Oratorian vocation; to be a son of St Philip is not to be burdened with a whole régime of obligations and prohibitions, but to be the prisoner of love; chained to your house, to your church, and above all to your confessional by a permanent readiness to woo souls for Christ. The Little Oratory, with its exercises and its recreations, the evening services, the popular hymns, the long martyrdom of the waiting-room, the encouraging murmur in the confessional—they are all manifestations of the same thing; of that charity—tenderness, Father Faber would have called it—which was, and is, St Philip's way of going to work. May his life be a challenge and an encouragement to us others; the life of a foreigner a long time ago, and yet so close in memory, as if it were a thing of yesterday.

18

ST CHARLES BORROMEO[1]

A great tempest arose in the sea, so that the boat was covered with waves: but he was asleep.—Matthew 8. 24.

IT is a common way of speaking in the Old Testament Scriptures to describe almighty God as sleeping and awaking from sleep. When Israel is at the mercy of its enemies, and prayer and sacrifice is vain, when there is no voice and no answer of any that regards, then, by a natural metaphor, the Jew tells himself that God is asleep. He watching over Israel slumbers not, nor sleeps—that is the habitual confidence of Israel's faith. But when persecution arises, that confidence begins to vanish: "Awake, Lord, why sleepest thou? Awake, and be not absent from us for ever"; and when deliverance comes, "the Lord awaked as one out of sleep". And you will find that in some of our Lord's parables almighty God is compared to a householder who slept—it is the same idea: wickedness flourishes on the earth, and divine Providence seems to take no notice, seems unwilling to interfere. So I imagine that when our Lord's apostles came to look back upon that terrible night in the Lake of Galilee, when they strained every nerve against the tempest while their Master lay sleeping in the boat, they found in it an allegory of their own situation, as they launched out the frail bark of his Church upon waves so troubled, with prospects so uncertain. And in every age the Church has looked back to that picture and taken comfort from it in times of adversity: "Yes, our Master seems to sleep; he gives no sign, vouchsafes no apparent answer to our prayers: no matter, we are safe from shipwreck, for he is still in our midst."

When Julius Cæsar wished to cross from Durazzo to Brindisi in a little boat, and the master of it wanted to turn back, because the wind had risen and he was in danger of shipwreck, Cæsar rebuked him for his cowardice in noble words that have come down to us: "Take courage, my friend, take courage, and fear nothing; Cæsar is your passenger, and Cæsar's fortunes are your freight." With greater, and with better grounded confidence, the Church of God, which is Peter's boat, has breasted the waves all through her troubled history. It is not upon the captain's judgment or the pilot's experience, not

[1] This sermon was preached at the Church of St Mary of the Angels, Bayswater, London.

upon human wisdom or human prudence, that she depends for her safe voyage: she rests secure in the presence of her inviolable passenger. Yet we should do ill if we grudged recognition and gratitude to those servants of his who at various times have steered our course for us through difficult waters, and especially to the saints of the Counter-Reformation—that remarkable group of saints whom God raised up at the time of Europe's apostasy, by whose influence, humanly speaking, the faith survived that terrible ordeal. And not the least, nor the least prominent, of these is your holy patron, who ruled the Church of Milan in the latter part of the sixteenth century.

Say what you will, Italy breeds the genius for government. So the greatest of Latin poets saw, and summed it up for us in a phrase:

> Others shall quicken bronze with softer grace,
> And from dull marble life's own features trace;
> Plead with more eloquence, the changing skies
> Map with more skill, and con the stars that rise:
> Roman, not these thy arts;—thy agelong skill
> To wield thy empire o'er the peoples still.

Anybody, in naming the world's great men, will give you almost at once the names of two Italians, Julius Cæsar and Napoleon. And, whatever verdict history may pass on our own times, it is in Italy that the anarchical tendencies of the last half-century have provoked the first reaction in favour of efficient government. St Charles came from a ruling family among that ruling race. Personal humility shone out in him as in the other saints; but there was something Latin all the same about the resolute competence with which he governed his diocese. Men called him a second St Ambrose; and St Ambrose, his predecessor in the See of Milan, was a civil magistrate before he was ever a bishop. It was no idle title to call St Charles a prince of the Church.

Whatever be the rights and wrongs of all the controversies we hear about the medieval Church, this at least is clear, that in the days of the Council of Trent its organization needed reform. And reform needs more than mere legislation to decree it; it needs administration to execute it. That is St Charles's characteristic legacy to the Church: it was the influence of his example, in great measure, that moulded her organization on the new model which Trent had decreed. The bishop has got to be the centre of everything in his diocese, and the clergy of the diocese are to be *his* clergy—a family of which he is to be the father, a guild of which he is to be the master. See how fond St Charles was of synods: the whole of his comparatively short episcopate is a long record of the synods he gathered amongst his clergy. See how enthusiastic he is for the seminary idea; the bishop, henceforth, is not merely to ordain people, he is to know whom he is ordaining. And above all what was characteristic of St Charles was the institute which he left behind him—a body of secular priests, putting themselves at the disposal of the bishop as absolutely as the religious puts himself at the disposal of his superior. Yes, there is much about St Charles's life which is more exciting, and much which is more attractive, than all this; his boundless generosity to the poor, the relentless mortification that regulated his busy, competent life. But what makes him stand out among the saints more than either is his intense devotion even to the most uninspiring details of diocesan routine.

In this church, where St Charles's own spiritual children minister to you, something of his influence must surely impart itself to you; there must be some response in your blood to the appeal, long strange to our countrymen, of "the Roman line, the Roman order". And it is only right that the faithful who worship here should have a special devotion to ecclesiastical authority, and to the expression of that principle in the archdiocese of Westminster. It is the aim of a decent Catholic to obey his superiors; it is the aim of a good Catholic to obey his superiors lovingly. The virtue of obedience, nowadays, is a specifically Catholic virtue. The Protestant or half-believing or unbelieving world around us does not understand that it is a virtue at all. English people by temperament, by habit, by tradition, regard obedience as a tiresome necessity. Useful as training, perhaps, for schoolboys or for soldiers, but not a virtue in itself. The Protestant, in fact, thinks that obedience exists because without it there could be no authority. The Catholic is more likely to tell you that authority exists because without it there would be no obedience. The Catholic admits, quite as much as the Protestant, that man ought to realize himself, to develop every side of his nature, as far as he can do so without sin. But he sees also that the faculty for paying cheerful obedience to the orders of a human superior is one side of a man's nature, and if he never recognizes a human superior, that faculty will go undeveloped. It is a good thing, says the *Imitation*, to be under obedience to a prelate, and not to be one's own master—a good thing, not a convenient thing or a necessary thing, but something good in itself, a source of merit.

You see, when your Protestant sits down, if he ever does, to read the biography of a man like St Charles, he says: "Ah, yes, that is where these Catholics have the advantage! These crafty ecclesiastical statesmen, who treat every human agent they employ merely as a pawn in the game, who always sees exactly what each man is fitted for, and where he will be most use, that is where the power of the Catholic Church lies! The Vatican issuing its orders to the bishop, and the bishops to their clergy, every one of whom is simply a cog in a great machine! These seminaries, of course, turn all the priests out on a mould, and when they come out of them the bishop can play his crafty game of chess with them, and the thing is done. A triumph of organization, but hardly suited to the English mind or to modern circumstances." That is the sort of picture of the Church which our obliging neighbours have invented for themselves in order to explain the fact that the Catholic Church is successful. We know that is a fable: we know that you have only got to live in the Catholic Church for a little in order to get the atmosphere of it, which is something totally different from that. But the Protestants are right about one thing; they are right in seeing that we have a tradition and a theory of obedience which they do not understand. Only it is not the obedience of blind tools that have lost all independence and all initiative. It is a submissiveness which we imitate from our Lady herself—*Ecce ancilla Domini!* It is a free act of loyalty by which Catholics acknowledge and accept the administrative authority of the Church, and hear in the commands of their superiors the voice of almighty God.

And above all, Catholic obedience rallies to the person of that Supreme Pontiff who holds his succession from the Pilot of the Galilean lake. With good omen, in these troubled times, we have seen a successor of St Charles in Milan elevated to the throne of St Pius the Fifth. In the present disintegration of Europe, that recalls to Catholic memory the storms of the sixteenth century, yet with cross-winds and cross-currents that are all its own, let us pray that the spirit of those two great saints may unite in their successor, as he grasps the tiller of Peter's boat, and finds, God be thanked, that she still answers her helm. And let us renew our own loyalty to his person and to his office, determined that those instruments of government which the saints of the Counter-Reformation perfected, shall not through our fault lose their edge or be baulked of their purpose, the glory of almighty God. To whom be praise and dominion for ever. Amen.

19

ST BERNADETTE OF LOURDES[1]

Put off the shoes from thy feet, for the place whereon thou standest is holy ground.—Exodus 3. 5.

ABOUT three thousand years ago, a man stood, thrilled with religious awe, on the slopes of Mount Sinai in Arabia. He was a shepherd, feeding on those barren pastures the flocks of his father-in-law; his attention had been aroused, at a distance, by the unwonted sight of a fire in the desert scrub. And now that he had drawn nearer, he saw that this was not merely something beyond the ordinary, but something beyond nature itself; the bush before which he stood burned continually, but was not consumed. At the same time a divine warning came to him that he must take off the shoes from his feet in sign of reverence. He did so, and when he had done so the divine voice came to him again; he was to bear a message to his brethren, the children of Israel, subject at that time to a barbarous captivity in Egypt. The God of their fathers, the God of Abraham and Isaac and Jacob, would deliver them from that bondage; and when they had come out of Egypt, they were to do sacrifice to him on this mountain of Sinai. And, in token of the new covenant he was to make with his people, the God of Abraham and Isaac and Jacob revealed himself by a new name: I AM WHO AM.

Rather less than eighty years ago, a little girl stood before the rock of Massabieille, in the township of Lourdes, on the slopes of the Pyrenees. No premonition of any divine event disturbed her thoughts; she was at play with her companions, and if she took off the shoes from her feet it was only to cross the stream that lay in their path. She heard a noise, like that of a strong wind; she turned, and saw that the trees in the valley were not bowed as a strong wind must bow them. She turned back towards the rock, and a rose-bush that grew in front of it. And now she saw the rose-bush flaming with something more bright, more pure, more beautiful than fire. She saw above it the figure of a Lady; what need to describe it in detail? Wherever Christendom reaches, the helpless aspirations of Christian artists have made that figure familiar to every human eye. The Lady said no word, but she made one sign, the sign of the cross; and the little girl, taking courage,

[1] This sermon was preached in February 1934.

said her rosary as if to defend her from harm. Then the Vision beckoned to her to come nearer; she drew back in alarm, and it vanished. She took off her other stocking, crossed the stream, and rejoined her companions, who had seen nothing. That was all; it was only in later visits that she realized what a grace had been bestowed upon her; that she, too, was to lead a world out of its captivity; draw it after her to worship God and celebrate the glories of his Mother on that mountain. It was only many days later that the gracious Lady revealed herself by name; lifted up her eyes to heaven and said: "I am the Immaculate Conception".

Moses was a shepherd, not by choice. A man of courts and palaces, he had been driven into exile, and served, in that exile, his apprenticeship among the flocks. It is curious how often God has chosen a shepherd when he has wanted to impart an inspiration that has revolutionized men's lives. Jacob was a shepherd, the founder of the Jewish race; David was a shepherd, the ancestor of its royal dynasty; Amos was a shepherd, the first of its sons to prophesy and to commit his prophecies to writing. And under the new dispensation it is not otherwise; the shepherds at Bethlehem were the first to hear from their cronies, the angels, of the divine-human birth, and you will find shepherd saints in every age of Christian piety—St Geneviève, St Paschal Baylon, St Vincent de Paul, St John Vianney. Curious, did we say? There is nothing curious about it when you come to think of it. For God himself was content to be described by his ancient people as a Shepherd; "Hear, thou shepherd of Israel", "The Lord is my shepherd", "He shall feed his flock like a shepherd"; and when the divine Word came to dwell among us, he chose for himself the title of the Good Shepherd, and handed it on to St Peter, his favourite apostle, when he committed to him the care of all the churches. He who would lead God's people must imitate the divine forethought, the divine patience, the divine gentleness which tends and pursues so lovingly the straying hearts of men. Shepherd to shepherd, God delegates to Moses his pastoral office.

St Bernadette, too, was a shepherd girl. Not that this was her business in her father's home; but when she went on a visit to friends of the family at Bartres, the year before her apparitions, she was given charge of a flock of sheep, among which, characteristically, she made the tiniest lamb her favourite. So she, too, was apprenticed to the shepherd's trade; for she, too, was to be the leader of God's people. And the gracious Lady who appeared to her over the rose-bush, was not she the daughter of a shepherd, St Joachim? And will not she, like

Rachel before her, have fed her father's flock? Shepherdess to shepherdess, our Lady delegates to St Bernadette her pastoral office.

Moses led his people, and they followed him, where? To the same
mountain in which he had first been privileged with the intimacy of
almighty God. We were picturing, just now, a solitary figure in the
desert, alone with God, no other human creature in sight. Carry your
mind forward a little space of time, and you will see the same man
closeted once more with the same divine Audience; but, at the foot of
the mountain, what is this? A vast array of Bedouin tents, the migration
of a people. More than six hundred thousand souls worshipping God
in the mountain he had chosen. With all that, the vision is still for Moses,
and for Moses only. The people stand at the foot of the mountain,
with limits appointed to them which they must not transgress; Moses
goes up into the mountain, and is hidden by a dark cloud from mortal
view. The people see the play of lightning round the summit, but the
divine Voice is not for them; it is only through Moses that the word
comes to them. Yet that word is sovereign; centuries go by, and the
nation of Israel increases as the sand by the seashore, but still the
memory of Sinai haunts them, and their dearest traditions are all
prefaced with the same rubric, "Moses said".

Bernadette stood before the grotto on the eleventh of February
with no other human creature near her, except two little girls, her
companions, on the other side of the stream. When she knelt there on
the fourth of March, just three weeks later, she was being watched by a
crowd of twenty thousand pilgrims. Yet still the vision was only for
her; for those others there was nothing but the grotto and the rose-
bush, and the mountains beyond. They could see the smile that lit
up the face of the visionary, but that was all. But the memory of her
smile still haunts the grotto, and all Christendom flocks there in its
hundreds of thousands, to worship in the place where her feet stood.
And still she haunts the place like a visible presence; when you offer your
lighted candle, you half expect to hear her cry out: "You're burning
me!" as she did when she woke from her ecstasy nearly eighty years ago.

When Moses came down from the mountain, his face shone, so
that the children of Israel could not bear to look upon it. They saw
there, as if reflected in a frail human mirror, the glory of him who had
spoken with him on the mount. And Moses covered his face with a
veil, lest even that reflected radiance should be profaned by human sight.

In May, 1866, the chapel which Bernadette's ecstasies had demanded
was inaugurated at Lourdes. That July she took the veil with the
Sisters of Charity of Nevers, and Lourdes was not to see her again. Did

we think that she would wait there to tell us all her story, to touch our rosaries and sign our autograph books? No, the face which had looked into the face of the Immaculate must be veiled thenceforward; thenceforward we should not even see her smile.

Moses was sent to deliver his people from bondage, and from a bondage to which they had grown accustomed, so that they loved their fetters, and were constantly turning on him and asking why he could not leave them alone. That was his chief difficulty—they did not want to be set free. And even when they had been set free, and led out into the wilderness, they were always hankering after the luxuries they had enjoyed in Egypt, always murmuring against the rough fare of the desert. While Moses was up in the mountain, the people he had left behind him in the valley made a golden calf and fell to worshipping it, as they had worshipped it in Egypt. All his life he preached to an incredulous race, condemned, for their hardness of heart, to forty years' wandering in the wilderness before they achieved their promised resting-place.

Bernadette was sent to a world in bondage, and to a world which rejoiced in its bondage. Those apparitions of hers took place in the very middle of the Victorian age, when mankind, or at any rate, the richer part of mankind, was enjoying material plenty to a degree, I suppose, unexampled before or since. And the presence of material plenty had given rise to a general spirit of materialism; a spirit which loves the good things of this life and is content with the good things of this life, does not know how to enlarge its horizons and think about eternity. She was sent to deliver us from that captivity of thought; to make us forget the idols of our prosperity, and learn afresh the meaning of suffering and the thirst for God. That is what Lourdes is for; that is what Lourdes is about—the miracles are only a by-product. You might have thought that in our day, when prosperity has waned and all of us, or nearly all of us, have to be content with less, we should have needed no longer these divine warnings from the rock of Massabieille. We know that it is not so; we know that in this wilderness of drifting uncertainties, our modern world, we still cling to the old standard of values, still celebrate, with what conviction we may, the worship of the Golden Calf. The year of Bernadette's canonization finds us no less in need of public reparation for our common sinfulness than the year in which Bernadette took the veil.

Do not think me fanciful, then, if I suggest that we ought to see in Lourdes a sort of modern Sinai; and that we ought to treasure the words our Lady spoke in the grotto as we treasure the words God spoke to Moses on the mountain. Ten words of God to Moses, which are enshrined, now, in the general conscience of humanity; ten words of our Lady to St Bernadette, ruling principles (surely) for the Church to whose altars the little prophetess has been raised. Let us meditate them, very briefly, as they come.

At the third apparition, St Bernadette took with her pen and ink and a sheet of paper, to write down the commands which, she felt, the strange Lady would want to express. And the first recorded utterance of the Immaculate bears on that point; "What I have to tell you, I do not need to set down in writing. Will you have the kindness to come here for a whole fortnight?" When Moses came down from Mount Sinai, he brought with him two tables of stone, on which the Ten Commandments had been written, we know not how, by almighty God himself. But the Christian law, St Paul tells us, is not written on tables of stone, but on fleshly tables of the heart. It is not a code of directions exterior to ourselves, but a spirit with which we are to be imbued, an attitude which we are to assimilate. And Bernadette, accordingly, must not expect her decalogue to be registered in pen and ink. She must come to the grotto for a fortnight, as continuously as she may, and the message will write itself on her heart. And from us, too, our Lady of Lourdes asks no laborious exercise of the intellect, no feats of memory, if we are to learn her lesson. We are to watch Bernadette, and see our Lady's own image in her.

That was the first word, and the second word followed immediately, with an almost cruel abruptness: "I do not promise you that you will be happy in this world, but in the next". Moses, the servant of God, brought his people out into a land flowing with milk and honey—but he was not allowed to enter that promised land himself. And St Bernadette was to open for us that miraculous spring from which healing has flowed into thousands of homes; the grotto in which she worshipped is hung about with a forest of crutches, the trophies of our Lady's clients; but St Bernadette herself, what reward was given to her for all her faith and endurance? Thirteen short years of life in the cloister; years haunted with the premonition, and crowned with the experience, of long and continued bodily suffering. We had so often been told, yet nothing really succeeded in making us believe, that it is eternity which matters, and time does not count. Bernadette should be a living proof of that doctrine; our Lady's favourite confidante, rewarded, not with health like us others, but with a short life and a long cross!

At the fifth apparition, during forty minutes of ecstasy our Lady taught St Bernadette, word by word, a special prayer she was to use. That prayer she learned by heart, and used it every day for the rest of her life. What was it? we ask, breathlessly. The answer is that we do not know, and shall never know till, by God's grace, we are allowed to use it in heaven. The message, I say it again, was for Bernadette, and for us only through her; we are not to go to Lourdes for this or that ceremony, this or that form of prayer; it is to be the shrine not of a ritual but of a life.

And the fourth word presses on to the heart of the mystery; it was during the sixth apparition that our Lady said suddenly, "Pray for sinners". That is not what we think of, is it, when people ask us what are the most characteristic impressions we carried away from the Lourdes pilgrimage. We think of those wasted forms in their invalid chairs grouped round the square in the afternoon, and the heart-rending petitions that echo round them: Lord, grant that I may see, Lord, grant that I may hear, Lord, grant that I may walk. Or we think of the torchlight procession in the evening, and the singing of the *Credo* which concludes it; we remember Lourdes as the embodiment of a great act of faith. But when our Lady stood at the grotto, the first command she gave was not, Heal the sick; was not, Convert the unbeliever. Her command was, Pray for sinners. Man's sin, that is our real malady; man's impenitence, that is the crying problem.

The fifth word is unique, in that it was heard by the bystanders, not indeed from our Lady's lips, but from Bernadette's. As she knelt there in ecstasy, she repeated several times, sobbing, the one word, "Penance". They learned afterwards that she was repeating it after our Lady. This, then, is our Lady's one public utterance; and, as I say, it is the message of Lourdes. We are to make there, in common, what reparation we can for our common faults. The true music of Lourdes is not the "Lord, he whom thou lovest is sick" that thunders across the square; not the *Ave*, *Ave*, that sweeps down the terraces. It is the *Parce, Domine, parce populo tuo*—the confession of our sins, and a desperate cry for pardon.

Then, not till then, at the ninth apparition, our Lady pointed to the sacred spring, and bade her prophetess drink and wash there. This sixth word is a kind of interlude; and, remember, our Lady never said that those who drank, those who washed, would be healed of their bodily infirmities. The faithful themselves were left to find out that gracious corollary; the ceremony performed at the time by St Bernadette was rather a pantomime of humiliation—to eat grass like the cattle, to drink and wash in a muddy spring. She dedicated herself and her mission to human scorn.

The seventh word emphasizes the lesson of humiliation, and connects it with the lesson of penance. "You will kiss the ground, for sinners." Because all our worst sins take their origin in pride, the penance we are to offer—we moderns at least—must be prefaced by the mortification of reminding ourselves, what and whence we are. So, next Wednesday, we open our Lenten fast by having our foreheads smeared with ashes, while the priest says to us, as God said to Adam when he had sinned: "Dust thou art, and unto dust shalt thou return". We must learn to grovel before we can learn to weep.

With the eighth and ninth words we come at last to practical, rubrical directions, which will serve to organize Bernadette's revelations as a cult. "Go and tell the priests to build me a chapel"; "I want people to come here in procession." Man is made of body and soul; body as well as soul must take part in his self-dedication to God. Material edifices, of wood and stone, outward gestures, pilgrimage and march and song, must be the complement and the expression of his inward attitude. So, when God issued to Moses his moral law, in all the grandeur of its austerity, he directed at the same time the building of a tabernacle, and the rites which were to be performed in and at the tabernacle; he would enlist material things in the service of a spiritual ideal. So, when our Lady preached to Bernadette her gospel of penance, she externalized it and eternalized it by prescribing the outward ceremonies that should be its expression.

The tenth word is the best known of all: "I am the Immaculate Conception". Why (people have asked) did she say that, rather than "I am the immaculately conceived"? It is, perhaps, rash to venture on explanations. But when God appeared to Moses, he revealed himself under the title I AM WHO AM; and theologians have read in those simple words the most profound truth about the divine Being—that there is no distinction of essence and existence, of attributes and personality, in him; his goodness, his wisdom, his power, his justice, are nothing other than himself. That cannot be said, obviously, of any creature. But, may we not suppose that the plenitude of grace which flowed into the soul of our blessed Lady so overshadowed and transformed her human personality as to make her little suppliant forgetful of it; make her see, there in the grotto, no longer a human figure but the embodiment of a spiritual truth? That the thought of what she was and is was obscured, in that moment of revelation, by the thought of what God wrought and works in her?

"Today, if you will hear his voice, harden not your hearts", was the message of Sinai. Moses struck the hard rock, and the waters gushed out; he could not wring tears, even so, from the hearts of a stubborn people. Surely, when she pointed to the miraculous spring at Lourdes, our Lady was telling a whole world to weep for its sins. So many years have passed, and do we still come away from Lourdes dry-eyed?

20

ST THÉRÈSE OF LISIEUX[1]

What if your mind should be corrupted, and lose that simplicity which is yours in Christ?—2 Corinthians 11. 3.

Is it a good thing or a bad thing, to be simple? Or doesn't it matter? Simplicity is one of the divine attributes; it comes first on the list; indeed, all the other perfections of the divine nature flow from it. That divine simplicity is something we mention with awe; it is a perfection, a splendour—whereas we don't think of human simplicity quite like that, do we? Not that we use the word in a contemptuous sense, meaning half-witted, as the Italians do; but always it has a slightly patronizing air about it. When we say "such a charming, simple person", we mean the description as a compliment, but a rather back-handed compliment; secretly we reflect, don't we, that people like that wouldn't be able to sit back and listen to the Third Programme, as we do.

There's very little about simplicity in the Bible. In the Old Testament, it describes people who are so helpless that they can't look after themselves; and in the book of Proverbs, where it comes oftenest, it is a term of abuse. Wisdom is represented as expostulating with the folly of mankind; "What (says she) are you still gaping there, simpletons?" The Hebrew word looks very much as if it meant going about with your mouth open, like the French *gobe-mouche*. In the New Testament, there are only a handful of references. Curiously, I think the word really owes its place in our devotional vocabulary to the

[1] This sermon was preached on the Feast of St Thérèse, 3 October 1954, at St Peter's Church, Birmingham, to the Catholic undergraduates.

Imitation of Christ. There, you will find some thirty references under "simple" and "simplicity", nearly all of them complimentary. To be simple, in the *Imitation*, is not just to be so helpless that almighty God feels bound to look after you; it is to have a quality which God wants to see in us and very often doesn't. He doesn't see it, for example, in those distinguished theologians against whom, somehow, Thomas à Kempis seems to have a bit of a grudge. Those later Middle Ages, when a degenerate race of schoolmen were boring Europe with their quodlibets and their quiddities—they taught us to value simplicity. But the possibilities of it weren't discovered till a modern saint put it on the map. Today is the feast of St Thérèse of Lisieux, and the collect by which we commemorated her just now asks that we may follow the footsteps of the holy virgin Thérèse in humbleness and simpleness of heart. To the best of my knowledge, that is the only place in the liturgy where this particular virtue is mentioned. You can't quite say that she invented it; but it was like her holy impudence to force it on the Church, wasn't it? The whole idea of the Spiritual Childhood is that we shouldn't just be innocent, as children are; we should be simple with the simplicity of children.

What is it, then, this quality which, as Christians, we have got to admire? Was Jesus Christ simple? We can't take it for granted that he had all the perfections of our human nature, taken as they stand; he had, for example, no faith, because faith has for its background the possibility of doubt, and for him doubt was impossible. He had not even got humility, as we understand humility. Had he simplicity? Yes, though it sounds a ridiculous suggestion, if we think of simplicity as if it meant being undeveloped, being under-educated. He was perfectly simple, because he was perfectly integrated. He, just like you and me, was compounded in his human nature of body and soul; the human surge of anger, for instance, which you and I feel welling up in us on so many inappropriate occasions, was made felt in him when he cried out against the formalism and inconsistency of the Pharisees. It would have liked to make itself felt when his own people turned against him and crucified him; only it didn't, because he was integrated, because his outlook was perfectly simple. Do you remember where it says that the people of some Samaritan village would not entertain him, because his face was set as if he were going to Jerusalem? That phrase is a symbol of his whole career; his face was *set*, wasn't always turning this way and that, looking to see what other people were thinking about him, looking to see where his own advantage lay, looking to see what was the best opportunity for striking an impressive attitude, or coining a memorable phrase. No, his face was set towards Jerusalem; the cross was the baton in his knapsack.

St Thérèse was simple, God knows she was simple; and on a hasty analysis we are tempted to say it was because she was just like a child —tell me, have you ever known a child like St Thérèse? No, her simplicity, too, lay in the fact that she was, as near as ordinary human nature can go, integrated; she knew what she was out for, and was determined to get it. Every moment of her day was built up conscientiously, laboriously if you will, into a pattern; every action of hers was a stitch in her divine needlework, her sampler, copied from the life of Jesus Christ. Her life, so short, was so businesslike; she cut out all the frills. And the reason why it makes you and me so ashamed of ourselves isn't really that she was young and natural and impulsive, isn't really that she was French, and had the French knack of intimacy with the supernatural, but that she knew what she was about, subordinated her whole life to a plan. She was simple because to her there was only one thing that mattered; she wasn't being distracted from her aim all the time by trifles and scruples as we are.

Well, it is all very beautiful, all very edifying; but I suspect that some of you are objecting that you did not come here to listen to a sermon about the saint of the day. Especially when the virtue held up to your admiration is that of simplicity—the last thing, surely, which ought to have any appeal for a group of University students, settling down to a fresh year of work. Surely (you say) the whole purpose of education is to make us less simple, more complicated sort of people. There are you, preparing to dissect skeletons, and map out nerve-reactions through a microscope; there are you, with your mind full of the causes and results of the Industrial Revolution; there are you, your head whirling with modern physical speculations which appear to outrun the very limits of common-sense; how are people in your position to cultivate simplicity of mind? Almost you wish that you were an agricultural labourer pulling roots, or a postman delivering letters, or even a nun in a convent laying out the vestments for to-morrow—life would be so peaceful, so simple! And you do not thank me for recommending, here in St Peter's, a quality of mind which you, of all people, must needs find it difficult to attain.

If there is anybody here who belongs to the teaching staff of the University, I hope they will not mind my saying—what is, after all, hardly better than a platitude—that the things we learn in such places are not the things which are taught us. What is handed on to us by our lecturers is taken down in a note-book, and languishes there until examination time comes round; it has not become part of our mental furniture. It is sealed off, for the most part, even from memory. What we are learning at the University is something quite different; we acquire it by a kind of unconscious absorption. Arguments we have had over a cup of coffee, points of view we have been introduced to at a debating society, or in reading the reviews—serious reviews, such as we feel bound to read now that we are intellectuals; stray pieces of information we have picked up on the wireless, or even at the cinema; all these penetrate under the skin, or say, if you will, that they are germs floating in the air which we breathe in without knowing it. You make heroes among your fellow students, and copy their hand-writing, their dress, their behaviour. You go on your travels in the vacation, attend conferences, meet people who impress you by their greater knowledge of the world. All that is, in the larger sense, your education. Your friends say, at the end of three years, how altered you are. But they are not thinking of lectures.

In all this you need simplicity. Simplicity is the filter through which all these competing influences have to pass, if they are to have the right effect on you. If you are simple, you will be integrated; you will assimilate these influences, and make them part of your way of thought; accepting here, rejecting there, according as they do or don't fit in. If you are not simple, you will pick up a lot of points of view, quite unrelated; or, worse still, a set of poses which you adopt in conversation; now one, now another, according to the company you are in. Simplicity does not mean crudeness of taste, or a low intelligence quotient; it means being yourself. May I explain that by hinting at one or two of the attitudes possible in a student which are the enemies of simplicity?

It is a violation of simplicity when you find yourself admiring some-thing, approving of something, maintaining some point of view, merely because everybody else seems to, when there is no genuine reaction in your own mind to ratify it. I don't mean that you oughtn't to be impressed by the unanimous judgment of a lot of other people But you ought to find out their reason for making such a judgment to go through the same process yourself, if you honestly can, before you give it your assent; otherwise you will only be shouting with the crowd, and often foolishly. Remember Hans Andersen's story of the Emperor's New Clothes, and how nobody, except one little child, noticed that they weren't there. If you are to be integrated, if you are to be all of a piece, it must be your own judgment, however immature, that dictates your opinions; your own tastes, however unformed, that underwrite your preferences.

It is a violation of simplicity, when you do just the opposite; when you court a reputation for originality by disagreeing with everybody else just for the sake of disagreement. The temptation is rarer, but it is not unknown at your time of life. What begins as an amusing affectation can harden into a habit of the mind; you may become cross-grained, precious, out of touch with your fellows; you will be forced out of your true pattern, and simplicity will be lost.

It is a violation of simplicity, when you allow partisanship to run away with your sympathies, unable to find fault with anybody who belongs to your crowd, unable to find any good motives in people who belong to the other crowd. This is a temptation which is very real to us Catholics. Our sympathies are so strongly engaged, we are so widely at variance with most of our fellow countrymen, that we are prone to bias. We try to simplify history, we try to simplify modern politics, by making them all black and white, all heroes and villains; and in doing that we only unsimplify ourselves. There is a perpetual conflict in us between our *parti pris* and our better judgment; our neighbours learn to shun us as people with a King Charles's Head. Oh, it is not all on one side, this simplification of the issues; nothing is more terrifying in the modern world than the way we are all drawing apart. But we shall not make things better by doing violence to our own instincts. We want to be ourselves, to see things as they are.

A new year of work lies before you; and I pray that you may graduate from this University as educated men and women, as good patriots and citizens, what you will. But I will pray above all, by your leave, that you may be simple; simple with the simplicity of St Thérèse, so good at dealing with ordinary life; simple with the simplicity of our Lady, so calm, so ready to make the best of things; simple with the simplicity of our Lord himself—your faces set towards Jerusalem, the city of peace here and hereafter.

21

LISIEUX AND ASSISI[1]

Except you shall be converted, and become as little children, you shall not enter into the kingdom of heaven.—Matthew 18. 3.

YESTERDAY, Christendom was celebrating one of the most recent, one of the most widely loved, among the memories of God's saints; the third of October commemorates St Thérèse of Lisieux, the Little Flower of Jesus. The prayer of the feast asks that we may follow her footsteps in humbleness and simplicity of heart. I am not absolutely certain, but I think that that is the only place in the whole of the Church's liturgy in which we pray God to make us simple. It is as if the Little Flower had discovered, for herself, a new Christian virtue. Of course, that is not really so. All the saints have practised all the virtues, except for some of those who reached their crown through martyrdom. But it may sometimes happen that one particular virtue shines out in the life of one particular saint more evidently than in the life of any other. The saints, you see, are our Lord's crown; and in that crown one particular jewel catches the light, now and again, so as to shine out more than ever. All the saints have possessed the virtue of simplicity; but it was not till God saw fit to give us a really glaring example of saintly simplicity in St Thérèse that the Church really noticed what a wonderful thing it is.

If we doubted that there was simplicity to be found among the saints, or even that there was a high degree of simplicity to be found among the saints, before the Little Flower came, those doubts were not able to last after October the third. October the fourth has brought with it the memory of another saint, once more one of the most dearly loved in Christendom, who also strikes the imagination by his simplicity perhaps more than by any other gift; I mean, of course, St Francis. In a curious way, the Poor Man of Assisi and the young nun of Lisieux stretch out hands to one another across the centuries, as if they were two children playing a children's game together—Ring a ring of roses, perhaps. I do not think it is fanciful, in spite of the difference in their centuries and their careers, to mention these two saints in the same breath. To take just one instance, and a not very important instance —you can see the same child-like quality in each of them if you consider their fondness for make-believe. The Little Flower, you remember,

[1] This sermon was preached in 1936.

when she was encouraging her novices to pray for the conversion of sinners, told them to think of those souls as a set of ninepins, and those prayers as a ball trying to knock down first one and then another. And she was always indulging in fantasies of that kind; so was St Francis. When he felt tempted, one extremely cold night, to regret his vows, he got up out of bed, and went out into the snow just as he was, and made a snow-woman and six snow-children; and he pretended that they were his wife and family. "There," he said to himself—for he talked to himself, as all children do—"these must all be clothed; see, poor things, they are dying of cold; here there will be all kinds of trouble." When you read stories like that, you realize that it is not a very long way from the Little Flowers of St Francis to the Little Flower of Jesus.

But, of course, there was all the difference in the world between the opportunities these two had of showing their child-like qualities to the world at large. St Thérèse says in her life, addressing her superior, who was also her sister: "An artist must have at least two brushes; the first, which is the more useful, gives the ground tints and rapidly covers the whole canvas; the other, a small one, is employed for the details of the picture. You, my dear Mother, represent the valuable brush our Lord holds lovingly in his hand when he wishes to do some great work in the souls of his children, and I am the little one he deigns to use afterwards to fill in the minor details." If you will put on one side the modesty of those expressions, they give you an admirable description of the difference between St Thérèse and St Francis. St Thérèse is the little brush; her work for God consists in etching in, very carefully, all the little daily details of a cloistered life with enormous care, like one of the pre-Raphaelite painters, drawing every leaf and every stone with minute precision. Whereas St Francis is the impressionist; he gets his effects with broad sweeps of the brush. He will fill the world with friars, men who have a roving commission to do nothing in particular except imitate Jesus Christ; his ideas are big enough, even, to make him go off to the East and try to convert the Sultan to the Christian faith; his vision cannot be bounded by continents—that is the difference.

Not that that was a difference of temperament; rather a difference of circumstances. St Thérèse's career reminds you of those lines of Henry Vaughan:

> If a star were confined into a tomb,
> Her captive flames must needs burn there;
> But when the hand that locked her up gives room,
> She'll shine through all the sphere.

God locked up St Thérèse in the tomb of a Carmelite convent; he would show a miracle of his power by making her suddenly shine through all the sphere only after she was given room, only after her bodily death. So she lived in her Carmel like a child that is shut indoors on a rainy day. She would have liked to be converting the heathen, shedding her blood as a martyr; that was not for her, so she made the best of the little world she lived in, as a child will make the best of staying indoors when it becomes clear that the rain is not going to stop. By her power of make-believe—and what it made her believe was no more than the truth—she would turn her Carmel and the little opportunities of her life at Carmel into a glorious mission for winning the souls of men. But St Francis was different—God never locked *him* into a tomb. Think of St Francis as you will, you always think of him as in the open air. He was a schoolboy out for a holiday, you might almost say a schoolboy playing truant from school.

All St Francis's life was a sort of holy picnic. There is one story of his sitting down to a meal, a very simple and we should think rather an unpleasant meal, beside a spring with rocks and trees round it; and all through the meal he kept on exclaiming: "What a treasure we have here, what a treasure!" Now, St Francis was not one of your sophisticated modern people, who could get enthusiastic about the beauties of nature because he thought it was the proper thing to do. No, he really enjoyed the treat as a child enjoys its picnic; it was so kind of God to have arranged a setting of rocks and trees for him like that. And that is the secret, of course, of his love of creatures. Do not, by the way, ever let anybody try to make you believe that St Francis was fond of animals; he was fond of creatures. His brother was the sun, his sister the moon; when he had to have an operation on his eyes, without anaesthetics, he asked his brother fire to be gentle to him, and when the last scene of all came, he could welcome his sister death. Anybody can be fond of live animals because they remind him of human beings; grown-up people often are, and some of them are very sloppy about it. But it is the child that can manage to be fond of inanimate things, talk for hours to a stuffed bird, for example. And St Francis was like that; he loved creatures, not because they reminded him of human beings, but because they reminded him of God.

Now, what is this gift of simplicity, which we admire so much in children, because it is natural; which we admire so much in the saints, because it is supernatural? Do let us get rid at once of a favourite mistake; that of supposing that to be simple means to be ignorant. You see, there is only one Being who is absolutely simple; that is almighty

E

God, and he knows everything. No, to be simple is to see things with the eye of God, that is, to see them as they really are, without the trimmings. To be able to distinguish what is important from what is incidental and doesn't matter; to get down to the broad, primary truths, and forget what is merely conventional. I think if you asked me who was the simplest person I have ever known I should mention the name of one of the cleverest men of our generation, Mr G. K. Chesterton, who died this summer. And it is not out of place to mention him here, because he was perhaps the best biographer St Francis ever had, and he died when he had just come back from a visit to Lisieux. I remember he says somewhere that, if you find a man lying dead under the sofa, you explain the situation to other people by saying: There is a man lying dead under the sofa; you don't say: There is a man of considerable refinement lying dead under the sofa. On such occasions you keep to the essential facts; and that is what simplicity means, to keep to the essential facts; not just at moments, but all your life.

And for the saint, you see, the essential facts are those of the next world, rather than those of this. God, your soul, eternity, sin, judgment, those are the essential facts; and the simplicity of the saints is to distinguish those facts all the time, without effort, from the unessential facts that do not matter, although human vanity and snobbishness and worldliness think they do. How are we going to get that spirit ourselves? I think it is easy to see how St Francis got it; what was the first stage, anyhow, in the getting of it. He cut himself off entirely from all worldly possessions. That is why I was telling you just now he soliloquized like that over the snow-woman, his imaginary wife. "Here there will be all sorts of trouble", he said to himself; he reminded himself that his vow of chastity had saved him from a whole heap of anxieties which might have distorted that simplicity of vision with which he saw God. It was the same with his poverty. When his father summoned him before the bishop, and said he would have no more to do with him and would cut him off from his inheritance, he immediately took off his clothes, because they really belonged to his father, and went about in a piece of old sacking with a cross marked on it. Now, he said, he could really understand what it was to have a Father in heaven. I have called St Francis a truant schoolboy, and that is what he was; he ran away from the world and its belongings so as to keep holiday in his heart to God.

Well, we cannot do that; our state of life and the demands which other people's lives make on our own will not allow us to do that. All right; but, remember, the less we cling to worldly enjoyments, the more we accustom ourselves to do without worldly enjoyments, the better chance we shall have of cultivating that true simplicity which is the simplicity of the saints. The world is very old nowadays, and we are all very grown-up; you can buy the wisdom of the ages for a shilling on a bookstall; the newspapers fling problems at us, and the advertisements tell us that it is our duty to get on, to make money, and to want as much as possible. That is what we call a high standard of living, to want as much as possible. Conventions of civilization, the second servant and the fresh suit on Sundays and the latest fashion in hats and in eyebrows make life expensive for us and complicated. But with all these wonderful opportunities, is our world really a happy world? Can we look back at the age of St Francis without feeling something of regret for our own childhood, something of that twinge which comes to us when we see, in the house where we were brought up, the familiar passage that leads to the nursery door?

The more we can resist the tyranny of these worldly embarrassments, the more we can be content to live according to our income, to be wise according to our opportunities, to be ourselves, to laugh at shams and see things as they are, the more we shall imitate St Francis, and the better compliment we shall pay him. May his prayers, and the prayers of our blessed Lady and St Thérèse, bring us out of this world, our schoolroom, into the glorious liberty of the sons of God.

II

THE ENGLISH MARTYRS

I

THE ENGLISH MARTYRS: I[1]

Therefore, seeing that we also have so great a cloud of witnesses standing over us, let us run with patience the race that is set before us.—Hebrews 12. 1.

I THINK it's a pity that, as Catholics, we never hear read out in our churches the eleventh chapter of St Paul's Epistle to the Hebrews. Partly because it is in itself a monument of noble writing, partly because its phrases cannot but recall, to English hearers, the memory of the persecutions which our forefathers endured, and of the martyrs whom we celebrate today. It is a long record of the great heroes of Old Testament history—Noe, and Abraham, and Isaac, and Jacob, and Moses, which shows that it was through faith they became pleasing to God. Faith is the substance of things to be hoped for, the evidence of things which appear not. It was through faith that Abraham left his country in obedience to God's call, through faith that he and his descendants dwelt in tabernacles in the wilderness. For they looked for a city which has foundations, whose builder and maker is God.

I'm afraid they're not very real figures to most of us, those heroes of the Old Testament, Abraham and Isaac and Jacob and the rest of them. We are rather apt to think of them as we see them in stained-glass windows in church. And on the stained-glass windows they are represented as rather angular old gentlemen with white beards, who wear heavy and cumbersome sort of robes, mostly in dull purple and brown. Their attitudes are stiff and conventional; they always seem to have gone for a walk with a stick in one hand and a thurible in the other. The background against which they are depicted is generally an uninteresting row of palm-trees. So we think of them, ordinarily, as if they were more like cardboard figures than our own fellow men. But in this eleventh chapter of the Hebrews a curious change seems to have come over them. A wind has sprung up, which lifts the heavy folds of their old-fashioned garments, and sets the branches of the cardboard trees stirring, and fills the whole picture with motion and with life. And what that wind is, St Paul tells us—it is faith.

Now in this particular chapter I don't think St Paul uses the word

[1] This sermon was preached at the Church of the English Martyrs, Sparkhill, Birmingham, in May 1924.

"faith" in its strict theological sense. It is, he says, the substance of things hoped for, the evidence of things which don't yet appear—the quality, then, of which he is speaking is not faith in the theological sense, but more like what we mean by hope, or confidence in God. The holy patriarchs—this is his point—were pleasing to God because they were perfectly content to go on in hope, obeying him and worshipping him, although they knew that the promise which had been made to them (the promise of salvation through our Lord Jesus Christ) would not be fulfilled in their lifetime, or for many centuries after it. They lived as exiles, believing that their children would have a country—that promise was not fulfilled until the time of Josue. They lived in tents without any fixed dwelling, and it was in a tent that they worshipped the God of their fathers (the tabernacle, we call it), believing that their children would be able to raise him up a majestic temple, in enduring stone—that promise was not fulfilled until the time of King Solomon. They endured this restless existence of living in tents in the wilderness, because their confidence in God made them believe that their children, one day, would have a settled home and walled cities to dwell in. But behind all that, they were looking forward also to another and a greater promise. And that was the promise of a Saviour, who should restore to exiled man his home in Paradise, welcome pilgrim man to his abiding city, the Jerusalem which is above.

And at the end of the chapter, St Paul gets tired of taking each instance separately; the list is too long. So he just mentions a few more names, and gives a summary of the heroic deeds and heroic sufferings with which these names are connected. And it is in the description of these that we are most vividly reminded of the saints whose memory enriches our own country. "Who through faith subdued kingdoms, wrought justice, achieved the promises . . . and others had trial of mockings and scourgings, of bonds also and of imprisonment; they were stoned, they were sawn asunder, were tried, were slain with the sword; they wandered about in sheepskins and goatskins, in want, in difficulty, in affliction—men of whom the world was not worthy. They wandered in wildernesses, in mountains, in dens and caves of the earth." Could there be a more vivid picture than that of the penal times, and of all that Catholics suffered, from Blessed John Fisher to Blessed Oliver Plunket? And then St Paul ends his chapter by drawing the moral of these lives. "All these," he says, "being approved by the testimony of their faith, did not receive the fulfilment of the promise, because God was providing some better thing for us, namely that without us they should not be made perfect."

Can you imagine what confidence in God it must have needed for Blessed Thomas More, Blessed John Fisher, and the Carthusians and the Benedictines, to stand their ground when the whole world seemed against them? To take their stand upon a mere ground of principle—after all, was there so very much harm in taking an oath merely because there was an objectionable clause in the preamble to it? Wouldn't it be wiser to let the King have his way for the time being, lest worse should come of it? Remember, King Henry had not repudiated the Catholic Faith. And there were thousands of people in England, quite good Catholics, who were ready to take the oath, and advise others to take it. How lonely, then, must have been the position of that handful of men who laid down their lives as martyrs in the first persecution! How little hope was there (it must have seemed) that posterity would ever ratify and applaud their solitary protest! But they endured, as seeing him who is invisible; these men had that confidence in God which sees behind the shifting panorama of politics, and rests in eternal truth. They were approved by the testimony of faith, laying down their lives in a hopeless cause, and leaving the promise of better times to posterity.

Can you imagine what confidence in God it must have needed for Blessed Cuthbert Mayne, Blessed Edmund Campion, and the long line of martyrs that followed them, to persevere in their mission to the English Catholics? To stand in hourly peril of their lives; to be outlaws when they set foot in England, forfeited criminals when they said Mass, that was not all, that was not the worst part of their affliction. To wander about by unfrequented ways, ill-clad, ill-fed, ill-housed, to hide for their lives in dens and caves of the earth—they could have borne all that. But to see the Faith, for all their efforts, gradually losing its hold, and persecution achieving its miserable object; to see soul after soul, family after family, wearying of the long struggle against an unrelenting enemy, and either conforming to a heretical Church, or losing their faith in religion altogether; to fight almost always and almost everywhere a losing battle—*that* needed confidence in God. "And truly, if they had been mindful of that country whence they came out, they might have had opportunity to return." English by birth, English by tastes, English by loyalty, they might, by being false to their creed, have become Englishmen once more. But they looked for a city which has foundations: they looked forward to times of peace and rest and reconstruction still far distant. As he lay close in his narrow hiding-hole, the Benedictine dreamed of spacious corridors in Downside or Ampleforth that were one day to be. As the secular priest whispered

EX

the Mass in his ruinous garret, he saw himself already—such is the power of faith—assisting at some gorgeous function in Westminster Cathedral. They were approved by the testimony of faith, and went out to meet death in the dungeon or on the scaffold, leaving the promises to us.

God had provided some better thing for us, that they should not be made perfect without us. You see, our faith, your faith and mine, is the fruit of their labours, purchased (under the mercy of Christ who redeemed us all) by their blood. Blessed Thomas More, not perfect without you and me! Blessed Edmund Campion, not perfect without you and me! Other men have laboured, and we have entered into their labours. There is a directness about our debt to the English martyrs which gives our devotion to them quite a special colour—we don't feel quite the same about the other saints, somehow. If St Augustine hadn't converted England, somebody else perhaps would have. But if the English martyrs hadn't kept the faith for us, who would have kept it for us? Humanly speaking, if it hadn't been for the martyrs, we in England might be in the same position as the Catholics of Norway or Sweden, a handful of two or three thousand, nothing more. We may have ten thousand schoolmasters in the Faith; we have not many fathers, such as these!

But remember, when we say that the prayers they offered and the martyrdom they suffered are made perfect through us, that doesn't mean that there is nothing more left to do. We have, by comparison with the Catholics of an earlier day, entered into rest; we can practise our religion boldly and openly, under the eyes of the police. Our bishops can go about in purple and hold synods and consecrate churches. But that doesn't mean that the fight is yet over; that doesn't mean that we can sit down and fan ourselves and say, Thank God that's all finished. What the martyrs prayed for was not the restoration of the hierarchy, but the conversion of England. And, although we have not the same dangers to run or the same sufferings to endure, we still need that faith, that confidence in God, which the martyrs showed, if we are to win through. The substance of things to be hoped for, the evidence of things which are not yet seen—do you hope, do you really hope, that England will be converted one day? If not, you are no true child of the English martyrs. And yet, is it so easy?

They have ceased to persecute us; yes, but is that because they are nearer than ever to our religion? Isn't it, in most cases, that they are further than ever from any religion at all? We talk of the decrease there has been, within these fifty years, of bitterness and of prejudice against the Catholic Church, and we do well to thank God for it. But isn't the root of it, very largely, religious indifference? We see around us a proportion of our fellow countrymen, we dare not ask how large a proportion, who are practically out of contact with any sort of Christianity. Not only do they doubt or cold-shoulder the claims of Christian doctrine, but they are losing even their hold on Christian morality. All that vital legislation of almighty God which protects the sanctity of marriage and family life is simply thrown aside as old-fashioned by the world at large; and what of those, even, who call themselves Christians? Those professedly Christian bodies, which might at least have fought by our side for sanctities such as these, debate the law of God as an open question, and decide to adopt it with a minority report! And is the battle finished?

There is, it is no use denying it, an urgency about this daily contact with a half-pagan world which threatens the faith of Catholics and tempts them to lose hope. In the labour of that mental strife, it is from the shrines of the martyrs, from the hiding-places where they lurked and the gibbets where they suffered, that the voice of comfort still hails English Catholics, and bids them fight on. Do we look few and lonely, when we protest at the laxity of our countrymen over the marriage law? Not fewer, not more lonely, than the martyrs who protested against the divorce of Henry VIII. Do we look weak and ill-equipped against the propaganda of our enemies and our rivals? Not weaker, not worse-equipped, than the little stream of missionaries that stole into England, year by year, in the days of the persecution. If we doubt, if we hesitate, how shall we bear comparison with these Old Contemptibles of the Catholic Religion?

We have, St Paul tells us, a great cloud of witnesses standing over us—witnesses, that is, martyrs: it is all the same word. And he tells us to run through patience to the prize that is set before us; he thinks of us, then, as competitors in some race, and of the martyrs as spectators who are watching us, looking down from heaven. And are they content with watching? Do they simply look on, and wonder which side will win? Is that the common attitude of spectators, when they watch an athletic contest? That is not my memory of the days, nearer thirty years ago than I care to think, when I used to watch football matches at the Aston Villa ground. My memory is rather of a small boy, wearing a claret-and-light-blue favour, who stood up on the seat and booed the referee. They are witnesses of our race, these martyrs of ours, but something more than witnesses, partisans who can cheer us to victory with the breath of their applause. For the applause of the saints is that prayer which goes up day and night before the throne of God: "How long, O Lord, holy and true, dost thou not judge and avenge our blood upon them that dwell on the earth?" And that prayer must be heard, in his own time.

Let us praise God, then, for the martyrs who are our fellow Englishmen, in heaven. These are no distant figures from stained-glass windows; they are men of our blood, sharing our common speech and our national ways of thought. Blessed Thomas More, with his hearty good humour, and his jokes on the scaffold; John Kemble, asking leave to smoke a last pipe before his execution—could they be of any race but ours? And surely, if they have not forgotten among the delights of eternity the soft outlines and the close hedgerows and the little hills of the country that gave them birth, their prayers still rise especially, among all the needs of a distracted world, for our fellow countrymen and theirs, whom error blinds or sin separates from God. It is Mary's month; she too, while a world lies prostrate at her feet, will not forget the land that was once called her dowry. May her intercession and theirs strengthen us and give us the confidence that never loses hope; and may our separated brethren, so long sought, so patiently wooed by the divine grace, return at last to their true allegiance, and make England a shrine of martyrs and a nursery of saints once more.

2

THE ENGLISH MARTYRS: II[1]

They that upset the world are come hither also.—Acts 17. 6.

WE enter this evening upon the Feast of the Invention of the Holy Cross, and tomorrow its relics will be exposed for veneration all over the world. Did you ever reflect, as you knelt before one of those chips of wood, upon its early history? Its history, I mean, before it became the instrument of our salvation. We have no record of its origin; in what forest the tree grew, or for what end it was first cut, or how it came to be brought to Jerusalem. Two planks, I suppose, lying about somewhere, and a soldier, the handy man of the legion, would fix them roughly together; not quite straight, perhaps, not

[1] This sermon was preached at Tyburn Convent, London.

quite true, but "after all", he would say to himself, "it is good enough for what it has got to do". A careless piece of carpentry, one of three jobs that had to be done by next morning, and in a hurry, because the need for it was unforeseen. And tomorrow a mere splinter of that wood, such as a man might run into his hand, will draw thousands of worshippers to their knees.

It is curious, is it not? Yet hardly more curious than the collection that is kept in this building; fragments of human bones and hair, patches of coarse cloth, shreds of linen with some dark stain on it. . . . Can you imagine what a stranger from some other planet would make of it, a man, if such were possible, without any idea or conception of God? You would persuade him that the collection was not one of mere odds and ends; that a certain interest attached to these things merely from the historical fact of their having been in contact with men of times past, the victims of a series of judicial murders. "Yes," he would say, "but, even so, is it not rather morbid? Is not one Chamber of Horrors enough for you people in London? Surely it is a perverted instinct in our nature that makes a story of crime so thrilling to us, that brings out a crowd on a cold morning just to see a flag hoisted when some murderer in a prison forfeits to justice the life he has misused; that throngs the inquest, and hardly allows the ambulance to pass? Is it well to feed this unnatural taste by keeping alive in perpetuity the trophies of a tyranny that has long since passed?" And we should try to tell him about the martyrs, and what they mean to us. And he would still persist: "Yes, but are you not making much of that very thing of which the martyrs themselves made so light? They handed over their bodies to the tormentor precisely because their bodies were of no account in comparison to their immortal souls; and you, in your ghoulish treasure-chambers, hoard up the very trappings of mortality they despised. Did not St Thomas More, as you call him, move his beard aside from the block because *that* had not committed treason? The soul, surely, not the body, is what matters. Cannot you bury the bodies of your saints in peace, and be content that their name should live for evermore?"

What answer should we make? I suppose this: That we do not treasure these relics as men treasure the ghastly evidences of some atrocious crime, but rather as the trophies of a conquest; we gather these bones as you might gather the droppings of some precious metal that had been tried in the fire, we catch the drops of blood as if it were some rare vintage flowing from the wine-press. If a housebreaker gave us the choice whether he should steal one of these bones, or the golden

reliquary that enshrines it, we should, without affectation, resign the
reliquary as a thing of smaller worth. We put a different value on these
historical events from those around us. These men, you see, were the
men who upset the world. And for us, their children, the world is still
topsy-turvy, and the meaning of things and the values of things are
stated, for us, in terms of a new currency. To us death is life, and defeat
is victory. I love that phrase, used of the apostles, "these men that upset
the world"—so much so, I am afraid, that I have taken the liberty of
translating it as it stands in the Greek original, although the present
text of our Latin Bible, by an obvious slip which I have no doubt the
Pontifical Commission will set right, has represented St Jerome as
writing *urbem*, the city, instead of *orbem*, the world. To upset the world
—it is the word that's used to describe the depopulating of a conquered
country, when the victor turns everybody out of house and home and
pulls down their roof-trees about their ears. The martyrs are the people
who have done that to the whole world. Whenever we feel inclined to
turn round and settle down and feel really comfortable in this world of
our pilgrimage, the example of the martyrs is there to evict us and make
us feel uncomfortable once more. God's saints don't content themselves
with overcoming the world, they are determined to make the place
quite uninhabitable for you and me. That is the boast of our religion;
it's also the reason why some people dislike it.

But I am going ahead too fast; let us tell our strange visitor who these
martyrs were and what were the circumstances of this deplorable miscarriage of justice. The question which sent St Thomas More and St
John Fisher, whom we commemorate especially at this time, to their
deaths, was the question whether they would take or refuse an oath
which recognized the validity of an adulterous union contracted by
their sovereign; the preamble to which oath—only the preamble—
cast aspersions on the right of the Holy See to judge (as it did judge, in
a contrary sense) matters of this character. This was long before any
considerable body of people in England had contemplated the possibility of being anything other than Catholics. To the mass of men,
even to devoted Catholics, even to the martyrs' best friends and kinsmen, the refusal of the oath seemed a scruple, an exaggeration of
conscience. Could not a man take the oath without committing himself
to all the bad doctrine that might be contained in the preamble? Was
it even wise to force an issue between the monarchy and the Papacy?
Do not let us blame the people who argued like that. They could not
see, as we can see now, what this defiance of ecclesiastical authority
was to lead to. The Chancellor, in criticizing St Thomas More's

conduct, said it reminded him of a fable of Æsop about a country where it was prophesied that a strange rain was about to fall,which would turn everybody it wetted into fools. All the wisest men hid themselves when it came, and expected afterwards to be able to have the fools at their mercy, but found instead that the fools persisted in governing themselves their own way, and they would have been wiser still to stay out in the rain and be turned into fools like the rest of them. It was true; the minds of the generality of men had been blinded, and the few wise men who had escaped that infection must either resign their sane opinions or pay for them with their lives.

But there were such people. The upsetters of the world had come hither also; had come even to England, to upset things just when everybody was going to be comfortable. They had that awkward, subversive temperament which sees everything upside down, which measures life only as the ante-chamber of death, time only as the preface to eternity. St Thomas More really could not see that he was any worse off in the Tower than at Chelsea; they were both equally close to heaven. And yet this was a man to whom his home was a sort of Paradise, who would have been unwilling, you would think, to spend a day out of reach of his library! He has learned, somehow, to measure things by the standard of eternity, and the peace of his own soul really does mean more to him than the peace of his country. He deliberately breaks up our home, our comfortable home, the world.

We do not forget, and God forbid that we should forget, the cause for which our martyrs died. Because the faith for which they suffered persecution was their faith in the privileges divinely conferred upon the Holy See, it is for us, their clients and their fellow countrymen, to be distinguished, if there must be such distinction, above the other nations of the world by our whole-hearted devotion to the Vicar of Christ. So much is due in expiation for the sins of our forefathers, in gratitude for the testimony borne by our holy patrons. But it is not for us to perpetuate, by letting the grim memories of past wrongs rankle in our minds, our personal quarrel with the Protestantism which sent the martyrs to their death. Bear a grudge against the Church of England for events that happened nearly four centuries ago? Believe me, it would be an unnecessary compliment. For the Church which— in some of its utterances—claims continuity with the Christendom of Augustine and Dunstan, cannot even claim the credit of continuity with itself. The Christianity which we see around us has little to do, for better or for worse, with the Christianity of the sixteenth-century divines. Brought up in the breezy historical tradition of Charles

Kingsley and the smaller Gardiner, it leaves the record of the martyrs a forgotten page in history. Well, in the face of that forgetfulness, it is good indeed that we should do everything to tend the memory of our martyrs, and to make public display of our devotion, but it should be with no feelings of resentment towards the mutilated Christianity which the evil tradition of the persecutors has left to our fellow countrymen. For, after all, what the martyrs triumph over is not the fury of the persecutor, it is the spell of the things which persecution takes from them: they triumph over the attractiveness of peace, of ease, of liberty, of comfort, of companionship, of health, and finally —the greatest attraction of all—of life itself. You do not tremble, when you read the story of St Thomas More confronting his judges, lest he should be brow-beaten or bullied into surrender. But you do catch your breath just a little for fear heaven should lose a martyr, when wife and daughter, not of any ill intent, but with misplaced affection, come to dissuade him from his holy purpose. A smaller man might have resisted the efforts of a Cromwell; it needed the martyr's heroism to resist the appeals of Margaret Roper. If we are to learn to imitate St Thomas More, we shall not do it by despising Protestants; we shall do it by despising Chelsea. It is the world that the martyrs trample under their feet; it is the world they would have us triumph over as best we may.

Of this attitude of defiance towards the world our English Catholicism ought, from the very circumstances of its past, to be a continual reminder. It is a matter of historical atmospheres. To have had the experience of teaching—if you will pardon my being autobiographical —in an Oxford College founded by Sir Thomas Pope, who was actually St Thomas More's gaoler in the Tower; to have gone on to teach at a school which acknowledged as its chief benefactors King Edward the Sixth and Queen Elizabeth; and then, as a Catholic, to find yourself teaching at the very college founded by an exiled cardinal for the training of seminary priests for England in the time of the persecution—that change means, so far as your historical perspective is concerned, a complete change of values. To have been brought up among the busts of portly gentlemen in semi-classical costume who became Lord Chancellors and Poets Laureate and what not, people who started as boys with your hopes, your ambitions, and succeeded, one way and another, in scrambling up the difficult slopes of fame, among portraits of bishops with puffy sleeves and lawyers in important wigs; and then to find yourself in a place where the most treasured roll of school successes is a long list of names the world has never

heard of, men who died convicted as traitors to their country—that
should be, to anybody, a sufficiently impressive sermon on the rewards
to be sought in this world and in the next. I was taught where, we are
assured on good authority, the battle of Waterloo was won. I am
teaching where the battle of Tyburn was won, and I thank God for it.

Oh, how they upset the world for us, these martyrs of ours, or if
they do not, how they ought to upset it for us! Where we seek our
gratification, they found their mortification; they blessed the discom-
forts we repine at, spurned the crowns we pant for, flicked their fingers
at the master that so easily whistles us to heel—human respect. To us,
eternity is a mere background, sketched in dimly behind this life, the
central incident on our mind's canvas. To them, the picture was the
landscape of eternity; the figures of this world were merely dotted
about in the foreground to give value to the rest. And at Tyburn,
whether it be the influence of their prayers or the continuous miracle
of the Eucharistic Presence, I cannot say, but there is a spirit that
communicates to those who offer their prayers in this place, something
of that other-worldly focus. The wheels hum and the motors hoot and
the cries of the street fall on your ear, but, praying here before the
monstrance, you know, somehow, that this, not that, is the reality,
here, not there, is the true current of human endeavour. We, too, if
only for the moment, feel that we could endure like the martyrs as
seeing him who is invisible, that amidst the world's changefulness our
hearts could there be set, where are the true joys. For a moment we
really see the world as the puppet-show it is.

Let us praise God, then, for our English martyrs, Thomas More and
John Fisher and the Charterhouse monks, and, from Blessed Cuthbert
Mayne onward, the long line of proscribed and hunted priests. Men
of our blood, they have left sayings which ring more familiarly to us
than the translated pieties of the Continent; men of our latter-day
civilization, they stand out with more of human personality than the
mist-wreathed heroes of the medieval world. And surely, if they have
not forgotten among those delights of eternity the soft outlines and the
close hedgerows and the little hills of the island that gave them birth;
if in contemplating the open face of God, they have not ceased to take
thought for the well-loved kingdom that exiled and disowned them,
the patiently evangelized people that condemned and hurried them to
the gallows, their prayers still rise especially, among all the needs of a
distracted world, for the souls we love whom error blinds or sin
separates from God. It is Mary's month; we hardly dare, so wide are
the sympathies of her immaculate heart, to think of our country as

singled out in her intercessions: yet we are her dowry, and while the world lies suppliant at her feet she will not forget the triduum we keep in these first days of May. God grant that through the power of such intercessors, whatever unworthiness and degeneracy he sees in us English Catholics of a later day may be pardoned and set aside, and that our brethren, so long sought, so patiently wooed by the divine grace, may return to the allegiance of the true Church, and make England a shrine of martyrs and a nursery of saints once more.

3

ST THOMAS MORE: I[1]

Thus did this man die, leaving not only to young men, but also to the whole nation, the memory of his death for an example of virtue and fortitude.
—2 Machabees 6. 31.

THE text which I have just read to you refers to Eleazar, one of the scribes, who suffered martyrdom under King Antiochus for the traditions of the Jewish religion. As a sign of apostasy from that religion, he, like many others, was bidden to eat swine's flesh, which (as you know) was forbidden under the ancient law. Kindly officials offered him, instead, a piece of some other meat which was clean according to the law of Moses; so that he could avoid the defilement as long as he would allow it to be thought that he had conformed with Antiochus' edict. His answer was a noble one; he would rather suffer martyrdom than give scandal to the younger men of his race by pretending to break the law in his old age. He died, it seems, under scourging.

You will not be at a loss to understand why I am recalling to you, this evening, the memory of unhappy things that took place long ago. The history conveys a striking parallel to other unhappy things which happened not so very long ago, only four hundred years ago yesterday. On 6 July 1535, a great Englishman died who has just been raised to the altars of the Church as St Thomas More. He died, like Eleazar, for something which seemed to many people of his time almost a scruple, almost a technical point; refusing to take an oath in support of a new statute, because there was something in the preamble to the statute of

which your conscience disapproved! Oh, you may be sure that St
Thomas More had no lack of plausible excuses if he had wanted to
avoid the crown of martyrdom; no lack of sincere people who urged
him to take refuge in them. Never, I suppose, was man so tempted
both by friends and foes to abandon his purpose. His own wife, his
own daughter took the part of his enemies, and entered into a loving
conspiracy to save him from himself. But to friend and foe alike he
opposed the impenetrable wall of his good-natured banter.

You see, he realized, long before other men of his time, that what
stood before England was a complete parting of the ways. He saw
that, in the conditions of his time, you must needs throw in your lot
either with the old faith or with the heresies that were beginning to
spring up all over Europe; that a nation which defied the authority
of the Pope, although it might do so merely in the name of national
independence, would be forced, sooner or later, into the camp of the
heretic. It is amazing to us, looking back upon all the intervening
centuries have brought, that so many good men of that age—men
who were afterwards confessors for the faith—were hoodwinked for
the moment into following the King when he incurred the guilt of
schism. But perhaps if we could think ourselves back rather more
successfully into the conditions of the time, we should pardon them
the more readily; and for that reason we should feel even greater
admiration for the few men who, like our martyr, were wise enough
to see what was happening. It was a time of national crisis, a time of
intellectual ferment. There were only a few people who kept their
heads, and those few who kept their heads lost their heads, like St
Thomas More.

Much, naturally, has been said, much has been written in the past
few months about him and about the holy Bishop of Rochester who
preceded him to his death. His portrait has become familiar to us
afresh; his praises are sounded everywhere, even in the most unlikely
quarters. What I should like to draw your attention to, this evening,
is a single fact about the life and fame of a many-sided man. This fact
—that his canonization has been a bewilderment and a blow to the
moderns, precisely because he was himself one of the moderns. He
belongs to the new world which came to its birth at the Renaissance;
of that new world he is a prophet and a pioneer. And, being all that,
he gave his life, unquestioningly and unquestionably, for something
which our moderns look upon as belonging wholly to that older
world which is dead—I mean, the Holy Catholic Church.

It is a curious thing about the attitude of our non-Catholic friends towards the Catholic saints; they always contrive to discredit, in one of two ways, their witness to the faith. Either they will say: "This was a very unpleasant, narrow-minded man, of ridiculous personal habits; and if that is what saints are like we would sooner hear no more of them", or they will say: "Yes, this man was indeed a saint; but then he was not really a Roman Catholic. He was just a good Christian, as I and my wife are; he only happened to be in communion with the Pope because everybody was in those days." They divide our calendar, in fact, into the nice saints who do credit to Christianity rather than to the Church, and the nasty saints who do no credit to anybody. St Francis, they will say; yes, what a charming character; what meekness, what cheerfulness, what love of animals! But then, St Francis was not a bit like a Roman Catholic. On the other hand, a man like St Thomas à Becket, although they admit that his martyrdom was an unfortunate incident, they dismiss altogether from consideration because his particular qualities, his salient qualities anyhow, were not the particular qualities which they happen to admire. And the Church gets no credit either way.

It is being a great puzzle to these people what to make of St Thomas More. So long as he was simply Thomas More it was all right; they were prepared to admire him as a pioneer of modern thought, or to praise him as a man who gave his life for his convictions, however mistaken. But now, we have taken to calling him a saint, and it is difficult to see which of the two categories he is to fit into. Is he to be regarded as one of the saints who were not really nice men, were not really admirable men? But nobody can help loving Thomas More; nobody can help admiring Thomas More. Or are they going to regard him as one of the saints who were not really Roman Catholics? But, unfortunately, his death makes that impossible. In life, if you will, he can be regarded as one of the moderns, as a pioneer of the Renaissance, as a cultured, liberal, broad-minded man, all that they are prepared to admire. But in his death, look at it what way you will, he is plainly a Catholic. He exploded the mine of controversy twenty-five years before its time; forced an issue between England and the Holy See before England had ever realized that it was going Protestant. Is it possible that we are to have, after all, an indisputably Catholic saint whom, nevertheless, our non-Catholic neighbours will find themselves compelled to admire?

Let us pause for a little over that apparent contrast in the life of a man whose sympathies clearly belonged to the new order of things, who yet died as a protest on behalf of the old order of things. Let me explain to you, at the risk of seeming to give you a lecture in history, what I mean when I say that St Thomas More has to take rank among the moderns. Of course, there is a certain sense in which all the English martyrs belong to our modern world, as compared with the English saints who went before them. If you think of St Edmund of Canterbury, or St Richard of Chichester, the last English saints who lived before Reformation times, you inevitably think of them, if I may say so without irreverence, as people in stained-glass windows, belonging to an era altogether different from our own. We do not know what they looked like, because there was little art of portraiture in their day, and of the art there was few specimens are preserved to us. And the medieval world to which they belonged is something we read about in history books, but something which has, so it appears, no living contact with our own. But our martyrs, even under Henry the Eighth and Queen Elizabeth, are living, human figures; in many cases we have authentic portraits, their writings have come down to us in abundance —we can imagine, or so we think, what it was like to live under the Tudors. Yes, the English martyrs are nearer to us than the saints who went before them; but in the case of St Thomas More it goes deeper than that. He was a humanist, one of the most prominent figures in that revival of learning, that broadening of culture, which followed upon what we call the Renaissance. All that, you say, is very vague; I am using long words, which leave no particular impression on your mind. Very well, then, let me try to put it in the concrete a little, and consider how it was that the men of the Renaissance differed from the men of the Middle Ages.

First, the men of the Renaissance looked backwards at history more than their predecessors did. The old classical authors of Greece and Rome, long hidden away in the shelves of dusty libraries, came to light and were studied eagerly. They tried to feel and to understand what other men thought, long centuries ago before our Lord came. And St Thomas More was steeped in all that; although he was such a busy man of affairs, he was one of the scholars of his age, the intimate friend of the great Dutchman, Erasmus. Many historians will tell you that the Renaissance, by opening men's minds to new avenues of learning, paved the way for the Reformation. It may be so, but among the greatest leaders of the Renaissance you will find St Thomas More, who died a martyr for the Catholic faith.

In the second place, the men of the Renaissance looked outwards at a world that had grown larger than the world which their fathers knew. "The world", as it was known to the Middle Ages, meant—

what? Europe, and the north coast of Africa, and a few strange, half-fabulous countries in the East, which only a few unreliable travellers had visited. By the year 1500 Columbus had discovered America, Cabot had sailed to Canada, and Vasco da Gama had doubled the Cape of Good Hope. Within a quarter of a century the known world had suddenly grown to three or four times its old size. Men's minds were fascinated by the thought that there were strange races in distant parts of the earth whose customs and traditions and way of looking at life were wholly different from their own. And not least, the mind of St Thomas More. Every schoolboy knows that he wrote a book called *Utopia*, describing the habits of an imaginary people on some remote island, and using that means to satirize the shortcomings of his own day. That imaginary island owed its existence, you may say, to the discoveries of explorers among real islands, twenty or thirty years before the book was written. The mind of such a man, clearly, was not bounded as men's minds were bounded in the Middle Ages by the horizon of Christendom. And yet it was for Christendom that St Thomas More died on the scaffold.

In the third place—this is more difficult to explain—the men of the Renaissance looked inwards, turned back upon themselves, watched their own thoughts, instead of being entirely wrapped up in objects outside themselves which challenged their attention. The proper study of mankind, said a great poet, is man; and the men of the Renaissance are called humanists because they rediscovered, in a way, the greatness and the complexity and the absorbing interest of man. You will find that all through the sixteenth century; you will find it in the art of Shakespeare, you will find it among the theologians of that age, in the enormously increased study of moral theology. And you will find it in the character of a man like St Thomas More; exemplified especially in that gift of self-criticism and of irony which distinguishes him; what we call nowadays, roughly, the sense of humour. A man passionately interested in men, allowing for their temperaments and sympathizing with their weaknesses. Yet a humanist, we see, could also be a man of stern principle; it was because he would not condone the weaknesses of the king who had been his friend that St Thomas More died.

All that enlargement of outlook, backwards, outwards, inwards, makes St Thomas More one of the moderns. If he lived in our own day —let us put it crudely—you can imagine him arguing over Plato with Dean Inge, or constructing imaginary worlds in collaboration with Mr H. G. Wells, or answering jest with jest, irony with irony, in a conversation with Mr Bernard Shaw. And if he had died in his bed, before the attack on the monasteries, before the question of King Henry's divorce ever arose, just imagine what the world would be saying of him. They would be telling us that he was, of course, a Roman Catholic, because that was how he had been brought up—indeed, in his youth he had been through a period of fanaticism, in which he thought of joining the Carthusians. But his whole mind, they would be telling us, had completely outgrown the narrow horizons of his youth; he was a critic of abuses in the Church, he was a friend of those Continental scholars who made, in great part, the Reformation. And had he lived, they would be telling us, this patron of the new learning would certainly have thrown in his lot with the Reformers, with Cranmer and Cromwell; perhaps, as an old man, he would have helped to build up the sonorous language of the Anglican prayer-book. All that they would be saying, were it not for the unfortunate fact that he died a Roman Catholic, died because he saw that you could not be a Catholic without being a Roman.

That seems to me the really extraordinary quality about our new saint, that he could bring forth out of his treasure, like the householder of our Lord's parable, things new and old; that he belonged to the new world, and yet died for something against which the new world was shortly to revolt. If he had been some member of the old English aristocracy, suspicious of the Tudors because they were upstarts, and resentful against their efforts to consolidate the power of the Crown as against the nobility—then we might have been afraid that political considerations affected his attitude. But it was not so; he was one of the new men, one of the King's friends, the last man in the world to stand upon ancient privilege for its own sake. If he had been some pedantic follower of a philosophy which had gone out of fashion, resolutely set against all new-fangled ideas, then we might have been afraid that there was something of mere human obstinacy, mere pig-headedness, that entered into his protest. But it was not so; as we have seen, he was a pillar and a patron of the new learning. If he had been some bluff, rude country squire, always ready to pick a quarrel with his neighbours for the sheer love of a fight, careless of what suffering he underwent himself or inflicted on others, then we might have been afraid that he took the risks he took, faced the scaffold as he did, out of a kind of insensibility, valuing his life little because he had never acquired the art of enjoying life intelligently. But no, St Thomas More was a sensitive man, of our modern type, very reluctant, as we know, to inflict punishment on others, and fully alive to the horrors of his own situation, as you or I would be. It was not temperament, it was not perversity, but sheer love of the faith he had been bred in that made a martyr of St Thomas More.

I wonder whether there is not something providential, I mean something that we can recognize as specially providential, about the delays which have attended the canonization of St Thomas More and St John Fisher, humanly speaking so long overdue? Whether, I mean, God does not mean us to understand that these two, and St Thomas More especially, are fitting patrons for our own age, because our own age is in so many ways like theirs? For in our age—it is a commonplace to say it—a new humanism flourishes, something like the humanism of four hundred years ago, but for better or worse a great advance upon it. We have dug further back than ever St Thomas More and his contemporaries did into the history of our race; unearthed the relics of civilizations far older than those of Greece or Rome, pushed back, by tens of thousands of years, the limits of human history. We have not discovered fresh continents—there were none to discover; but we have entered into closer contact with men of alien ideas, studied their history, and puzzled out the secret of their attitude towards life. And we have turned back more than ever on ourselves; analysed the background of our own minds, tried to trace the origins of our own mental processes. Our age, more than ever, is lost in admiration of man's greatness, so as to forget the God who made us; at the same time, more tender towards man's weaknesses, more tolerant of his wrong-doing, more merciful to his faults. And in this age of increased reverence for man you and I have got to live, reminding ourselves and reminding our neighbours of that higher reverence which is due to God.

Times like these, do not let us deceive ourselves about it, are difficult to live in for a Catholic who loves his faith. There is a continual apparent contrast between the restless speculations of the modern intellect, and those abiding certainties by which we live. The question continually arises: Is such and such a view, which I see propounded in the newspapers, consistent with Catholic truth? Is such and such a political expedient, which I see prominent men are advocating, justifiable in the light of Catholic doctrine? We are hurried along breathlessly by the spirit of the age in which we live, yet protesting all the time, questioning all the time. Our neighbours, our non-Catholic neighbours, look upon us as an obscure survival from the Middle Ages, a kind of museum piece, whose beliefs they find it interesting to study, but impossible to share. Here and there, one or two of our Catholic friends drop out of the ranks, abandon their religion for no better reason than that they have been caught by the glamour of modern movements. There is no acute conflict, but we are perpetually ill at ease, like a ship that drags its anchor.

In such times, let us thank God's mercy for giving us the example and the protection of a great saint, our own fellow countryman, who knew how to absorb all that was best in the restless culture of his day, yet knew at once, when the time came, that he must make a stand here; that he must give no quarter to the modern world here. His remembrance has long been secure in the praise of posterity; it only remained for us to be assured by the infallible voice of the Church, what we could not doubt already, that he is with our blessed Lady and the saints in heaven. He knows our modern needs, let us turn to him in our modern troubles; his prayers will not be lacking for the great country he loved so, for the great city in which he lived and died.

4

ST THOMAS MORE: II[1]

WE are celebrating two saints of Christendom so famous in this world, and, we doubt not, so glorious in the next, that it seems a kind of irreverence to leave one out of account and focus all our attention on the other. If I do so, it is not because the thoughts I mean to offer you would be inapplicable to the story of St John Fisher. It is only because, after all, St Thomas is your fellow villager here in Chelsea, whereas St John belongs to Southwark. Like the two men Daniel saw in the last of his visions, they stand one on either side of the river, and St Thomas is the more manifestly ours. It is this I would say of him (and I would say the same of both), that we English people are privileged to have a saint here whose martyrdom, if I may put it in that way, is the type of sensible, English martyrdom. There is no rhetoric about it, there are no dramatic gestures; you are not tempted for a moment to suppose that hysteria or vanity played any part in it. Here is a man whose life is so well documented that you feel as if he had died only yesterday; we can plumb his motives, watch his reactions, and see for ourselves that he never strikes a false note. We can point to him, and tell the doubter that if he wants to understand what stuff the

---

[1] This sermon was preached at the Church of Our Most Holy Redeemer and St Thomas More, Chelsea, on the Feast of St John Fisher and St Thomas More, 9 July 1948.

martyrs were made of, he has only to read the history of St Thomas More.

The Henrician martyrs belong to our epoch. St Joan of Arc died only a hundred years before them, and her process is fully documented, but how remote her world is from ours! Almost she seems a figure of fairyland. But St Thomas is of ourselves. We have his portrait, painted by a master's brush, and painted from the life; you can imagine meeting him. We have works from his own pen, written in vigorous English, whose secret, unfortunately, we have lost; but it is not Anglo-Saxon, or Norman French, it is our own tongue. We have a hundred details about his daily life, a hundred gracious anecdotes about the way he managed his household, about his way of talking in his own intimate circle; he kept a monkey—what other saint kept a monkey? And these reminiscences of him are not the idle chatter of some gossip-writer; they come to us from the pen of Erasmus, the greatest scholar of the age. St Thomas More is not, if you shut your eyes and think about him, a figure in a stained-glass window, like St Thomas à Becket, he is a real person. When St John Fisher was climbing the scaffold, there was a burst of sunshine, and he quoted a verse from the Psalms: "Come ye to him and be enlightened, and your faces shall not be ashamed"— a strong light beats on the faces of those sixteenth-century martyrs, illuminating them in almost photographic detail, and they can stand the test; they are saints' faces still.

That fact I find strangely comforting. After all, if you talk about the early martyrs to some friend who is not of our religion, you will find that he respects them as brave men, but there is a certain hesitation about the tribute which he pays them. Shocking, no doubt, that men should have been put to death for their private beliefs; but, are we certain there was nothing to be said on the other side? Were they not, perhaps, men of a somewhat twisted psychology, determined to bring persecution on themselves merely out of a morbid love of suffering? Were they not, perhaps, one-way thinkers, over-clear about their own side of the argument, over-impatient of compromise? Were they not, perhaps, men wedded to old fashions of thought, stupidly conservative, and always ready to put a spoke in the wheels of human progress? To which we answer, "Perhaps; but look at St Thomas More".

Psychologists talk, I believe, of a "martyrdom-complex"; and most of us have friends to whom, in a small way, that ungenerous description seems to apply. People, I mean, who are so convinced the world is treating them hardly that they almost resent a benefit conferred on them, as if it were an attempt to rob them of their precious grievance;

people who work themselves to the bone over some quite unimportant purpose, as if to have the satisfaction of assuring us that they never get a minute to themselves. Now, if somebody suggests to us that there was a morbid streak of that kind in St Thomas of Canterbury, we shall all of us reply that that is not the picture we have formed of him, but we cannot prove our case, because we have not enough evidence to prove it. If somebody likes to insist that Thomas à Becket saw himself in the role of St Anselm, as a champion of the Church's liberties threatened by an impious tyrant, and, falling in love with that vision of himself, played for martyrdom, was consumed with a hysterical desire for martyrdom, almost forced King Henry to martyr him— well, it may be a curious reading of history, but we have no materials for proving that it is a false one. But St Thomas More! Assuredly there is nothing of the hysterical patient there. He shows that clearest proof of sanity, the capacity for seeing a joke, and indeed for seeing a joke against himself; did he not love to play upon the Greek significance of his name, "Morus", the fool? So far from exaggerating his afflictions, he will pooh-pooh them in a bluff, hearty voice that rings down the centuries; what does it matter being confined to the Tower? Is not the world itself a prison? One remembers Dr Johnson, paradoxically maintaining that a man on board ship is no better off than a man in gaol; there is a kind of splendid commonsensibleness which is the property, equally, of Dr Johnson and St Thomas More. No, there is no morbid streak here; St Thomas enjoyed life to the full, loved his books and the society of his friends. If such a man went to the Tower and the scaffold, it was not some kink of temperament that sent him there, it was a conviction of the soul.

Again, it is an arguable thesis, though it is not in the least a plausible one, that St Thomas of Canterbury was a man wedded to his own opinion, incapable of seeing the other person's point of view, incapable, therefore, of devising some formula of agreement which would be acceptable to both sides. It is an arguable thesis, because we do not know St Thomas à Becket sufficiently from the inside to be able to say outright, "No, he was not such a man". But if you try to maintain that plea against St Thomas More, you have not even got a case to go into court with; you are contradicting known facts. Never was a man better qualified, whether by training or by disposition, to frame an honourable compromise, if the circumstances had permitted it. Never was a man more humble about his own opinions, when they were merely opinions of his own.

And again, you might represent the struggle between St Thomas à

Becket and Henry II as a struggle between two world-orders, an old and a new. Becket (you might say) thought with the mind of the Dark Ages, when kings were people of no great importance, when Europe was in the melting-pot, and the institution of the Papacy stood out as the one fixed point in a world of change. He didn't understand the importance of those principles of national sovereignty which were being worked out in his time. He died, not for the sake of any theological principles, but because he clung, with obstinate conservatism, to the old order of things. All that is quite untrue; but you cannot prove it untrue from your knowledge of the man, because for practical purposes you have no knowledge of the man. With St Thomas More it is different; you know where you are with him. He belonged to the reforming party in the Church; in happier times, he might have done something to correct the abuses of which he, like Colet and Erasmus, was fully conscious. He was the child of an age thrilled with the discovery of new lands across the ocean, with the rediscovery of an almost forgotten past. He belonged, not to some narrow national clique, but to the cosmopolitan intelligentsia. Whatever were his reasons for rejecting the royal claims, they had nothing to do with the intransigence of an unimaginative mind.

No, but he lived in an age when the children of this world were, all too evidently, wiser than the children of light. How wise they were, after their fashion, those newly-made gentry, those go-getting clerks, those court adventurers, who flourished under the Tudors! How quick they were to foresee and to forestall the whim of a royal master! Those others, the children of light, who loved the old ways and had been brought up in them, were not so quick to discern the will of their royal Master in heaven. They could not see what was happening; events moved too swiftly for them; the Church's cause was lost before they knew it. The Mass was still said, our Lady still venerated; what was wrong? Only a few, St John Fisher, St Thomas More and the rest, saw just where it was the breaking-point came; just when it was you must make a stand, if a stand was to be made at all. They made their protest, and left it on record; ineffectual then, it should be an encouragement and a warning for Catholics of a later time.

We live, like the men of the sixteenth century, in an age of new horizons; and for us, as for them, the old question still presses, How much can we afford to fall in with the spirit of our times? I say, "afford"; I am using commercial language, as our Lord used to. There comes a point at which, in reaching out for earthly prizes, we may lose the heavenly. The Church, it is true, speaks to us with more particularity of guidance than formerly. On the other hand, in countries like our own, the Catholic tradition is so much forgotten that we find ourselves constantly at cross purposes with our next-door neighbours. In such times, let us thank God for the inspiration he has given us in histories like those of St Thomas More and St John Fisher, so far from us in date, so near to us in living influence. And let us ask them to pray for us, and make us good stewards of the heavenly wealth committed to us, wise in our fashion, as the children of this world in theirs.

5

THE OXFORD MARTYRS[1]

Remember the days of old; think upon every generation.—Deuteronomy 32. 7.

You will probably have seen in the papers this week, if you did not know it before, that the claim of some two hundred and fifty of our fellow countrymen to the honours of martyrdom are now being considered at Rome; and that a large number of them, some two hundred in all probability, are likely to be beatified either this month or in the very near future. By a fortunate accident, the feast of the Oxford martyrs, which we celebrate in this archdiocese, falls this year on a Sunday, this Sunday. The whole total of the English martyrs, if you include those who have already been beatified, is three hundred and fifteen; and in view of the historical circumstances it is not a little remarkable that exactly one-fifth of these were Oxford men. No less than seventeen colleges are represented out of a possible twenty. It would be out of place, I think, to go over the old ground of controversy and remind ourselves once more how monstrous was the attempt of politicians, and later of historians, to brand the great majority (at least) of these names with the stigma of treason. Instead of that, I thought I would just give you a few thumb-nail biographies, if I may so call them, of a few among these many; and I have chosen, for that purpose, the names of those Oxford men who have already been beatified, and who suffered as seminary priests in the earlier years of

---

[1] This sermon was preached at the Undergraduates' Chaplaincy at Oxford, 1 December 1929.

Queen Elizabeth's reign, before the Spanish Armada. This selection will reduce the whole number to a dozen or so; we have hardly time for more.

You must begin any such list with the Jesuit Blessed Edmund Campion. He was one of the original scholars of St John's when it was founded in 1555; he became public orator of the university and junior proctor. He was generally regarded as *the* Oxford man of his period, and Queen Elizabeth herself was delighted with his eloquence. But of course he enjoyed all this fame under a miserable condition; he had to take the oath of supremacy, and was ordained deacon according to the ritual of the Protestant Prayer-book. He thought, perhaps, as many have thought since his time, that he could do better work for the Catholic cause by "staying where he was". Like Newman, he exercised an extraordinary influence over the minds of others; like Newman, he must have felt that his choice lay between Oxford and Rome. He left Oxford, and went over to Dublin, still as a Protestant; but his conscience was being too strong for him, and after witnessing the trial of Blessed John Story in London he went abroad, first to Douai, and then to Rome, where he entered the society. He worked first in Bohemia; then was sent on the English mission, and, among other vast apostolic labours, printed his "Ten Reasons" at a secret printing press. He was apprehended at Lyford Grange, near Wantage; was offered life and preferment by the Queen herself if he would return to Protestantism; was mercilessly racked, and finally, by an afterthought, condemned on a ridiculous charge of treason. He suffered at Tyburn on this day, in the year 1581.

St John's also claims the first martyr among the secular clergy, Blessed Cuthbert Mayne. He was educated by his uncle, a priest who had conformed to the new religion. He was apparently already ordained when he came up, first to St Alban's Hall—that is, for practical purposes, to Merton—and then to St John's, where he took his M.A. in 1570. In the same year, when he was already considering the question of his religious allegiance, like other members of Campion's circle, a letter addressed to him from abroad fell into the wrong hands; he disappeared from Oxford, and we next meet him in 1573, at Douai, where he was ordained, and sent back to England in 1576. He worked in Cornwall, where he passed as the steward of a well-to-do Catholic; but after a year of this the pursuivants found him, and he was led off to trial. No charge was brought against him which could be supposed to have any political bearing whatsoever. One of the judges protested against his sentence, and the case had to be remitted to London; the

Government simply ordered his execution, and he was murdered on November 29, 1577.

When Sir William Petre extended the foundation of Exeter in 1565, one of the first scholars he nominated was Ralph Sherwin, who took his degree there in 1574, and was reckoned an accomplished scholar both in Greek and in Hebrew. By the next year he, too, had left for Douai. Not much is known of his life, and he was apprehended when he had only been on the mission for about half a year. But the story of his imprisonment, of his twice-repeated torture on the rack, and of the five days during which he lay without food or drink, and found at the end of them "no distemper in his joints by reason of his racking" are among the most noteworthy of our martyrs' records. He should also be remembered for some of his last utterances; it was he who, after his condemnation, pointed up at the sun and said: "I shall soon be above yon fellow"; he who said on the scaffold: "If to be a Catholic only be to be a traitor, then I am a traitor"; he who died with the words "*Jesu, Jesu, Jesu, esto mihi Jesus*". He was martyred at the same time as Blessed Edmund Campion.

In 1574 a strikingly handsome young man came up to Hert Hall, which we now call Hertford. His name was Alexander Briant; he came from Somersetshire, where the old faith had died hard. It was a Somersetshire man, Robert Persons, who was afterwards a member of the Society of Jesus and one of the most active, if not always one of the most discreet, partisans of the Catholic cause in England. Persons was then a fellow of Balliol, and young Briant was his pupil, so that he must have been early attracted towards the Catholic cause. He must have gone down without taking his degree, for by the year 1578 he had already gone out to Douai and been ordained priest there. He returned to England, and went back to his own county of Somerset, to reconcile heretics and minister to Catholics. Among others he reconciled the father of his old Oxford tutor. When he was apprehended, as he very soon was, he had to suffer for this connection; the Government were particularly anxious to lay hands on Persons, who was then himself in England, and they tortured Alexander Briant unmercifully in the hope of information, driving needles, for example, between his finger-nails and fingers. Soon before his martyrdom, he applied for and was granted admission into the Society of Jesus. He suffered with Campion and Sherwin, on this day, at the age of twenty-eight.

For myself, I feel specially bound to pray to Blessed Thomas Ford, fellow of Trinity in 1567. He was a Devonshire man, and perhaps as a Devonshire man he was already acquainted with Cuthbert Mayne at

St John's; certainly it was he who warned Mayne of the danger threatening him when that letter from abroad went astray. Nor was it long before he himself followed his friend abroad, arriving at Douai in 1570. He took a long course at Douai, and did not come back to England till 1576; he was sent to work at Lyford Grange, not far from Abingdon—indeed, it is not a dozen miles from where we sit; and it is clear that there were close relations between the Catholics who remained in Oxford, and the safe moated grange in Berkshire where they could go off to hear Mass. It was quite an establishment that Mrs Yate kept there; there were eight Bridgettine nuns sheltered in her house. Then one day there was great excitement in the little colony —Edmund Campion was to pay them a visit. He came, stayed the night, and left; then Thomas Ford had to ride after him and bring him back, because a crowd of sixty or more, from Oxford and elsewhere, had come over to hear him preach. His return was fatal to him, and to Thomas Ford as well; both of them, with another priest, were observed by a spy and captured in a hiding-place where they had taken refuge. So Thomas Ford shared the ignominious ride to London with Campion, and Campion's imprisonment; he was finally condemned on the accusation that he had taken part in a conspiracy, or an alleged conspiracy, in Rome and again at Rheims, during a time which he had, as a matter of fact, spent entirely in England. He was martyred some time after Campion, in 1582.

As Campion and Ford were being taken from Lyford to London, they were passing through a part of the country where the faith still had its strongholds, notably at Stonor Hall, near Henley. It was at Henley that another priest incautiously tried to speak with Campion, so giving himself away and being carried off with the others. This was William Filby, an Oxford martyr in a double sense; for he was a native of the town, and had been up as an undergraduate at Lincoln. He matriculated in 1575, and was at Rheims by 1579; there he was ordained, and must presumably have been sent to work in Oxfordshire, but as he was only ordained in 1581, the year of Campion's apprehension, he must have had a short missionary life. From the November of that year till the following May he was kept in handcuffs, and then executed at Tyburn.

Two other Oxford priests were executed with him, both from Brasenose. One of these, Laurence Richardson, was a Lancashire man, and not only came from Lancashire, still so largely Catholic, but from Great Crosby, still intimately connected with the name of a Catholic family. It seems pretty clear that he must have been a "born Catholic", as we say, and we may perhaps look upon him as a member of this congregation in a sense in which Edmund Campion and the others were not. Nevertheless he seems to have managed to take his degree; that was on November 25, 1573; and Challoner says that he was a fellow of the College, though Gillow seems to deny this: the family from which he came were recusants right up to 1717, and it seems hard to understand how he could conscientiously have taken a fellowship under the religious conditions of those times. In any case, he left Oxford almost immediately for Douai, where he was admitted in 1573. He returned as a priest, four years later, to Lancashire, and acted as chaplain at Ince Blundell—the Blundells were his cousins. In Lancashire persecution was not so easy to organize as in the south, but he was apprehended in London, and charged with complicity in the same plot in which Thomas Ford was supposed to have been involved, though he too had never left England during the time in question. He was martyred in 1582, repeating St Stephen's words: Lord Jesus, receive my soul.

The other Brasenose man who was martyred at the same time was, like Laurence Richardson, a man of good family, and came like him from Lancashire. His brother, who succeeded to the estates, appears on the recusants' rolls, but he, it seems, must have been reconciled to the Church, for the parents were Protestants. Thomas Cottam, therefore, will have come up as a Protestant; he took his degree in 1568, and then went off to teach at a grammar school in London. Here he was converted, and went abroad; his desire was, apparently, to join the Society of Jesus and go out to the Indian missions. His health prevented this, and he was ordained at Rheims in 1580. The moment he landed at Dover he was arrested, on the evidence of a spy who had met him abroad. Then an extraordinary thing happened. The Mayor of Dover gave him into the charge of a gentleman who was travelling to London, to be delivered into safe custody there. This gentleman was really a Catholic and a priest, Dr Ely by name; and he insisted on Thomas Cottam going free when he got to London, though somewhat against his own conscience. Later, Dr Ely was in danger of getting into trouble for not delivering up his prisoner, and Cottam voluntarily gave himself up to save the situation. He was taken to the Marshalsea and tortured; out of sheer wantonness, it would seem, because they did not try to extract any secrets from him. He was thirty-three when he went to his eternal reward.

The same college produced another of these martyrs, John Shert. He was a Cheshire man, and took his degree from Brasenose in 1566; like Cottam, he was for a time a schoolmaster in London, then went to

F

Rheims, and came back to England in 1579. His work lay in London, and there for two years he managed to escape detection; he was then committed to the Tower, and condemned with Thomas Ford for the conspiracy which he, like Thomas Ford, knew nothing at all about; he, too, had been in England at the time alleged. He suffered immediately after Thomas Ford, to whom he boldly prayed on the scaffold as to one already in heaven.

Lincoln, too, has another beatified martyr, Blessed William Hart. He came from Somersetshire and caught the infection of Catholicism which still lingered in Oxford; went abroad to Douai and afterwards to Rome, and was ordained priest, it seems, when he was only twenty-one. He worked on the mission at York, where his charity and his eloquence made him almost a public figure; yet even in York, where sympathy with the old religion was still strong, he went in danger of his life, and on one occasion had to climb down the walls of the castle and hide in a moat to save his life. They arrested him on Christmas Day, 1582; and the charges at his trial were so frivolous that the foreman of the jury demanded to be dismissed, and had actually to be dismissed before a verdict was brought in against him. A most touching letter, written to his Protestant mother on the eve of his execution, has been preserved to us. He suffered in 1583.

Two months later, in the same city of York, they executed another Oxford martyr, Blessed Richard Thirkeld. He was up at Queen's in 1564-65, but it is not known what became of him between that time and his ordination at Rheims, fourteen years later. He was a native of Durham, and when he came back to England he was stationed at York, where he was confessor to the well-known martyr, Margaret Clitherow. He was one of those martyrs who have longed for martyrdom from the first; for eight years he had prayed for it. Accordingly, when he was arrested on York bridge and accused of being a priest, he immediately admitted it, instead of leaving it to his prosecutors to prove the charge. He actually appeared in court in his cassock and biretta; and he was condemned without difficulty on his willing confession that he had reconciled the Queen's subjects to their allegiance to the spiritual power of the Pope. When he was executed, the Mayor of York held a general meeting of the citizens elsewhere, for enrolling the militia; so doubtful was the effect, in York, of public executions for religion.

Well, there are eleven martyrs for you. I have not included two Oxford martyrs who suffered under Elizabeth, Blessed Thomas Plumtree of Corpus, and Blessed John Storey, master of Broadgates

Hall (now Pembroke), because although they suffered under Elizabeth they were not seminary priests; they had been brought up at Oxford when it was still a centre of Catholic learning, before the death of King Henry the Eighth. Remember that these names are only a fifth of those martyrs, beatified or waiting to be beatified, whom Oxford numbers among her sons; remember that the Oxford martyrs in their turn have to be multiplied by five before you reach the total of the English martyrs.

I am not going to draw any elaborate morals from what I have told you. I would just draw your attention to the ages of these men; I suppose their average age was about thirty-one; they did not live long, and they knew that they would not live long. When they were up at Oxford the world was all at their feet, and a world which held out greater opportunities, one would say, than our world, for men who wanted to make a name and get the best out of life. They could hope to become paragons of chivalry like Sidney, courtiers like Raleigh, adventurers like Drake, poets like Spenser; or, if they were determined to embrace a clerical career, there were easy openings for them, and ample emoluments for them, in the Church of England. But conscience beckoned them, and they gave up all that prospect, to go and live in a little dusty Flemish town, which promised them the life of an outlaw, and death at thirty-one.

They were our fellow students; as they lay in prison, little vignettes of Oxford must have danced before them; the Cottages at Worcester, and Mob Quad at Merton, and Christ Church Hall, and Magdalen Tower, and New College cloisters, and the old library at Trinity, and the front of St John's, were as familiar sights to them as to us who follow them; they must remember them still, if heaven is to be the completion of our life on earth. St Silvester, whose feast we celebrated last Tuesday, was converted by the sight of a young man's corpse in an open grave; "This man", he said to himself, "was what I am; what this man is, I shall be." Let us take a kindred lesson from the martyrs of whom we have been speaking. They were what you are, Oxford undergraduates. God grant that you may be what they are, citizens of the kingdom of heaven.

6

THE DERBY MARTYRS[1]

For we are the good odour of Christ unto God, in them that are saved and in
them that perish; to the latter indeed the odour of death unto death, but to the
former the odour of life unto life.—2 Corinthians 2. 15.

ON July 24, 1588, at a moment when the Spanish Armada was
cruising off the south coast, somewhere between Plymouth and
the Isle of Wight, three Catholic priests were put to death in this town
with the horrible tortures then prescribed for those guilty of high
treason. Their offence, as usual, was a merely technical one, that of
being priests and of celebrating Mass; there is no record which suggests
that they had been concerned with political activities. The name of the
best known among these three priests was Nicholas Garlick.

Garlick—it is not a pretty name. It reminds you, inevitably, of a class
of plants with a very pungent smell, which most of us dislike. And I
have no doubt that on that day of July, more than three hundred years
ago, the street boys of Derby made merry on the subject, holding their
noses, as likely as not, while Nicholas Garlick was drawn on his hurdle
to the gallows. They will have thought of garlic as the name of a
nasty scent; they will have forgotten that this plant, however distressing
it may be to the nostrils, has a high medicinal value. The smell of it may
be deadly, but its properties are life-giving. If they had thought of
that, their minds might perhaps have travelled back to another preacher
of the Christian religion, fifteen centuries before; they might have
remembered how he wrote to his friends in Corinth: "We are the
good odour of Christ; to them that perish, the odour of death unto
death; but to them that are saved, the odour of life unto life."

An odour of death unto death, an odour of life unto life—that
means that the Christian message is what you make of it. If you find it
deadly, then it is deadly, to you; if you find it life-giving, then it is
life-giving, to you. I do not mean that at the time when our martyrs
suffered, all those who took part in tormenting them, all those who
joined in the cry against them and jested at them on their way to
execution, involved themselves thereby in eternal damnation. The
tendency to shout with the crowd is one of the strongest, and on the
whole one of the most pardonable, tendencies in human nature; nor

[1] This sermon was preached in the market square at Derby.

can there be much doubt, I suppose, that at the time of the Spanish Armada, the English public was worked up into an attitude of intense antipathy to everything which it suspected of being foreign. Fear is a great promoter of cruelty. But I do say that when you read the history of the martyrs you will find in it an admirable illustration of how the doctrines of our holy religion, which seem, and are, so life-giving to us, can seem, and be (so far as their rejection is culpable), deadly to those who reject them.

An odour of death—the Catholic religion had already begun to seem, to the young people of that day, a dead thing, a back number, a page from the history of the past. Human memories are lamentably short; there must have been old folks in Derby who could remember the old religion well enough; who had seen, when they were young, the habits of the black monks and the black nuns, and had experience of their charity. But the younger people—remember that the Protestant religion had been in the saddle for thirty years. The days of Queen Mary were exactly as remote from them as the days of Queen Victoria are from us. If you think of all the changes that have come over England since 1901; if you think, for example, of the growth of the Labour Movement in these thirty years, that will give you some idea of how remote the Catholic religion must have appeared to the people who were just growing up and marrying at the time of the Spanish Armada.

These priests, then, these seminary priests who slunk about the town in their disguises, must have seemed to Englishmen of the day part of a dead world, like ghosts from the old graveyards which housed the bones of their Catholic ancestors. And yet there must have been old-fashioned people about the town, with their families, who had never accepted the new religion; had conformed to it outwardly, perhaps, through fear of consequences, but had never come to believe in the claims of the usurping ministers who occupied the parish pulpits. And to them, these seminary priests were an odour of life; they brought back memories of the old days when Mass was said at St Alkmund's, when the figures, the emblems of our Lady and the saints were to be seen everywhere, in a brighter and a freer England. In this dead world of Protestantism the sight of Father Garlick or Father Ludham, passing by them without recognition in the street, was like a ray of sunshine piercing through fog. For these men brought with them that Bread of Life which had been interdicted to a starving England these thirty years. An odour of life unto life.

An odour of death—how they must have marvelled, those ordinary

Englishmen of the day, at the persistency with which priest after priest came back from the Continent to work on the English mission, only to fall after a year or two into the hands of the pursuivants, and atone for their heroism by death! These three priests of whom we are speaking had only been able to work for souls half a dozen years before they met their end; and in each case with an interval of banishment. How mad they must have thought us, to suppose that we were going to keep alive the embers of the old religion, when a seminary course of six years only qualified our priests for six years of apostolate! If ours was not a dead religion, at least ours was a dying body; a few years more, and it would be bound to come to an end, from sheer attrition of numbers. Poor Garlick, only another weed rooted out, as all the weeds must before long be rooted out, from the beautiful, ordered garden of Protestant England!

And yet—an odour of life; those others, those few who still clung to the faith of their ancestors recognized, with whatever doubts, with whatever failings of the heart, that this long pageant of butchery, so far from threatening the Catholic religion with extinction, was in reality deepening and widening its influence; that every judicial murder meant another martyr praying before the throne of God for our apostate country, another model of fortitude, to encourage fresh souls to embrace the same hazardous career, another outrage, to sicken Englishmen at last of the brutal work. One after another, political hopes failed them; but they clung on, none the less jealously, to the tradition of their forefathers, and left a stock surviving to be fertilized in God's own time, and to grow and flourish beyond all the measure of their hopes.

Still doomed to death, and fated not to die—so wrote our Catholic poet of the faith he had embraced; and this has been, everywhere and at all times, its history. For it seems, our faith, a thing rooted in the past, wrapped up with a great deal of venerable imagery, of forgotten ceremony, of exploded treadition; so that even those who hate it will sometimes speak of it in tones of hushed respect, as men speak of the dead. But the fact is that it is alive; that in the midst of all this modern hurry and heedlessness of the past, all this frantic worship of tomorrow, our Church is attracting converts to itself as no other religious body in England is attracting them, is expanding its borders as no other religious body in England dares to expand them. It looked a dead thing compared with the Protestant religion which had superseded it, thirty years after Elizabeth came to the throne; today, thirty years after Queen Victoria ended her reign, does the same comparison survive? Is it not rather true that those who are frightened of us, and there are still many who are frightened of us, attribute those fears, openly, to the growth in Catholic numbers and Catholic influence which our generation has witnessed?

The Catholic Church always seems to despise all measures which would promote her own survival. She takes some of her most devout sons, and bids them follow, in the priesthood, a life of celibacy; she takes many of those women whom you would expect to become the mothers of pious Catholic families, and immures them in the cloister. You would say she was pursuing a policy of ecclesiastical race suicide. And yet in our own day, when parenthood has ceased to be held in honour, and thoughtful men are directing our attention to a decline in the birth-rate, and the possibility that the English stock will die out, it is the Catholic body more than any other which is resisting that tendency and breeding the Englishmen of the next generation. It is the odour of life, not of death, that breathes from the Catholic Church, now as then.

Only, now as then, we Catholics have to keep alive among us that same spirit of devoted sacrifice in which the martyrs gave their lives for the Church. These are hard times all round, and we may well meet harder times before long; and we Catholics shall feel them not least, with the burden of large families and the burden of supporting our children's education. We shall grumble, sometimes, at the sacrifices demanded of us. But before we grumble, let us pause awhile on the old bridge and think of three men, Nicholas Garlick, Robert Ludham, and Richard Simpson, who were butchered there in cold blood, when times were worse than ours. God grant, through the prayers of all the English martyrs, that we ourselves may not be found wanting in whatever trials his mercy may suffer us to undergo.

7

BLESSED EDMUND CAMPION[1]

THE University of Oxford can point to three famous sons of hers, widely differing both in temperament and in historical setting, whose destiny was yet strangely similar. Each of the three belonged to his age, was characteristic of his age; yet each felt bound in conscience

[1] This sermon was preached at the Church of the Immaculate Conception, Farm Street, London, on the Feast of Blessed Edmund Campion, 1 December 1949.

to set his face against the whole tendency of his age. None of them succeeded in carrying his point, yet each registered a protest, so that the cause of religion did not go by default. Each in his own day, each in his own way, held up the progress of the reformed Church in this country; it could not win all along the line; a flaw became patent in its title-deeds, there was a minority report to be considered.

Thomas More, Edmund Campion, John Henry Newman—it would delay us overlong, if we stopped to consider how they differed in natural complexion or in historical context. Let us be content to remind ourselves of the resemblance between them. It would be hard to pick out three men who were more characteristic of the periods they lived in. Thomas More, such a child of the Humanist Renaissance, a realist, something of a cynic, something even of a reformer. Edmund Campion, born with such talents, with such energy of mind, in an age that promised so many prizes to the adventurous. John Henry Newman, such an incarnation of Oxford, and of an Oxford that for once was giving the nation a lead, after fighting so many rearguard actions. Yet More must die as the champion of a Papacy that seemed, then, discredited and outworn; must challenge the rise of nationalism and of absolute government, when so many men of his time, even men like Gardiner, were prepared to fall in with it. Campion must abandon his brilliant chances of helping to create Elizabethan England, and devote himself to shoring up the breached walls of Rome. Newman, who had thought to re-quicken the energies of the Established Church, so as to resist the growing infidelity of the day, must become the hesitating mouthpiece of an uninfluential minority. Each of them floated away, by a kind of fatality, from the main current of the times, and was lost, so it seemed, in a back-water.

It was not a solitary protest; great names were associated with theirs, and if a resolute minority had been able to carry the day, carried it must have been; there was no slackening of effort. Yet the despoiling of religion went on, as if More and Fisher had never existed; Allen and Campion might retard the process by which England lost the faith, they could not reverse it; Newman and Manning released a stream of conversions which has not dried up since, but it was a stream, not the torrent men hoped, men feared to see. What a sad thing it is, the history of the Church in our country! So often nearly retrieving her position, and never quite. Worse still, there is an unworthy doubt that suggests itself to us, or is suggested to us by reading unfriendly accounts of the matter. Is it possible that the gesture these men made was in each case, however generous, a mistake?

Arguable, that if Fisher and More had taken the oath, preamble and all, they might have remained in favour at court, prevented some of the mistakes of Henry's reign, perhaps even restored peace between England and Rome. What if Campion had allowed himself to fulfil his early promise, and become the scholar-courtier men expected him to be? The friend of Sidney, he might have gained, at least for a time, the shuttlecock favour of the Queen, might have won easier terms for the Church he still cherished at heart. Or at least, if he must go abroad and join the exiles, let him be a plain secular priest from Douai, with his roots in the English tradition; why must he go off to Rome and turn Jesuit, bringing back with him the shock troops of the Counter-Reformation? Naturally the Government took alarm; they smelt treason. As for Newman, we see how influential the Oxford Movement became without him; what if he had continued to lead it?

Would it still have been possible, in Campion's day, to effect a compromise; to secure a kind of contemptuous recognition for the old religion, if only he and his friends had had more patience, more prudence? If we think that, it is because we were taught so in earlier, more peaceful days, when all the world paid lip-service to the principles of democracy. It is one of the few satisfactions you get out of living in times like these, that they help you to understand history. The emergence of the modern gangster-State has made it much easier for you and me to realize what it was like, living in the golden days of Good Queen Bess; the spies, the informers, the agents provocateurs, the search-warrants, the faked accusations of conspiracy, the crushing fines, the rack and thumbscrew, the scheming of unscrupulous men at the head of affairs, the sudden rise and fall of favourites—it is all happening now. In Elizabethan England, as in so many parts of the world today, a new gang had worked their way to the top, and they meant to stay there. The old religion could not be tolerated, because it was part of the old order, on whose ruin their hopes depended. Catholicism might be allowed to die out, if it cared to, by a slow process of decent inanition. But to give it artificial respiration, to perpetuate its orders and its sacraments—that would not do. If the Government had really been frightened of foreign plots, their remedy was simple, they could have allowed the old hierarchy of Queen Mary's reign to go on ordaining. But no, that would have been no better than foreign seminaries; it would have been a link with the past.

Did Campion ever see things in a different light? Did he ever wonder whether a policy of secret infiltration would serve his turn better than open defiance of the Government's policy? I doubt it. Allen may have

had his doubts; Robert Persons may have had his doubts; either had
the makings of a conspirator. By that, I do not mean that the charges of
treason brought against them by the English Government had any
foundation; a Government which relies so much on fraud and forgery
cannot hope to justify itself in the eyes of posterity. And indeed, as an
acute biographer of Campion has pointed out,[1] if these men really
hoped to engineer a rising of Catholics against the Queen, they went
about their business very foolishly. It was all-important, if they had
that end in view, that Catholics should conceal their sympathies,
pretend to be ordinary citizens like their neighbours. Instead of which,
the exiled priests were always encouraging Catholics to declare
themselves, to make themselves marked men by refusing to go to the
parish churches. No, I feel certain that Allen and Persons, no less than
Campion, believed in the policy of open defiance. But I can imagine
them toying with the other alternatives, making up their minds after
a careful weighing of the advantages on either side. Whereas Campion,
once he had seen the way lie clear before his own conscience, never
hesitated; there was a great simplicity about his mind, for all his
uncommon powers of reasoning.

You cannot judge safely about the thought of a man who has left so
little of himself on paper. But the impression I get of him is that he saw
the faith with a kind of mathematical clearness, such as makes it very
difficult for you to understand why the other man cannot see it as
clearly as yourself. There, he is quite unlike Newman; Newman sees
the other man's point of view almost better than he sees his own. Even
when he is being interrogated by his judges, or browbeaten by
Protestant theologians, men briefed to put the Government's case, you
feel Campion is wondering all the time how on earth they can manage
to be so dense about it. The long interval between the moment at
which Newman first "saw a ghost" and the moment when he knelt
at the feet of Father Dominic, was an interval of real intellectual
indecision; he could not make up his mind whether the claims of the
Church were a bright bubble or no. With Campion, are we wrong in
guessing that he saw his way clearly from the first, knew himself even
at Oxford, even at St John's, to be a square peg in a round hole? And
if he trifled with his conscience for a little, it was very understandable;
there were so many others in his own case, encouraging him to bide
his time; the young experiment at Douai seemed so hazardous, and so
insignificant; Oxford, of all places in the world, is the one most apt to
carry you along tranquilly in its own stream, postponing decisions. . . .

[1] Evelyn Waugh, *Edmund Campion*.

But I think he did some violence to his conscience by accepting Anglican ordination; I doubt if he ever really believed that was a possible solution. That is why, as a missionary, Campion had a more immediate success than Newman. Newman was an ex-Anglican, urging Anglicans to follow his example, but all the while obsessed by a penetrating sense of their difficulties; about the Immaculate Conception, about the Vatican Decrees. Campion had never really been an Anglican; he had been a lapsed Catholic, and he was urging lapsed or semi-lapsed Catholics to follow their consciences, as he had followed his. The one-volume *Dictionary of National Biography* describes him as sent over to England to coerce temporizing Catholics in England. "Coerce" is good. Here are men threatened with crippling fines, with sudden, arbitrary arrest, with execution on trumped-up charges, if they will not adopt the religion of the gang, and a missionary who goes about, carrying his life in his hand, to give them the contrary advice, is described as "coercing" them. No, the only sort of coercion which Campion knew was a very simple one. He had nearly stumbled over the edge of a precipice, and he stood there at the brink of it, warning other passers-by to mind their step.

Why did Campion turn Jesuit? It is the least explained incident in his career. There were English Jesuits already, but they were few; it was Campion who set the fashion. If we did not know our man, we might have suspected him of running away from danger; Douai was the road to martyrdom, and it looked for a time as if he would end his days teaching school at Prague. My suspicion is that at Douai they made too much of him, hailed him as a great intellect; he might be left there to write controversial treatises, be turned on, perhaps, to translate the Bible. That mathematical clearness of mind would not be content to make a sacrifice without going the whole way; he had turned his back upon fame and popularity, and he must join the novitiate which would cut him adrift most effectively from the very memory of such things. He joined the Society for what is, I suppose, the best reason for joining the Society; he read the Exercises, and they said to him, "This means you".

So he came to us, in the disguise of a servant; the same disguise his Master had worn, all those years ago. And, at the beginning of Advent, they murdered him, as such Governments will. In these dark times, may his blood avail us.

8

BLESSED PHILIP HOWARD: I[1]

I, therefore, the prisoner of the Lord, beseech you to walk worthy of the vocation wherewith you are called.—Ephesians 4. 1.

BLESSED Philip Howard, Martyr. It would seem that, in the very earliest age of the Church, all those who had suffered for the Faith were acclaimed as martyrs, even those who suffered ill-usage without actually shedding their blood for Christ. It was only later that these came to be distinguished by the title of Confessors. And—I do not know for what reason—the man whose holy memory you Catholics of Arundel will fitly be celebrating tomorrow, his towns-people, on the anniversary of his death, is included among the English martyrs, although he died, probably from natural causes, in prison. Legally, Philip Howard, Earl of Arundel, was a martyr; for, during the latter half of his imprisonment, his death sentence had been passed. Morally, he was a martyr; for an imprisonment which takes away more than a quarter of a human life, takes away the full half of a promising manhood, is a kind of death; and a life cut short at thirty-eight was cut short, it can hardly be doubted, by the inhuman conditions under which that imprisonment was inflicted. Philip Howard, then, met a fate which did not differ in its essentials from that of his contemporaries, the seminary priests. But let us seize upon the point of difference which does distinguish him. We think of Cuthbert Mayne and Edmund Campion and those others as the victims of the hangman's knife. Let us think of Philip Howard as a prisoner, with a message of comfort for prisoners, with a message of warning for those who enjoy their freedom.

St Paul was fond of referring to himself as the prisoner of Christ. And you will find his commentators discussing the question, whether that means that he was, as in literal fact he was, a prisoner of the Roman Government for Christ's sake; or that he was, in a mystical sense, a prisoner whom Christ held bound. That is, I think, the sort of question which St Paul left his commentators to discuss without bothering about it himself. What difference did it make after all? Everything that befell him, even if it befell him through the malice of his enemies,

---

[1] This sermon was preached at the Church of St Philip Neri, Arundel, on Sunday morning, 18 October 1942. The following sermon was preached on the evening of the same day.

was Christ's will for him, was Christ's way of seeing to it that his witness should be borne in the most effective way possible. And he likes to think of himself, I should say, as one whom Christ has laid by the heels and shut up in a dungeon because it is the safest way of ensuring his sanctification. In this passage from which I have quoted, he even seems to go further, and contrast himself with his converts at Ephesus because they enjoy their liberty, while he is not allowed to enjoy his. I, the prisoner of the Lord, tied hand and foot so that it is impossible for me to do much harm in the world, call upon you, who enjoy your liberty, to walk in a way worthy of your vocation. To walk —the sense of the word is, to stroll about at your own pleasure, as your own masters, the thing the prisoner cannot do. Because you have been entrusted with your liberty, it is for you to see to it that you make a right use of that liberty; that your actions, and the whole bent of your lives, shall be such as become men called to Christ's service.

And I think Philip Howard would have liked us to look upon his imprisonment in the same way. True, it was a punishment, for no crime whatever, inflicted upon him by his enemies. But I think he saw it in a different light; he had enjoyed, in earlier years, the gift of liberty, and what bad use he had made of it! He had dedicated himself to the service of the world and of the Court, putting the call of Christ aside; till Christ met him, as he met St Paul on the way to Damascus, conquered him, and made him give up his sword. Having made him give up his sword, Christ held him as his prisoner. Was he to let him free on parole? Hardly; he had been put on his parole years earlier, when he was brought to the font, and he had broken his parole when he dedicated himself to the service of the world; you do not give such a man a second chance. So Christ, this time, made a prisoner of him; shut him up in the Tower, where he had no opportunities of going wrong, no temptation to retrace his steps and resume the worldly thoughts he had abandoned.

And he would want us, Catholics of a later day, who can practise our religion without incurring the danger of arrest and imprisonment, to be all the more careful, for that reason, about the steps we take, the paths we choose, because, in these days, the choice is left to us, and it is so easy to go wrong. The prisoner's lot, after all, is a type of the conditions under which every human life is lived; is a type, especially, of human life as it has to be lived by us Christians in a fallen world which is not our true home, only a place of detention. Every man born into this world lives in a condemned cell; the warrant for his death will be issued not at an hour of his own choosing. Meanwhile, the environ-

ment of his life, his social ties, his limited opportunities, interfere with
his liberty of action; when all is said and done, he has little of real
freedom. And we Christians, whose faith forbids us to think of this
world except as the ante-chamber of the next, can think of death as the
warrant for our release; there is a window high up in our cell which
gives us tantalizing glimpses of a wider world beyond, and we long to
taste its more generous air. We must look, then, to the prison life of
Philip Howard as a sacrament of human life in general; we must learn
from him to face the ten years, twenty years, whatever it may be of
life that remains to us, in the same spirit in which he faced those ten
years which saw him a prisoner in the Tower of London.

We shall be able to find, in Philip Howard, a model of detachment.
All of us in these days are accustoming ourselves, rather ruefully, to
do without some of those little indulgences which seemed, till yesterday, necessities of life to us. And we do it with an uneasy feeling that
we have not yet nearly reached the limits of what may be expected
from us. We know, all the time, that we are at this moment the most
pampered nation in Europe. And yet we give way, sometimes, to
self-pity; sometimes, too, when we think of the future, we are inclined
to wonder whether we shall get back, any of us, after the war to the
standards of comfort we cherished before the war. Will things ever
be the same again, or have we to reconcile ourselves to a sterner mode
of existence, with our pleasures, our holidays, or opportunities of
cultivating friendship and family life limited, henceforward, by
narrowed means and greater regimentation? When we feel like that,
let us remember the story of Philip Howard; a man born to enjoy the
ease and plenty of an age in which ease and plenty seemed, as never
before, within man's reach, yet sentenced by his own conscience to
live the life of a prisoner, within sight and sound of all the amenities
he loved. He had, unquestionably, the chance of buying back his
liberty at the price of denying his faith; if he would not consent to do
that, he was not even to be allowed sight of his wife and children—a
harder sacrifice than even St Thomas More had been called upon to
make. But Philip Howard, I think, never stopped to ask himself the
question, "What have I done, to deserve all this?" He was the prisoner
of the Lord; in all the circumstances which preyed upon his health and
restricted his liberties, he saw nothing but the conditions of an honourable confinement. Cannot we learn from him to think of ourselves as
Christ's prisoners, ready to offer to him, in small things or in great,
whatever sacrifice is demanded of us by the bestowal of that honourable
title?

I have said, he did not ask himself what he had done to deserve all this. I was wrong; I think Philip Howard did ask himself what he had done to deserve his fate, and found a ready answer to his question in remembering the sins of his youth. That is why I think we shall once more be able to find, in Philip Howard, a model of abiding penitence. If he was denied the sight of his wife and children, that (he felt) was only just, because, when he was free to see as much of them as he would, he had neglected them. He had had all the chances life could give him, before his imprisonment, and had made bad use of them; the Tower of London was a kind of purgatory, in which he suffered appropriate punishment for his careless living of yesterday. If only *we* could learn, when *we* look back, and attempt to trace the causes of our modern difficulties, to find the explanation of them, not in the short-sightedness of our politicians, but in our own love of comfort and security, our own selfish use of the prosperity God still gave us, only a few years back! Cannot we learn from Philip Howard to think of ourselves as belonging to a civilization which has its purgatory to undergo, here and now, for so many opportunities wasted, so many warnings misread?

And I think we shall be able to find in Philip Howard a model of self-effacement. Here was a man—I shall hope to direct your attention to it in more detail this evening—who might have been a candidate, and indeed was, when he began life, a candidate for some of the highest prizes the world had to offer; and that in an age of unexampled splendour. When he became a Catholic, and as a Catholic had to spend the last ten years of his life in gaol, he put those brilliant hopes behind him. Can we not imagine what a temptation it must have been to him to fret and to chafe, when he found himself so cut off from all the life of his time? To be unable to assert himself, to make his influence felt, to strike a blow for the causes he had at heart—what an ignominious sense of frustration it must have given him! When they wanted to trump up a charge of high treason against him, what was the figment in which they took refuge? Why, that he had had Mass said for the success of the Spanish Armada! Malice itself was unable to credit him with any more active interference in the political events of his time. Can we not learn from Philip Howard to curb that self-assertiveness in us which makes us want to interfere with the running of things every-where; to be at the head of every movement, or, if that is impossible, to be always criticizing the people who are at the head of it, as if we could have done it better ourselves? Can we not learn to be content with the work, however humble its sphere may be, which God has given us to do; content to be overlooked and passed by, to have our opinion disregarded, to be left out in the cold? The prisoners of Christ, happy, if need be, on a treadmill, because that is how he wants us to serve him!

Meanwhile, as we remember Philip Howard's chains, and the spirit of detachment, of penitence, of self-effacement in which he wore them, do not let us forget to think of him as the patron of prisoners everywhere. So many of them, all over the world, soldiers and civilians, men of political importance and men of no importance whatever, caught up in the machinery of a world war and laid by the heels for three years, four years, who can tell how long? Let us remember the sense of frustration which makes their lot specially bitter; soldiers who were outmarched before they ever struck a blow, patriots who paid the penalty for having sympathies, before they could translate those sympathies into action. No class of men is more forgotten, I think, in war time, than the prisoners; and if their existence is remembered, it is only in some evil moment when their captors are tempted to hold them as hostages. Let us ask Philip Howard, a prisoner no longer, but a courtier of the Queen of Peace, to remember the days of his low estate, and pray for all that multitude of human beings who lie, justly or unjustly, necessarily or needlessly, in prison. May the slow years that pass over them, and pass them by, bring them nearer to God, instead of making them disappointed in themselves, embittered against their fellow men. May he win freedom for the souls that are crushed by captivity; and for us, who go free, may he do more; may he bring every thought of ours into the captivity of our Master, Jesus Christ.

9

BLESSED PHILIP HOWARD: II[1]

He was taken away, lest his mind should be altered by wickedness, or his soul seduced by deceit.—Wisdom 4. 11.

THE Blessed Philip Howard—the Church calls Philip Howard blessed—that is, happy. It was a paradox with the old heathen philosophers, that you should never call a man happy until he was dead. A living man may, at this moment, be in prosperous circum-

[1] This sermon was preached at the Church of St Philip Neri, Arundel, on Sunday evening, 18 October 1942.

stances, be enjoying health and good spirits, but you must not call him happy, they argued, because you cannot tell what is going to become of him later on. Croesus, the enormously rich king of Lydia, was angry with his wise friend Solon for not counting him a happy man; but later, when he lost his kingdom and became a prisoner at the court of King Cyrus, he acknowledged that Solon was in the right. So it is with the judgments of the Church—only she is more guarded still. For her, death is not the end. A man may die full of years and honours, peacefully, surrounded by his mourning children and friends, after a career of congenial activity pleasurable to himself and useful to others; is he happy? Yes, says the heathen philosopher; the Church is more doubtful. There remains for him a dreadful moment of judgment, at which all he did and the motive of all he did will be tried in the balances; only if he comes triumphantly out of that ordeal will she pronounce the epitaph, This was a happy man. And, because much of man's action is hidden, and still more of his motive is hidden from the view of his fellows, she will very seldom pronounce it officially. Of a very few of her children she says, This was a saint, a man set apart by God for the manifesting of his power in a human life. Of a few more she says, I do not say that this man was a saint, but assuredly he was a blessed man; his life was, if you will, a happy life. And she says that about Philip, Earl of Arundel.

Not merely, remember, in the sense that he is happy, now, in heaven. There is a unity, a continuity, between our life here and our life here-after; so that God's friends, in spite of all the persecutions they endure, in spite of all the mortifications they encounter, are happy here and now; read St Paul's letters, and he will tell you how in prison, in ill-health, in his moments of gravest anxiety, he rejoiced continually. We are to say, not merely, Philip Howard is a happy man, but Philip Howard was a happy man. In what, then, did his happiness consist?

His was an age, you would think, for men to be happy in. There are few periods in human history so rich with the memory of adventure and romance as the second half of the sixteenth century. There have been few milieux in which a man of spirit and imagination could so fulfil himself, win so many prizes in action, or leave such a mark on the literature of his country, as that milieu which centred round the court of Queen Elizabeth. She, a gross creature of moods and vanities, yet knew how to queen it among her subjects, how to make those who served her feel, even if she gave them little tangible reward, that they were her knights, fighting with her favour on their sleeves. Think of the great names that have come down to us from that Elizabethan world.

Courtiers like Leicester and Essex, statesmen like Burleigh, men of thought like Bacon, men of high susceptibilities like Philip Sidney, adventurers like Raleigh, sea-captains like Hawkins and Drake and Grenville, poets like Shakespeare and Marlowe and Spenser; how their names have lingered on in our national heritage, so that a schoolboy would be ashamed not to have heard of them! What a halo of romance crowns those men, what a grace there is about the poise in which they stand out to view, carved in the imperishable marble of their achievements! Into that world, so rich with promise, Philip, Earl of Arundel, was born.

True, he belonged to the old aristocracy, and it was the day of new men. True, his father had been executed on a political charge, and the Norfolk title was under attainder. But there were prizes, then, even for the nobly born; and, in the year 1581, when his career was launched amid the splendours of the Elizabethan court, you might have said that the world was at his feet. He might have become a great commander in the crisis of the Spanish Armada; he might have led successful privateering expeditions against the enemies of his country; he might have discovered new lands, and bequeathed his name to them. There might be at this day, somewhere in the United States of America, a town of New Arundel, all skyscrapers and luxurious hotels and business enterprise, whose citizens would visit *this* town, in pious pilgrimage, because it was here that the founder of their fortunes once lived. Or he might have become a great poet, a great dramatist; have written lines which still kindled English hearts to adventure, or scenes which still drew rounds of English applause, still drew tears from English eyes. Statesmen would have quoted, at the end of their glowing periods, a few well-known lines from the poet Arundel. May a stranger be forgiven for reminding you of it? Your town has a name surpassed by few English place-names for its beauty; and that name Philip Howard might have connected, for all times, with the history of his country. Surely, in the year 1581, with all the world before him you might have counted him a happy man? "Bliss was it in that dawn to be alive, But to be young was very heaven";[1] now, Philip Howard, bliss, blessedness, is within your grasp!

Was there anything yet lacking to him, that young man of great possessions? Two things, or one, if you prefer to count them as springing, after all, from the same root in a man's character—human love, and divine. He was married, and had children; but he seems, at this time, to have been estranged from them, and indeed to have neglected them.

[1] William Wordsworth, *The Prelude*, Book XI.

His teachers, if their names have been correctly reported to us by tradition, were men of piety. One was Gregory Martin, that indefatigable scholar who gave us our English version of the Bible, almost as one man's work. What veneration Philip Howard might have conceived, as the result of his teaching, for the old religion of his forefathers! The other was John Foxe, author of that very untrustworthy but immensely popular work, the *Book of Martyrs*. What indignant championship of the Protestant cause might have stirred the bosom of Philip Howard, after the one-sided picture such a man must have given him of the issues which the Reformation involved! The influence of both teachers seems to have passed him by. There was no harm in that, from the point of view of his worldly prospects. It was no bad thing to leave your religion behind you when you embarked on a career in Queen Elizabeth's court. And it was not a bad thing to forget you had a wife and children, if you were to accommodate yourself to the loose morals of that strangely tolerant society. But there was a gap in Philip's life which was soon, in God's providence, to be filled.

Towards the end of that year, 1581, he was present among other courtiers at a long and wearisome religious disputation, staged by the Government of the time in order to bring discredit on the Catholic cause. The Protestant side of the quarrel was upheld by this and that divine who had won all the comforts of ecclesiastical preferment, by combining court opinions with a reputation—then easily come by—for theological learning. The rival disputant was a very different man; the official description of him was Edmund Campion, the seditious Jesuit. Here was a man who, a few years earlier, had had the world at his feet as it was now at Philip Howard's. The paragon of Oxford scholarship, already holding high position in the University, he had gone abroad, done his studies in a Catholic seminary, joined the Society of Jesus, and come back to England to restore his countrymen to their old allegiance. He had been caught, in hiding, brought up to London, and cruelly racked in a vain effort to make him give information about his fellow priests. And now he stood there, without books, without friends, without advisers, pleading the cause of religion before these impudent nobodies, who did not fail to taunt him with his helpless position as a prisoner. It is a scene difficult to match, for injustice and brutality, in the annals of modern Germany. But it passed, unfortunately, as an every-day affair in sixteenth-century England. Probably, when Philip Howard learned that he was to form part of the audience at this debate, his first thought was that it would be a tedious business, listening to these divines chopping logic and capping texts from the

New Testament; a September afternoon had better have been spent
out hawking. But it was the Queen's wish that he should be there;
and, as her loyal knight, he must sit through the wearisome pro-
ceedings, to witness the discomfiture of error.

Of the impressions he formed there, no record survives to us; it
only remains clear, from what followed, that as the result of the
disputation Queen Elizabeth lost a courtier. It may well be that the
logic, it may well be that the texts, made little impression on him one
way or the other. He is more likely to have been moved by the reflection that the New Learning, if it could not give its opponents more
generous treatment than this, was a poor substitute for the religion of
yesterday. Perhaps the wasted, tortured figure of Edmund Campion
had a majesty about it not of this world; some reflection of that Majesty
which had spoken the word long ago, Sell all thou hast, and give to the
poor, and come, follow me. All we know is that within three years
Philip Howard embraced, in secret, the religion for which Campion
had sacrificed everything. By a gracious coincidence—it seems to have
been no more than a coincidence—the claims of the Catholic Church,
which have so often brought strife and division into families, brought
peace and harmony into his. His wife was reconciled to the Church
about the same time as himself, and during the rest of his life he evinced
a tender affection for her, and an abiding penitence for his unworthy
treatment of her. Not that the couple, so reunited, were to enjoy, in this
world, the fruits of their reunion. Betrayed and captured in a vain
attempt to escape to the Continent, Philip was committed to the
Tower, and spent the last ten years of his life in confinement. When he
asked for the favour of a meeting with his wife and children, he was
told that he might have it on one condition, that of apostasy. So
reunited and disunited, the story of their married life reaches its strange
ending; he died, a witness for the faith, she outlived him for thirty-
five years, and the persecuted cause found in her an ever devoted
patroness.

Meanwhile, during those ten years between 1585 and 1595, the prizes
which the world had once offered to the young Earl of Arundel went
to others, and passed him by. The splendid pageant of Elizabethan
England became a peepshow seen, for him, only through the bars of a
prison. Drake and Hawkins witnessed the defeat of the Armada, while
Philip Howard remained in prison. Raleigh set out to colonize Vir-
ginia, and Philip Howard remained in prison. Spenser began publishing
his great epic, the *Faërie Queene*, Marlowe founded the greatness of the
English stage with *Tamerlaine* and *Faustus*; Philip Howard remained in

prison. A young dramatist, still little known, brought, in the autumn of 1595, a tragedy entitled *Romeo and Juliet*; and Philip Howard died in prison.

Did he do his best, as prisoners will, to compensate his frustrated energies by authorship? When Raleigh found himself in the Tower, some ten years later, he began writing his *History of the World*; did Philip Howard undertake a history of the world? No, he and the world had said goodbye to one another. In strict penance, full of contrition over the false start his youth had made, he began a long apprenticeship to qualify himself for the prizes of a world more durable, and to him a less hard task-master, than this. What he has left us in writing, a poem or two and a few translations, are only the by-products of his prayer. Some thought he died of poison; it is perhaps more likely that he succumbed to the rigours of his imprisonment, to gaol fever. But ten years were granted to him, a man under public sentence of death, to make his soul and prepare it for meeting its God in judgment. During those ten years he could never wake in the morning with the confidence that he would live till sundown. And was not this gift of angry fortune the gift of a happier life than any her smiles could have offered him? To see life, always, as the embryo state of a being framed for eternity; to see death as a release, the only possible release, from a prison-house? To live dead to the world, within grasp of immortality?

Tell us, Francis Drake, what does it avail you now, to have captured all those treasure-ships, beaten off all those enemies, to have been, in life, the idol of your fellow countrymen, to have become, in death, a legendary figure to symbolize their greatness? Tell us, William Burleigh, what reward have you reaped in the end for all those watchful labours in defence of the dynasty whose cause you had espoused? What satisfaction is there, now, in having founded the fortunes of a race still influential in English council-chambers? Tell us, William Shakespeare, of what advantage is it to you now that your name is known all the world over, that fragments of your poetry will haunt the imagination of Englishmen so long as the English tongue is spoken? What does it avail you, that after three hundred and fifty years your plays should still be played to crowded houses, you who cannot take the call of "Author", now that the curtain of death shuts you off from the scenes you loved? Does the earth lie the lighter on any of you, for being famous; does the world's applause weigh one scruple in the balance against the account you had to pay when God called you before him in judgment?

But the just shall live for ever; their reward also is with the Lord.

We do well, especially in times of emergency like these, to remember the past, and God's mercies to us in the past; we do well to honour the feats of enterprise and heroism which, long ago, made our country great. But we must not forget, in doing so, that our estimates go for nothing in eternity; that the judgments we pronounce are only froth blown upon the wind; can take no rank with that terrible judgment which is passed on every child of Adam when he passes from death into the world beyond. God reads the secrets of the heart; he is not impressed by successful careers, or by solid earthly achievements; it is our motives, the use we have of our opportunities, small or great, that he will judge. And, not seldom, he will show us that the choice of his predilection fell upon a soul which was never the world's candidate, never the world's hero; he will floodlight with the aura of sanctity some obscure niche in a convent cell or within the walls of a prison. He who chose for himself, when he came to earth, the obscure home of a carpenter's wife, and an ignominious death of the cross, will repeat that same lesson, not seldom, in the annals of sanctity. Let the world pay its homage to Charles Howard of Effingham, who led the fleet of England against the Armada; we will not grudge him his mortal laurels. But, for us, the issues which are fought out on the battle-ground of a single human soul are issues more real and more momentous; for us, Philip Howard of Arundel, who had news of the Spanish threat and of its passing only from his gaolers, is an inspiration more poignant, because he did nothing that we may not be called upon to do ourselves; is a patron more venerable, because he put the world behind him, instead of competing for its crowns? When we call, as we called just now, on the names of those others, a Burleigh, a Drake, a Shakespeare, we know that we are only indulging in an exercise of rhetoric; our voices die away upon the faint echoes of the past. But when we call upon Philip Howard, we know that his voice is raised in answer to ours; that he, once so unsuccessful a courtier in the splendid world of Queen Elizabeth, is a courtier now amidst splendours which surpass all our human imagination; that he can exert an influence no earthly patron could exert for us, with a King whose favours are not the uncertain favours of caprice. To Charles Howard we turned long ago, in the time of our country's peril; now, in perils not lighter, it is to you, Philip Howard, that we turn. Pray for the country which gave you so little, which treated you so cruelly; pray for the Church whose battles you fought, pray for all of us, whom you see so distracted with worldly cares, so deluded by vanities, so much in need of detachment, of your fortitude, of your great simplicity of heart.

10

BLESSED JOHN SOUTHWORTH[1]

Knowing that the same fellowship of suffering is shared by the brotherhood you belong to, all over the world.—1 Peter 5. 9.

WHEN we recall, with our faltering praises, the memory of some human being now in glory, should we be concerned to emphasize marks of individuality? To say, "in this or that characteristic, the man we celebrate was unlike his fellows"? John Southworth, who was martyred exactly three hundred years ago, at Tyburn, offers several points of contrast with those martyrs who preceded and followed him. His life is little documented, but he stands out, recognizable, in the glorious company of seminary priests that were his schoolmates.

For one thing, he was the only one of the English martyrs who suffered under a dictatorship. As the Civil War drew to an end, and the triumph of Parliament over the Crown was assured, the troubles of our Catholic forefathers were not diminished. They had been accused of plotting against the King; the King lay murdered, and still the persecution went on. They had been fined for refusing to accept the Elizabethan Prayer-book; the Elizabethan Prayer-book was exiled from the parish churches, and still the persecution went on. But when the last remains of the Long Parliament were ignominiously sent packing, and Cromwell was left, for all practical purpose, ruler in his own right, there seems to have been a change of policy. Cromwell, man of blood though he was, belonged to the sect of the Independents, and shared their theoretical distaste for all religious coercion. Liberty of conscience was proclaimed, with disturbing effects; in 1653 the eccentric prophet Muggleton was imprisoned for blasphemy; in 1656 James Nayler stood in the pillory, after being hailed as the Messiah at Bristol; and before long the Fifty Monarchy Men were being denounced as a peril both to Church and State. But, all the time, all through the last four years of Cromwell's rule, the seminary priests came and went on their secret errands, and only one paid for it with his life.

Why was John Southworth distinguished from the rest? We can only suppose that he was, somehow, an unmistakable figure. Seventeen

[1] This sermon was preached at Westminster Cathedral on 27 June 1954, at the Pontifical High Mass to mark the tercentenary of the martyrdom of Blessed John Southworth.

years earlier, when the plague was devastating Westminster, he was
seen coming out of an infected house, and the curate of St Margaret's,
guessing the business on which he came, got him arrested. He was set
at liberty through the connivance of friendly authorities, so that the
clemency with which he was treated gave scandal to the Puritans. He
was a marked man, and the warped natures that played informant in
such cases must have felt confident that he, at least, would not escape
for a second time with his life. He is a marked man still, for he comes
at the end of a chapter; no other priest followed him to execution till
twenty-four years later.

There is a second distinguishing feature about him, no less honourable. It was and is a principle of English law that an accused man,
whatever be the real facts of the case, has a right to plead *Not Guilty*;
it rests with the prosecution to break down, if they can, his defence. To
be a Catholic priest living in England was at that time a criminal and a
capital charge; and it was the common if not the universal practice of
the missionaries to plead *Not Guilty* when they were accused on that
count. To John Southworth, it seemed that a denial of his priesthood
would be a denial of his faith. Was it just a scruple? I think there may
have been a reasoned calculation behind it. The days of smug Erastian-
ism were past; the court was not unfriendly, and the Recorder of
London, when he passed sentence, actually wept, with the ready tears
of the enthusiast. Quite possible, if he had pleaded otherwise, John
Southworth might have saved his life; but he did not want to save his
life by a legal subterfuge. He admitted to being a priest, I think by
way of showing up the monstrous injustice of those laws which treated
the priesthood itself as a crime. In his speech at the gallows' foot, he
pointed out that almighty God did not punish the whole hierarchy of
angels when some of the angels rebelled; why should the innocent
suffer with the guilty? He may, at his trial, have conceived the hope
that his own unblemished record would lead to a reconsideration of the
penal laws. Of that hope he was disappointed; he was not disappointed
of the dearer hope of martyrdom.

His life was not spared, but a curious concession was somehow
obtained; his mortal remains came into the possession of the Howard
family, and by them were conveyed overseas. Thus John Southworth
has a third claim to distinction; he is the only English martyr, so far,
whose body has been preserved for Catholic veneration almost in its
entirety.[1] I say "so far" because the earth has still its secrets to give up,

---

[1] The quartered body of Blessed John Southworth is preserved for veneration at the
Altar of the English Martyrs, Westminster Cathedral.

and our present craze for tearing up the ground with bull-dozers produces, now and then, fortunate results. So it was with John Southworth. For a hundred and fifty years his body rested at Douai, there among his old schoolfellows, the object of a veneration which they might not publicly express. Then, at the time of the French Revolution, the seminary was taken over by the Government, and the relics which were treasured there had to be hastily buried, because there was no chance of removing them. The secret of the *cache* was handed on, but somehow, it seems, inaccurately; when a search was made, about seventy years later, the relics, including those of John Southworth, could not be found. At last, about a quarter of a century ago, the authorities at Douai took to town-planning; and it was in driving a new road through what had once been the English College that they unearthed, by mere accident, the forgotten secret. The hair-shirt of St Thomas à Becket was destroyed, under the impression that it was rubbish. But the embalmed body which rested close by was a different matter; it was examined, and identified, and it lies in the shelter of this Cathedral.

The only one of our English martyrs to suffer under a dictatorship. The only one who notoriously pleaded guilty to being a priest. The only one, so far, whose body is preserved to us entire. Let me go back to my starting-point—*should* we be concerned, in such a case, to emphasize marks of individuality? To say, "in these three characteristics, John Southworth was unlike his fellows"? Let us make an oracle of the hallowed body that lies beneath us, and ask John Southworth himself. "Who, I?" he will say. "Different from the others, distinguishable from the others? Never while eternal life lasts! Did not Bartholomew Roe, who suffered so short a time before me, greet his fellow priests at Tyburn with the words, 'Here's a jolly company'? And shall we not be a jolly company still, now that we have won through to the other side, we, who all suffered the same ill-usage, bore the same witness to Mary and the Mass and the unity of the Church? No, if my body is here in Westminster, where I loved to labour, it is only as a specimen; in me you see, representatively, all the long line of English martyrs from the Dissolution of the Monasteries down to poor Oates' plot. What difference does it make, if we did not all go to the scaffold at one time, or after one fashion? We are all fruits of the same tree, and it was in God's hands, when we should ripen and be plucked, part of his pre-destined harvest. What if we fell out sometimes and had quarrels among ourselves, while we lived on earth? It is all forgotten now. When you invoke me here, you invoke all these others, my fellow bedesmen; we were, and are, nothing else than your servants in Jesus Christ."

The English martyrs—how we love them for being so specifically English! English in their bluff directness, English in their obstinacy; English above all in their determination to face death, though the death were martyrdom, with a jest. From St Thomas More refusing to have his beard cut by the axe, to John Kemble having his last pipe and his last drink with the sheriff, they are of our blood. Different, somehow, from the other saints—why, here we are falling back into the same mistake of picking and choosing! We have resolved not to treat Blessed John Southworth as different from his fellow priests, only to find ourselves treating the English martyrs as different from other martyrs. How wisely does the *Imitation of Christ* warn us against that parochial tendency of ours! "Some people", it complains, "feel drawn towards this saint or that with a kind of competitive love; and all the while the motive which influences them is human, not divine." The saints are the lights of the world, but the light which shines in them is borrowed. They are like the glass reflectors by the roadside which guide the motorist at night, not from any illumination of their own, but as they are caught by the glare of the headlights. So Christ, who is the valiancy of martyrs, is reflected now in this life, now in that; now in this group of lives, now in that. Martyrdom is only the after-glow of that good confession which he made before Pontius Pilate; it is the same everywhere, and in all ages. Three hundred years ago, it was men of our blood and our character that flashed back the rays of his sacrifice; today, over a vast tract of the world from Berlin to the Pacific, the same light shines; the same witness is borne under a persecution, God knows, not less terrible. As we say our prayers before the broken body of John Southworth, let our hearts go out in fellowship and in sympathy towards our brethren on the other side of the Curtain. Let us pray that the faith, driven underground, may in God's good time be restored to the light and the air, like the body of John Southworth buried away, there in the vaults of Douai, so long lost, and so providentially found.

III

OCCASIONS

I

ROGER BACON[1]

There shall be no remembrance of the wise, no more than of the fool, for ever;
and the times to come shall cover all things together with oblivion. The learned
dieth in like manner as the unlearned.—Ecclesiastes 2. 16.

ROGER BACON, whose memory is perpetuated by that tablet in the
wall in front of you, is one of the world's great men. He left
behind him a living tradition, in Oxford especially; so that men looked
back to him as if he had been a great magician, something like Doctor
Faustus; and you may still see prints of the gate-house that used to stand
on Folly Bridge, which is described, in the legend underneath the
picture, as Friar Bacon's study. But while his memory in men's mouths
thus passed into something legendary, his works remained scattered
through the libraries of Europe; probably there are more of them to be
unearthed yet. And as these were found and published he acquired a
new reputation in the learned world, as if he had been a man vastly
ahead of his time, both in the methods of his research and the results
of it. Not because of his most characteristic views, the views he expressed
with most warmth and courage; as, for example, that the philosophers
of his day were all taking the wrong course because they could not
study the works of older philosophers in the original Greek and Arabic;
or that theology was at fault because it was not strictly based on a careful
examination of Holy Scripture, which was, to Roger Bacon, the ultimate source of all knowledge whatsoever. No, the moderns have been
interested in Bacon because he did know something about optics,
could tell you how to make a telescope or a microscope, though it
does not appear that he had either; dreamed, perhaps, of steam traction
and of aviation, had a secret recipe for making gunpowder; sought,
even, in the very latest fashion, to set out all physical reality in mathematical formulae. One of the world's great men; we do well to put
up a tablet to him.

At the same time, Roger Bacon is not a saint. He is not, that is to
say, a saint canonized by the Church; we can never say with certainty

1 This sermon was preached at the Roger Bacon memorial tablet, on the site of the
old Franciscan Friary at Oxford.

that this man or that, who has died, is not reigning already in heaven; only God knows that, who can read our consciences. But the character of Bacon, as you find it in his own writings or in the impressions of his contemporaries, is not apt to strike the reader as a saintly character. Indeed, if the truth must be told, within earshot, almost, of all these venerable institutions, Bacon was not much of a saint—he was more of a don. He had the don's unalterable conviction that all the other dons were going the wrong way about things; that they were not profound enough, not accurate enough; that nothing could be done until the whole of learning had been reorganized on his own lines. It was not that Bacon was attempting to glorify his own order by belittling the work of other orders; he was quite as fierce about Alexander of Hales, the Franciscan, as about anybody else. And if he lived a troubled life, and incurred the suspicion of his superiors, it is difficult not to believe that it was partly his own fault. He had the irritable temperament of the scholar, and he minced no words when he wanted to put other people right.

But although he may not have been a saint, Bacon was a perfectly good Catholic. He was, in every way, a child of his age. It is very tempting, but it is a great mistake to hail him as the prophet born out of due time, who anticipated this or that later movement, and deserves to be regarded as the father of it. He wanted to revive the study of Greek, but he is not the forerunner of humanism; he cared nothing for the classical culture, he only wanted people to read Aristotle, and the New Testament, in the original. He believed in getting back to Scripture, but he was not the forerunner of the Reformation. On the contrary, he was befriended by a pope, and everywhere treats the papacy with due respect; nor is his complaint against the worldliness of bishops or prelates, but against the ignorance of scholars. He shows a wonderful *flair* for science when you consider the limited possibilities that existed in his day for the study of it; but he is not the forerunner of the Empiricists; has no kinship with his namesake, Francis. To him, as to all the men of his day, metaphysics was the highest form of science in the human scale; and metaphysics was only the handmaid of theology. If Roger Bacon came back to Oxford today I believe you would find him quarrelling with all the other learned men as heartily as ever. The philosophers would find him a back number and the scholars would find him a pedant, and the scientists would find him a chopper of logic, and the theologians would find him a fundamentalist; and there would be fresh trouble all round.

But Roger Bacon is dead. And by that I do not mean merely that his soul long since underwent separation from his body, as all souls must. I mean that his very memory is by now a thing of the past, belongs to an old world, which is still the subject of antiquarian interest, but is not near enough to us to feel as if it were a part of ourselves. With the saints, you see, it is otherwise; just as their bodies, in many cases, have been found uncorrupt long years after they were buried, so their lives remain embalmed for us in the odour of sanctity, belong to us, if we are faithful Catholics, as if they were men of yesterday. Saint Francis is not dead, in the sense in which I am now using the word. He is removed from our company, because he is in heaven; but his story is of yesterday; he is like an elder brother who died, more is the pity, before we were born. You cannot think of him as remote, uncongenial, shut off from us; his sanctity bridges the centuries that lie between us. But Roger Bacon belongs to the past, for all those precocious speculations of his which made him seem ahead of his time. There shall be no remembrance of the wise, no more than of the fool, for ever; and the times to come shall cover all things together with oblivion. The learned dieth in like manner as the unlearned. That is the law under which Roger Bacon is forgotten.

And yet, is he forgotten? Not altogether; not in Oxford. He is remembered here because his own Grey Friars have come back here and will not allow the site of their old residence to be altogether obliterated. So they have chosen Brother Roger as the type, the representative, of all those many Franciscan friars who must be waiting, not far from this spot, for their Resurrection. We are to pray, not "grant him", but "grant them" eternal rest; not only Brother Roger, but all those cloister-mates of his whose names we do not know; the ones who worked for him without acknowledgment, copied out manuscripts for him and verified facts for him and pointed out slips he had made, helped in one way and another to make his name the great name it is; the ones who did not quite approve of him, and thought his studies were all waste of time, if not worse; the ones who laughed at him, and thought him a crack-brained old fellow; the learned people (for there were plenty of others in that beautiful dawn of Oxford scholarship) who never managed to achieve fame like his, and the simple people who were content to be simple people like St Francis —all the old Grey Friars you must have seen once, walking up and down behind the old battlements, as you came upon Oxford from the south, across the windings of the Thames.

All alike, Brother Roger with the rest of them, belong to the past now; the conditions under which they lived, the problems they had to face, were not our conditions or our problems, and we cannot really put ourselves in their place, or them in ours. The world is so full of anxiety about the present, of speculation about the future, that it has no time to waste, no tears to shed, over the ruined glories of the past. But we, Catholics of Oxford, assemble once a year to remember these fellow townsmen, fellow gownsmen of ours, and to pray for their souls; that gracious bond of unity is not destroyed for us by any lapse of years or any change of manners. Let us commend, then, to the mercy of God and to the prayers of his blessed Mother that restless soul, so long ago laid to rest, and the souls of all who in times past ministered or worshipped in this place; and let us pray also, in this place, for a restoration to the university of the faith in which it was cradled, and of the sacramental life which it once lived by, and has lost.

2

KING HENRY THE SIXTH[1]

These are they whom we had some time in derision, and for a parable of reproach. We fools esteemed their life madness, and their end without honour. Behold, how they are numbered among the children of God, and their lot is among the saints.—Wisdom 5. 3.

FOUR hundred and fifty-five years since, a week ago last Saturday, died the only king of England since the Conquest who has ever been within measurable distance of being raised to the altars of the Church.[2] And because, in our day, there is some hope that his cause will be proceeded with afresh after a long lapse of centuries; because I am particularly bound to him as the Founder of the school at which I was educated, I want to represent to you very briefly this morning the true facts about King Henry the Sixth, and to ask—if what you hear interests you—your prayers for his eventual beatification.

King Henry the Sixth? The mind fumbles nervously in the dusty pigeon-holes of memory. Echoes from the small green Gardiner respond unwillingly to the call. Yes, Henry the Sixth, let me see, was not he the king who was always going mad? An innocent creature, to be

---

[1] This sermon was preached at St Catherine's, Chipping Campden, on 14 May 1926, the 455th anniversary of the death of Henry VI.

[2] King Henry VI in fact died on 21 May 1471.

sure, not responsible for all the calamities which befell England during his reign; his murder in prison was, I quite agree, one of the most brutal in English history. But . . . a saint? Surely this harmless type of character, under-developed and barely capable for better or worse of moral action, has nothing to do with the manly virtues of the saints? They felt temptation, and triumphed over it; they dominated their fellow men, left their mark on the world through sheer force of character. Surely you are not going to set up this weakling, this half-idiot, beside men like Dunstan, and Anselm, and Thomas More?

These are they whom we had in derision, and for a parable of reproach. We fools esteemed their life madness, and their end without honour. Behold, how they are numbered among the children of God, and their lot is among the saints. . . . Let me tell you a story. Possibly it is not true, but it is a story which was affirmed on oath and duly chronicled at the time. A little while after King Henry the Sixth died, when it had begun to be rumoured that miracles were being wrought through his prayers, a near neighbour of yours, a certain John Robins of Inkberrow, was making his way to Stratford-on-Avon. And it will have been soon after Abbot's Moreton, where he turned into the main road, that he met with another countryman, George Luffar from Crowle, who began to talk to him about the holy King Henry and his wonderful miracles. I daresay George Luffar was a tiresome enthusiast, but anyhow John Robins got weary of it, said he did not believe a word of it, said that King Henry was just an innocent creature who hardly knew his right hand from his left, and no more a saint than anyone else. And so they went on arguing until they got to Stratford. The same day, while he was in Stratford, John Robins went stone blind. There was no explanation of it, and there was no cure for it, until he vowed that he would make a pilgrimage to King Henry's tomb at Windsor—a vow which was afterwards duly paid—and then he recovered his sight on the spot.

Well, I would not trouble you with that story if it were the only story of its kind. But it is one out of one hundred and seventy-four similar stories which are preserved for us in a manuscript now kept at the British Museum. And we know, from that manuscript, that in St George's Chapel at Windsor they kept a list which contained the record of at least three hundred and sixty-eight miraculous cures and deliverances as the result of prayers offered to King Henry; all of which date during the thirty years between his death in 1471 and the end of that century. What does it all mean? It means that at the end of the fifteenth century the pilgrimage to Windsor was one of the great English

G

pilgrimages, like those to St Thomas at Canterbury and our Lady at Walsingham. It means that in churches all over the country pictures and statues of King Henry were being put up as if he were one of the saints—a dozen or so of them may still be seen today—that lights were kept burning, and hymns were written in his honour. It means that in those days the natural thing to do, if you were in any trouble, was to appeal to a dead king for his prayers. Why, in the reign of Richard the Third, who was King Henry's murderer, there was a girl over at Honeybourne, called Agnes Freeman, who suffered from what was called the King's Evil; it was a skin disease which could be cured, men said, only by the touch of the reigning monarch—and so it continued down to the day when Dr Johnson was touched for the King's Evil by Queen Anne. But Agnes Freeman did not go to Richard the Third; she went to the dead king's tomb instead, and found relief from her malady there.

Now, it is quite true that King Henry is not the only popular hero who has been regarded as a saint by the people who could remember him. The body of Simon de Montfort, the leader of the Barons against the king two hundred years earlier, was kept in the Abbey Church at Evesham, and there is record of miracles happening there. But there is this difference, you see; the devotion to Simon de Montfort died out: the devotion to King Henry did not die out, it was simply swamped by the Reformation. In 1528, the year before Thomas Cranmer became Archbishop of Canterbury, it is historically certain that the envoys of King Henry the Eighth at Rome, while they were urging the Pope to sanction the divorce from Catherine of Aragon, were also urging him to proceed with the beatification of King Henry the Sixth. And the Pope was perfectly willing, he was only waiting for the arrival of fresh evidence from England. And that evidence never came, because the breach between England and Rome came first. The cause had dropped, but the devotion to King Henry did not drop. It is historically certain that pilgrims from Devonshire and Cornwall were coming in large numbers all the way to Windsor as late as the year 1543. 1543, that is seventy years after King Henry the Sixth died, and only half a dozen years before the Mass was abolished in England. England did not lose her faith in King Henry until she lost her faith in the Catholic Church.

Well, I have taken the risk of giving you all this dull lecture in history because, as I say, the reopening of the cause at Rome after nearly four hundred years does seem to be practical politics just now. But nothing will come of it unless people in England will offer prayers for that intention. After all, St Joan of Arc was neglected for more than four hundred years and then canonized; and now that England, more than ever since the Reformation, is beginning to count among the Catholic countries of Europe, it would be a pity if through some want of patriotism, some want of feeling for our Catholic past, we missed the opportunity of publicly invoking a saint of our own royal lineage. Pray, then, for his beatification, you who love the English countryside which he loved; and commit to him sometimes your prayers for temporal or spiritual favours; if experience goes for anything, it will not be in vain.

We esteemed their life madness. It is true that twice, during the fifty years of his life, King Henry was deprived, for a time, of the use not only of his senses, but apparently of his limbs. The attack, upon either occasion, lasted less than two months. For the rest, although he was a weak king in stormy times, nobody ever doubted that he had the full use of his reason. The founder of Eton, and of King's College, Cambridge—and in either case he drew up the statutes himself, with particular care—has left to the nation a legacy which is more enduring than those of most English monarchs. There was, in his whole character, a child-like innocence which the men of his own day took for sanctity; it was left for later generations to suggest that this innocence was a form of feeble-mindedness. Is it, perhaps, that in our day we have lost the faculty for appreciating sheer innocence, for understanding the temperament of one who is brutally treated by his enemies, yet bears it all without complaint? If so, I think that King Henry has yet a work to do in schooling and in softening our English hearts.

3

CATHOLIC EMANCIPATION[1]

And we cried to the Lord God of our fathers, who heard us, and looked down upon our affliction, and labour, and distress, and brought us out of Egypt with a strong hand, and a stretched-out arm, with great terror, with signs and wonders, and brought us into this place, and gave us this land flowing with milk and honey, and therefore now I offer the first-fruits of the land which the Lord hath given me.—Deuteronomy 26. 7.

THE Church, in her Easter liturgy, finds everywhere in the deliverance of the Israelites from Egypt the type of our Lord's Resurrection from the dead. In the *Exultet* which is sung by the deacon on Holy Saturday, which is probably one of the oldest and most primitive features of our modern Christian worship, we find this notion continually insisted upon. "This therefore is the night in which thou didst bring our forefathers the children of Israel out of the land of Egypt ... this therefore is the night which set free the children of Israel, and despoiled the Egyptians", and so on. The Paschal candle, which is blessed while the *Exultet* is being sung, is meant to remind us of that pillar of fire which guided the Israelites through the wilderness; and the waters of the font represent to us that dark passage through the Red Sea, when the waters stood up in a heap on this side and on that while God's chosen people passed through. So, on Holy Saturday, Christ who is our Light passed through the dark gates of the tomb, and brought his people out with him into the sunlight of Easter morning. Just as their deliverance from Egypt was, to the Jews, the supreme turning-point of their history, the one unforgettable incident which must be annually celebrated with every circumstance that could recall it to memory; so, to us Christians, it is our Lord's Resurrection from the dead which must overshadow, for us, all other triumphs and all other deliverances.

Yet, as the Church journeys on through the centuries, and the threads of her experience are interwoven with the tangled skein of human history, fresh crises must arise which are worthy of record, worthy of perpetual commemoration. The whole story of the Church is one which imitates the story of her divine Master; she dies, and she rises again. She was buried in the catacombs; she rose again with Constan-

[1] This sermon was preached in the diocese of Nottingham on the occasion of the centenary of Catholic Emancipation (1829).

tine. She died in the Dark Ages; she rose again with Charlemagne. She died with the Renaissance; she rose again with the saints of the Counter-Reformation. You cannot kill the Catholic Church. The heresies spread themselves like weeds, and like weeds come up when and where they are least expected; small wonder that they should flourish to the end of time. The miracle of Catholicism is of another kind; the same trunk, attacked again and again through the centuries, always puts out fresh branches, decks itself in fresh leaves, as the centuries go by; shoots all the more generously where it is pollarded. Men think that they have killed the Catholic Church, and go to sleep on it; and while they sleep, she pushes back the stone which they have set over her, casts aside the grave-clothes in which they bound her, and celebrates, for each of her Calvaries, a fresh triumph of Easter.

So it was with us a hundred years ago. For what we celebrate this year is not this or that enactment, this or that concession wrung with difficulty from a government tenacious of its prejudices and jealous of its privileges. No, what we celebrate is the termination of long centuries of flagrant injustice; of bloody laws wantonly passed against the faith in which England was cradled, against the Church which was her nursing-mother. What we celebrate is not the triumph of the hopes by which O'Connell or Charles Butler lived, but the triumph of the hopes in which Edmund Campion and Oliver Plunkett died. Our interest is not confined to those forty or fifty years during which the struggle for Emancipation took place. Our minds travel back over those many years, nearly three centuries in all, during which our religion was penalized and its free exercise was denied to us. We suffered like Israel in Egypt; as the Egyptians laid grievous burdens on them, so we were ground down with iniquitous fines and disabilities; as the Egyptians tried to kill the male children of the Israelites, so it was made impossible for us to educate our children in the faith. Nor was there even the excuse that we were foreigners; it was against men of their own blood that the English Government, for a full two centuries, enacted and tried to enforce hostile legislation. What wonder if we celebrate our deliverance as a new Passover, a new Resurrection of the Church in England from a legal death, that threatened to be a death in reality?

Picture yourself as one of the Israelites standing, on that spring morning, by the shores of the Red Sea, looking back at the land of your captivity. Those waves, that were parted last night by a long path of sand, are now an impenetrable barrier set between you and your enemies. Over them hangs the mysterious pillar of cloud which is the token of the divine Presence; and through that cloud the land of Egypt appears dim and distant; a few palm-trees here, a Pyramid there, are all that is left to remind you of the country in which for all those years you toiled and were a slave. What would be your first instinct, in the flush of gratitude for your deliverance? Why, surely this, that now more than ever your people was the people of God, a nation that he had chosen out for himself by redeeming it from captivity; a nation which had died and been buried and risen again; it had passed through the Red Sea as through a tomb, and this morning in the new sunlight, in the new springtime of the year, you feel that you belong to a new people altogether; yesterday and all the yesterdays that went before it are only a dream, a bad dream that is over, no true part of your experience. Yours is a nation which has no history; for its history begins today; begins with the day when God took it out of the land of Egypt and out of the house of bondage.

And that is exactly the point God wanted them to see, God wanted them to realize. They were to be his own peculiar people, and he was to be their God; they were to hold up before the world, a world sunk in heathenism and idolatry, the truth that there is only one God over all the earth. In order to do that they must, before all else, keep alive the religious traditions of their nation. And that was not going to be such an easy thing to do. He was leading them out into a land that flowed with milk and honey, the land of Chanaan; and it was inhabited, remember, by heathen tribes, who worshipped the gods of the harvest and the vintage. If once the Israelites mingled with them, intermarried with them and learned their ways, the tradition of pure religion which insisted upon the worship of the one true God would become fatally contaminated. His own peculiar people—whatever else they did, the Israelites must keep pure, in that land whither they went, the stock of their race and the traditions of their history. They must remember, wherever they went, that their forefathers were once sojourners in Egypt, and that in being redeemed from that captivity they had become a new people, holy to the Lord.

That was the message which Moses preached to the children of Israel; that was the message which St Paul preached to the early Christians. Delivered from a worse captivity than ever the old Israelites had known, from the bondage of death and sin, they had become a holy people, dedicated to the Master who had redeemed them. When he passed, on Holy Saturday, through the dark gates of the tomb, he was a new Moses crossing the Red Sea; and every soul that passed through the waters of baptism—in those days, I need hardly remind you, baptism meant total immersion in water—became mystically associated with the death, burial, and Resurrection of the Redeemer. You are dead, and your life is hidden with Christ in God . . . being buried with him in baptism . . . if you then are risen with Christ, seek those things which are above—baptism is a death, a burial, and a rising again. Christians are dead—to what? Why, to the world, to the heathen world all around them; they must keep themselves clear of that if they are to be worthy of their Christian vocation. The man who has been baptized should look at the world as something he has left behind, dim and distant, as the land of Egypt looked to the Israelites when they stood on the further shore of the Red Sea.

We too, as I say, we English Catholics, have experienced a great persecution and a great deliverance. It was effected with the utmost difficulty; Pharaoh, you will remember, refused for a long time to let the children of Israel go; and the king of England a hundred years back was only just restrained by his ministers from exercising the royal prerogative in order to veto Catholic Emancipation. We too, surely, are the peculiar people of God, called to show forth his truth in a world of misbelief and unbelief. Now, what has the effect of Catholic Emancipation been on us? Has it made us English Catholics more careful than we were a hundred years ago, or less careful than we were a hundred years ago, to keep ourselves unspotted from the world? Let us answer that question with all sincerity; let us see how far our attitude towards the world is justified, and, if we are wrong, where we are wrong.

If you look at a copy of some old manual of devotion such as they used a hundred and fifty years ago—Bishop Challoner's *Meditations*, for example, or his *Hell Open for Christians*—I think you will find the tone of it somewhat foreign to our modern taste. You will find it, I fancy, severe; and in particular you will notice that it refers to "the world" in the good old theological sense of the word rather more insistently than a modern manual of devotion would. If you are clever enough, you will explain that difference by saying, "Ah, yes, Jansenism; the Gallican influence!" But I do not think it was only that. I fancy that Catholics in the days before Emancipation lived such isolated lives, kept so much together and saw so little of their neighbours, that the world around them did seem to them an unknown and a formidable thing. The life of the court and of the camp, the life that flatters and demoralizes, passed them by; they lived on their country estates, entertained little, gave themselves to leisured pursuits. The world —what did they know of the world?

And then Emancipation was secured, and Catholics began to come out of their hiding-places; they began to get commissions in regiments, to take silk at the Bar; in one way and another, to take their share in the national life. And they found, probably, that the world was not quite such a wicked place as they expected it to be. After all, the world of Queen Victoria's reign was not a particularly wicked world to come out into. It had a high tone of morality, it was a world of spaciousness and of endeavour. Catholics began to meet Protestants for the first time, and to realize for the first time that they did not bite. Catholic and Protestant society began to intermingle; marriages helped it, the Oxford conversions helped it, the restoration of the hierarchy helped it; we ceased to be a little nation all to ourselves within the nation; we became merged and scattered among the general population. That was inevitable, and I think you can say without much hesitation that it was desirable. If Catholics never went about among their Protestant neighbours, their influence would be far less felt, and there would not be nearly so many conversions to record. By the end of the century, Catholics were even beginning to go to the universities; mixed marriages were becoming common; everywhere we had lost our individuality and our exclusiveness (save where in some of the northern towns little colonies of Irishmen managed to hold their own as a separate world, cut off from the world which surrounded them).

That is the England into which you and I have been born; an England in which Catholics and Protestants mix freely, and no questions are asked; it is perfectly possible, nowadays, to have been working side by side with a man for months, in the same office, and then suddenly, through some chance turn in the conversation, to make the unexpected recognition, "What! Are you a Catholic? Why, so am I." There is still a great deal of misunderstanding about our religion, a surprising amount of misunderstanding, everything considered; but on the whole nobody thinks worse of you for being a Catholic; people do not look at you nervously, as if you might suddenly turn into a Jesuit. And that is natural, after all, considering our numbers. A hundred years ago, I suppose you would find one Catholic in every hundred of the population. Today you will find one Catholic among every twenty of the population. If I get into conversation with a stranger in the train, and he learns that I am a Catholic priest, he can nearly always mention some link which he himself has with the Catholic Church, how he used to work for Canon so-and-so, how his sister-in-law married a Catholic, and so on. We are no longer a little patch sewn on to the English nation somewhere at the edges; we are interwoven with its texture; we are part of its life.

All that is as it should be. It means, from England's point of view, that a particular element within the nation, once a minority with a grievance, but now an integral part of the population, strengthens the Government with its Catholic instincts of discipline and order. It means, from the Church's point of view, that the Catholic religion spreads more easily, in proportion as it is better known, in proportion as its atmosphere is more familiar. And I think it is even possible to say that the Catholic body itself has benefited in some ways by its contact with the world outside. I think it is fair to say that in the days before Emancipation the Catholic body was a little behind the times, rather insular in its outlook, rather angular in its cast of mind; old-fashioned in its devotions, exacting in the rigidity of its principles. We needed fresh blood, perhaps, and Emancipation made it possible for us to absorb fresh blood into our system.

But when you have admitted all that, it remains true that the diffusion of Catholics among the population has its dangers as well as its advantages. There is the danger that all this rubbing shoulders with the world outside—more especially when it means mixed marriages, and children being brought up in a different faith from one of their parents—will weaken the purity of our stock and the firmness of our resolve. Are we Catholics really the men we were a hundred years ago? Let me remind you of a Catholic whose name is not much remembered nowadays, but ought always to be remembered in this diocese at least, Ambrose de Lisle Phillipps. In the year 1828, just a year before Catholic Emancipation, he was an undergraduate at Cambridge, and had just been received into the Church. Every Sunday morning he used to go on horseback to St Edmund's College, Ware, the nearest Catholic centre; always fasting, so that he could make his communion at the other end; he did this in a weak state of health, and once very nearly died of it. Now, it so happens that I once had to do that journey fasting, on a bicycle, and I can tell you that I did not enjoy it; it is every step of twenty-five miles. Twenty-five miles, fasting, every Sunday—it makes you a little impatient, doesn't it, with the modern Catholic who cannot often get to church, because it is more than three miles to go. Am I right in expressing the fear that we are not quite the men we were, have not quite the spirit we had, a hundred years ago?

And yet we ought to be. We owe it, in loyalty, to our forefathers who preserved for us the faith of England. We owe it in gratitude to God who delivered us, only a century back, from our house of bondage. He has brought us out of our captivity, but he has not brought us out into a land flowing with milk and honey—not yet. The conversion of

England is happening; is happening before our eyes; but anyone who thinks that it is going to happen without effort and generosity on our part is a fool. We live in a selfish age, in an age distinguished by lack of principle. And if we are going to conform to the standards of the world around us and take our line of behaviour from the world around us, then it is nonsense for us to talk about Emancipation. What is the good of talking about Emancipation, if we Catholics are still slaves?

During the last century, the hold of religion upon the masses of the English population has been steadily declining; and in our own time we are seeing the results of that—England is losing hold of the principles, even of common morality. More and more as that happens we Catholics become a civilization to ourselves, a nation within the nation. The world says to us, What peculiar people you Catholics are, not recognizing divorce! And we have to reply, Yes, we are a peculiar people; to us marriage is the sacrament which expresses Christ's union with his Church; and as our forefathers upheld the indivisibility of the Church, and suffered for it, so we uphold the indissolubility of marriage. What peculiar people you are, says the world, with your large families! Yes, we reply, we are a peculiar people; we trusted in God to provide for us during the dark days of persecution; we trust in him still, the absolute Lord of life and death. What peculiar people you are, insisting that your own children should be brought up in your own schools! Yes, we are a peculiar people; the faith we teach was saved at the price of men's blood, and we dare not compromise it.

A peculiar people; that is the true lesson of Emancipation. The memory of penal days and of the martyrs who suffered in the persecutions is a memory burned deep into our consciousness, as that of the captivity in Egypt was burned into the consciousness of the Jewish nation. Please God, the bitterness is dead; the injury is long ago forgiven. But the heroism and the generosity of those days is not forgotten; God help us if we ever allow ourselves to forget it. We should be unworthy of the Catholic name if we shrank from any sacrifice, or feared any criticism, until England becomes the Island of Saints and our Lady's Dowry once more.

4

THE OLD ROAD[1]

And the places that have been desolate for ages shall be built in thee. Thou shalt raise up the foundations of generation and generation, and thou shalt be called the repairer of the fences, the restorer of paths.—Isaias 58. 12.

IT was an understood thing, in those unsettled days when the Hebrew prophets wrote, that invasion by a foreign enemy caused the high roads of a country to fall into decay. "In the days of Samgar the son of Anath, in the days of Jahel, the highways were unoccupied, and those that travelled went through by-ways." You would not drive your cattle or carry your crops along the main arteries of the old civilization, where you might encounter, at any moment, the marauding bands of the enemy; you cultivated, instead, the little hill tracks where his chariots could not follow you. And, as time went on, the old main roads would be overgrown with grass, and the hedges that fringed them broken down. So that whoever took in hand the reconstruction of the country when the foreign danger was past must see to it first of all that the old means of communication were made fit for use again. Thus it is that the prophet Isaias, by a metaphor natural to the men of his day, speaks of the man who would reinstate the true worship of God in its purity and simplicity as one who would repair the fences, one who would restore the old roads to their use.

And I cannot preach at Watlington upon such an occasion as this without remembering that there runs, within a mile of your town— yet disregarding it, and disregarded by it—one of those ancient track-ways that scar the face of our countryside with a sense of history and a sense of mystery all in one. Who built the Icknield Way, who used it, when did it fall out of use, whence is its name derived, what was its starting-point and what its terminus? All those questions you may ask, and the antiquarians quarrel amongst themselves over it, or are dumb. Through eight counties, from Suffolk on the east to Wiltshire on the west, it has left its traces; now losing itself altogether, now occupied by a modern crossroad, now stretching for miles, grass-grown between its hedges, now splitting up into a hill road and a valley road, as beyond Chinnor. Almost certainly it goes back beyond the Roman conquest;

[1]This sermon was preached at the opening of the Church of the Sacred Heart, Watlington, Oxfordshire, on 14 May 1930.

it does not travel between Roman centres, nor has it the military straightness the Romans cultivated; it may be that, as a single road, it has remained in disrepair ever since the eagles marched between Dorchester and Bicester. It lies there, like a solitary protest against our modernity, teaching you citizens of Watlington to recall the old days, and the forgotten races from which we are sprung.

There is no excuse for men who live by the Downs or the Chilterns to lack the sense of mystery, that should be kept alive in them by the old roads, the old camps, the old stone huts upon the hills. There is no excuse for them to lack the sense of history, dwelling under the barrier that stretches from White Horse Hill, where King Alfred rallied his men against the Danes, to Dunstable, where Cranmer pronounced sentence of divorce against Catherine of Aragon. You ought to see time in its true perspective, living here by the Icknield Way. The great turnpike roads superseded it; and they, when their time came, were superseded by the railways, and now, under our very eyes, the roads are threatening to supersede the railways after all. And still the Icknield Way stands plain to view; and the holidaymakers in their cars, as they sweep over the bridge at Aston Rowant Station, or breast the top of the hill that lies above Benson, catch, for a moment, a vista of its patient progress between the hedges. If they have any imagination, it must give them, too, a momentary sense of history. How long will it be before we, too, with our motor-cars and our petrol-stations, will be forgotten like the generations that went before us, and the relics of our civilization buried among the silent hills?

I believe it is impossible, for a person with any imagination, to read the history of our country during the last three hundred and fifty years without having something of the same experience. Every now and again in the course of that history, he meets with some mention of an institution which is older than all this modern greatness of England, which was once part of England—nay, was the breath of her life—yet, during these last three hundred and fifty years, has fallen into neglect and all but become obscured. I mean, of course, the Catholic Church. It goes for nothing in the development of modern England; our thought, our habits, have been formed on an altogether different model. It was a Protestant England that achieved that greatness among the nations which began with the triumphs of Elizabethan seamanship and ended, perhaps, with the Treaty of Versailles. And in reading the history of that development you only come across the Catholic Church now and again, crossing the page of our history for a moment, just as the Icknield Way will cross, just at one point, the great arteries of our modern road transport. The Gunpowder Plot, the Titus Oates Plot, the reign of James II, the rebellion of '15, the rebellion of '45, the Gordon Riots—you realize, with a shock, at such points, that there were still Catholics in England even in the days when they were un-relentingly persecuted by the Government. But for the most part, you hardly come across the mention of them; they have disappeared from view, like an old road that has lost itself in the open fields.

And yet it *was* the old road. It is bitten deep into the soil of English history; you cannot obliterate the landmarks. During a thousand years and more of our history England was but a part of the Catholic Commonwealth of Europe; all the institutions which we revere as old, our Parliament, our civic procedure, our universities, still reek of a Catholic origin. The old road, but it had served its turn, men thought, three hundred and fifty years ago; and they struck out on newer paths, and let the old sign-posts rot away and the old milestones become grass-grown. The Catholic faith became, in England, a thing of by-ways and of retired corners; it flourished most where new movements were felt least; it was remote, provincial, unfashionable. You find the traces of that survival still scattered over the map of Oxfordshire and Berk-shire; at Hethe, at East Hendred, at Buckland, at Stonor. But it was Hethe, not Bicester; East Hendred, not Wantage; Buckland, not Faringdon; Stonor, not Watlington. Not in the market towns, but in the little villages where the Catholic squires held out, the faith still lived, precariously; they were content to shun the world's eye, and to live in retired corners; yes, our religion was a religion of the by-ways. Like the palace of the Sleeping Beauty in the fairy-story, the religion that had been England's pride was moss-grown now, and grass-covered; it would never, you thought, be used again.

There came a time, a little less than a hundred years ago, when the Catholic Church in England began to emerge from that isolation, to revive from that oblivion. How it happened, you could hardly say; it was as if you have gone out one morning along the road to Nettle-bed, and found gangs of workmen, with steam-rollers and barrels of tarmac, laying down a fresh surface on the Icknield Way. You may think of an old man dying on the G.W.R. platform at Pangbourne; he had been taken ill in the middle of his untiring journeys, to and fro, by which he sought to convert England again to the faith he loved. That was Father Dominic, of the Passionist Order, an Italian priest whose earliest dream was to convert the distant country of which he knew nothing. Or you may think of this same Father Dominic, a few years before, making his way to a cottage in Littlemore on a night of

October, to receive into the Church a convert whom he knew only by reputation—John Henry Newman, afterwards Cardinal of the Holy Roman Church. No one knows exactly how it happened, but since that day the Catholic Church in England has ceased to be what it was, a remnant, half-pitied, half-despised, to be hated perhaps, but certainly not to be feared. It has grown into a vigorous movement, perhaps the most vigorous movement in contemporary English religion; you brush up against it everywhere, in the newspapers, on the wireless, in the street corners of London, even in the walks of daily life; it is something present and active; half-feared, half-admired; to be hated perhaps, but certainly not to be despised. Two generations of missionary endeavour have repaired the fences, and restored the old paths once again.

The Catholic Faith is coming back. I do not say that it is coming back suddenly, sensationally, issuing a violent challenge to the public attention. But if you merely look at the figures for the last thirty years since the beginning of the century, you will find the progress steady and unmistakable. At the beginning of the century, I suppose that one in every twenty-three Englishmen was a Catholic; today, one Englishman in every nineteen is a Catholic. Today, one out of every twelve children born in England is brought to a Catholic font. Thirty years ago, there were 2,800 priests in England; today, there are more than 4,200; we have increased by fifty per cent. Thirty years ago, we had 1,500 churches and chapels; today, we have more than 2,100. The work is going on, the hedges are being repaired, and the old paths restored.

That work is perhaps slowest of all, most difficult of all, in the country towns of moderate size; the kind of town where it is not quite clear whether there are just enough or just not enough Catholics to make a permanent church worth while. For in most of these country towns no whisper has been heard of the Catholic religion since it was eclipsed three hundred and fifty years ago. Here in Watlington, for example, though the very messengers who carried Campion's tract, the *Ten Reasons*, from the secret press at Stonor where he had printed it to Oxford, must have passed through your streets, the Catholic faith has been something apart from your experience, the fad of an old family somewhere on the other side of the hill. Today, it comes down into your valleys, meets you with the old challenge, and offers the old consolations. It will not skirt respectfully round Watlington at a little distance, like the Icknield Way; it will come into your midst, look you in the face, offer you its companionship for your life's journey, a highway to the city of God.

What answer will you make? These are days of stumbling and hesitation; men look for guidance to the faiths in which they were born and nurtured, and too often they find none; or, if guidance is offered, there is a confusing variety of utterance; one preacher extols what another preacher condemns, and one generation burns the idols which the last generation worshipped. Is it possible that the faith in which Europe was cradled is after all the faith which man was made to live for; that all the improvements which men have devised upon it have shown themselves worthless, like short-cuts that tempt the way-farer, only to mislead him, and leave him to hark back, as best he may, to his starting-point? That is the question with which today's ceremony poses you; meanwhile, whatever you make of that question, it is certain that you have now, in Watlington, a fresh witness in these evil days to the power of God and the faith of Jesus Christ. A fresh centre, where the venerable mysteries of our religion will be celebrated from week to week, where men will hold up holy hands of prayer, in inter-cession for their own and their neighbours' needs; a fresh heart, that will quicken the slow pulses of the spiritual life, a fresh channel through which God's blessing will descend upon your undertakings. May that blessing, through the prayers of blessed Mary Ever-Virgin and St Joseph and the saints of our country, prosper our handiwork this day and sanctify these humble beginnings we make here to the glory of his Name and the salvation of souls; may he bring both those who planned and those who built this church, and us too who are gathered for the dedication of it, to the Jerusalem which is above, a city eternal in the heavens.

5

BISHOPS IN COUNCIL[1]

God prepared a worm, when the morning arose on the following day, and it struck the gourd, and it withered.—Jonas 4. 7.

THE prophet Jonas was sent to preach in the city of Nineveh, and to prophesy its destruction. Moved by his warnings, the people of Nineveh repented, and God spared them. And Jonas, we are told, was angry—not, I suppose, merely from a kind of professional disappoint-

[1] This sermon was preached in July 1930.

ment, but because he probably regarded the kingdom of Assyria, of which Nineveh was the capital, as a dangerous enemy to the kingdom of Israel. God taught him his mistake by a parable. On a day of intense heat, Jonas sat under the shade of a gourd, a trailing plant which grows and dies very rapidly, and throws plentiful shade. Next day, its roots had been attacked, and it had withered away. When Jonas complained, God asked him why he showed such regret for the gourd which had covered him, and yet longed so for the destruction of Nineveh. There was, I think, at the time a special appropriateness in this comparison. For the king of Assyria, by his continued wars against the people of Damascus, was preventing them from harassing the Israelites, their neighbours on the south. And in consequence, Israel achieved at that time a greatness which it had not known since the days of King Solomon. Nineveh, then, instead of being the natural enemy of God's people, was acting as a kind of shelter which saved them from their enemies at Damascus, just as the gourd protected Jonas from the heat of the sun. And the purpose of the parable was to show Jonas that he ought to be rejoicing instead of grieving, over the unfulfilled prophecy which he had made.

Sometimes we do make that mistake. We Catholics, for example, are apt to grow exasperated at the continued existence of other religious bodies, and to ask God why he allows people to go on believing in these half-truths, to the dishonour of the Catholic Church. We forget that God, in his providence, may permit these other religious bodies to exist, and even to flourish; for the reason, if for no other, that their existence is in some sort a protection to the Catholic Church, in days when the atheist and the materialist are making such determined attacks upon every form of organized religion. Is it not possible that the Protestant Christianity of our country, instead of being a menace to us Catholics, as it was in the centuries gone by, is now a protection to the Church, a breakwater against the flood of infidelity, a gourd whose shadow stands between it and the glare of the world's sun? Are we sure that we want the breakwater destroyed, the gourd withered away, so soon?

This feeling, which is often in my mind, affects me particularly on those occasions, rarer than they used to be, when the Established Church of this country stands in the limelight of public attention, figures largely in the Press, shows signs of renewed energy. And during this month, as we know, the eyes of the news-editors are fixed on Lambeth, where some three hundred bishops, from all parts of our Dominions and from the United States of America, are meeting in conference. At first sight it might be objected that after all this has nothing to do with us. Standing, as we Catholics do, for an unalterable tradition of faith, and for the principle of a unique, indivisible Church, we cannot conscientiously make any gesture of welcome or gratification; we cannot hold out the right hand of fellowship as the Nonconformist bodies do, nor share the pleased interest which is shown by the orthodox Christians of the East. On the other side, it would be ungracious and indeed unchristian in us to greet an occasion like this with contempt or with ridicule; we can dispense, I hope, with such methods of controversy. How then can we have an attitude towards the Lambeth conference, whatever publicity it achieves in the papers? How can it possibly have anything to do with us?

If anything, we are tempted to feel resentful, as Jonas did over Nineveh. We feel, perhaps, that too much fuss is being made about the occasion altogether. After all, if we collected all the Catholic bishops from the British Dominions and the United States of America, they would muster not three hundred but well over four hundred. Tricks of phrase in the published reports, which assume that the modern Church of England is in some way continuous with the Church which existed in England before the Reformation, irritate us and make us turn over the page impatiently. And yet I think we shall do well to regard the present gathering as important for ourselves, and even as a suitable subject for prayer. For it will have a certain influence—not a binding force, but an influence—over the future attitude of the Anglican Communion towards some of the most important problems of our day. Bear with me, then, if I tell you, in outline, my hopes and fears about it.

There was a letter in *The Times* the other day from one of these bishops, which compelled attention by the evident goodwill and earnestness with which it was written. And there was one passage in that letter which I should like to read to you, because it seems to me to throw into strong relief the difference there is between conferences such as that which is being held at Lambeth and the great councils of Catholic Christendom.

"All the bishops go to Lambeth", it says, "having tried their best to learn the opinions of their diocese and to form their own opinions on the subjects in the agenda. They are conscious that other bishops will have gathered and formed other opinions. They do not go primarily to persuade the others to adopt their own opinions; they go in order that the whole conference may reach together a truer opinion than any one bishop has reached singly." You will see at once what is the leading idea in that passage. The word "opinion" occurs no less than five times in a dozen lines of print. When I read it, a contrast immediately occurred to my mind with Abbot Butler's newly published history of the Vatican Council, which I had just been reading.[1] The Vatican Council, as you know, was suspended in the year 1870, and might reassemble at any time, now that the Vatican has become a sovereign State once more. In that Council, as in all ecumenical councils, the bishops were present primarily in order that each might testify what was the tradition of Catholic antiquity preserved in his own see. They might be called upon to express opinions; to express an opinion, for example, whether it was opportune, at that moment, to define the Infallibility of the Roman Pontiff as an article of Catholic Faith. But in the first instance, they were expected not to contribute opinions, but to give voice to a testimony. Each bishop has received, from his predecessors in his own see, a Catholic tradition; that is why, when a bishop feels his end approaching, he calls his canons together and makes a protestation of faith. The Fathers of the Vatican Council, though many of them held the opinion that it was not a suitable moment for defining Papal Infallibility, all agreed that the infallibility of the Pope was part of the doctrine commonly received in their sees, doctrine which had been handed down to them by their predecessors.

Of all that, you see, there is no word in this Anglican gathering. Nobody is interested, it appears, to find out what opinions have been held by the occupants of the various Anglican sees in time past; nobody wants to know what the Victorian bishops thought about it. The point is, what opinions are held now, in the twentieth century? What opinions have the bishops formed, and what opinion has been formed by the clergy and laity of their respective dioceses? Now, it is no doubt a very excellent thing to compare the impressions of Christian truth which have been formed by various members of the English-speaking races, and of the races which own the authority of the English Crown, in different parts of the world. But it is exactly the opposite of an ecumenical council, as Catholic doctrine understands that term. It assumes that the truths of the Christian religion, instead of being a set of truths handed down once for all, which it is the duty of the Church to maintain and to teach, are in some way dependent on, and capable of being revised by, the ordinary Christian believer. The principle of democracy has been grafted on to the notion of conciliar authority, and the result of that is Modernism in the making.

If you trace the history of the Christian councils, you will find that

[1] Abbot Christopher Butler, o.s.b., *The History of the Vatican Council*, two volumes (1930).

each was a little more severe, a little more exacting than the last. There
has been no modifying of beliefs, no explaining away of doctrine
previously defined; rather, each new council has anathematized some
fresh error which previous councils had left unnoticed. That is natural;
it is, after all, the emergence of fresh doctrinal errors that makes a
General Council desirable. But with these Lambeth conferences it is
not so. Rather, it seems to me, each of them represents a fresh stage
in the whittling away, the watering down, of those doctrines which the
Anglican Church is still supposed to abide by. Each is a little less
positive than the last over the value of Christian tradition as against
the suggestions of historical and biblical scholarship, over the importance of episcopal ordination, over the points in Christian doctrine
which most draw the fire of the world's criticism, as for example the
Christian doctrine of marriage. And that is why, to my thinking, each
conference at Lambeth has a special importance, if only as a sort of
barometer to show how far Anglican thought has contrived to travel
since the last one.

Now, this progressive weakening of front, this gradual abandonment of old positions, on the part of our Anglican neighbours has one
reaction which is of immediate interest to us as Catholics. Each
successive crisis in the Church of England produces a fresh little crop
of conversions. And that, not because the Church of England has
changed, so that it is no longer possible for one who venerates Catholic
antiquity to have part or lot in her. No, the Church of England has
not changed; but one or two souls have at last clearly discerned what
the Church of England is, and what she stands for; hitherto they have
been blind to her true nature, this last experience has been, as we say,
an eye-opener. The present Lambeth conference will be invited to
approve or to disown a scheme of reunion drawn up by the various
Protestant bodies in Southern India, in which the Church of England
body is included.[1] If this scheme is approved, it will mean that, for an
interim period, Anglicans in India will have to recognize as validly
constituted ministers of religion men who have never been ordained
by a bishop, and to receive the sacraments from them. And consequently, the approbation of that scheme will probably mean a slight
increase, a very slight increase, in the stream of conversions from
Anglicanism. Some few souls, which hitherto have struggled to believe
that the Church of England was really a part or branch of the Church

---

[1] This is a reference to the proposed union of Anglicans and Nonconformists in the
South India Mission, which raised the whole doctrine of Apostolic Succession. The same
question came up at later conferences.

Catholic, will now be convinced that this was only an illusion, and they will find rest for their souls by making their submission. To that extent, we have nothing to fear from the lowering of Anglican standards; if anything, we stand to gain by it.

But there are other issues over which a capitulation is to be feared; yes, feared by us Catholics. For example, in the Lambeth conference of 1908 the bishops debated the question whether the innocent party in a divorce might legitimately remarry. They decided against the possibility of remarriage; but the decision was only carried by 87 votes against 84. Now, I believe it is true to say that on that occasion the weakness shown was chiefly on the part of those bishops who came from the United States; and in the present assembly the United States bishops will pull less weight as a matter of numbers. But the whole attitude of the English public towards divorce has altered so much in the last twenty years that I am afraid of what this conference may decide if the subject is brought up again. I say, I am afraid, because in a matter like this, where the pressure of social opinion is of such importance, we want all the allies we can get. If Anglicanism generally abandons the principle that marriage is indissoluble, then for practical purposes we Catholics will be left alone in our protest. And the more that happens, the harder is it going to be for the world to understand our attitude; the harder is it going to be for Catholics themselves to obey the teaching of the Church about the sanctity of marriage, when the whole opinion of the world is against them.

There are other questions of which I might say the same: questions of education, questions of the family, and so on. But the one instance will serve to illustrate my point. There is a canker, I am sorry to say, which is threatening to infect, fatally, the other Christianities of our time, a canker of Modernism. They are giving up the old certainties; they are content, more and more, to take their standards, not only in belief but in morals, from the debased philosophy of our time. We would hope great things, if we dared, from the Lambeth conference. We should like to see the United States bishops lead the way in a determined and unanimous reprobation of divorce. We should like to see the Colonial bishops urging, for the sake of the Empire, the need of a higher birth-rate. We should like to see, on every side, a fearless demand for the Government recognition of Christian education. I do not think we are likely to see any of these things. Inoperative resolutions about war, about labour difficulties, about the need for more clergy—these are more what we have to expect; nothing more than expressions of opinion.

I would not have said all this, if I did not feel that it contained a direct moral for us Catholics. We cannot expect to live much longer under the shadow of the other Christianities; as time goes on, we shall have to face, more and more, the glare of the world's hostility. For that reason, we must rally closer than ever round our bishops, our clergy, our churches, our schools; we must be active Catholics, instructed Catholics, if need be combative Catholics, to meet the demands of the new age. And in the meanwhile, let us beg the prayers of our blessed Lady and of the English martyrs, that more and more of our fellow countrymen may receive the gift of faith, and be brought out of images and shadows into that eternal Truth whose guardian on earth is the one Holy Catholic Church of Christ.

6

VESSELS OF ELECTION[1]

And the Lord said to him: Go thy way: for this man is to me a vessel of election, to carry my name before the Gentiles and kings and the children of Israel.—Acts 9. 15.

THINK for a moment of the infant Church as it was in the days just before the martyrdom of St Stephen. There's no doubt, I think, that in Judea itself that martyrdom had an extremely disheartening effect. The holy apostles, I take it, were still too much occupied in going after, and reclaiming, the lost sheep of the house of Israel to have much time as yet for the conversion of the Gentile world, even in and around Palestine itself. But already among the body of men known as proselytes, Gentile adherents, that is, of the Jewish religion, there was growing up a nucleus of faithful Christians; the seven deacons who were appointed to help the apostles in the organization of the Church had all of them Gentile names, and probably Gentile sympathies. And one of them was distinguished above the rest for the fearlessness with which he argued against the old Jewish prejudices and brought the claims of the Gentiles forward—that man was St Stephen. In him the Gentiles must have felt that they had a formidable

---

[1] This sermon was preached at Westminster Cathedral on the Feast of the Commemoration of St Paul, 30 June 1930, at a Mass offered for the Converts' Aid Society.

champion; able to meet the Jewish theologians on their own ground and prove to them from their own Scriptures that the salvation which Christ brought into the world was not for the Jews only but for their Gentile neighbours as well. And then there was an acrimonious debate between this champion of theirs and the Jewish theologians; there was a cry of "Blasphemy!", a hurried pretence of judicial procedure, and in an evil moment mob law got the upper hand. St Stephen was dragged out and stoned to death. So soon, so tragically, the first voice of Gentile Christianity was silenced.

It is not difficult to imagine what despair the Gentile Christians must have felt. "Where shall we find another", they will have said to themselves, "who will plead our cause so eloquently? The twelve apostles, indeed, have power to stir men's hearts by their preaching; through their means, we simple folk are being drawn to the worship of the Crucified. But they are, as the world goes, unlearned and ignorant men; the chief priests and the rulers of the people, the Pharisees and doctors of the law, are not impressed by any arguments such as they can bring forward. And the result is a relentless persecution which is undoing all the good work of the last two years. Christians are being hauled off to prison and even to death, or escaping from such perils by taking refuge in foreign countries. Where shall we find another apologist like Stephen to make the world of intellect and of fashion respect us? Where shall we find a Christian controversialist who will be able to stand up and refute the learned argument of this rising Jewish theologian they call Saul of Tarsus? Here is a man steeped in the tradition of the Scriptures; a man who has been to a foreign university and learned the wider outlook of the Greeks, their quickness in debate; and what does he make of our Gospel? What does Jesus of Nazareth, or the cross, mean to Saul of Tarsus? Everywhere he persecutes the name of Christ. Who can be found to meet him on his own level, answer him in his own coin?"

So the Christians of the day must have argued, and divine Providence in a moment made all their speculations look foolish. Who, they were asking, is to controvert the bitter anti-Christian logic of Saul of Tarsus? And divine Providence answered, Why, Saul of Tarsus! All these elaborate sophistries which Saul of Tarsus has discovered in order to excuse the inexcusable conduct of the Jews towards Incarnate God— Saul of Tarsus will expose them. All these ingenious calumnies, which Saul of Tarsus has circulated in order to explain away the evident fact of Christ's Resurrection—Saul of Tarsus will refute them. All this long catena of texts which Saul of Tarsus has collected from the Old

Testament to show that the Jews, and the Jews only, are to be the inheritors of the divine promises—Saul of Tarsus will answer them. In the full flush of his zeal for the cause which he had persuaded himself to think was the cause of God, Saul of Tarsus set out on a journey to Damascus; his object, to persecute and imprison whatever Christians he might find there; his passport, a warrant from the high priest. He exults to feel the even pace of his horse as it moves under the saddle, tracking down relentlessly the enemies of his religion. The sun, that stands high in the heavens, seems to him a parable of that lucid clearness ... convictions, the force of his ... walls of Damascus, power— ... something happens in a ... ndist is at an end. A light ... of that sun; he loses his ... him so near his destination. ... rd for thee to kick against ... ts new to him, or familiar? ... God, whom he has fanati- ... Voice of Jesus whom he has ... ew, surely, before he asked. ... It is not Stephen, whose ... or for their bloody act, not ... ly await their sentence, not ... w are hiding in fear at the ... u persecute. It is Jesus of ... It is his hands you are nail- ... wilt thou have me to do?" ... ecutor is led away captive; ... tchdog of the fold he once

POPE JOHN XXIII
November 25, 1881
June 3, 1963

"O God, in your ineffable providence you chose your servant John as supreme pontiff. Grant that he who ruled on earth as the vicar of your only-begotten Son, may be admitted into the company of your holy Popes forever. Through the same Jesus Christ, our Lord."

... own the suddenness of this ... rse on the road to Damascus ... ss of conversion. Ever since ... ver since he saw that head ... voice that prayed for the ... has been at work; he has ... of the Christians and their ... the voice of conscience that ... Well, all that makes a very

touching story, but, you know, there's no sort of authority for it in any of St Paul's writings or utterances. No, he was at the time, he tells us, "exceedingly mad against the Church"; he was in the heyday of his pride and his fancied conviction. The conversion which he experienced was a complete conversion; the direction of his thought boxed the compass all in a moment. Oh, I grant you, he was in bad faith really; he knew behind it all that what he was doing was wrong, when he persecuted the saints. God help us all, how easily we men deceive ourselves, how easily we persuade ourselves, when we act against conscience, that we are doing God service! But being in bad faith about the course you are pursuing doesn't necessarily mean that your conscience is working, that you are being gradually drawn towards the truth. Unless God's grace interferes, you may go on sinning against the light, and die in your sins. Not as the result of any train of thought already at work in his mind, not as the reward of any aptitude he had shown for receiving divine illumination, was that vision vouchsafed to St Paul on the Damascus road. Grace came, as first grace always comes, unmerited and unsought.

God will not be beholden to us, his creatures, for the accomplishment of his designs. It is as if he deliberately avoided making the choice which human preferences would have approved or human calculations indicated. Ask any Christian of that time who was the last man in the world likely to be brought under the influence of the Gospel, and he would have said unhesitatingly, "Saul of Tarsus". And it is Saul of Tarsus whom God chooses. He is a vessel of election unto me—a vessel of election, that is, a chosen vessel; but why a vessel? St Paul himself gives us the answer to the problem, in his Epistle to the Romans, where he tells us that the vessel in the potter's hands has no right to say to the potter, "Why hast thou made me thus?" The potter may, at his discretion, make one vessel to honour and another to dishonour. So almighty God will rule our destinies in his own way, not abiding our question, not accepting our excuses. A *vessel* of election, clay in the potter's hands; that is how saints are made.

That is how saints are made, and that is how converts are made. I hope I shall not be understood as suggesting that every convert who is brought into the Church is just the precise man who was [required] at that moment, to meet, in some important particular, the needs of that moment. On the contrary, one is sometimes tempted to wonder why God saw any use in making this or that particular convert at all. I know one case like that, anyhow. No, my point is that God's election is free, and for that reason must always be, to our human calculations, unforeseeable. If we converts are ever inclined to think too well of ourselves, let us turn away from that inglorious entry of St Paul into

Damascus, and think instead of our Lord's triumphal entry into Jerusalem. Do you remember how he sent forward two of his disciples to
loose the ass for him; and how, if anybody asked why they were loos-
ing it, they were to reply simply, "The Lord hath need of him"? That
is more like the explanation how some of us came into the Church;
the Lord had need of us; why, we cannot think. When we are doing
our best to help some doubting spirit into the Church, it sometimes
happens that Anglican friends will say to us, "Why worry about So-
and-so? Surely he is much better off where he is; surely he can't be
very much use to you"—as if we only made converts because we saw
that in some way they would be useful. But our answer is the same
answer which the apostles were told to make when they loosed the
ass, "The Lord hath need of him". We don't know why; we can't
think why, but the Lord hath need of him.

That is how we come aboard the ark of salvation, we converts, not
a picked crew, but a set of stowaways, shanghaied, here and there, by
the grace of God, not of great importance, not of much use to anybody,
but not through our own choosing. And there are some among us who
are worse off still; who seem to lose, through the force of circumstances,
such usefulness as we had; ministers of religion who can no longer be
ministers of religion, in the new surroundings to which God has called
them. No use blaming *them* for not providing against such a contin-
gency; you cannot provide against the act of God, and what is an act
of God, if conversion isn't? No use telling us that these are not the
converts we ought to have made; it was none of our doing—the Lord
had need of them. That means, that an abnormal situation arises.
Where an abnormal situation arises, you can only meet it by abnormal
expedients. And the Converts' Aid Society is an abnormal expedient.

I say "abnormal" in the sense that there is no need for such an
institution in other countries. Not in the sense that the need of it
exists only for the moment; that we shall be able to say in twenty
years' time, or in fifty years' time, that it has done its work. On the
contrary, the conditions which called it into existence will intensify,
must intensify, as the years go on; and in the meantime our converts
from the ministry will be more than ever in need of help, owing to the
difficulty of saving, in these times, on a clerical income. In this next
month, those who enjoy authority in the Church of England will be
concerned with fateful decisions.[1] What will be their ultimate issue, we
cannot foresee; but it is difficult not to believe that there will be a
backwash of conversions, which will mean more work for the Society

[1] The Lambeth Conference, held in July 1930.

and more need of funds. Let us ask the prayers of our blessed Lady and of St Paul, the patron of conversion, that this next year may see the funds of the Society taxed to their utmost, the nets full so that the ship begins to sink; and then, that the generosity of Catholics will rise to that opportunity, and shoulder that burden, as God may ask of us in his good pleasure.

7

EGO SUM[1]

I am.—Exodus 3. 14.

THOSE are two simple words I have taken for my text; but they are not for that reason words whose import is to be despised, whose meaning is to be lightly taken for granted. So at least the Jewish people thought, to whom those two words were a title of divinity; and we Christians value them yet more, because our Lord, speaking with the language of the Jews, used them of himself on five separate occasions, and on each occasion, unless I am being unduly fanciful, there was something of challenge in his utterance; I think he was, by the use of that simple formula, inviting an act of faith. Sometimes our Bible renders "It is I", sometimes "I am he", but always whether in the Greek or in the Latin the words are the same, *ego sum*, I am.

He used them when he sat by the well of Samaria, tired out with travelling, reduced to asking from a stranger the gift of a cup of water; she mentions the Messias, and he takes her up at once, *Ego sum*, I am he. He used them when he came to the disciples walking on the waters of the lake, and they cried out in terror, thinking that it was some unreal phantom which mocked their sight; unreal? Rather here is the source of all reality, *Ego sum*, It is I. He used them when the band of temple officers came to arrest him in the Garden of Gethsemani; they told him they were seeking Jesus of Nazareth, and they went backwards and fell to the ground, overawed by the majesty with which he replied, *Ego sum*, I am he. He used them before the tribunal

[1] This sermon was preached at the Pontifical High Mass sung by the Bishop of Northampton at the Church of Our Lady and the English Martyrs, Cambridge, on Sunday, 27 July 1930, at the opening of a Summer School of Catholic Studies.

of the high priest, when he was adjured in the name of the living God
to say whether he were the Christ, the Son of the living God, or no;
he passed his own sentence of condemnation when he answered,
Ego sum, I am.

The blasphemy, so the Jews thought it, the irony and the mystery,
so we Christians see it, of those words defiantly repeated on the lips
of a Galilean peasant, must be sought in the passage from which my
text is taken, the passage where God reveals himself to Moses in the
burning bush, the bush that burns but is not consumed. The tireless
energy of that portent was witness to them of God's nature, his un-
changing, unfading, effortless power. Let me remind you a little of the
circumstances. The Jews had settled down long since in the land of
Egypt, honoured guests at first with the best pasture land in the whole
country for their domain. And then a new dynasty had arisen, and all
the popularity of the Jewish people was gone; their jealous neighbours
turned against them, and made them into slaves. Under cruel task-
masters, doomed to eternal subjection if not to actual extermination,
they were beginning to lose (and no wonder) the proud hopes which
they had cherished as being the heirs of Abraham, Isaac, and Jacob.
What use to remind them that they were to inherit a blessing above all
the nations of the earth, as they plied their hated task and dragged their
interminable loads, making bricks to serve the architectural whim of
their conquerors? They knew, indeed, that the God whom they
worshipped had been the God of their forefathers, and, if only out of
national pride, they professed his service still. But he could do little, it
seemed, in defence of his own servants now. All around them they saw
the symbols of idolatrous worship, monstrous shapes of bird and beast,
the false gods of their heathen neighbours. Likely enough that in their
despair they may have gone some way towards making terms with
these unfamiliar powers, accustomed themselves to joining in the
religious ceremonies of the country. At no time, probably, in the history
of their race can it have seemed more likely that the worship of the
one true God would lose its last witness and pass from human memory
altogether.

Such was the position of the Israelites when Moses was born; such
was the servitude in which they were resolved to persist, even when
Moses tried to rally their national sentiment and lead them forth into
liberty. Like so many misunderstood patriots, he was forced to fly
for his life and take refuge in a foreign country. He married the
daughter of a Madianite chief, and fed, on the lonely slopes of Mount
Sinai in Arabia, the flocks of his father-in-law.

On those lonely slopes, remote from the jarring life of the court in which he had been nurtured, communing with himself under the pitiless sun and amid the spacious silences of the desert, Moses passed, like our Lord himself at the beginning of his ministry, like St Paul after his conversion, a period of spiritual retreat. If only he could bring out his degraded fellow countrymen into these pure airs of the wilderness, away from the stifling atmosphere of pagan Egypt, how much more chance there would be of turning back their hearts to the God of their fathers! Such, perhaps, is his thought, when one day he is interrupted by a sight strange to that wilderness, a fire in the shrub. He goes nearer to it, and knows it at last for the supernatural thing it is—sees in amazement, and approaches with reverence, the bush that burns yet is not consumed by burning, the symbol of that pure Act, which is God.

So his vocation comes to him; he is to go back to Egypt, and appeal to his fellow countrymen once more. But this time, he is fortified with a special message; God will reveal himself under a new Name. We know how a name can be a mark of intimacy, how calling a friend by a Christian name or even a nickname can be a definite step forward in the history of our acquaintance. And when almighty God sees fit to reveal himself by a new Name, it means that he will enter into a special relation with the people so privileged; he invites them to a certain familiarity of friendship; they are to be his people, he is to be their God. And the Name itself will be a jealously guarded secret; who is there that has ever loved, that does not know what it is to treasure a name as his own personal secret? So, from that day onward, almighty God was to the Jews something more than the God of Abraham and Isaac and Jacob. He was to be known now by the sacred Name which he had chosen for himself. We will not pursue the scholars into their exact researches over the meaning and the origin of it; enough to say that to the Hebrews as a matter of history it had this simplest of all possible meanings: I am, *ego sum*.

I AM—the gods of the heathen, what are they? The genealogy by which they are connected, the stories of their birth, may be multitudinous and exact. The images by which they are represented may be awful to the imagination through long centuries of reverential tradition. Their influence on men's minds may be powerful; in their names the juggling magic of the East may profess to exercise occult powers. But what are they? They are not. Only foolish dreams, that have gained credence through man's love of the mysterious. Only abstract notions which popular religion has falsely credited with existence. Only superstitious echoes of common things—sun and rain and harvest and the other processes of nature that affect, daily and intimately, the life of man. Their temples rise gorgeous over the cities; worshippers throng their courts; countless victims are immolated at their altars. But there is one word that must be added—they do not exist.

I AM—there is no past and no future in my timeless existence. The old days when I walked with Abraham and Isaac and Jacob may seem very far away now, dim and legendary, but I am still the same God. You, my people, have experienced great vicissitudes of fortune; once masters in the land of Egypt, you are now its slaves; the greatness of your history is a dead and almost forgotten greatness, seven times have passed over you; but I am the same God. The promises which I now make to you are not for today or tomorrow, it is not you or your children or your children's children that will see the fulfilment of them, but they will come to pass long years hence; I am, then as now, the same God. Behind the age-long riddle of man's birth and death lies the promise and the terror of my timeless Being.

I AM—the Christian philosophy of later ages has read in those words a further message. God alone IS; that is to say, he alone exists in his own right and of his own nature; we, all created beings, exist only as dependent on him, depend on him from moment to moment for our existence. As the images of the dream you dreamt last night existed only in dependence on you, the dreamer, so you and I and all created things have only a contingent existence, depend on God. He is Being itself; in him the act of being and that which he is are one; essence and existence cannot be distinguished in the indivisible simplicity of his nature. And did we say that there was not much of a sermon to be made out of the two words, I AM?

For the Jews, the great lesson of this apparition on Sinai, a lesson hardly learned through a long history of rebellions, tribulations, and repentances, was the uniqueness of the True God. He was not to be thought of as one tribal God among other tribal gods, defending his own people because there were his own people, unconcerned with the fortunes of any other nation than theirs. He alone had real existence; the others were only shadows. He was present everywhere; they did not, as heathen tribes would, exchange one theology for another when they passed from the fertile valleys of the Nile into the barren spaces of the wilderness, or from the wilderness again into the plenty of the promised land. He was omnipotent; he controlled, not the destinies of a tribe, but the destinies of a universe. He was all-righteous; there could be no blindness in his justice; he was unchangeable, there could be no faithlessness in his promises. But above all, he was unique in his majesty, no created thing could contain him, or even represent him; nothing less than himself could ever share with him the honours of human worship. For twelve centuries, that was to be the theological lesson of mankind.

In our day, however far they may travel from the Christian tradition, men do not fall, like their forefathers, into a habit of idolatry. They no longer think of divine influences as limited to one particular spot or to one particular function; they do not need, accordingly, to conceive a whole pantheon of rival deities, like the old generation of pagans. Whatever else it has done, the Christian revelation has left this mark on the world—it has left men convinced that if there is a divine Being at all, he is one and unique; the many gods of antiquity are a nursery toy of the world's childhood, which the world has put away. But there is a new kind of paganism springing up, in these days when men turn away contemptuously from the contradictory utterances of so many rival pulpits, and fashion a God for themselves after their own imaginations. The danger, now, is not polytheism but pantheism. Men will agree with us that God exists, will agree with us that he is one; but when we examine their meaning more closely we find that they do not think of him as almighty, as existing before all worlds and independent of all other existence besides himself. Rather, they will tell you that as the body of man and the soul of man form one single being, so God and the universe form one single being; God is the soul, and the universe the body; it is no more possible to think of God as existing without the universe than to think of the universe as existing without God. That is the modern blasphemy we have to encounter.

And we encounter it still by the revelation made to Moses, the revelation of the bush which burned and was not consumed. The Church encourages us to see in that portent a type of our Lady, giving birth to a Son without losing her virginity; it is natural and right that we should do so. But surely we may also find a type, there, of almighty God himself, and of his dealings with creation. As the bush in the wilderness fed the fire continually, yet never lost anything of its own substance in doing so, no branch scorched, no leaf shrivelled, so God gives life to his Creation without losing anything of himself, without exerting energy, without abandoning, for a moment, the eternal changelessness of his being. I AM—he is all reality, not a part of reality; he gives existence to all things, derives his existence from nothing, depends for his existence on nothing, outside himself.

Some of you will be attending, this week, the Summer School of Studies, which this year is taking no less a subject for its considerations than God himself. Let me counsel you to remember the warning which Moses received when he approached the burning bush, "Loose thy shoes from off thy feet, for the place whereon thou standest is holy". Much that we know about God's nature, the fact for example that there are three Persons in one God, we know only by revelation; it is self-evidently a mystery. But even what our own intellects can learn about God through philosophical reasoning plunges us into mystery too; we can affirm, we must affirm, but the intellect which affirms cannot gauge the content, cannot plumb the depths, of its own affirmations. Let us approach, then, in the spirit of Moses; ready to learn, yet ready to admit that what we learn is what we shall never fully understand in this life; we are like men staring at the sun. May God of his mercy enlighten our minds and humble our hearts, and give us grace to worship him, as he seeks to be worshipped, in spirit and in truth.

8

REUNION[1]

If it be possible, as much as lies in you, have peace with all men.—Romans 12. 18.

IT is one of the compensations of growing older, that we achieve the experience of having lived through a slice of history; of being able to compare, with the knowledge only possible to an eye-witness, things past with things present. Only, of course, on a very small scale; even the centenarian who is interviewed by the newspapers nowadays cannot remember the time when there were no railways—his mind cannot really travel back very far into the past. And there are times (like our own) when history seems to speed up, when great changes seem to take place within the compass of a very few years; and those who live in such times can achieve the experience which I speak of even in middle life. One of the favourite forms which our habit of historical reminiscence takes is this, to ask ourselves the question, Who would have thought, so many years ago, that such and such things would come to happen, which we see happening now?

There are all sorts of things happening now, which nobody would

[1] This sermon was preached in 1931.

have been likely to anticipate ten, still less twenty years ago. I was trying to indicate some of them this morning. But tonight I only want to allude to one aspect of the moment in which we are living, its personal aspect. If you take a glance for a moment at the names of the men who are now prominent in public life, you will find the topsy-turvy situation of today mirrored in their personalities. If your mind can travel back for thirty years, and remember the days when Mr Joseph Chamberlain launched his proposals for revising the fiscal system of the country; remember the storm of Liberal and Labour opposition which that suggestion aroused, in many parts of England but above all in Lancashire, would you have thought it possible that, in thirty years time, a man like Mr Philip Snowden would be holding office in a Government which is considering the question of protective tariffs? Or, if your memory is shorter, and only goes back say fifteen years, to the time of the Great War, put the question in this way: who would have believed it if he had been told, in 1916, that fifteen years from that date Mr Ramsay MacDonald would be at the head of a Government in which Conservatives and Liberals were co-operating with the utmost loyalty; that he would be being hailed, from one side, as a man who knows how to put country before party; that he would be being criticized, from the other side, as a man who lets down the workers to suit the convenience of the bankers? We have lived to see that happen; and the very natural consideration which is thereby suggested is that prophecy is uncommonly dangerous work. It is dangerous work to say that such and such a thing is impossible, when you cannot look into the future and see the altered conditions which the future will bring.

Now, one of the things which plenty of people would have called impossible, say thirty years ago, was the reunion of the various Christian bodies, whether in England or in the world at large. I suppose it was about that time that the present Bishop of London went out on some kind of state visit to Russia, and I remember his being reported as saying, when he came back, that it was impossible there should ever be any reunion between Anglicans and the Eastern Church until the Eastern Church had had a reformation. And at the same time, feeling was running high between Anglicans and Nonconformists over the question of the schools. Prominent Nonconformists refused to pay their rates because of the Balfour Act, and prominent Churchmen threatened to do the same if Mr Birrell's bill should ever become law. It seemed quite impossible there should ever be any good understanding, let alone any suggestion of co-operation, between the two parties.

Once more, our prophecies have not been justified. At the present moment, Anglican dignitaries are busily discussing terms of mutual recognition with the representatives of the schismatic Eastern Church; and at the same time the Archbishop of Canterbury has invited the Council of Evangelical Free Churches to re-open friendly conversations in something of the same sense. So much for historical impossibilities.

Circumstances, we say, alter cases. What are the circumstances that have altered the case, so as to make it possible for the three great political parties to merge into a National Government? It was a financial situation which threatened a depreciation of our currency. Unless we were prepared to unite, and balance the next budget, so we were told, the pound sterling would drop. It would still look the same, be printed by the same people, carry the same nominal purchasing power, but its value would be something different; you have only to go across the Channel now to be unpleasantly reminded of that. And the leaders of the late Government decided, rightly or wrongly—I am not here to talk politics—that in the face of an emergency like that they must get together; even if it meant the apparent sacrifice of principles which had always been held inviolable by the party to which they belonged. Better, they thought, the sacrifice of certain principles which divided them from other parties, than a depreciation of the currency which would bring dismay to all British citizens, whatever their party colour might be.

And I think you may say that the better understanding between Christians, the movement for reunion both at home and abroad which has lately become so prominent, has been in the same way dictated by a threatened emergency; and the threat is one which you may describe as a depreciation of the currency. Only this time a depreciation of the moral currency; the threat was not to the gold standard, but to those moral standards which are, and ought ever to be considered, more enduring than gold itself. After all, wrap up the facts as we may, England during the present century has been travelling very fast towards paganism. Even a merely outside observer, if he had been abroad for the last thirty years and came back to British shores nowadays, could see symptoms of that change, not so important perhaps in themselves as for what they pointed to. Let me suggest one small instance. Less than thirty years ago I remember staying at a place in Scotland close to a local branch of the railway. And on that branch it is a fact—I have seen it myself—that the signalman, when he left his cabin on Saturday night, put down the signal for the first train on Monday

H

morning. All through Sunday it remained down; so confident was Presbyterian Scotland that not even a belated goods train could possibly want to make its way along that line on the sabbath. The other day, waiting at a station in Scotland, waiting for a Sunday train, I am afraid, I saw an excursion train full to bursting with trippers, who may possibly have been to kirk in the morning, but were certainly making up for it in the afternoon. Now, I do not suppose that all that will sound very reprehensible in Catholic ears. I am only pointing out that there has been a change of values. We still talk about Sunday as a day of rest, but we do not mean the same thing when we use the same term. And it is hardly necessary to point out that in other directions, which to us at least seem very much more important, there has been within recent years a wholesale depreciation of the moral currency.

We still talk about decency, and we mean in general the same thing by decency that we meant thirty years ago. But it would be idle to pretend that our standards of decency have not changed during that time, and when you think of some of the books that are published and some of the entertainments that are provided nowadays, it is affectation to pretend that they have not changed for the worse. We still celebrate a marriage with all the old formalities, the bridesmaids and the orange-blossom and the wedding-cake and the confetti and all the rest of it, but isn't it true that a great many of our fellow countrymen do not really mean what they used to mean when they enter upon that holy contract? They used to mean what they said, when they uttered the words "till death do us part"; now, those words have become for many people a mere legal formality, and marriage is hardly looked upon as more than an experiment. The same symbols, but a different interpretation is being put on them; that is what I mean by a depreciation of the moral currency.

Now, with England threatening to go Pagan, it is no wonder that we find Christians in England determined to get together, in the hope of resisting that peril. And it is no wonder that they are prepared to think of making sacrifices with a view to closer union, which would have been regarded by most people some time back, and would still be regarded by many, as sacrifices of principle. Meanwhile, at the other end of things there is, as I say, a movement for closer union with those Eastern Churches which were once in communion with Rome, but have been separated from her now for many centuries. The need for such reunion is not so apparent at first sight. For, after all, the spheres of Anglicanism and Greek orthodoxy do not really touch; there is no country in which both bodies are considerably represented. But here, too, I think you will find that circumstances have altered cases. England, ever since the war, has been growing less insular and more European. I can still remember a leading article in one of the London newspapers during the war, which roundly declared that England would never have anything to do with a League of Nations in which foreigners were in the majority. A delightful use of the word "foreigners", but it has come for all that; and now that we see how closely our own financial stability is bound up with the financial conditions of Europe, it is probable that we shall cling to our insularity less than ever in future. And, in waking up to take more interest in Continental affairs, we have become conscious that the religion practised by these foreigners has a meaning and an importance for ourselves. A few years back, if religion was being attacked in some Continental country, as for example in Portugal immediately after the revolution there, we did not pay much attention; it was only these foreigners who were concerned, and Roman Catholics at that. If the Turks massacred thousands of Christian Armenians, we were very sorry of course, but after all it was only in Armenia; and we felt vaguely that Armenian religion was something as distant from our own as that of the Mussulmans themselves. But since the Russian revolution all that has changed. English people have begun to realize that there are forces at work on the Continent which are not merely hostile to the Pope, not merely concerned to wipe out a few pockets of obsolete and corrupt Christianity. We know now that there are really people who hate the Christian name, and are prepared to do battle against religion of any kind.

So, once again, there is a movement for getting together. And, because any hopes of reunion with the Church of the Papacy must needs be distant, even if they were entertained at all, the Anglicans have turned to the so-called Orthodox Christians of the East, and are trying to plan out, in common with them, terms of mutual recognition. We might well be surprised, that it should be possible for one religious body to hold out its hands in both directions at once. On one side you have the Nonconformists, with their dislike of sacerdotalism, of theological niceties, of antiquated ceremonies; on the other side, the Orthodox with their insistence on the hierarchy, their inherited loyalty to party in disputes which date centuries back, and the complicated formalism of their worship. Indeed, many sincere Christians feel that no good can come of these two contradictory gestures; and that if things go too far the result is more likely to be a split in the Church of England, than a healing of differences with those outside.

But others, more sanguine, delight in the apparent inconsistency, and claim that the place of Anglicanism in the designs of Providence is now evident. It has been permitted, they say, to hold together in spite of the large differences of opinion which divide its members, precisely for this purpose, that it should act as a bridge between the old Christianities of the East and the new Christianities of the West. A bridge; that is the metaphor they commonly use, and it is obviously an appropriate one. Only, even if you assume that both sets of negotiations are completely successful, and that Anglicanism can devise terms of reunion with the Nonconformists and with the Easterns at one and the same time, it will be a bridge, unfortunately, still in the making. For it will be a bridge with an arch missing at both ends, and the value of such a bridge can only lie in its hopes for the future.

At one end, you see, there is this distressing fact—that the Nonconformists nowadays are not, any more than the Anglicans, in any effective touch with the great bulk of our fellow countrymen, even with those who still say that they believe in God, and do not disown the title of Christian. It is common, I fancy, for Continental observers who are interested in reunion schemes to imagine that, if they found themselves in alliance with the Anglicans and with the English Nonconformists, they would have practically the whole of England united on their side. Unfortunately that is very far from being the truth. I doubt if the effective numbers of all the non-Catholic denominations in England put together amount to a sixth of the population. Behind that you have a mass of people still nominally Christian, wanting to be married and buried with religious rites, and often bringing their children to be baptized, who do not trouble to go to church, who do not hold with organized religion, who see no need for the existence of a clergy, or of sacraments, or of creeds. In these last days Nonconformity has done its best to satisfy their demands, offering all it could in the way of fellowship and attractive services and undogmatic teaching; but the appeal falls on deaf ears for the most part. The chapels in our day, no less than the churches, afflict the ordinary Englishman with a sense of constraint and artificiality; he can worship God better, he says, by hiking over the moors. At that end, then, the bridge is broken; it does not touch the bedrock of the population at all.

And the other end? At the other end, too, the bridge is broken. The Catholic Church stands aloof, as she has always stood aloof, from every movement which threatens to sacrifice the unity of Christian truth for the sake of peace and good fellowship. If the Anglicans were restored to full communion with the Orthodox Christians of the East tomorrow, and if, through that alliance, their ministry recovered the validity of orders which it lost at the Reformation, they would still be no nearer to reunion with the Catholic Church. Now, why is that? What is it that dictates this exclusive attitude—so our critics call it—to the authorities of the Catholic Church?

Many non-Catholics believe, others have persuaded themselves to believe, that such reunion will come in the course of time. "You tell us it is impossible", they say, "but impossibilities, historical impossibilities, are always happening, as you told us just now. And the reason (they say) why you Catholics are so unsympathetic in England at present is because, at present, you are winning. You are making your twelve thousand converts a year; your numbers are increasing, while ours are diminishing, your priests are multiplying, while we can hardly keep our parishes staffed, you are building new churches and schools, while we are selling the old ones. And because for the moment you are in a winning position, you can afford to despise our overtures. But, if times change and things go against you, we shall hear of reunion from your side, too."

But you know, it isn't that. As God sees us, it isn't that. If you or I were the last Catholic left in England, it would still be impossible for you or me to make terms with Anglicanism, or with any other Christian body. If we did not believe that, we would open negotiations to-morrow. But for us there is a fatal obstacle. All this talk about reunion assumes, necessarily, that the one Church which Christ founded on earth has, in process of time, been split into a set of fragments—the Easterns, the Anglicans, the Wesleyans, and so on. Each of these will have preserved some part of Christian truth, some more than others. But since it is impossible now to determine which was right in the old dead controversies, we ought to sink our differences as far as possible (it is argued) and remake the Church out of its fragments once more. To us Catholics such language is meaningless; we have not so learned Christ. For us, the Church is nothing less than his Temple, his Bride, his own Body; and the idea that it could, by any conceivable historical circumstances, be split into fragments, is a blasphemy. The reunion of the Churches is to us not merely impossible, it is unthinkable. You cannot reunite what has never been divided. For the Catholic Church to take part in a reunion of the Churches would be a paradox, a contradiction in terms.

For that reason, and not for any other, we stand outside the reunion movement. And I have ventured to take my text from St Paul's exhortation to the Romans, to live peaceably with all men if it was possible, as much as lay in them, because I think we need to remind ourselves sometimes that we ought to be very careful to show charity towards non-Catholics. If we are always sneering at them, always making light of the good they do, always seeking a quarrel against them, we shall give them a wrong impression about our attitude towards reunion. We shall make them think it is because we are proud, because we are prejudiced, because we have not forgotten the persecutions, that we will have nothing to do with them. And that means disedifying our neighbours, and delaying the conversion of England. If it be possible, as much as lies in you—it is not always possible to be at peace with our non-Catholic neighbours. But where their own attitude makes it possible, let us sympathize with their difficulties, let us give them credit for good intentions. By doing that, we shall perhaps help forward more than we know the day when Christians will really be reunited in obedience to the Holy See, and the martyrs will come to their own, and England will be our Lady's Dowry once again.

9

RUIN AND RESURRECTION[1]

Amen I say to you, unless the grain of wheat falling into the ground die, itself remaineth alone; but if it die, it bringeth forth much fruit.—John 12. 24.

TODAY, 1,900 years ago, it looked as if the fortunes of the great Galilean Prophet, Jesus of Nazareth, were at their height. It was the time of the feast; a great multitude of people from Galilee had come up to celebrate it, and these, plainly, were proud of their fellow countryman. At home, where his family was known to many of them, they might criticize him and laugh at his pretensions; but here in Judaea it was a different thing; they were not going to have their own Prophet laughed at by the Jews of Judaea. That is human nature. And then, just a day or two before Palm Sunday, an extraordinary rumour went round Jerusalem itself. A man of Bethany, a well-known figure there, had died and been buried; and when he had already been four days in the tomb, Jesus of Nazareth had called to him and he had come

---

[1] This sermon was preached at St Catherine's, Birmingham, on Palm Sunday, 25 March 1934, and was an appeal for funds for the reconstruction of St George's, Dorridge and Knowle, recently destroyed by fire.

out alive. Bethany was only about two miles from Jerusalem; it was as if you heard that somebody had been raised from the dead, say, at Harborne. Naturally, crowds of people came out from Jerusalem to look at the man who had been buried and come to life again; to question his sisters, and have their own assurance about the facts. And these, convinced by what they saw and heard, were hardly less enthusiastic on behalf of the Prophet than the Galileans themselves.

The result was a kind of public demonstration. Word got round that he would be coming into Jerusalem on the first day of the week; they lined the roads, prepared to shout "Hosanna" in his path. And he seemed, curiously, to welcome this demonstration rather than otherwise; he came, though the distance was so short, riding on an ass; and so deliberately reminded them of an old prophecy which said that a King would come into Jerusalem so mounted. At that, their enthusiasm passed all bounds; they climbed up the trees, and cut down palm-branches to spread them in the way; others, not to be outdone, took off their coats and made a carpet of them. Hosanna, they cried, blessed is he that cometh in the name of the Lord, the King of Israel! You would have said, wouldn't you, that now the career of the Galilean Prophet was at its very zenith. Who could tell what might happen? The Roman Emperor was far away, a recluse, hated by his subjects. The Roman governor in Judaea itself had made himself profoundly unpopular. Was this not the opportunity for the multitudes to shake off the Roman yoke altogether, and proclaim a kingdom with the Son of David at its head? So at least the Pharisees feared; it was the only excuse they found for silencing their own guilty consciences, that this Jesus of Nazareth was a dangerous pretender, who would get them into political trouble; and then, they argued, the Romans would come and take away their place and nation. Which, they asked, was more valuable—the life of one man, or the existence of the Jewish people? Why, already the very Gentiles were beginning to be impressed by these tales of miracle; and a deputation of them had asked for an audience with the Prophet as if they, too, were ready to attach themselves to his cause! It was expedient that one man should die, rather than that the whole nation should perish.

And he? What does he make of it all? When this last evidence of his popularity is brought to his notice, does he go out and make a speech to them? Does he begin to appoint lieutenants, and form plans of campaign for the deliverance of his people? No, his comment is a sad one, and a mysterious one. "Unless the grain of wheat falling into the ground die, itself remaineth alone; but if it die, it bringeth forth much fruit." He is speaking—who can doubt of it?—in the first instance about himself. He is the grain of wheat, that is to be buried in the ground when his mangled and crucified body is committed to the sepulchre. He is to be buried in a garden, in the first days of spring:

> Here's an acre sown indeed
> With the richest, royallest Seed
> That the earth did e'er suck in
> Since the first man died for sin.[1]

And his Resurrection is to be a harvest, a world-wide harvest of human souls, ransomed by him and raised into supernatural life. He knows that success must come through failure, triumph through suffering; he knows that the royal progress which befits Incarnate God is not this pageant of popular welcome, but that *via dolorosa* which he is to tread five days later, with his enemies reviling him and the crowds jeering at him. "I, if I be lifted up, will draw all men to me"; if I be lifted up, not upon a throne, but upon a cross. He thinks of that mysterious harvest of the Holy Eucharist, in which his natural body, in which he took flesh from his blessed Mother, is to be reproduced in all the myriad hosts of the world, to be the spiritual food of Christians, imparting life to them through its own death. "Our Lord", says St Ambrose, "was himself the grain that was to be mortified and to be multiplied; mortified by the infidelity of the Jews, multiplied by the faith of the Gentile peoples."

But I wonder—when he spoke those words, wasn't he thinking of something else as well? Wasn't he thinking, perhaps, of Jerusalem, his own city, so faithless and so beloved; that had but now welcomed him in triumph, and was so soon to reject him? It was natural that he should be thinking about Jerusalem just then. He was revisiting it after an interval, at the risk of his life, for the great festival. He had approached it, that day, from the east, where you get, they say, the perfect view of it; had seen its walls and the roofs of the temple gilded with the spring sunshine—had seen it, and had wept over it. "If thou hadst known, in this thy day, the things that are to thy peace! But now they are hidden from thy eyes. For the days shall come when thy enemies shall cast a trench about thee, and beat thee flat to the ground, and shall not leave in thee a stone upon a stone." The Hosannas of the crowd were still echoing in his ears; shall we not suppose that he was still thinking of Jerusalem, when he spoke those words about the grain of wheat?

[1] Francis Beaumont, "On Westminster Abbey".

You see, he loved the city. Loved it with that divine love which his Incarnation mirrored on earth; "the Lord loveth the gates of Sion more than all the tabernacles of Jacob". Loved it, too, with a human love; for when he became man he would become complete man, sin only excepted; he would experience all the emotions which are proper to our nature—why, then, he too must have felt the thrill of patriotism; he must have known what it was to love places, because of the memories which they enshrined and the traditions which they preserved. Only, for him, that love was always clouded with sadness, because its memories for him were memories of benefits vainly bestowed; its tradition for him was one of ingratitude and rebellion. "Jerusalem, Jerusalem, thou that killest the prophets, and stonest them that are sent unto thee, how often would I have gathered thy children, as a hen gathereth her chickens under her wings, and thou wouldest not." He loved his own city, and dropped natural tears over its apostasy from his heavenly Father, and from himself.

And yet, knowing as he did that within the lifetime of his generation that city would be razed to the ground, he recognized and accepted its fall as part of God's purposes. "Except a grain of wheat fall into the ground and die, itself remaineth alone; but if it die, it bringeth forth much fruit"; so the destruction of that earthly Jerusalem was no loss in reality. Out of its ashes was to rise the heavenly Jerusalem; the Church of the Old Covenant was to be replaced by the Church of the New Covenant—the Catholic Church which he himself had come to found on earth. "Itself remaineth alone"—the city, perched up there on the hills which shielded it everywhere from attack, which seemed to keep every foreign influence at bay, was typical of that isolation in which the Jewish people lived, despising the Gentiles and keeping them at a distance, instead of asking whether God might not have a purpose for them too. "But that Jerusalem which is from above", says St Paul, "is free, which is the mother of us all." The Church of the Old Covenant, buried under the ruins of what had been till now God's holy city, was to rise again a glorious Church, not having spot or wrinkle or any such thing, ransomed with the blood of Christ.

This principle, that a death is needed as the gateway to a resurrection, is verified not only in our Lord's life but in the life of his saints. Above all, in that of the martyrs; my text is used by the Church as a special Gospel, for example, for the feast of St Laurence, the Roman deacon who was martyred just after Pope Xystus. From the earliest times, Christian people recognized that the blood of the martyrs was the seed of the Church. Their tombs, in those grim underground passages which

HX

you may still see at Rome, shot up above ground in a harvest of conversions and of repentances, procured by their intercession. Do we talk as if it were a thing of the past? Those relics of the catacombs still have power to work miracles above ground, as Europe knew a century ago, when St Philomena's body, the body of a saint whose life and legend were unknown, was discovered by what seemed an accident, and a fresh crop of divine favours sprang from her forgotten sepulchre. So, they say, the grains of wheat buried in the tombs of the old Egyptian kings can be sown afresh, after all those centuries of darkness and neglect, and grow into flourishing plants. Dead and buried, yet still alive; rather, still alive because they were dead and buried.

And if that principle is verified in the lives of the saints, it is verified also in the life of the ordinary Christian. Every Christian life will be fruitful for God, exactly in proportion as it has been crucified with Christ, and buried with him, and lives now with that risen life of his which is the seed of the supernatural. You will see it especially, perhaps, in the lives of the religious; the sacrifice which men and women have made in devoting themselves to the life of the cloister, the breaking of their wills under the hard discipline of the novitiate, produces in them noticeably, even to us others, a kind of serene purposefulness which effects more, achieves more, than all the bustling activity of the unsupernaturalized character. If any of you heard or came across that light of the Dominican Order, whose early death we English Catholics have been mourning this last week,[1] you will know what I mean. Father Bede Jarrett had natural gifts which would have marked him, I think, among his fellow men, whatever state of life he had embraced. And there must have been some who thought it a pity that one so talented should bury away his talents—so the world calls it—in the service of religion. But it was because it was buried away in religion that his life became so fruitful. The radiance—I know no other word for it—which those who met him even casually discerned in him was the effect, under God's grace, of a will beautifully mortified; it was the risen life shining through. And the great work which he achieved for his own Order and for the Church at large, the strong influence he had in so many lives, came from the same source; it was given to him to do a great deal in a short life, and a life which never seemed to be hurried, because, in St Paul's phrase, he was dead, and his life was hidden with Christ in God. May he rest in peace after all his labour for souls.

And notice, once more, that this principle holds good not only in

[1] Fr Bede Jarrett, o.p., died on 17 March 1934.

the life of individual Christians, but in the life of Christian institutions
as well. The Christian Covenant cannot, indeed, be revoked, like the
old Jewish Covenant, and replaced by something better; we have our
Lord's own promise that he will be with his Church to the end of time,
and the gates of hell shall not prevail against her. Yet even the Church
herself repeats through the ages, in a mystical sense, the history of her
divine Master; she lives through a hundred deaths, and a hundred
resurrections. She died under the persecutions, and rose again with
Constantine; she died under the barbarian invasions, and rose again
with Charlemagne; she died under the European apostasy of the sixteenth century, and rose again with the saints of the Counter-Reformation; she died with the French Revolution and the Napoleonic Wars,
she rose again with the Catholic reaction which followed on them.
"Still doomed to death, and fated not to die"—so wrote Dryden of the
Church in England two and a half centuries back; and do we doubt, as
we look around us today, that the prayers of our own martyrs have
won for us a resurrection of Catholic life in England, whose scope is not
achieved, whose vitality is not exhausted yet?

I stand before you to make an unusual appeal to your charity. The
districts of Knowle and Dorridge were served, till the other day, by a
church built during the war, and dedicated to our unknown warrior
saint, St George. It was a temporary church, built of wood; but, as is
common in such churches, the ornaments inside were valuable out of
proportion to the shell which enclosed them. There were Stations of
the Cross, such as you might have expected in a flourishing parish;
there was a shrine of St Philomena, whose name we were remembering
just now. A few weeks ago, a fire broke out during the night, and the
church was gutted, ornaments and all. The insurance money has sufficed
to pay off the debt; and the little congregation of Knowle and Dorridge,
some two hundred souls not much encumbered with worldly goods,
find themselves back again just where they were in 1917, hearing
Mass in a hotel and wondering where they are going to get a church
from.

I would like to see your faces if you came to St Catherine's one
Sunday morning, and found a blackened ruin here with a notice on it
to say that Mass was being said in the Grand Hotel. But remember,
these poor people at Knowle are in a worse position than you would
be; it is their own pinchings and savings for charity, these years past,
that they have seen go up in smoke during a single night. St Catherine's
stood here before most of you were born; those Knowle Catholics
love their church with a kind of motherly affection; it is the offering

they themselves have made to God. And now it is a burnt offering.[1]

Unless the grain of wheat falling into the ground die, itself remaineth alone; but if it die, it bringeth forth much fruit—why shouldn't that principle prove true, here too? Isn't it possible that this burial of their hopes which our brethren at Knowle are going through, the swallowing up in one night of all those little acts of self-denial which built the church for them, will bring them a harvest beyond their expectations? Will make it possible—that is their Rector's plan—to begin on a permanent church, once and for all? It is possible; but we've got to help to make it possible; that's why I'm standing here. Oh, I know it's all very irregular, to appeal to Catholics for help in building a church somewhere else; but it's the kind of help which, just because the thing is no concern of yours, wins you more gratitude on earth, more favour in heaven. Why, a contribution made by a big church like this to a small parish half out in the country like Knowle has the same effect as giving a stick of chocolate to a child; the benefit you confer is out of all proportion to the expense you incur. Help them to build a more fitting home for our Lord's Eucharistic presence than they have had hitherto; throw your garments in his path, in the spirit of Palm Sunday—that new jumper you were going to buy, which you don't really want. God will reward you for your charity; and St Philomena, who's done such great things and still does such great things for her clients all over the world, won't forget the people who helped to build her shrine afresh. Dead, buried, and risen again—let that be the boast of St George's, Dorridge, as it is the secret of all sanctity, as it always has been, and always will be, the history of all Catholic endeavour. God bless you all, and give you a holy Passiontide, and a happy Easter.

[1] The church was re-built and re-opened in 1935.

10

THE LONDON ORATORY[1]

And when Jacob awaked out of sleep, he said, Indeed the Lord is in this place, and I knew it not. . . . This is no other but the house of God, and the gate of heaven.—Genesis 28. 16.

WHEN the patriarch Jacob went into exile, to avoid the anger of his brother Esau, he came to a city called Luz; and there, lying down to sleep on the bare earth, a fugitive and a wanderer, he dreamt a dream rich in its consolations for posterity. It seemed to him that a ladder was set up on the earth reaching to heaven; that almighty God himself, from the top of this ladder, looked down as if in pity on his creation; and that the angels went up and down it in their busy traffic over the needs of men's souls. That vision, as we know, was prophetic, and looked forward to the day when, in the fullness of time, almighty God bridged the gulf between our lowness and his inaccessible Majesty through the Incarnation. Angels that sang over the fields at Bethlehem, coming down as the escort of the Incarnate; angels that comforted his Church, when they returned with him in triumph at the Ascension —these, had Jacob but known it, were the celestial passengers of his dream. That promise he could only behold afar off; but this message of divine encouragement must be perpetuated somehow in memory before he proceeded on his journey. He took a stone, and poured oil on it, dedicating it to God; "surely", he said, "the Lord is in this place; this is none other than the house of God; this is the gate of heaven". So it was that, then or later, the city called Luz was renamed Bethel, the House of God. And Christendom, when the dedication of a church is to be celebrated, still falls back on those old memories; still loves to see, in every building consecrated to God, the image of that ladder set between heaven and earth, and the angels who climbed it.

Almighty God does not dwell in temples made with hands. And it is a mark of our human imperfection that we are for ever trying to localize his presence, to tie down his gracious influence to this one plot of earth, this one fabric of human workmanship. When our Lord came, after all those centuries of incomplete revelation, he found the Jews and the Samaritans still lost in controversy, whether the One God ought to be

---

[1] This sermon was preached on the occasion of the Golden Jubilee of the Consecration of the London Oratory, 16 April 1934.

worshipped in the temple at Jerusalem, or on Mount Garizim. And to this day, there is no motive, I think, which so powerfully retards the conversion of our fellow countrymen to the Catholic faith as the pathetic illusion that because Westminster Abbey and Canterbury Cathedral were God's chosen temples once, they must be God's chosen temples still. God is a spirit; and those who worship him must worship him not just here or just there, not in this building or in that, but in spirit and in truth.

Yet we are men, and the monuments of human workmanship have power to seize our imaginations, and to touch our hearts. A church that has stood even for fifty years has become part of our history. Although there may be those present who saw this church when it was first opened, how much of human life has come and gone since then! How many Christian children have been reborn in that font; how many Christian lovers have breathed their vows at those altar-rails; that bell has tolled over how many Christian dead! And what shall we say of the daily commerce between earth and heaven these walls have witnessed, all the renewals of Calvary in the Mass, of Bethlehem in holy communion, all the flood of sins that has flowed through the gratings of those confessionals, to meet and be stemmed by the merciful tide of absolution that ebbed back? No wonder that God allows us, even under the New Covenant, to consecrate our churches, that are the focus of so many memories, the meeting place of so many associations. We look for the Jerusalem that is from above, a city not made with hands; but her image is expressed in these earthly temples, so close to our daily walks, so saturated with the experience of our mortal lives.

And, above all, these multitudinous memories throng around us when we contemplate a church set, as this church is, as Oratories must ever be, in the heart of a great city. Medieval piety loved to bury itself in remote fastnesses of the countryside; *Bernardus valles, colles Benedictus amabat*.[1] Bernard loved the valleys, and Benedict the hills, but each alike would build for God where man seems nearest God, out in the open spaces, and close to wild nature. St Philip, in whose days the growth of commerce was already beginning to crowd men into cities, St Philip, in whose heart the love of souls was wedded so closely to the love of God, would follow neither. To Bernard his valleys, to

[1] This is part of a medieval saying. The full rhyme runs:
  Bernardus valles, montes Benedictus amabat,
    Oppida Franciscus, celebres Dominicus urbes.
  (Bernard loved the valleys, Benedict the mountains,
    Francis the towns, Dominic the populous cities.)

Benedict his hills; if you sought Philip, you must go to find him in the market-place.

And it was surely providential that after the great economic changes of the early nineteenth century, when rich and poor found themselves huddled together, in uneasy neighbourhood, the Oxford converts should have fallen under the spell of St Philip and founded their two great institutes in the heart of towns: in London, that industrialism had transformed, in Birmingham, that industrialism had created. Not immediately, in Father Faber's case; there are little villages in the Derbyshire hills where you may still come across Catholics whose grandparents were converts of Father Faber. But he, too, must throw in his lot with the others; he, too, would bring spiritual consolation where it was most needed, among the broken hearts in the great cities. A Catholic poet had not yet written the lines:

> When so sad thou canst not sadder,
>   Cry, and upon thy so sore loss
> Shall shine the traffic of Jacob's ladder
>   Pitched between Heaven and Charing Cross;[1]

but it was at a stone's throw from Charing Cross, in King William Street, that the Oratory came to London; to take root here, eighty years ago, in Kensington, to build here, fifty years ago, its permanent church.

And this church, whose golden jubilee we celebrate, is in a very special sense the life-centre of the Institute which serves it, the reason for its existence. People will talk of the Jesuit church at Farm Street, of the Dominican church here, of the Franciscan church there; nobody yet ever talked of the Oratorian church in the Brompton Road. This is the Oratory, and these are the Fathers of the Oratory; they belong to it, not it to them: Father Faber was exiled, like Jacob, from the world of his birth and education, from the scenes he knew; like Jacob, he spent some of the best years of his life toiling for a false ambition —Lia instead of Rachel. Tractarianism instead of Catholic unity. But he has left us this church to be the memorial of his short life; to be the Bethel of London, its house of God; a meeting-place of heaven and earth; Jacob's ladder pitched here in the Brompton Road, in the midst of the great swirl of traffic, and the hurrying life of London, that deafens and bewilders us and makes us forget God and our souls' destiny, if we will heed its clamour.

Yes, for those of us who have money and leisure to get away, the

[1] Francis Thompson, "The Kingdom of God is Within You".

Benedictines still offer, in the seclusion of their remote abbeys, a haunt of peace. But here is peace brought to London, to be had for the pushing of a door. Has the distraction ever overtaken you, when you came into the church to say a prayer for some private intention, of wondering what all these others are praying about; these other casual worshippers, fellow Christians whose path has crossed yours for a moment, whose faces you will perhaps never see again? And then, have you thought of the number and variety of the prayers which are offered in this church between sunrise and sunset of one day? Now, cast your mind back over these last fifty years, and think of the sum of human aspiration which has beaten against these walls, which has poured itself out at the shrines of our Lady and St Philip. The sick, the poor, the hungry, the undecided, the timorous, the anxious, the sinful . . . prayers for the health, the happiness, the salvation of others; conversion for heretics, change of heart for the sinner, recovery for those who have fallen away from religion, rest for the departed . . . acts of faith, of love, of contrition, of confidence in God's mercies . . . fifty years of them. My house shall be called a house of prayer (so runs the title over that apse) —shall be *called*? Surely the name of the Oratory has been deserved; ask those doors at the end of the church how often they have revolved by now, to admit a worshipper. And all the while, if we will follow the symbolism of Jacob's dream, the angels of God have been thronging up the ladder in their myriads, to present the petitions of all those worshippers, your petitions and mine.

I said just now that, in the mind of our liturgy, each church that we consecrate to God is an image of the heavenly Jerusalem. And in the office for the dedication of a church one phrase occurs which belongs to the description of the heavenly Jerusalem in the Apocalypse, a phrase of infinite tenderness; "God shall wipe away every tear from their eyes". God shall wipe away every tear from their eyes—that promise cannot be fully verified except in heaven. Mourners come to this earthly temple, and leave it with their tears unstaunched; sinners come to it, and return before long to their sinful habits; the anxious come, and their fears are not always dispelled; the distressed come, and their wants are not always relieved. And yet, what gracious showers of consolation have fallen upon Christian hearts in this place! Favours bestowed, not always the favours we asked for; difficulties overcome, not always in the fashion we had in mind; strength to undergo the ordeals from which we would fain have been delivered; patience to bear the misfortunes we laboured to avert. Oh yes, the angels of God have been thronging *down* the ladder too; no prayer ever went up, but some grace came down. Fifty years of that busy commerce between heaven and earth; and did we say it was lost labour, wasted money, that raised those pillars, and rounded that dome?

It is the fashion of the age we live in, to look back on the day before yesterday with a kind of antiquarian interest; to speak of the Victorian period, fifty years or less than fifty years ago, as if it were a closed chapter, a memory of dead things. This want of conscious continuity with our immediate past is the sign of an unsettled civilization, possibly of a return to barbarism. We are not likely to make that mistake in our celebrations today; we are not likely to imagine that because the Oratory has stood here for fifty years already its work is done, its reserves of vitality exhausted. Rather, while we thank God for all that fifty years of the Oratory have meant, let us pray that the next fifty years may be even more fruitful of achievement; more worshippers still crowding these courts, more numerous prayers besieging heaven, more purity of intention, to draw down heaven's favours in return. And when the Jerusalem which is from above is revealed in all her beauty, may we find all those who worship here pass safely through the gates into the city, *ubi non praevenit rem desiderium*, where prayer is made perfect, because desire is accompanied by its own fulfilment, and there shall be no more death, or sorrow, and God himself will wipe away every tear from our eyes.

I I

THE CORONATION OF GEORGE VI[1]

O Lord, save the king.—Psalm 19. 9.

IT is a characteristic of our modern publicity that it misses, as often as not, the central nature, the characteristic quality, of the event which it is celebrating, because its attention is caught by casual details, by unessential features which have more "news value". What have the newspapers made us understand, these last few days, about the Coronation? That multitudes of visitors have flocked to England from all parts of the world to witness it; that the streets of London will be lined by enormous crowds, that vast sums of money have been spent on accommodating the spectators, on decorating the streets in London,

---

[1] This sermon was preached at St Aloysius's, Oxford, on the occasion of the Coronation of King George VI, 12 May 1937.

and elsewhere. Or, getting nearer to the point, but still missing the point, the newspapers will instruct us about the private life of the Royal Family, their tastes, their habits, their domestic virtues. What does not emerge from all these columns of print is any material for answering the question—What is it that we, citizens of this unwieldy Commonwealth of Nations, are doing today?

We are performing an act of homage; that is to say, we are abasing ourselves. You and I—for in this matter those fellow citizens of ours in London are only our proxies, only our representatives—you and I are putting a gold crown on the head of a fellow mortal, a man like ourselves, and telling him and ourselves that he is a more important person than we are. An act of homage; not the admiration we pay to some great athlete or some profound genius; not the envious felicitation which we accord to one who is richer, happier, more influential than ourselves; something which is at once more simple and more subtle than that—homage. It is a more human relation; we are the King's men; men who, as such, have set up a man, as such, to govern us. His title to kingship is our title to humanity—the accident of birth. He happens to be a king, not a subject, as we happen to be men, not beasts. His sense of long lineage, his early apprenticeship in the discipline of Courts, may make it suitable that he, and not another, should occupy a position so beset with dignity. But it is birth, not training, that makes a king of him. We ask who he is, not what he is, before we delight to honour him.

Why do we do it? Not because he wants it; be assured of that. A king, today at least, is the victim of his people; he is sacrificed to their continual demand for his public appearance, pelted to death with their garlands. What is happening today is happening not because his Majesty insisted upon it but because we insisted upon it; not because he wanted to have our homage, but because we were determined to give it him. You and I today, are satisfying a need, humouring a tendency in our own natures; we have a natural aptitude for loyalty; we want to be subjects; we want to say to a fellow man, "Be thou ruler over us". We thrust him out, reluctant, from our midst, telling him that he may no longer be a subject like ourselves; he is to be King, for a king we must have. It is not that we want somebody to govern us; a statesman, chosen at random, will do that for us. We want somebody to whom we can do reverence; whom we can set on a pedestal apart from ourselves. We reverence him, not as the man who signs the proclamations, but as the mystical representative of his people. And that position must come to him as of right, not by delegation from below; he is the nation's other self, not its creature.

Why are we like that? Why do we find this tendency, this need in our nature, to do reverence to something higher than ourselves? Because we are made for God; made to worship. Man is, I suppose, the only species in creation to which kneeling is a native posture. We are built that way; built for worship. The faculty of reverence by which we do homage to King George is the same faculty by which we worship God. Do we then wrong God, take away something of his honour, when we crown a man to rule over us? No, not if the heart of the nation is sound. Where a nation loses sight of God, it tends to deify man; you will read that lesson without difficulty in the story of tyrannies, whether they be ancient or modern tyrannies. But, where the sense of God is not lost, our reverence for Royalty does not conflict with our reverence for Deity; the two complement one another. On the one hand, the kingship is a kind of natural sacrament by which our loyalty to God expresses itself, externalizes itself. As the sun above us, with its generative warmth, its all-pervading light, is a natural symbol to us of the Power which created us, of the Wisdom which observes all our actions, so the King on his throne is a natural symbol to us of the God who rules, the God who defends, the God who judges us. And on the other hand, we know that it is the higher order of things which lends reality and significance to the lower, not the lower to the higher. St Paul tells us that the Fatherhood of God is the model, the eternal type, after which all fatherhood in heaven and earth is named. So the Kingship of God is the explanation and the basis of all other kingship.

We shall do ill, then, to treat this day's crowning as if it were no affair of ours, as if it were merely a matter of routine or merely a matter of sentiment. And we shall not do much better if we treat today as merely a fresh occasion for merry-making and sight-seeing, in days when sight-seeing is so cheap, and merry-making so laboriously cultivated. Rather, we must let the thought of this day's pageantry, and the professions of loyalty which accompany it, carry our minds up, as they should be carried up in Ascensiontide, to the unfading glories of heaven, their inspiration and their antitype. There let us greet the crowned Christ in the words of the Church's liturgy:

> Called from above, you, as your own,
> In right of God resume the throne,
> And thence this universe survey,
> Whilst all your creatures homage pay.[1]

[1] *New Westminster Hymnal*, No. 59.

And so, turning our thoughts back again to this earthly crowning, let us ask for God's blessing on those who are so closely present to our thoughts; ask the soldier St George to protect the King against his enemies, ask Elizabeth, the royal saint of Hungary, to crown our Queen with the rose-garland of her own charity. And as we remember their names, we will remember, too, the name of the Queen Mother; asking Mary, our Queen and our Mother, to protect the dowry that was her own—is her own—and bid it take its place once more as a jewel in the undivided crown of Christendom.

12

CHURCH AND STATE[1]

The kings of the earth stood up, and the princes met together, against the Lord and against his Christ.—Psalm 2. 2.

THE struggle between Church and State is as old as the Church, and has lasted all through her history. In the very earliest days, it was a struggle between the Christian Church and a pagan empire which openly persecuted it. Then came the Emperor Constantine, and with him the apparent triumph, the external triumph, of the Church. But the christianizing of the world—perhaps we ought to say, the external christianizing of the world—led almost at once, by a kind of fatality, to dissensions within the Church herself. The Arian heresy, the first really great heresy which divided Christendom, managed everywhere to lift its head, managed everywhere to hold its own, because it caught the ear of the secular powers. It was patronized by several emperors, especially by the eastern emperors; it was the religion of the Spanish kings; and an Arian, Ulfilas, succeeded in converting the powerful nation of the Goths. And the first time when the influence of the Papacy is written large on the page of history is the time when the ancient doctrine of the Church, supported by the Popes against this powerful coalition of error, maintains itself and wins its way in defiance of the secular powers which opposed it.

In the Dark Ages, you see the spiritual power not merely a match, but more than a match, for the secular. You see the old kingdoms

[1] This sermon was probably preached in July 1938.

being broken up and the old landmarks obliterated; the tide of heathenism and Mohammedanism sweeping up as if to engulf the now Christian civilization of Mediterranean Europe; and when the secular unity of Europe is broken into fragments, it is the Papacy, the principle of ecclesiastical unity, that pulls Europe together. All the modern nations, you may say, had the Church for their nursing-mother; they borrowed from her the first rudiments of their culture. It was, for example, so the historians tell us, the devotion to our blessed Lady which first produced that feeling of respect for womanhood which we call, in Christian Europe, by the name of chivalry.

In the medieval period, you see the Church once more apparently flourishing, as she was apparently flourishing in the time of Constantine, but in reality exposed to great dangers of disunion. In the first place, because the kingdoms were growing in power, and the kings were continually at issue with the central authority of Christendom in the attempt to strengthen their royal prerogative—you see it, of course, in the quarrel between Henry II and St Thomas Becket. In the second place, because the Papal court itself tended to grow corrupt, and the lives of Churchmen were often openly scandalous, so that there was a quite legitimate cry for reform; and when you start reforming things there is always considerable danger that you will break them up in the process. There was a reforming movement, which wanted to replace the authority of the Pope by the authority of a General Council. That movement failed, not because moral reform was unneeded, but because the instinct of Christendom would not buy reform at the price of unity.

Reform did come; it came with the Council of Trent. It is quite impossible to exaggerate the importance of the Council of Trent as a reforming council; what it did, for example, in raising the whole tone of the clergy. But by that time Protestantism had begun in the Northern countries of Europe, and it was necessary, as a condition of reforming the Church, to define the doctrines by which she stood. The Middle Ages asserted the unity of Church Government; the Council of Trent asserted the unity of the faith. And that meant a new kind of disunion in Europe; It meant that whole countries were separated from the Church, and consequently from the main stream of European culture. The notion that you could devise any sort of concordat between Lutheranism and Catholicism was only a dream. The kingdoms were now at the height of their power; it was the age of the despots. And consequently in the reformed countries the secular power got the upper hand, and subordinated, for all practical purposes, the spiritual power to itself. Meanwhile, what happened in the countries that remained Catholic? What effect had the Reformation there in defining the positions of Church and State?

You would have thought that the Council of Trent, with its general tightening up of ecclesiastical discipline, had established in the Church once for all a principle of central control. But as a matter of fact you find in France, between the Reformation and the Revolution, attempts more determined than ever to make the Church a national institution, owing allegiance to the crown before it owed an allegiance to the Papacy. When the Gallican movement was at its height, you may say that the position of the Church in France was not much different from that of the Church in England under Henry VIII, although there was in fact no breach of relations with Rome. It was only as the monarchies themselves began to decay in power, from the time of the French Revolution onwards, that the independence of the Church really began to be recognized. Wherever you had a powerful Catholic monarchy, in France, in Spain, in Austria, there was unceasing trouble between Church and State.

Today, the Austrian Empire has been dismembered; and with the revolution in Spain we have seen the last of the old Catholic monarchies of Europe unseated. Now at least, you would think, the troubles of the Church in this particular direction must be over. However much the theories of Roman canonists may hanker after a Catholic state on the old model, it is quite clear that such an ideal cannot be realized in the conditions of today. The best we can hope for, surely, is the notion of a free Church in a free State, the State either refusing all recognition to religion, or treating all religions on the same footing; the Church existing as a legal corporation, and qualified as a corporation to hold its own property, to elect its own officials, to reject those who are in disagreement with the principles of its foundation from the privileges of its membership. There is no reason, surely, why the Catholic Church in the modern State should not hold the same position which is held by, say, the episcopal Church in Scotland; legislating for its own members, directing its own internal policy, without seeking or pretending to influence, otherwise than indirectly, the life of the nation as a whole; without, on the other side, needing any national legislation to curb its activities or to control its destinies.

Once more, what you would have expected is what you do not find. Everywhere, even nowadays, in a hundred different forms, the old trouble between Church and State continues to crop up. So much so that Protestants loudly say, and we Catholics are sometimes tempted to think, that there must be something wrong with a Church which always seems to prove a storm-centre of political debate, even where it has no longer any temporalities to defend. "Why cannot you Catholics leave politics alone?"—that is the cry which greets us everywhere, and sometimes wearies us. Just when it looks as if we had managed to persuade the British public that the claim we make to support for our schools is not a deep-laid plot to reintroduce thumbscrews into English life, the Maltese quarrel breaks out, and the whole business has to start again. Now, I think it is very often a fair answer to that question to say that the Church is quite prepared to leave politics alone when politics will be content to leave the Church alone. After all, there are very few countries in the world even now where the Catholic Church does not have to work under artificial handicaps owing to political interference. Most people would tell you, for example, that the persecution in Mexico is a thing which has happily died down. Yet only a few days ago you could read in the newspapers that the state of Vera Cruz had decided to ration the clergy on a basis of one priest to every hundred thousand of the population. Well, that may be some people's idea of a free Church in a free State, but it is not ours.

A long time ago now there was a picture in *Punch* representing the consternation of an old gentleman whose wolf-hound has just eaten a prize rabbit, the property of a neighbour; and there is a small boy leaning over the fence in an ingratiating way, saying, "Gi'e me a tanner, guv'nor, and I'll swear it was the rabbit as begun it". Ordinarily speaking, when you read that some Government measure has been taken as the result of persistent interference of the clergy in politics, it is safe to assume that it is the small boy over again, saying it was the rabbit as begun it. But when you have said that, obviously you haven't given the full account of the matter. It would be against reason and against nature to suppose that almost all the statesmen of almost all the countries in the world deliberately set out to injure the Catholic Church out of sheer perversity, with no grudge to satisfy and no advantage to gain. There must be something about the Catholic Church, whether it be creditable or discreditable, which will account for the way in which it is singled out by politicians sometimes for repression, and always for distrust.

There is that something about the Catholic Church. It is not easy to pin it down with a definition, especially in the course of five or ten minutes. But roughly I think you can say this—that there is such a thing as the Catholic culture, the Catholic philosophy of life, call it which you will, and that it is commonly at variance with the outlook of the generality of men, non-Catholics or slack Catholics, at any one given moment in any one given corner of the world. I think we are wrong if we describe that culture, that philosophy of life, as Latin, or dwell too much on its connection with the culture of Imperial Rome. The Catholic culture is something much wider than that. It depends on the whole history of nineteen hundred years, on the whole geography of five continents. A religion which has its roots so deep and its *rapports* so wide necessarily forms in the mind which lives by it an attitude, not merely to the next world but to this, traditions about the State and society, about marriage and the family, about the values of life, about the relative importance of various duties in life, and so on; these traditions would hold their own even if they were not reinforced, as at certain points they are reinforced, by the solemn judgment of the Church herself. And wherever you get a large body of Catholic citizens, especially when they have freedom for the interchange of ideas and opportunities for corporate action, they will necessarily form a kind of clique within the State, holding to, and defending, their own philosophy of life, which is a universal philosophy of life, against those particular fads and fashions which please that particular country at the particular period in history.

It is not hard to give instances. In England, this Catholic culture is opposed to the propaganda for small families. In Italy, it is opposed to that ultra-nationalism which would insist that children should be educated, first and foremost, in a tradition of violent and intolerant patriotism. Now, mark this—nobody in Italy wants small families; there is no kind of conflict between Church and State about that there. Nobody in England wants to replace Catholic education by the doctrines of the Empire Crusade; there is no kind of conflict between Church and State about that here. But in either case something strange and eccentric has cropped up since yesterday, and to that fashion of today the Catholic culture opposes itself. So you see in the United States the Catholic culture opposed, on the whole, to the Prohibition movement, a modern fad and a local one; so in England you would find it on the whole opposed to that kind of Puritanism which prosecutes people for holding tickets in a sweepstake. In Germany you will find it on the whole opposed to that militant nationalism which endangers the peace of Europe; in France on the whole you find it distrustful of an internationalism which would jeopardize the rights of small peoples. Very often, statesmen find this Catholic influence useful to them, as a kind of pendulum which redresses the eccentricities of the political machine, which stands for law and order and commonsense. But where a whole people is stampeded by some new fashion of thought, it cries out against this influence as something sinister, hostile, anti-social; Catholics cannot be good citizens, must be taking their orders from abroad, if they do not fall in with the catchwords which the fashion of a moment has made dominant.

I wonder what this generation of Englishmen is going to do about all this mess the world is getting into? It is getting into a mess, don't let us make any mistake about that; extraordinary things are going to happen in Europe within the next thirty or forty years. Well, thank God one can get to heaven without taking any interest in politics. And there are many really good Catholics who never seem to take much interest in what is going on in the world, especially when they are Englishmen and the affairs in question concern foreign countries. But this I do say, that in so far as you are an active Catholic, really try to appreciate the Catholic culture and what it stands for, really learn to rejoice with the triumphs of the Church and sympathize with her defeats, you will find yourself in the full stream of the life of your generation, you will know the joy of conflict, without which there is little savour in living, except for those few who live very close to God. The difference between being merely Catholic by creed, and being a full citizen of the Catholic world, in times like these, is, if I may degrade the subject by an undignified metaphor, all the difference between merely watching a race and watching a race you have money on. The question is whether you will be a spectator merely, or whether there will be a part of yourself in the issues that are being fought out during your generation. You must make your choice—only may God grant that if a real trial of our faith comes, you and I may be found ready for it, and worthy of that opportunity.

13

A NATIONAL DAY OF PRAYER[1]

ONCE again, on Sunday, September 8th, we are being aroused by a national call to prayer. It is not to be wondered at; such an appeal chimes in admirably with our national mood at the moment. Let a

[1] This article, written on the occasion of a National Day of Prayer, 8 September 1940, is taken from *The Tablet* (7 September 1940).

scratch party of travellers be snowed up at an inn, they will fall to fraternizing at once. People who hitherto glared at one another suspiciously from opposite sides of the chimney corner, thaw into friendliness and exchange anecdotes about their families. So, cut off for the moment from a Europe in quarantine for German measles, we are beginning to feel a strange neighbourliness towards our fellow islanders. We may have disagreed with some of them, we may disagree with them still, but after all, on certain outstanding questions, how right they are! This spirit of party truce has invaded even the primordial sanctities of religious controversy. The jangling bells which, Sunday after Sunday, cried up Carmel against Bethel and Bethel against Carmel, are hushed now in the expectation of celestial visitants. Not unwilling to derive what support we can from synagogue or conventicle, we fall severally, but not competitively, to our knees.

Alas, that the moment when we most feel the need and the desire to pray should be the moment when distractions assail, most importunately, our prayers! Distractions are pitiably frequent at the best of times. The unconscious, bottled up and raging after the efforts of concentration we have expended on adding up the monthly books, or doing the morning crossword, is looking out for an opportunity to get its own back; and finds that opportunity when we betake ourselves to prayer. The truths of religion claim, after all, only a tenuous hold on the imagination; attention is stupefied by the familiarities of routine. No time is more favourable for the recurrence to our minds of memories, anxieties, grievances which have been driven under, for the moment, by the stress of daily living. How often, for example, we remember a letter that has got to be written only when we come to say our prayers at night! And if the imps of distraction always take their holiday in prayer-time, prayer-time in wartime affords them in a positive carnival.

I am not referring to external distractions, among which air-raid alarms are perhaps the most inculpable. It can hardly be in this sense that the *Imitation* forbids us *aurem blandienti praebere Sirenae*. I am thinking of alarms and excursions which come from within. Every war is a war of nerves; and those of us at least who are sensitively, who are imaginatively built, will be full, all the time, of half-suppressed echoes left over from the last newspaper we read, the last bulletin we heard. We carry about with us a kind of buzzer which is ready to be set off by any stimulus, even remotely connected with the war; and for the most part, in company especially, we know how to put the stopper on it. Then we kneel down to pray, and at once it goes off. To pray about the war must involve in some degree thinking about the war; and thinking about the war is to set the buzzer racing in our minds, to the confusion, it seems, of all holy influences.

These echoes are infinitely various. We may be set thinking about some danger to ourselves, near or remote; about the inconveniences or problems in which war involves us personally; about the safety of friends or relations; about the future of our country or of Europe. We find ourselves in the opposite predicament to Balaam's, cursing where we set out to bless. Theological problems may arise and pester our brains—the apparent deafness of heaven to so many petitions, the justification of so much misery and bloodshed, and all the rest of it. Worst of all (I think) we may discover, after a quarter of an hour spent in the attitude of prayer, that we have been devising ingenious schemes for the enemy's undoing, working out plans for the imagined benefit of the General Staff, asking the Almighty to suggest such and such an idea to the Prime Minister. . . . The Devil is an excellent tactician, and inspires us to unimagined flights of generalship when we ought to be thinking about something else.

True enough, these distractions have no power to defeat our purpose, unless we parley with them; the essential act of prayer consists in wanting and trying to talk to God as best we can, not in "succeeding"; to speak as if prayer was effective in the measure in which it "comes easy" and makes itself felt in the form of sensible devotion, is pernicious Jansenist stuff. (When will somebody re-write the answer to Question 143 in the Catechism[1] much more carefully?) But for all that, it is a continual disheartenment to many of us to realize that, when we talk to God, we treat him with an absent-mindedness at which an earthly friend would take justifiable offence. And the worst of it is that the distractions do not break in upon our prayers from without; they seem to spring from the prayers themselves. We pray for those we know to be in peril; and the thought of their peril leads us into an attempt to picture it. We resign ourselves to what the future may bring; and in doing so we are betrayed into wondering what the future *will* bring, a theme which opens up endless vistas of day-dreaming. We pray for victory; and we cannot resist the temptation to speculate how, when or where victory will be achieved. Every step we take lands us deeper in the morass.

Is there any remedy for those who find themselves afflicted with this

---

[1] The answer to the Catechism Question 143 is: "Those who, at their prayers, think neither of God nor of what they say, do not pray well; but they offend God, if their distractions are wilful."

kind of impotence? The one I have in mind is one which will suggest itself, perhaps, to those who read Mr Watkin's recent article on *The Cloud of Unknowing*, and perhaps also that by Fr Corbishley on Père de Caussade.[1] I mean that outside our times of statutory prayer—those prescribed for us by obligation—we should fall back upon a much simpler method, or absence of method, which aims at throwing us back directly, and if you will confusedly, on the bare acceptance of God's will. Such prayer dispenses not only with formulas of words, but with formulas of thought; puts on one side even those considerations, those exercises of the affections, those acts of the will, which have at other times proved, and might at other times prove, attractive and salutary; concentrates on the bare thought of God, the bare aspiration that his will may be done in us, and in everything.

In its essence, this method (or absence of method) is what is called the prayer of stupidity. You are content to hold yourself in readiness before God (like a beast of burden, Père Grou says, quoting the Psalmist), and let him choose, as it were, the subjects of conversation. Even holy thoughts and good inspirations only float on the surface of the prayer; the true stream of it is a steady attention to him. In its application to the needs of the moment, it is the prayer of abandonment, preached by de Caussade. Accepting what he calls "the sacrament of the present moment", you concentrate your attention on the thing that is your job here and now, as manifestly his will for you. You put blinkers over that tantalizing outlook into the future which brings with it so many unruly day-dreams. Invasions, privations, Red revolutions must be left as part of a confused background, consisting of the things that may possibly be God's will; your eyes are focused only on the present, and on your contact with the present, as certainly his will.

I do not suggest that prayer of this kind is not liable to distractions; obviously, in so far as it gives you less to fill your mind with, it invites their assault. But it has this advantage, that the distractions no sooner present themselves than they are recognized for what they are. With the prayer of petition or the prayer of acts they tone in, so that you are uncertain from moment to moment whether you are praying or wool-gathering. In the prayer of stupidity they give themselves away, and can, very often, be gently brushed aside as they come: "I am not thinking about that just now" is the soul's response.

It need hardly be added that when I speak of accepting God's will, I

---

[1] The reference is to an article by E. I. Watkin on *The Cloud of Unknowing* (*The Tablet*, 4 May 1940) and to an article by Fr T. Corbishley, s.j., on *L'Abandon à la Providence Divine* (*The Tablet*, 13 July 1940). The articles form part of a series entitled "The Catholic Classics".

mean something very much more than a mere "Oh, very well; if it must be, it must". You must love God's will, desire it, will it: drawing a blank cheque on your powers of submission, so that you are prepared to welcome it, however little nature, or your common habits of thought, may understand or appreciate it. If, with the spiritual writers of the French school, you want to unite yourself in your prayer with some "state" of our Lord in his Incarnation, you have the perfect model before you in Gethsemani. In our worst times, could we pray better than by asking God to send the Spirit of his Son into our hearts, by which we can cry "Abba, Father", as our Master did?

14

THE RELIGIOUS LIFE[1]

You are dead, and your life is hidden with Christ in God.—Colossians 3. 3.

IF there were a girl in the school here who had no knowledge what-ever of the Christian religion, and no knowledge whatever of the English language, I wonder how she would describe today's ceremony in her next letter home? I imagine she would either say, "One of the nuns was buried today", or, "One of the nuns was married today". And she would have some ground for making either of these mistakes. The ceremonies used at the profession of a religious are, and are meant to be, a cross between a funeral service and a wedding service.

"You are dead, and your life is hidden with Christ in God." St Paul wrote those words, not to a religious community, but to all the Christian people of Colossae. In his thought, baptism meant a burial; you were engulfed for a moment under water, in token of the fact that you were being associated, sacramentally, with the death and burial of Jesus Christ. As Jesus Christ passed through the dark gates of the tomb, and rose to a new life on Easter Day, so the soul which received Christian baptism died to the world, and rose again to live with a new, a spiritual life. Christians, for St Paul, were people who

---

[1] This sermon was preached at Aldenham Park, Bridgnorth, when the Bishop of Shrewsbury received the final vows in religion of Mother Mary Dominic of the Order of the Assumption, on 6 May 1941.

had died and been buried; the world, with its honours, its pleasures, its temptations, was a scene they had left behind, a childhood they had outgrown; it could mean nothing to them now.

We find it difficult to believe that; we find it difficult to live as if we believed that. The world left behind, its honours left behind, its pleasures left behind, its temptations left behind—do we really feel like that about it? Because we find it so hard to live up to the facts of our spiritual situation, we worldly people look towards you, souls vowed to God in holy religion, to point the way for us, to take upon yourselves in a visible, tangible form, the baptismal responsibilities we find it so difficult to shoulder. The three vows of poverty, chastity and obedience, the seclusion, the silence, the simplicity of your lives, are a concrete advertisement to us of that new, that risen life which we know to be ours by right of baptism, but find it so difficult to live.

The profession of a religious, then, is a funeral; it is the separation of a soul from earth. It is also a wedding; it is the closer uniting of a soul with heaven. Once more, this is, or ought to be, the striving of every Christian soul—to be united, by an irrevocable determination of the will, to our Lord. It is not to some few, cloistered friends, but to the general run of Christians at Corinth, that St Paul writes: "I have betrothed you to one husband, so as to present you, a virgin undefiled, to Christ".[1] To be in love with Jesus Christ—that is the destiny for which every baptized soul is marked out; but how far we are from really feeling like that! So, once more, you religious have to point the way for us, to live the life we are trying to live, by signing away your liberty and making the love of Christ, nothing less, your visible vocation.

I expect some of you are inclined to say, "Aren't we making too much fuss about all this? After all, it isn't as if Mother Dominic was going to disappear, and we should never see her again except behind a grille. She will still be taking her classes, won't she, and running the Guides, and rolling the tennis-court? Why do we hold ceremonies and make speeches, as if we were parting from Mother Dominic for good?" Yes, I know; but something is really happening when a religious makes her profession, although everything seems just the same as before, except that she wears a ring. Because that ring is the symbol of the interior act by which she signs away her liberty—locks the door in the world's face, and belongs, henceforth, only to Jesus Christ. It is a parting, in a sense; she is leaving us behind, to belong to Jesus Christ.

Dear Mother, how impatient you must feel over all this time spent in talk, when you are in such a hurry to enter that glorious slavery we

[1] 2 Cor. 11.2.

are speaking of! We are like people standing about on a railway-platform, with bags of confetti in their hands, waiting for the bride to go off. Let us just give you, then, our last messages, before you start on your wedding journey. The first is this; you mustn't, after all, leave us behind. We want you to take us with you in your prayers, and bring us nearer to God. We are so stupid, we others, we haven't learned the language of heaven properly—only just a smattering of it, like the French you pick up from a phrase-book. So we want you to be our ambassadress; to take our prayers with you, and make them known to God. That is the first of our last messages; don't forget to tell our Lord, who now espouses you to himself, that we too love him, and want to love him more.

Oh, and one more last message; really the end, this time. We are wishing you nothing less than a life-long romance. So we say, it's true, when our friends get married; but I'm afraid the best that most of us really expect them to enjoy is a life-long comradeship. For romance will feed on nothing less satisfying than perfection; and the perfections we human creatures have aren't enough to go round. They outlast a year or two of married life; but after that husband will find in wife, and wife in husband, some points that fall short of the ideal they once formed. You have chosen that good part which shall not be taken from you. The Bridegroom who claims your soul is of such fathomless perfection that a lifetime of intimacy can never exhaust its fullness. Your romance, then, is not a sunset splendour which fades, but a dawn that rises more and more towards the perfect day. Thy youth, says the Scripture,[1] shall be renewed as the eagle's; to the eyes of us worldly people religious never look old. That is because life lasts while love lasts, and life beats high until love burns low. We wish you, then, a life-long romance.

And so we commend you to God, and to the word of his grace, who is able to give you an inheritance among the sanctified; and to the prayers of our blessed Lady and St Augustine. And may this earthly parting bring you at last to that heavenly union which has no name on earth.

[1] Psalm 102.5.

15

PRIESTHOOD[1]

We have this treasure in earthen vessels.—2 Corinthians 4.7.

MANY of you have been witnessing, this morning, the ordination of a priest. We Christians make much of it, when that sort of thing happens. It is our instinct—not a rule, prescribed by authority, not a doctrine, set out in text-books, but one of those instincts which bloom, self-sown, from the soil of Christian piety—to crowd round when there is an ordination, and make the most of it. We must kiss the hands of the newly-ordained priest while the oil still glistens on them, obtain his blessing before that ceremony is staled by usage. A virtue and an influence, we feel, must hang about the first sacerdotal acts which he performs. We can quote Gospel precedent; our Lord would be born of a Virgin, he would be laid in a tomb wherein never man yet was laid, and when he rode into Jerusalem before his Passion, the beast that carried him should be a beast no man had ever ridden before. Does not this same Lord rejoice, we ask, in the fresh fervour of a priest newly ordained? Of course he does. And it will be no harm if we finish our Sunday's worship with a sermon about the priesthood; that is no slight to the feast of Pentecost, for it was at Pentecost that the glory of the priesthood first began to stream out upon the world.

I am taking my text from a passage in which St Paul is talking about the Christian priesthood, I think, chiefly; though it is always difficult to know when St Paul is talking about the priesthood and when he is talking about the laity as well. "We have this treasure in earthen vessels", he says; these strange, supernatural gifts of ours are enclosed in so frail a casket! A priest is only human; and man, the book of Genesis tells us, was made of the dust of the ground. Perhaps St Paul was thinking of that; for there is a very close and a very curious parallel, if you come to look into it, between the creation of Man and the institution of the priesthood. I hope you will bear with me if I draw out that parallel rather in detail.

When did God make man? Why, at the very end of his creation, and (if we may say so without irreverence) by a kind of afterthought. Already he had made, on the seventh day, the beasts of the field; you quite expect to hear, after that, "And there was morning and evening,

[1] This sermon was preached at the Church of Our Lady of the Assumption, Latchford, near Warrington, on Whitsunday, 13 June 1943, on the occasion of the ordination of Father George Evans and Father Gerald McDonald to the priesthood.

a sixth day". But no, all was not over yet. God said, "Let us make man, after our own image"[1]—almost as if it were a kind of sudden inspiration, like that of a child inventing a new game: "Let us make man". That puts us in our place rather, doesn't it? To think that God might have been content to make a world in which plants grew with no human hands to weed or tend them, a world in which the animals survived or perished according to the law of their nature, with no human master to kill them, or to tame them to his purposes. But at the last moment, God said, "Let us make man".

When did our Lord institute the priesthood? Well, in a sense on Maundy Thursday, on the last evening of his mortal life. But he did not make his intention clear until he met his apostles again on Easter Day in the Cenacle; when he breathed on them and said, "Receive ye the Holy Ghost".[2] Once more, you see, it is a kind of afterthought;[3] the work of our Redemption is finished, death has been vanquished, and hell harrowed, and the holy patriarchs have gone to their reward, and the reign of grace has begun—and our Lord did all that without any priests to help him. He trod the winepress alone, and of the people there was none with him. And he could have achieved your sanctification and mine, could have spread his gospel through the world and given mankind faith to justify them, charity to sanctify them, without any priests to help him, if he had decreed to do so. But no, at the last moment, a thought seems to strike him, "Let us make priests".

Why did God make man? Partly, no doubt, because he wanted, from his creation, a conscious response of gratitude. When he made sun and moon and stars and the earth with all its delicate beauty, its intricate workmanship, he pronounced it very good, and the sons of God shouted for joy, we are told, at this new thing that had come to be. But within the material universe itself there was no answering cry of recognition. True, the stars in their courses, the orderly process of the seasons, showed forth the glory of God; true, the living animals could enjoy some confused pleasures of memory and hope, and in doing so rendered a kind of mute homage to their Creator. But amid all that wealth of multitudinous life no conscious response was given, until he made man, to be, as we say, the priest of creation; to praise God on behalf of those dumb, material things, with a mind that could reason and a voice to express their thankfulness. The priest of creation; the

[1] Gen. I. 26.   [2] John 20.22.
[3] Mgr Knox clearly is not questioning the institution of the priesthood on Maundy Thursday. He is drawing a parallel between our Lord's bestowal of the power to forgive sins on the first Easter Sunday and the completion of God's work of creation on the first sabbath.

J

instrument through which the chorus of its praise should thrill and become vocal at last.

But there was more than that; Almighty God wanted his creation to be taken in hand for him. Why, we do not know; but the want is clearly expressed in the account which Scripture gives us, "There was not a man to till the ground".[1] God did not make man to be a kind of toy, a final piece of craftsmanship more subtle, more delicate than all the rest. He made him to bear rule over the birds and the beasts and the fishes; to be the viceroy of his new dominion. He was to impose God's will on this planet; he was to be a kind of tool by which God's action would express itself, through the long centuries during which the visible order was to persist.

Why did our Lord institute the priesthood? Partly because he wanted to have a special set of men who would have the freedom and the leisure to make a whole-time job of his service. The rest of us would be so busy, earning our daily bread and looking after our families and fulfilling our various duties as citizens, that we should not be able to attend on him as continually as we should have wished, to think about him as uninterruptedly as we should have wished. Partly that, but partly also because he wanted this new supernatural creation of his, the Christian Church, to be taken in hand for him. As he would have man to look after the dumb beasts, to fold them and guide them and feed them in the ways of the supernatural life. He could have done without us, but he preferred to have, once more, a kind of tool through which his action should express itself. Tools in his hand, that is what we priests were to be.

How did God make man? Doubtless you have to make some allowance for the use of figurative speech; we do not go to the book of Genesis for exact chemical formulae. But when we are told that the Lord God formed man out of the slime of the earth, it surely must mean this, whatever else it means—that man on his physical side is one with the material creation which surrounds him. We may strut and give ourselves airs, and tell one another that we have conquered practically the whole of nature and it is only a matter of time before we conquer the rest of it; but the fact remains, we were made of the slime of the earth; dust thou art, as the priest says to us on Ash Wednesday, dust thou art, and to dust shalt thou return. If we are anything more than dust, it is only because God saw fit, of his free bounty, to do something else. "God breathed into his nostrils the breath of life, and man became a living soul."[2] That lifeless thing, a mere toy of dumb

[1] Gen. 2. 5.   [2] Gen. 2. 7.

clay, which lies there on the ground—it is only God's inspiration that
has turned it into this wonderful creature we know and are, Man.

How did our Lord institute the priesthood? "When he had said
this, he breathed on them, and said, Receive ye the Holy Ghost. Whose
sins you remit, they are remitted unto them, and whose sins you retain,
they are retained."[1] With one breath, God created the whole human
family; with one breath, our Lord instituted the whole Christian priesthood. As man is a beast among the beasts, so the priest is a man amongst
men; he shares their passions, their weaknesses, their disabilities. And
yet, when God breathes into the face of a priest, a new thing, in a sense,
comes into being, just as when God breathed into the face of that clay
image he had fashioned. It was a kind of second creation, when our
Lord spoke those words in the Cenacle. It brought into the world a
new set of powers, infinitely exceeding all that man had ever experienced, all that man could ever expect. It was a fresh dawn of life—
supernatural life. Man could not more have evolved into a priest than
a beast could have evolved into a man; it was a special creation, this
time too.

It would have been possible, it might even have seemed natural,
that our Lord, having won our redemption for us, should apply the
fruits of that redemption to our souls without any kind of priestly
ministry to aid his purpose. Many who value the name of Christian
still find it reasonable to believe that he did just that; the priesthood,
they will tell you, belonged to the Jewish covenant, to the old Law;
when the mercy of God shone out to us in the face of Jesus Christ,
the need for all ceremonies and sacraments was done away. But it is
not so that the courtesy of our Lord Jesus Christ treats us. When he
turned water into wine at Cana of Galilee, he used no word, no touch,
no gesture, to claim the miracle as his own. "Fill the water-pots with
water . . . Draw out now, and bear to the governor of the feast"[2]—the
miraculous transformation should take its effect between the hands of
the servants who were waiting on the guests; they should have the
apparent credit for it. And so it was when he multiplied the loaves
in the wilderness. He gave the loaves and fishes to the disciples to
distribute; it was in their hands, it seems, that the multiplication took
place. It is part of his courtesy, you see, that he will thus associate
human agents with himself, just when he gives us the most startling
proofs of his miraculous power.

And so it is with the Christian priesthood. Not only when he gives
us, under the forms of bread and wine, his own body and blood to be

[1] John 20. 22-3.   [2] John 2. 7-8.

our food; in *all* the sacraments he is the true author, the true fountain of grace, yet he will suffer a human ministry to intervene. "Receive ye the Holy Ghost; whose sins ye shall remit, they are remitted unto them, and whose sins ye retain, they are retained." But most, and most characteristically, in the sacrament of Holy Eucharist. When a priest baptizes or absolves, he stands there, sits there, only to unseal the fountains of grace to the faith, to the penitence, which knock to receive them. But when he stands at the altar, the priest does something more; he takes upon himself the Person of Christ, re-enacting in his name the ceremony which he performed on the night of his Passion. A priest clad in the sacred vestments (says the author of the *Imitation*) is the viceregent of Christ himself. He uses our Lord's own words, identifies himself with the offering which our Lord continually makes before the Father, of his own body and blood. How is it that men can be found with the assurance, with the presumption, to do that?

The difficulty is solved for us by one golden phrase of St John Chrysostom's. "When you see a priest offering the Sacrifice", he says, "do not think of it as if it were *he* that is doing this; it is the hand of Christ, invisibly stretched forth." The hand of Christ invisibly stretched forth—that is the picture we should conjure up to our minds if we are to think of the Mass as it really is. The philosopher Aristotle, in defining the position of a slave, uses the words, "A slave is a living tool". And that is what the priest is, a living tool of Jesus Christ. He lends his hands, to be Christ's hands, his voice, to be Christ's voice, his thoughts, to be Christ's thoughts; there is, there should be, nothing of himself in it from first to last, except where the Church allows him, during two brief intervals of silence, to remember his own intentions before God. Non-Catholics who come to our churches complain sometimes, don't they, that the ceremonies of the Mass seem so lifeless, so mechanical. But you see, they ought to be mechanical. What the visitor is watching, so uncomprehendingly, is not a man, it is a living tool; it turns this way and that, bends, straightens itself, kneels, gesticulates, all in obedience to the orders given it—Christ's orders, not ours. The Mass is best said—we Catholics know it—when it is said so that you do not notice how it is said. We do not expect eccentricities from a tool, the tool of Christ.

Those of you who witnessed the ordination ceremony this morning saw the future priest stretched out at full length, face downwards, like a corpse, like a dummy, while the solemn chant of the litany rolled over his head. He was waiting there like a dead thing, for the Holy Spirit to come and quicken him into a new form of life; as Adam's body waited, slime of the earth, for the informing touch of the Creator's hand to turn it into a living soul. He was yielding his body to Christ to be his instrument, as if he had no life, no will of his own. And even when he had risen from the ground, his hands must be tied together with a purificator, in token that he was the captive of Jesus Christ; his slave, to drive and control at will. "I live, now not I, but Christ liveth in me"[1]—that is the protestation which these ceremonies make on behalf of the newly-ordained priest. No life of his own, no liberty of his own; henceforth he is Christ's.

You see, the slavery to which the priest commits himself does not begin and end when he is saying Mass, when he is performing cere-monies. Ah, if only it did! No, it is a lifetime of service; a lifetime during which the priest must consecrate himself, keep on consecrating himself afresh, to his Master, for the sake of that flock which his Master has entrusted to him. Please God, the new priest you saw ordained this morning will be a faithful servant, salt of the earth, a light to the world. But that will not happen automatically. The merely mechanical part of a priest's life, the ceremonies he has to perform, the sacred words he has to utter—those come easier to him with use as time goes on. It is not so with the consecration of the heart; that needs ever fresh outpourings of divine grace if it is not to become a more difficult thing, God forgive us, a more irksome thing, with each year that passes. The thrill of fervour with which a new priest approaches the altar—that will grow less, in the ordinary course of things. It will lose its novelty, and for us human creatures whatever loses its novelty loses something of its zest. He will be tempted to settle down into a rut, to be satisfied with formal pieties and think he is doing well enough. Then will come disappointments and discouragements, to make him cynical and disillusioned. If the grace he received this morning fails to take its full effect in him, he may well grow up into a workaday priest, good enough for his job, but he will not love souls, or convert souls; he will be a crooked tool in the hands of Christ.

In the notices this morning, you were told that Wednesday, Friday and Saturday of this week are Ember Days. What were your reflections on that announcement? "Well, that doesn't mean I'm bound to go to Mass those days." True enough. "And thank God, there's no fasting or abstinence in war time." No, no fasting or abstinence. Was that all? Did you never reflect what the Ember Days are? They are the days on which we ought to pray for one of the greatest of all the gifts our Lord has for us, a good clergy. What would be the use of our war effort, if

[1] Gal. 2. 20.

we had no factories to make machine tools? And how can you expect the Church of God to flourish, how can you expect England to be converted, if the instruments which Christ uses for the sanctifying of his people are shoddy instruments? Pray, pray for your priests; every nation, every diocese gets the clergy it deserves. We priests are only earthen vessels; you know for yourselves many of the shortcomings, hasty temper and slovenly habits and so on, by which we often disgrace the livery we wear. But, when you observe such things, you merely shrug your shoulders, and say, "Pity Father So-and-so isn't more like poor Canon So-and-so". You should be on your knees, this next week, praying for the clergy everywhere, from the Holy Father himself down to the new priests ordained this morning; praying for the seminaries too, the factories where the tools of Christ are made. God protect his Church in the anxious, bewildered days that are coming; and give us a supply of good priests to work as the martyrs worked, to live as the martyrs lived, and if need be to die as the martyrs died, to the glory of his holy name.

16

ONE HEART AND ONE SOUL[1]

The multitude of believers had but one heart and one soul. Neither did any one say that aught of the things which he possessed was his own, but all things were common unto them.—Acts 4. 32.

IT is a curious fact that the Christian Church began with an experiment in Communism. The example does not seem to have spread beyond Jerusalem, and the experiment itself was a failure. For at least a quarter of a century the Church at Jerusalem had to be helped out by the alms of the faithful; alms collected in great measure from the Gentiles, by the Apostle of the Gentiles. And if the record of it has been preserved to us in the Acts of the Apostles, that is not because St Luke wanted us to draw any political moral, one way or the other. He wanted us to see, in the common life those early Christians lived, the sacramental expression, the outward symbol, of the spirit in which those early Christians loved. The multitude of believers had but one heart and one soul—that is the point, that is what matters. There is a spirit of brotherly love which the Christian regrets in her origins, and is ever striving to recapture.

[1] This sermon was preached at Westminster Cathedral on Low Sunday, 16 April 1944, in connection with the Centenary of the Society of St Vincent de Paul in England.

Of that happy dawn, the religious orders are the abiding reflection; they are working models of primitive Christianity. We others, so wedded to our possessions and our private comforts, must be made to feel that it is possible for men, or for women, to live together on a system of common ownership; we see them using the community typewriter, riding the community bicycle, wearing (in some cases) the community hat. It is all a throw-back to the days of the apostles. And now, why was it that the Church, in the innocence of her childhood, instinctively adopted the principle of a common purse? She had no theory of government, no democratic prejudice to justify. No, it was a simple calculation, almost child-like in its simplicity. They were not, they felt, a collection of people, they were one person. There was one body of the faithful, daily refreshed with a common food. There was one head, Jesus Christ. There was one spirit that organized the whole body, the Holy Spirit who had animated them on the day of Pentecost. They were one person, therefore they were one legal personality; whatever any of them possessed was the property of them all.

It belongs to the essence of the Church that it should enjoy, at all times, this inner unity of life. It belongs to the welfare of the Church, that this inner unity should be expressed in outward brotherhood; that there should be a bond of practical charity perfecting it and making it manifest, transforming a spiritual reality into a fact of tangible experience. We do not need to be reminded, just now, that there are moments of history at which the brotherhood of all Christians is very imperfectly realized. A world in which Catholic Germans are dropping bombs on London, and Catholic Englishmen are dropping bombs on Berlin, is a nightmare world which those who live long enough will look back upon, please God, as a nightmare. Yet this wholesale inter-ruption of social commerce and of kindly thoughts, which has over-taken the world in the last five years, has not severed that bond of unity which knits together, in every land, the members of Christ. Suppose a man asleep or unconscious, suppose him paralysed and numb to all sensation—that man still lives. It is easy to tell us that he does not speak, does not move, does not take in what is going on around him; all that is beside the point—the man still lives. And so it is with the Church, Christ's mystical body. It may be rent by a thousand discords, but its supernatural unity goes on undiminished.

Only, just as a body in normal health enjoys, not bare life but active, conscious life, tingling in every nerve and pulsing in every vein, so the Catholic Church, in so far as it is true to itself, should be bound together by a conscious, active bond of unity. We must not be content to *be* one in Christ; we must *feel* that we are one in Christ, own ourselves one in Christ, behave towards one another as being one in Christ. Have I been guilty of saying something very obvious? It may be an obvious thing to say; believe me, it is not an obvious thing to do. You see, when a new movement starts, it is natural that its members should be united together by the spell of an enthusiasm they all share; it is common, human *esprit de corps*. And common, human *esprit de corps* helped the Church, in those days of its first beginnings, to deserve the tribute which is paid to it in the Acts, "The multitude of believers had but one heart and one soul". They were a small body, a young body, and instinct told them to rally side by side.

But the years go on, and the first fervours of that natural enthusiasm spend themselves; and the Church grows larger, and embraces men of different classes, different cultures, different nationalities. Sympathies begin to diverge. It is one body still; heresy and schism only cut away the rotten members without impairing its essential life. But the conscious charity of its sound members for one another is less generously shown, less easily maintained. There is not the same co-ordination between them, the same quick reaction to rally them against assault. And the work of the Church is crippled, and the enemies of the Church blaspheme; and men look back with regret to the old days of faith, when the heathen stood in amazement, and said: "See how these Christians love one another!"

Many people will tell you that the Church is dead. How are we to prove to them that she is still alive? To do that, we must give them proof, tangible, exterior proof of that supernatural unity which is the bond of us all. We must show them, not the laborious breathing of a giant in his death-throes, but the liveliness of an organism, with its quick reactions, the delicate rippling of its muscles. Ours must be, not merely a living Church, but a live Church, if men are to take notice, and seek to understand. They think of it as belonging to a world which is passing or has passed away; a world of privilege and of tradition, with its eyes fixed on the past instead of the future; unsuited to the conditions of our time. Where shall we find a remedy, since no remedy lies to hand? Shall we, after all, look back into the past, take counsel, after all, of our traditions; ask whether the Church has not, before now, shown even graver symptoms of lethargy, only to startle the world by a rewakening?

A hundred years ago, a little more than a hundred years ago, the spiritual state of Europe was almost as desperate as it will be when this war is over. In France especially, demoralized by long years of revolution, and still more by long years of victory, the pulses of religion beat low. It is true, the monarchy had been restored, and with the monarchy the Church; but it was only an empty façade of Christianity that remained. Faith seemed dead, the sacraments were almost universally neglected. The revival of religion in France in those years, which is one of the most amazing triumphs of the Christian genius, was, under God, the work of a mere handful of men; and of these, not the least memorable was Frédéric Ozanam. A layman, without any great connections, without any obvious opportunity for influencing public thought, a chronic invalid, who died when he was not yet fifty,[1] Frédéric Ozanam retrieved the credit of religion in the cultured world, the world of the universities, beyond all that would have seemed possible. And how did he do it? His activities were manifold, but the most important, the most characteristic, the one that will be longest remembered, is the foundation, in 1831, of the Society of St Vincent de Paul.

He and his companions saw, or, if they did not see, they knew by unconscious instinct, that if you wanted to restore the spirit of faith you must first restore the spirit of charity. In those days of fierce political controversy, theirs should be the programme of the cenacle, "the multitude of believers had but one heart and one soul". They would visit the poor in their homes—not to inspect them, report on them, and legislate about them, but to bring them what help they could, material or spiritual. They would look in like good neighbours to ask if they could be any use. And by such acts of charity, very obvious, very primitive, they would see if they could not chafe the numbed limbs of Christendom into vigorous life once more. The movement rapidly became world-wide; it was introduced into England only thirteen years after its foundation. In the more complex scheme of modern society it has enlarged its scope, taking in youth movements, probation work and many other activities into its programme. But always its first business is its old business, to establish personal contact between the more fortunate and the less fortunate members of the Catholic body. "He that hath this world's good, and seeth his brother hath need"—impossible not to be conscious of it, now that the bombers have come and knocked down the walls of so many poor streets; we can see at a glance what kind of home it is that our brother lives in. And if any Catholic, who has some means, some leisure of his own, feels the rebuke of St John's words as they are reflected in his own life, there stands the Society of St Vincent de Paul,

[1] Frédéric Ozanam died at Marseilles on 8 September 1853, at the age of forty-nine.

ready to give him the *entrée* to these human homes which he might, otherwise, be too shy to visit.

But you are longing to interrupt me and point out a flaw in my argument. Frédéric Ozanam planned the Society of St Vincent de Paul to meet the needs of his own time, and no doubt it did meet the needs of his own time. But all that is so long ago! The Society was introduced into England a hundred years back, in 1844, before the restoration of the Hierarchy, before Newman's conversion. And must we set out to impress our very modern contemporaries by pointing to the activities of a Society which is, no doubt, excellent in every way, but whose whole inspiration is early Victorian? Why, all this talk about "the poor" has, in itself, an old-world sound about it; what is the use of encouraging people to visit the poor, when we have all agreed that poverty is to exist no longer; when the Government undertakes to see that every working man in England enjoys "security" for himself and his family henceforward? Do we not need some new movement altogether, to meet the challenge of our time with its own appropriate answer?

Very likely we do need such a modern movement; it may be already in existence. But I think it would be a grave mistake to suppose that visiting the poor has become useless and out of date because we are abolishing poverty. God grant we may abolish poverty, but it is not going to be done all at once; the most optimistic of our planners only hope to breed it out within a period of years. And for the time being, people who can hardly read a newspaper, people who hardly know how to sign their own names, are expected to read through long lists of regulations, are expected to fill up the most complicated forms, are expected to find out what the law is as it affects them, from day to day —a law which changes every day. I do not think there was ever a time at which the poor folk of this country were more in need of a friendly visitor with some education, some experience of business, who will help them to find out what their rights are, what they are allowed to do and what they aren't, what money they are entitled to, and when, and how to get it. More and more, as the beneficent schemes of our modern legislators take effect, the poor man is being reduced to the status of a bewildered slave. To help him understand and assert his own rights may, in the years that are coming, be a very important exercise of Christian charity.

And meanwhile, man does not live by bread alone. The spiritual care of our scattered Catholic populations is going to be a more difficult business than ever when the population has been redistributed and rehoused; when young men and young women who have been torn away, all these years, from the influence of home and family, come back and settle down again to civilian and to civilized life. Youth movements are to have an established place in the national economy; and if our Catholic youth movements are not well organized, we shall fall out of the running. Nothing, unfortunately, suggests that the ordeal which the nation has been through in the last few years has recalled English people to higher standards of purity, of decency, of honesty, of public discipline. No, if the English Society of St Vincent de Paul should become less numerous or less active in this second century of its existence, it will not be because there is less work to be done. It will be because Catholic laymen are prepared to face their judgment with the plea of Cain on their lips: "Am I my brother's keeper?"

We must not think of it as one among many Catholic societies competing for our support. Rather, it is the Catholic Church herself, organized for beneficence. Those who accept relief from it escape the sense of inferiority which hurts a man when he takes money from an individual; they escape, at the same time, that sense of pauperism which disgusts men with the more mechanical forms of organized relief. It is public, without being impersonal; it is charitable, without the detestable suspicion of patronage. It is the Catholic Church bringing help, mother-like, to her needy children. It is the Catholic Church appealing to you, her children, for the support which you owe to her. It is the Catholic Church remembering her origins, the days when our Lady and the apostles were still alive to link her with her divine Master, and reflecting that now as then she has but one heart and one soul.

Meanwhile, we are asking for your alms. The money which you put into the plates held by the brothers at the door will not be devoted to any of those world-wide schemes of relief which in these days are so numerous and, alas, so necessary. What you give, you will be giving to your own neighbours, to the parishioners of Westminster, the people whom you pass, day by day, in the street, the people who kneel side by side with you, brothers and sisters sharing in a family meal, when you receive holy communion. If these have no claim on you, whose claim will you recognize? If these make no appeal to you, what appeal will melt you? What answer will you have when you meet that terrific challenge at your judgment: "Inasmuch as you did it, as you did it not, to one of these my least brethren, you did it, you did it not, unto me"?

17

THE CONVERSIONS OF NEWMAN AND FABER[1]

I said, I have laboured in vain, I have spent my strength without cause and in vain; therefore my judgment is with the Lord, and my work with my God.
—Isaias 49. 4.

ALMOST every great religious genius has felt, at some time in his life, many a great religious genius has felt at the very close of his life, the sense of failure—he has laboured in vain, spent his strength without cause. And yet he dares not doubt that his mission came from God; must he infer, then, that God has failed through him? Rather, he is driven to the conclusion that through his failure God has succeeded; the purposes of the Divine Wisdom lay deeper after all, were destined to work themselves out more slowly after all, than the prophet, in the warm glow of his inspiration, had imagined. His judgment is with the Lord; history, somehow, will reverse the verdict of failure. His work is with his God; there will be a recompense for labours heroically endured, even though the labourer returns from the furrow empty-handed.

Among the great men of the world, I do not know if there is anyone whose life is more consistently written down a failure, by friend and foe alike, than the man whose submission to the Catholic Church will be a hundred years old this autumn: John Henry Cardinal Newman. The popular impression of him is that in his Anglican days he devoted himself to an impossible task, that of re-Catholicizing the Protestant Church of England. Baulked in his attempt by the opposition of those bishops whose privileges he had laboured to defend, of that Oxford whose atmosphere was the very air he breathed, he acknowledged defeat; took the line of least resistance, and gave in his loyalty to a Church which thought as he did. Tragic miscalculation! In his new surroundings he found himself scarcely less of an outlaw, scarcely less of an ugly duckling, than in the old. Suspect of that very Liberalism which, in his Anglican days, he had fought so strenuously to oppose, too much of an Oxford man for the Catholic Church, as he had

---

[1] This sermon was preached at a Mass offered at the London Oratory for the Converts' Aid Society, on 26 June 1945.

formerly been too much of a Catholic for Oxford, he set on foot scheme after scheme for the betterment of the Church's position in these islands, was encouraged up to a point, and then told it would not do. . . .

That picture we are apt to see, I think, somewhat out of perspective. It has been distorted by the anxiety of many historians to convince us that the Catholic Church does not really want converts, does not know what to do with them when she gets them. It has been distorted for us, a little, by Newman's own sensitiveness; he was too ready to suspect unkind motives; he made the most of his disappointments. And yet, when you have made allowance for that, read the whole story again; what is the upshot of it? He spent some of the best years of his life trying to found a Catholic University in Ireland; it failed. Owing to the apathy of the very people who had imposed the task on him, it failed. Twice he thought he saw the way clear for establishing an Oratory in Oxford, which would neutralize the growing spirit of infidelity there; and twice the nervous apprehensions of his fellow Catholics in England secured the defeat, at the last moment, of his project. He was invited to edit a new English translation of the Scriptures; had begun allocating the various portions to his collaborators, was already out of pocket through the venture, when suddenly the scheme was abandoned. He consented to edit a Catholic review,[1] in order to repress the dangerous speculations in which a set of younger men were indulging; he only succeeded in acquiring a reputation for heterodoxy himself. Oh, he had literary triumphs; few literary triumphs have ever been so complete as the writing of the *Apologia*. But always when he thought to strike a blow for the Catholic cause, he found his hand knocked up, by his own seconds. He left, as his monument, only his Oratory and the Oratory School. Of all his patrons, St Philip was the only one who never abandoned him.

Our Anglican friends are not slow to point the moral. Either they will tell you that no convert is ever happy in the Catholic Church, or, more cautious in the face of facts, they will tell you that it is all a matter of temperament; by all means become a Roman Catholic if you have the right temperament for it. If you love to exaggerate, to proclaim defiant paradoxes, to swim with the tide of exuberant spirituality which foams down in flood from the Seven Hills, then the Church of Rome is the place for you. It is otherwise if you are critical in your outlook, guarded in your judgments, tender towards the inherited prejudices and the robust common-sense of Protestant England. Rome is for the

[1] *The Rambler.*

Roman-minded. There are such men, and we should do ill to forget it
here. We should do ill to forget that the year 1845 witnessed the conversion of another fellow of an Oxford College—Frederick William
Faber.

Newman and Faber, twin products of the Oxford Movement, twin
sons of St Philip: how poignantly the very similarity of their destinies
illuminates the contrast between them! Father Faber, with all his tender-
heartedness, had a mind that ran to extremes. If Newman had been an
Evangelical in his youth, Faber had been a roaring Calvinist. Give the
two men the grace of conversion, and how admirably they illustrate
the two types of convert we have all of us noticed: the convert who
retains, to the last, some trace of his Anglican scruples, and the convert
who strikes out boldly in the opposite direction, as if determined to
be a better Papist than the Pope! I do not mean to suggest that Father
Faber had a wholly uncritical mind; on the contrary, there is much
more brain behind his spirituality than there is behind a great deal of
modern writing; but he loved mystery and welcomed it. I do not
mean to say that Newman was deficient in Catholic piety; such a
notion would be absurd; but he had a mind too well disciplined to let
any unfamiliar proposition pass without challenge. While Faber is
introducing the British public to the most luscious legends of the
Counter-Reformation, Newman is still concerned over the difficulties
of Anglicans, still asking how and in what sense Catholic doctrine has
developed, still cautiously delimiting the spheres of faith and reason.
Faber, you would say, took to his new Catholic allegiance as a duck
takes to water; Newman, to the last, is something of a square peg in a
round hole.

Are we to conclude, then, that Faber did right, and Newman did
wrong, in following that same call of conscience which came to both
of them, a hundred years ago? Are we to conclude that Catholic ways
of thought, of life, of worship are well suited to some temperaments, ill
suited to others; that you and I, who have followed in the footsteps of
Newman and Faber, ought to look back over the years we have spent
as Catholics and ask ourselves, Has it made me feel happy, has it made
me feel comfortable, this change of my spiritual allegiance? And if,
sometimes, we have felt the strain of belonging to a Church so little
loved by our fellow countrymen; if, sometimes, the morning paper
has brought us more of bad news, because we were Catholics, and our
fellow Catholics were undergoing persecution abroad; if, sometimes,
we felt inclined to criticize the policy of our own leaders, or found
matter for offence in the personality, in the attitude of the priests with

whom we came in contact, are we to say to ourselves: "No, I have not been happy; if looks as if, after all, I made a mistake"? Should we feel tempted, in that way, to make our own feelings the measure of eternal truth, there are two witnesses, believe me, who will rise up in scornful condemnation of us, and their names are Frederick William Faber and John Henry Newman.

There are, indeed, two temperaments, not among converts particularly, but among Catholics in general; I mean, among those whose minds are accustomed to criticize, and to reflect. There are those who seek to enlarge the province of piety; to heap fresh honours on the memory of our Lady and the saints, to flout the maxims of worldly wisdom, to extend the rights of ecclesiastical authority. There are others who keep a jealous eye on the documents of antiquity whose concern is to safeguard the balanced edifice of Christian doctrine; and to these, not seldom, the zeal of the enthusiast seems full of danger. Humanly speaking, it is the equilibrium of these two forces that makes Catholic theology what it is—ever a living study, yet ever rooted in an unforgettable past.

Newman did not fail. It is doubtful whether even his writings have been so powerful a means of effecting conversions as the spectacle of his life; a life so crossed by disappointments and misunderstandings, yet so vividly illuminated, from first to last, by the beams of that kindly Light which he had invoked at the time of his youthful struggles. It has been an inspiration and will yet be an inspiration, to thousands; a perpetual witness that the Catholic Church is not merely a resting-place for this temperament or that. It is the resting-place of all minds, learned as well as simple, critical as well as enthusiastic; it has a welcome and a home for all.

A welcome and a home; we must not forget, in casting our eyes back over the events of a hundred years, the needs of those who make their submission to the Church, Newman's younger brothers, today. It is, I think, a happy symbol that the Converts' Aid Society should be appealing to you for a special purpose: to buy a house which will offer to the convert clergyman, what is often his most immediate need —a roof over his head. A symbol all the more happy, because the house whose purchase is contemplated was the home of a man who, more than any other in our day, has taught men to love their homes; Gilbert Chesterton's house at Beaconsfield.[1] Newman and Chesterton —the two greatest minds, perhaps, that have been drawn within the luminous circle of Catholic truth, in the century that followed Catholic

[1] "Top Meadow", acquired by the Converts' Aid Society in 1945.

emancipation. And Chesterton, were he with us, would be the first to own, what every English convert owns, that under God's grace the example of Newman was the beacon that brought him to the faith. Newman is alive; through the breach he made in the walls of English prejudice, a multitude of souls still find their way, year by year, into the liberty of the sons of God; grope their way after him, not without his guidance, *ex umbris et imaginibus in veritatem.*

18

THE CONVERSION OF NEWMAN: I[1]

There must be a renewal in the inner life of your minds; you must be clothed in the new self, which is created in God's image, justified and sanctified through the truth.—Ephesians 4. 24.

WE have met this morning for a particular purpose, and a strange one. Have we come here to proclaim the glories of a saint? Why, no; the Mass is a Mass of the Blessed Trinity. Have we come here to implore God's mercy for the soul of a fellow Christian, now dead? Not exactly; there is no apparatus of sombre vestments, of unbleached candles, to remind us of the holy souls in purgatory. No, we have come here to thank God for the grace of conversion bestowed, a hundred years ago, upon a great Englishman, John Henry Newman.

And why in Liverpool? Say what you will, the glories of the Church in England are unevenly distributed between north and south. We in the south boast of our conversions; you in the north of your native Catholic stock. Run through a list of the great names in English Catholicism during the last hundred and fifty years, and you will see the justice of that observation. Think of Dr Lingard, Squire Waterton, Bishop Hedley, Francis Thompson, Napier Hemy—all Northerners, and all cradle Catholics. Think of Newman, Manning, Pugin, Chesterton, Eric Gill—all Southerners, and all converts. You yourself, as you sit here, are conscious of the Faith as something you have inherited, a precious heirloom, from generation after generation of Catholics, here

---

[1] This sermon was preached at St Clare's, Sefton Park, Liverpool, on 30 September 1945, in the presence of the Archbishop of Liverpool, to commemorate the centenary of the conversion of John Henry Newman.

in Lancashire or over the water. If there had been no Oxford Movement, if John Henry Newman had never made his submission to the
Church, you, by the mercy of God, would be Catholics all the same.
Am I the right person, you ask, to be throwing up my cap and shouting
because an Oxford man became a Catholic, and turned into a Birmingham man, a hundred years ago?

Not that you have any grudge against converts; you have known
some very decent people among them, and when they've been settled
down in the Church for ten years or so, you can scarcely recognize
them; but the whole idea is strange to you. All your life you have
breathed the air of the Catholic religion; it's as familiar to you as the
multiplication-table; and you can no more imagine yourself as a
Protestant, wondering what it is like to be a Catholic, than you can
imagine yourself as a Hottentot, wondering what it is like to be an
Englishman. You know your catechism, and you've learnt it intelligently; you are familiar with all the gracious usages of the Catholic
religion; you obey, to the best of your power, the commands which
the Church enjoins upon you. But what these things would look like
from the outside, to a person brought up in quite another way of
thinking; what it would be like to hear for the first time about the
Immaculate Conception, or to be taught how to take holy water, or
to be persuaded, with great difficulty, to go to confession—all that,
which the convert knows well enough, is to you something unimagin-
able. How are you to enter into the spirit of that great event—for it
was a great event—which took place in such humble circumstances—
for they were very humble circumstances—a hundred years ago?

You must picture to yourself a little village a mile or two from
Oxford, on the main road to Henley and London, but little affected
by that accident of its position. Away to the left, as you approach
the rather uninspiring parish church, is a row of cottages, adapted so
as to hold a little community of religiously disposed persons. In one of
the rooms, small, bare, and not very comfortable, you see a man praying
on his knees; a man forty-four years of age, just at his life's meridian;
you can tell him by his brow for a scholar, by his mouth and the lines
round his mouth for a sensitive nature, much alive to human friendship.
He is listening for a knock at the door; a knock which will alter his
whole destiny. His decision has been taken, but not yet put into effect;
and the thoughts that possess his mind, while he tries to subdue them
into resignation, are thoughts of what the decision will mean; the
unknown world into which he is banishing himself, the familiar things
he is leaving behind, his reasons for leaving them; the faces of his

friends, who will be thrown into doubt, consternation, and something like despair, when they hear of today's news; the faces of his critics, as they toss aside the morning paper with the contemptuous cry, "I always told you so". And, interlaced with these, a string of quotations from the early Fathers, centuries ago; what St Athanasius said about the Arians, what St Cyril said about the Nestorians, what St Augustine said about the Donatists. Those long-dead controversies of the first six centuries are almost more real to him than the actual world of his day, so absorbedly has he studied the documents of antiquity, so resolutely has he cut himself off from Oxford, with its noisy theological debates and its cosy common-room life. All his human sentiments are pulling him one way; all his dry, academic convictions the other. And he knows that his dry, academic convictions have got to win. There is a knock at the outside door; it is Father Dominic.

Tell me, is there about that picture any suggestion of breathing, human realities, for you—for you who have been brought up in the faith, and never known what it was to make a decision in conscience, which claimed the obedience, not of your will precisely, but of your intellect? Can you really throw yourself into the feelings of this man, so much a child of his own age, of his own university setting—you, living a hundred years later, in a world so much wrapped up in its own hopes and its own problems, so unsympathetic with the past? Confess that though you feel sorry for the man, though you admire him, the spirit of his sacrifice is something strange to you. When you have heard a sermon in church on Sunday morning, you like to come away feeling that a message has been given which makes Christian doctrine clearer, or Christian duty easier, to you personally. But these remote intellectual struggles of an early nineteenth-century scholar only bewilder you.

Let me say, then, this: essentially, all conversion is one. The same thing happens when a Protestant receives the gift of faith as happens when a drunkard at a parish mission gets the grace to live sober; as happens in a retreat, when some soul, after many hesitations, decides to give itself up more completely to God—perhaps in the life of the cloister. It is God's will taking over, and man's will saying "Carry on". Oh, I know that theologically speaking conversion to the faith is a different process; what is required is not an act of the will, but an act of the intellect commanded by the will. But, if anything goes wrong at the last moment, believe me, it's not because the intellect won't obey orders; it's because the will won't issue them. Essentially, what the Protestant gives up in becoming a Catholic is not this or that doctrine which he believed, this or that doubt which he found congenial, but the privilege of having his own way, of choosing for himself. And for that reason I say that the conversion of John Henry Newman is not an event of remote ecclesiastical importance which we English Catholics feel we ought to commemorate somehow, for fear it should look as if converts weren't welcome. It is one of those breathless moments in history when a great soul has given up its hesitations and handed over the control of its destinies to almighty God. There are only a few of those conversions that really catch the imagination: St Paul, St Augustine, St Francis, Pascal, Louise de la Vallière,[1] and so on. But we should never read the story of them, you and I, without stopping to think to ourselves: "Here a much greater man or woman than I stood once at the parting of the ways; had to decide whether a human will or a divine will should have the precedence. And grace triumphed. May grace always triumph in me! Speak, Lord, for thy servant heareth."

And I leave that with you as the moral of Cardinal Newman's conversion all the more willingly, because he himself has recorded for us in poetry, with one of those strokes of the pen which change thousands, perhaps millions of lives, the aspirations of a soul which resolves to submit itself to the divine guidance. Twelve years before his conversion, when he was travelling in the Mediterranean, he wrote three stanzas of which, I think, he did not know the meaning at the time; he will have felt that anybody, however circumstanced, might have written them. He had not the faintest consciousness, then, of any attraction towards the Catholic Church. He had just been to Rome, had had an interview, even, with Monsignor Wiseman, but his impressions of religion abroad were unfavourable. Really, I think, the call of grace had got under his skin, although he did not know it. Certainly anyone who has been through the same experience will tell you that, during the struggles which preceded his own conversion, those stanzas haunted him, had more influence with him than anything else Newman ever wrote. How familiar they are to you, I do not know. Every English-speaking Protestant in the world knows them by heart; but it was only ten years ago that "Lead, kindly Light" found its way into our official Catholic hymnal.[2]

"Lead, kindly light, amid the encircling gloom, Lead thou me on."

---

[1] Louise Françoise de la Vallière (1644-1710): mistress of Louis XIV; in 1671 entered a Carmelite convent, where she led a most saintly life until her death. See Joan Sanders, *The Devoted Mistress, a Life of Louise de la Vallière* (Longmans, 1959).

[2] The new Westminster Hymnal, which the Hierarchy commissioned Mgr Knox to revise in 1936. See Evelyn Waugh, *The Life of Ronald Knox*, p. 253.

For Newman, no doubt—though at the time he did not know it—the light of theological truth was meant; in that gloom of liberalizing doctrines that was beginning to settle down over Oxford and over England (still only a faint haze, compared with the Egyptian darkness which now envelops them, but discernible already to watchful eyes like those of Newman and his friends), one ray of hope seemed to offer itself. They must recondition the Church of England, bring it back to that high sense of its own position which it had had two centuries earlier. A will-o'-the-wisp, or some reflection from a fuller blaze of illumination? Who shall say? But at least it was the best light he had—then; and he resolved to follow it. We, who enjoy that fuller illumination, ask for no fresh theological certitude on this side of the grave. But to each of us, in the management of his own interior life, God is ready to make his will plain to us in proportion as we ask him for enlightenment. Not one of us but needs to pray, "Lead, kindly light"; we are surrounded on every side with the false maxims of the world, with a general sense of apathy and despair which has come down on us since the war ended, and brought us no nearer the solution of our problems; the lights of civilization seem to be going out around us, and we have, somehow, to make our souls; "Lead, kindly Light".

"The night is dark, and I am far from home." Newman, indeed, was still far from the bosom of that Church which is our home, here on earth. Like most souls to whom God means to give the grace of faith, he was at once farther from the Church, and nearer to it, than he knew. For us, there is no such sense of homelessness; you cannot be a displaced person while you have the passport of God's kingdom in your pocket. But we, too, are exiles; our true home is in heaven; and most of us, though we may be near our end, are very far from that purity of heart in which alone man can be privileged to see God. That more perfect purity we need, that better thing he would have us do, he will make known to us if we will pray faithfully for his light.

"Keep thou my feet; I do not ask to see The distant scene; one step enough for me." By very gentle, gradual stages Newman was led on to the discovery of Catholic truth. You would almost think divine Providence—or is that an unworthy suspicion?—meant him to make a great name for himself as an Anglican, so that his conversion, when it did take place, might have all the more profound effect. But that readiness to keep his eyes blindfolded, to follow the divine call wherever it might lead him, looking not to long-term results but to the achievement of God's will here and now—*that* was an attitude which stayed with Newman through life, a life which involved, even when he had joined the

Church, many ups and downs, many disappointments. And it is an attitude which God loves to find in you and me. His "sacrament of the present moment", the thing which we ought to be doing here and now, concentrating all our attention on, here and now, because it is his will; blindfolding ourselves to all the future has in store for us or for others, not wasting ourselves on day-dreams, on unnecessary alarms. To be always asking to learn more of God's will, always perfectly resigned to the consequences of following it, never looking ahead in nervous anticipation of what those consequences will be—that is the character of the real Christian. "One step enough for me."

Not a saint, John Henry Newman, as far as we know; God has his own saints *in petto* who are never canonized. Not a canonized saint, but a man full of human tenderness and human lovableness, who, to the end of his life, scrupulously obeyed his conscience as the voice of God. A man who suffered much, and suffered keenly, yet never allowed disappointment to spoil his usefulness, or to sour his temper. It is not only in his saints that God gives you and me an example of how we ought to get through this difficult world. If we cannot invoke Newman, at least we can pray for the grace to follow him. "Let me die the death of the just, and may my last end be like this."[1]

19

THE CONVERSION OF NEWMAN: II[2]

Great is truth, and has the mastery.—3 Esdras 4.

VERY few people know the source of that quotation, although it is one which every Englishman is accustomed to misquote, and to misunderstand. The story—there is no reason whatever to think it is true—is that King Darius had three lords-in-waiting, who argued the question, which was the strongest thing in the world. The first said, Wine; the second, A king; the third, Zorobabel, said, Women; but he added, And yet there is a stronger thing than any of these, Truth. With that, all the company cried out, Great is truth, and has the mastery. They meant, not that truth will sooner or later prevail in

[1] Numbers 23. 10.
[2] This sermon was preached at the Birmingham Oratory on 9 October 1945, in the presence of the assembled Hierarchy, to commemorate the centenary of the conversion of John Henry Newman.

men's minds over error; but that truth enjoys an intrinsic sovereignty of its own, more compelling than the lure of pleasure, than the sword of earthly authority, than the glamour of a woman's looks. It beckons to the mind, and the mind, under penalty of abdicating its own nature, must needs follow.

We have met to celebrate Cardinal Newman in the Oratory which was his home; the home of one who was, as every Oratorian must be, a great home-lover. This is not a funeral panegyric. If long keeping of his own fireside could impress a man's image indelibly on his surroundings, you would say that the Cardinal is waiting for us upstairs; too tired for attendance at the High Mass, we should expect to find him there, at least in the room where so little has been altered since he took his last journey to Rednal.[1] We are talking about him behind his back; about the thing which happened on October the 9th, 1845—his conversion. What is, precisely, the spiritual event we are discussing? When a soul receives, not in infancy, the grace of faith, two things happen: the Church gains a convert, and the convert gains a Church. Which of those two considerations is uppermost in our minds?

If a preacher stood before you who could boast that the sunshine of the Catholic faith had lit up his nursery days, that the same authority which taught him his alphabet had taught him his *Hail Mary*, that the message of the Gospel had come down to him direct through the preaching of the English martyrs—then, courtesy would demand that he should sum up for you what the Catholic Church gained, when she gained John Henry Newman. But since you are in the mood to listen to one who worshipped as a schoolboy in that other church of another St Philip, am ile from here;[2] to one who served the same apprenticeship Newman himself served, of Oxford Anglicanism, held a fellowship in Newman's own College, and watched Newman's snapdragons fade on the walls of it at the beginning of every autumn term—if a convert must speak to you, let him speak of what John Henry Newman gained, when he gained the Catholic Church.

Loss and Gain, the Story of a Convert—few of us can look along a row of his works, reading the titles on the backs, without pausing as we meet those words to consider what loss, what gain the author himself experienced. When Newman knelt there, in his Oratory at Littlemore, waiting to hear Destiny knocking at the door, the timid "May I come in?" of Father Dominic, he was forty-four years of age; he died at

---

[1] The burial ground of the Fathers of the Birmingham Oratory. The land was acquired by Newman in 1854; a chapel was built there in 1857.

[2] A reference to the Anglican pro-Cathedral, dedicated to St Philip the Apostle. Mgr Knox's father was Rector of this church before becoming Bishop of Manchester.

eighty-nine, and I suppose that, if the moment of grace could be of our choosing, our advice to Protestants would be, "Make your submission to the Church, either at nineteen or at seventy". "The more than Michal of his youth, the Abishag of his age"—if it were ours to woo the Catholic Church for the sake of her companionship, we should take her either for the inspiration of a whole career, or for the comfort of a lonely old age. To become a convert, as Newman did, at the meridian of your days, is to miss, humanly speaking, the best she has to offer. You are too old to be any longer adaptable; you have made most of your life-long friendships; you have become settled in your habits, and, to a great extent, in your ways of thought. Few men can afford to change their whole setting at that time of life; least of all, John Henry Newman. On the other hand, for you as for other converts the gracious influence of the honeymoon period will fade; you will be disappointed, sometimes, not with the Church, but with the human machinery which represents her, which so often misrepresents her; you will have ups and downs, periods of dryness and of staleness—it will not be, with you, as it was yesterday and the day before. Few men can welcome life's rebuffs, when they seem to come from the hands of that very institution to which a life has been dedicated; least of all, John Henry Newman.

Wine, and the king, and women; those are crude terms under which the third book of Esdras would image for us three great appetites of our nature, the love of pleasure, the taste for power, the craving for human affection. To all those appetites we may have to say, "Get behind me", when the paramount claim of truth rules them out of consideration. There are few more comfortable lives than that of an unmarried Fellow at one of the grey-stone universities. To Newman, comfort did not mean much; but I think the mere routine of a familiar life was very dear to him; if he kissed the door-posts of his meagre cottage at Littlemore when he went away, it was because they stood for something that had become a matter of custom with him, something he had grown into—he was not fond of moving. To leave the atmosphere in which he had been nurtured would have meant a wrench for him, even if there had been nothing else. But there was, much else. He must leave behind him that position of dominance in a world of thought which comes to few men, and is all the more treasured because it is so rare. And he must make up his mind to the parting of friends.

I do not mean to ask here whether Newman's influence as an Anglican was wider or less wide, profounder or less profound, than his influence as a Catholic. But this I think is certain; that the kind of

fame and of opportunity which Newman had when he was an Anglican
were of a more enjoyable sort than the fame and opportunity he
enjoyed as a Catholic; and he must have foreseen it. To be part of a
movement, of a growing and a winning movement; to see, in all your
personal contacts, in all your literary projects, an opening for spreading
the influence of that movement; to dominate, in large part, by force of
intellect, the intellectual world around you—I do not know that any
kind of publicity can be so sweet to a man's taste as the kind of publicity Newman had before 1838. Opposition, criticism no doubt there
will be, but you hardly feel them in the excitement of the struggle.
Contrast that with the orbit of Newman's influence after 1845.
Writing, on the whole, for a smaller world, and always with an eye to
unknown critics ready to scent unorthodoxy; being employed on
projects more likely to bring distrust than fame; the suspicion, magni-
fied perhaps by his sensitive temperament, that he was watched, that
he was being weighed—all that, for which it is easy to blame his contemporaries too much, was a poor exchange for the academic splendours of the past. And further, to be the spokesman not of his own
ideas, but of an international body perhaps not always wisely governed,
certainly wanting in sensitiveness towards English feelings, was
cramping to a mind of great intellectual integrity. "The advisers of the
Holy Father", he said (in discussing the *Syllabus Errorum*[1]), "seem
determined to make our position in England as difficult as ever they
can." More of a liberal than he knew, in days when liberty was suspect,
a pioneer of Catholic Action in days when a Roman Monsignore could
tell us that the province of the laity was "to hunt, to shoot, to entertain", he lacked intellectual elbow-room. He had not borne the yoke
in his youth.

Not all that, perhaps, was foreseen; it was none the less implicit in
the act of submission Newman made, a hundred years ago. He paid
over, and knew that he was paying over, a blank cheque. It was otherwise, I think, with the sacrifice of his friendships. As it proved, many
of his near friends followed him into the Church; some remained his
close companions, and shared with him that gracious family life which
is the gift of St Philip. He even picked up, though only after an
interval of years, the threads of his old intimacy with men like Church[2]
and Rogers.[3] But all that, at the time of his conversion, he could not

[1] The name given to a series of propositions containing modern religious errors condemned by Pius IX in 1864.

[2] Richard William Church (1815-90), Anglican clergyman, Tractarian and dean of
St Paul's; buried at Whatley, near Frome.

[3] Frederic Rogers (1811-89), Fellow of Oriel, Tractarian, co-founder of *The Guardian*;
raised to the peerage as Baron Blachford, 1871.

foresee. To an intensely affectionate nature, like his, the dreariest cloud which hung over that autumn day at Littlemore was the thought that he was going into a new world of human beings. To those others, his comrades in arms, gathered about him there in imagination, he preached his parting sermon. "Oh hard destiny", he told them, "had not the All-Merciful so willed it, that such companions might not walk in the house of God as friends!"

And all that he bartered away, or was prepared to barter away, for what? For truth. Day-to-day comforts, familiar ways of living, the nest a man has made for himself as he turned round in the world about him, have a pull that tends to keep him anchored. Ambition, the instinct of command, of wanting to see things carried out according to his own prescriptions, will make a man think twice before he deserts his own proprietary concern to work under the orders of another. Human affection, so subtly, so invisibly prehensile, casts a noose round his heart from which he will find it difficult to disentangle himself. But the claim of truth is absolute. Sooner than live a lie, a man will consent to any laceration, no matter how violent, of his own feelings. And Newman, in his meditations at Littlemore, had reached a point at which any further parleying with Anglicanism would have been living a lie. Truth beckoned to him, offering no credentials except its own innate royalty: "Rise, take my hand, and come". Have I exaggerated the sacrifice he made, or thought he was making, in becoming a Catholic? I do not care; Newman's spirit was so finely tempered that he would have answered the call at whatever cost. What he gained, the only thing he substantially gained, the only thing it mattered to gain, was the consciousness of telling, of living the truth. He went where he belonged; that is all the convert asks; all that the convert *can* ask with safety.

When the grace of conversion first comes to a man, still very far off, like the sound of a gnat singing in his ears, he does not know that anything has happened to him. He is like Eliseus, when Elias said to him, "Go back; what have I done to thee?" But thenceforward he is a haunted man. I suspect that this happened to Newman a full twelve years before 1845. When he lay desperately ill in Sicily, you remember, he said, "I shall not die; I have not sinned against the light". As it is the first sign of drunkenness when a man tells himself he is not drunk, so it is the first sign of bad faith when a man tells himself that he is in good faith. Grace had got in under his skin, although, except in a moment of delirium, he was not aware of it. Sooner or later, he must either succumb or, at the grave peril of his soul, gag the accusing

Voice. He gave way by inches, rationalizing as he did so. In 1839 he abandoned controversy, telling himself that it was because of the way in which the public had received Tract Ninety. In 1841 he made his solemn protest to Lambeth about the Jerusalem bishopric. In 1843, conscious that the Anglican hierarchy looked on him with mistrust, he resigned his living and went to Littlemore. "One step enough for me"; in all this, the *Apologia* has proved for ever that he acted with full sincerity, as far as conscience was concerned. But, behind the scenes, grace was at work, and in 1845 he made his exit. Truth stood before him, fully embodied, and he gave way.

I say then that Newman was, as in a measure all converts are, a witness to truth. The martyrs are witnesses to the truth, but for them, it is mixed up with other considerations; with loyalties, with ideologies; the convert sees truth, as truth is represented proverbially, naked. And I say that this witness to truth is all-important in our time. In our life-time the sovereignty of truth itself has come to be assailed. For the sake of cause or party, for the sake of efficient government, men will silence, expressly and deliberately, that sovereign voice. A hundred years ago our enemies blamed us for thinking wrong; today they blame us for thinking. They hustle the unwelcome metaphysician into the concentration camp, into the gas-chamber. Men are to think as the State wants them to think, whether it is true or not. And not only Catholics, but all lovers of truth as such ought to celebrate, with reverent rejoicing, the ninth of October. If you do not celebrate the ninth, you have no choice but to celebrate the twenty-sixth.

And yet, for us Catholics, truth is something homelier and friendlier than bare intellectual conviction. Revealed truth does not merely claim the homage of our intellects, it satisfies the aspirations of our hearts. What Newman gained in 1845 was not the mere saving of his own intellectual honesty; it was a system of spiritual values which lit up the world for him; not a cold glare but a warm blaze, a kindly Light which made the darkness more congenial than the garish day he loved once. A man of intellect, but very human, he preached to us, not from the rostrum, but from the pulpit. He followed truth, not as one who demands mere leadership; it was a wine he thirsted for, he was love-sick for its romance. His great name lives imperishable in the annals of the Church, a man who lived haunted by the truth, and died desiring it.

20

THE CONVERSION OF FABER[1]

A necessity lieth upon me. For woe is unto me if I preach not the gospel.—
1 Corinthians 9. 16.

IN the early morning of 17 November 1845, the rector of a village in Northamptonshire left it for ever. It was Monday morning, a black Monday for the people of Elton. The evening before, their rector had preached them a sermon announcing that his position as an Anglican was no longer possible for him, then threw off his surplice and left it lying on the floor. He had chosen the early morning, so as to avoid publicity; but as he went windows were thrown open everywhere with cries of "God bless you, Mr Faber, wherever you go". He was accompanied by two servants, seven of his parishioners, and a young friend who had just taken his degree at Cambridge; a young man with a good Protestant name, well known afterwards as Father Thomas Knox, of the London Oratory. When they reached Northampton, Bishop Wareing, of the Eastern District, received them all into the Church, and gave them confirmation next morning. There was not much in all this to arouse the interest of the public. Stars had fallen from heaven, only a month ago Newman had joined the Romanists; what difference would one country parson make? They were not likely to hear of him again.

The public was wrong, as it usually is. Mr Faber was to be heard of again. There is a curious resemblance between the Methodist Revival in the eighteenth century and the Oxford Movement in the nineteenth. We think at once of Wesley and Newman, two men who set about the difficult task of converting Oxford; each of them experienced conversion (in one case an emotional, in the other an intellectual conversion) in middle life, each became a figure of national importance, a name we have all heard of. We forget George Whitefield, who in his day was a preacher not less known, perhaps better known, than his master John Wesley. We forget Faber, who in his day was a figure hardly less significant than Newman himself. What is the meaning of that partial eclipse?

To some extent it is a matter of longevity. Wesley and Newman

---

[1] This sermon was preached at the London Oratory on 17 November 1945, to commemorate the centenary of the conversion of Father Frederick William Faber.

died as very old men; indeed, between 1700 and 1900 there were only twenty years in which neither Wesley nor Newman was alive. White-field (born in 1714) died, worn out, at the age of fifty-six. Father Faber (born in 1814) died, worn out, at the age of forty-nine. Less than a generation of men came under his influence; and perhaps a presage of mortality bade him work at high pressure, leaving things unpolished. But, more importantly, Whitefield and Faber were both, really, men of the pulpit, not of the study; their preaching demanded a living personality to carry it off. Whitefield, breaking off in the middle of a sermon to exclaim, "Stop, Gabriel, stop, ere you enter the sacred portals, and yet carry with you the news of one sinner converted to God!" How cheap it sounds, repeated like that! And yet it nearly made a Methodist of David Hume. Faber, when a mission sermon of his was going badly, crying out, "How can I touch your hearts? I have prayed to Jesus, I have prayed to Mary; whom shall I pray to next?" And then, as he fell on his knees, "I will pray to *you*, my dear Irish children, to have mercy on your own souls"—we do not care for it, perhaps, but the whole congregation fell on its knees with him. Preaching like that does not live between the pages of a book.

When I say that Father Faber has suffered a partial eclipse, I do not doubt for a moment that his hymns will be known and loved, several of them even among Protestants, as long as the English language is spoken. And his devotional writings, if they have not the vogue they had formerly, will never collect dust, like Mr Gother's sermons.[1] It may be, they will leap into popularity again. But at the moment, we are out of tune for his writings. A child of his age, he cultivated the florid style we admired once, but no longer admire, in Macaulay; he aimed at the pathetic effects which the modern reader frowns upon as sentimentalism in Dickens. Those long sentences—I have counted one of three hundred and seventy words—those crowded epithets, do not suit our present taste. We remember him by some of his weak lines almost as easily as by his good lines; Wordsworth was his master. Nay, the man himself had a trick of throwing himself so completely into the thing he was doing, that he never stopped to think about the figure he was cutting. We have all been brought up on the story of Father Faber, at the end of a magnificent procession of our Lady, bursting into tears and ejaculating, "Won't Mamma be pleased?" He does not accommodate himself to our prejudices; he is of yesterday.

If you had told him that a hundred years after the date of his leaving

---

[1] A convert minister who died in 1704. Most old Catholic libraries contain many volumes of his sermons.

Elton people would be picking holes in his hymn-writing, and in his prose style, and even in his personal approach, I don't think Father Faber would have taken any offence; and I don't think he would have changed a line, or altered his habits by *one hair's breadth*. He was a conscientious Philistine; he would not understand how Christian people could take pleasure in reading Milton or Byron, considering how bad their theology was. "Art for art's sake" had no meaning for him; the glory of God and the conversion of souls was the only thing that mattered, and if a bad verse would have more chance of winning souls than a good verse, down the bad verse would go. If somebody composed a tune for "Oft in the stilly night" which caught his fancy, he would sit down and write a hymn, to the same air. It was his conviction that the Catholic body in England had been miserably impoverished by its long ostracism in a Protestant country; the pious practices, the spiritual reading, the saints' lives, the church ornaments which contributed such diverse splendour to the devotion of Catholics on the Continent, were all unknown. *He* must supply the need, picking up his material from here, there and everywhere; he was rebuilding a ruined city, and if it became necessary, now and again, to use trumpery material, it couldn't be helped.

And all that because he was fundamentally, and to a rare degree, an ascetic. I do not think he was naturally humble; naturally he was rather self-centred. But, as an act of mortification, he was perpetually *bullying* himself into humility, as a son of St Philip should; he was *always* choosing the harder way. "One of the Fathers", we are told, "finding in his room a large heap of letters ready for the post, expressed envy of his talent for answering letters. '*Talent!*' exclaimed Father Faber. '*It's the fear of God!*'" That was Father Faber all through. Had he consulted his own wishes, he would have spent his life roaming about in the Lake country, with Wordsworth, and writing poems on it. What sent him to win souls in the Brompton Road was the fear of God. Always he was allowing himself to be torn up from the surroundings, from the work he loved. Newman was converted after two years spent in retreat; Faber was converted after two years of strenuous parish work, in which he had transformed a degenerate country village into a kind of Paradise. He gave *that* up to become a Catholic; founded a Wilfridian order of his own; went to live in the country again and did something no other man had done, or has done, since the Reformation, turned a whole English village Catholic; gave *that* up, to become an Oratorian. Then came the hardest test of all; people didn't like his series of saints' lives, wanted it stopped—and he gave *that* up. It was too much; divine Providence remembered Abraham and Isaac, and the series was recontinued. All through the most active part of his life he suffered, almost incessantly, from violent headaches; he was continually forcing himself out of a sick-bed to devote the last ebbing powers of his life to the service of his Master. We laughed at Father Faber; which of us is worthy to loose the shoes from his feet? He caught something from today's saint[1] as a memento of his conversion; the spirit of faith, which can move mountains. With faith, we may save our own souls; we need the *spirit* of faith, much more of it than we have, if we are to save the world.

21

THE JUBILEE OF CAMPION HALL[2]

Et dixi in corde meo, Si unus et stulti et meus occasus erit, quid mihi prodest, quod majorem sapientiae dedi operam?
Why then, I said to myself, if fool and I must come to the same end at last, was not I the fool, that toiled to achieve wisdom more than he?—Ecclesiastes 2. 15.

THE Jesuits in Oxford! What a temptation, when you are invited to celebrate such a theme, to go back over the history of the past! To recall the tradition that always, from the day when Edmund Campion was laid by the heels at Lyford, to the time of Catholic Emancipation, there was a Jesuit priest somewhere within call of Oxford, if you knew where to find him! To remind ourselves that Oxford really was, once, the home of lost causes, an Oxford which accepted the Reformation so slowly, so grudgingly the Hanoverians. To sigh for the old days of Antony à Wood and Tom Hearne, when Oxford was content to be a backwater, because the tide of fashion ran foul!

The Society of Jesus, too, is the home of last causes; what other institution in the world looks back on such a long record of failures that nearly succeeded; from the theocracy of Paraguay to those

---

[1] St Gregory Thaumaturgus (Wonderworker).
[2] This sermon was preached at St Aloysius's, Oxford, on 30 October 1946, in the presence of the Cardinal Archbishop of Westminster, to commemorate the fiftieth anniversary of the establishment in Oxford of the Jesuit house of studies, now named Campion Hall.

Christians, come down from Francis Xavier, who were wiped out by the atom bomb at Nagasaki? Is there, perhaps, something in common between these two great products of Christian civilization, the University of Oxford and the Society of Jesus; are their destinies somehow linked, their tempers somehow congenial?

St Ignatius, we all know, was himself a university man. But we should not be tempted to describe St Ignatius as a man of the universities. We think of him not as a don, but as an undergraduate. And at the same time, we think of him not as a youthful undergraduate, but as one of those older men who (as the late head of my own college used to say) "make all the trouble". By the Paris authorities of his own day, he was no doubt remembered as the disturbing influence which prevented that ripe scholar, Francis Xavier, settling down as he ought to have. All very well, to go round buttonholing people and asking how a man is the better for it, if he gains the whole world at the expense of losing his own soul; but the men come up here to work, and they will never get the best out of the place if they are at the mercy of these stray evangelists. To the Paris authorities St Ignatius must have seemed typical of those predatory idealists who come up to the university, not to complete their education, but to enlist recruits for some movement, some organization of their own. Little wonder if the Company of Jesus was hardly more popular in sixteenth-century Paris than in seventeenth-century Oxford.

And were we right in supposing that the Society which began life with such a record would fit, as a matter of course, without friction, without need for adjustment, into the life of a university? With the older religious orders, not cradled in times of controversy, the concordat is easy. The university is ready enough, in ambition at least, to exchange mottoes with them. The sons of St Benedict, with their patient researches into the history of which they feel themselves to be a part, may serve as good models for what the ideal scholar should be, if only he could secure the leisure to imitate them. Pax is the motto every college would fain write up over its library—if it were not for the men. And the Black Friars, with their fearless attempt to solve the central riddle of existence—that is an ambition with which the academic philosopher finds it easy to sympathize, even when, in an age of disillusionment, he has come to the conclusion that the riddle has no answer. Dominus Illuminatio Mea; he, like themselves, is in search of enlightenment, and a single sentence will cover his aim and theirs, if you do not inquire too closely into the grammar of it. But, Ad Majorem Dei Gloriam—that sounds a note of challenge. It limits too narrowly the scope of human achievement, the range of human motive. As a phrase it is all right, but the intention of it is more questionable. Does it not simplify the whole of life too much, by reducing it all to a mechanical hierarchy of ends and means? *Quid hoc ad aeternitatem?* ask the meditation books: "How does *this* bear on eternity?"—as if *that* were the only question that mattered. Is not this to reduce the rest of our human values, the quest of knowledge for its own sake, the quest of beauty for its own sake, to the level of childish games?

I am, deliberately, overstating the terms of the contrast. But Matthew Arnold described Oxford, in his day, as a city which had never given herself over to the Philistines; and there *is* a kind of holy Philistinism about the *Exercises* of St Ignatius; they do preach a kind of utilitarianism *in excelsis*. They are a counterblast necessary then, and perhaps not quite unnecessary now, to the humanism of the Renaissance. They disturb our complacent habit of mind, so dear to the academies, with an echo of the verse which saint murmured to saint[1] in the crowded classrooms of Paris: "How is a man the better for it, if he gains the whole world at the expense of losing his own soul?"

Notoriously, there is no department of human learning which does not reckon Fathers of the Society on the list of those whose labours have adorned it. Notoriously, there is no Order in the Church that cultivates so generously, and utilizes so fruitfully, the varied talent which is to be found among the members. But always, or so the world reasonably suspects, there is a hesitation, an *arrière pensée*; not learning as such, not art as such, but the glory of God as these can serve to promote it, is the object consciously envisaged. And all the humanist in us is ready to rise up and take offence. We are so schooled to an essentially pagan way of looking at things that we suspect a certain dilettantism, a certain want of naturalness about the learning that runs thus harnessed to the thought of eternity. Unconsciously we assume that a man cannot be a real scholar, a real scientist, a real historian, unless he is a monomaniac on his subject.

And yet we know that we are wrong. We know that the pursuit of learning, if it goes unchecked, can lead to a kind of idolatry. Historical truth, scientific truth, the method of philosophy, that delicate balance of the mind which we call scholarship, are in themselves values which can claim our reverence; you can think of them as worth cultivating for their own sakes, although in fact the light which shines from them is not theirs; God is their Sun, and it is from him their radiance is borrowed. But all these desirable aims, if you see them against the

[1] St Ignatius to St Francis Xavier.

background of a single human life, are only toys after all, only extras; they are not, taken alone, worth living for. The scholar who lives only for his subject is but the fragment of a man; he lives in a shadow-world, mistaking means for ends.

I would suggest, then, that the completeness of being which the very word "university" implies is not achieved, in this modern world, unless the Fathers of the Society are there to leaven it. As they slip into their shiny black gowns, of a different cut from ours—gowns (you would say) not eagerly possessed but picked up absent-mindedly, at the last moment, in the porter's lodge—they warn us that human learning is only a part of life, not life's end or life's essence. They will make, to be sure, a brilliant and varied contribution to the academic perfection of our institute, enriching it with the profound thought of a Rickaby,[1] the political vision of a Charles Plater,[2] the literary genius of a Hopkins. But all that will be, from their point of view, a by-product: sparks struck out incidentally from the anvil of a dedicated life. Predominantly the Fathers of the Society are with us as university demonstrators, demonstrating what is, to flesh and blood, indemonstrable—that all our studies are, in a certain sense, toys; their subject-matter passes with the passage of time.

St Ignatius, persuaded by the omen to spare the blaspheming Moor, is still the model his sons imitate.[3] They ride on, with their faces set towards a dawn which is not of this world; and we are left, babbling of this and that, in their wake, stretching out our hands towards the unattainable, and, by the example of their pregnant silence, consciously belittled.

[1] Joseph Rickaby: b. 1845; entered Society of Jesus 1862; d. 1932; published many philosophical works, including God and His Creatures.
[2] Charles Plater: b. 1875; entered Society of Jesus 1894; Master of Campion Hall 1916-1921; d. 1921; chiefly known for promoting the Catholic Social Guild and for occasional writings on social topics.
[3] It is recorded that on the way to Manresa, St Ignatius Loyola fell into argument with a Moor about the virginity of our Lady. The Moor broke off the discussion and rode ahead. Left to himself St Ignatius was tempted to revenge the Moor's blasphemy with his dagger. For some time he was in doubt. Then he decided to leave the matter to his mule, giving it free rein to choose its road. The beast turned aside from the path which the Moor had followed and St Ignatius accepted its guidance.

K

22

A LONDON PARISH[1]

*After this, many of his disciples went back to their old ways, and walked no
more in his company. Whereupon Jesus said to the twelve, Would you, too,
go away? Simon Peter answered him, Lord, to whom should we go? Thy
words are the words of eternal life.*—John 6. 67-69.

EVERY year, when the Gospel of this Sunday is read out, we feel a
slight sense of monotony, of anticlimax. Surely we have heard all
this before, and not very long ago—the fourth Sunday in Lent, wasn't
it? We are wrong; that other Gospel described how our Lord fed five
thousand men, with their womenfolk and children, on five loaves,
leaving twelve small baskets of bread unconsumed. This morning's
Gospel referred to a later occasion, when he fed four thousand persons
altogether, on seven loaves, leaving seven great hampers of bread unconsumed. Fewer people, more food, and more waste; if there is
monotony, if there is anticlimax here, the liturgy is not to blame; it
happened like that.

What is the explanation of the figures? It is to be found, surely, in
those words I quoted just now from St John. After the miracle of the
five thousand, our Lord put a heavy strain on the faith of his followers,
by telling them about the doctrine of the Blessed Sacrament. And for
some of them, the strain was too great; many of his disciples went back
to their old ways, and walked no more in his company. May we,
perhaps, picture the holy apostles as going round on their hospitable
duties with a sense, this time, almost of disillusionment? The freshness
of the miracle has worn off; they are tired, themselves, after three days
of fasting; and, worse still, the popularity of the movement is not what
it was—they have thrown their lot in with a losing cause. Bread
enough for everybody, and more than enough; there is no falling-away
in the divine munificence. But, alas, how much of it will be left over!
There is a falling-away in human loyalty.

What a curious subject for a sermon, you complain, on a day like
this! We are all in holiday mood, and we are to be told, not of the
progress which the Church of Christ has made, in these last hundred

---

[1] This sermon was preached at the Church of St Thomas of Canterbury, Fulham,
London, on Sunday, 27 June 1948, on the occasion of the centenary of the consecration
of the church.

years, but about the leakage which has crippled her work, tarnished her reputation! Yes, but consider this. We are here to thank God for the devoted lives of a long series of priests, here in Fulham; let me mention a good friend of my own, whose name many of you will remember with gratitude, dead not ten years since, Father Joe Warren. And the greatness of those men lies largely in this, that they worked, much of the time, under a heavy sense of disappointment. So many labours of the priesthood are, or seem to be, thrown away, bread cast on the waters, in the drifting tide of modern London. Modern London? Let us reflect how it seemed, a hundred years ago, when the paint in this church had hardly dried, to a great preacher of those days.

"In this huge city," he said, "amid a population of human beings, so vast that each is solitary, so various that each is independent; which, like the ocean, yields before and closes over every attempt made to influence and impress it; in this mere aggregate of individuals, which admits of neither change nor reform, because it has no internal order, or disposition of parts, or mutual dependence, because it has nothing to change from and nothing to change to; where no one knows his next-door neighbour, but everywhere are found a thousand worlds, each pursuing its own function unimpeded by the rest, how can we, how can a handful of men, do any service?" Thus spoke Father Newman, not when he occupied this pulpit just a century ago, but a year or two later, when he opened (not then in your neighbourhood) the London Oratory. It was the dawn of the Second Spring, but even then those silver tones vibrated with a note of disappointment.

Newman was thinking of his own preoccupations, his own experience. Just four years ago that steady stream of conversions had begun, influenced by his own, which had threatened to breach the dykes of English Protestantism altogether. It looked, for a moment, as if there could be no end to the process, once it had started; as if the full tide of English religious life were destined to flow back again into those old channels which it had deserted since the Reformation. And then, somehow, a reaction set in; the stream died up, and English Protestantism was flowing between its accustomed banks as placidly as ever. Newman, always sensitive to the least breath, was the first to be conscious of that check; and in sending out the Fathers of the Oratory to their mission in King William Street, he was at pains to warn them that theirs would be a difficult task. The religion they preached had suddenly lost the charm which it had exercised over English minds; it had gone back to the lumber-room of forgotten superstitions, and the apostles of it were everywhere cold-shouldered.

But in fact it was not merely the work of propaganda, of extending the kingdom of Christ, that was going to be difficult. Just at the same moment, the potato famine across St George's Channel had driven Irish Catholics, hundreds of thousands of them, to look for work and food in England; an epidemic had broken out, which was decimating their ranks and making them an object of dread to their neighbours. Few in numbers, the English priesthood found it difficult to meet the spiritual needs of such an invasion; meanwhile, charity was being offered to the wretched Irish which was accompanied, more or less openly, by the danger of apostasy. In the late forties of last century, the Catholic body in England were not merely committed to a desperate struggle to save the souls of their Protestant fellow countrymen. They were threatened, at the same time, with wholesale perversion among themselves. In so far as they failed to meet that situation, the return of England to the faith would be as distant as ever. Of what use were conversions, if all the time we were engaged in filling a bucket that leaked?

This church is one of those—alas, comparatively few—that were built in the early days of Cardinal Wiseman's appointment to the London district. And I think it may stand to us for a type of those patient pastoral labours which are designed, not to impress the world without, but to protect the faith, and deepen the spiritual life, of the Church's own children. We must win the world by hook or by crook; St Peter was called as a fisherman, but he lived to become a shepherd. Let it be for those others, then, our neighbours, to produce an effect on the heedless throng that passes their doors; the Oratorians with their splendid music and ceremonial, the Servites with their peals of bells ringing out defiantly down the Fulham Road. St Thomas's shall be a plain parish church, looking after the needs of plain parish folk, passing generations of Christians on, not unprovided, from time into eternity.

That is the history of the last hundred years. Do not be deceived into thinking that history is the record of wars or crises, of social developments or the changing fashions of human thought. Such things are only the backwash on the current. History is the life of John Smith, of the parish of Fulham, his birth, his marriage, his death. All that you will find set down in the parish registers; and always with the priest's name appended, to show that the blessing of the Church was there: *Ego*, Josephus Warren ... *Ego*, Ernestus Hanifin ... *Ego*, Carolus Flood[1]

[1] These are the names of recent rectors of Fulham: Fr Joseph Warren (1935-39); Fr Ernest Dominic Hanifin (1939-47); the Very Rev. Canon Charles Bernard Flood (1947-53).

—so, year after year, the ruling moments of human destiny stand dispassionately recorded. And meanwhile, how many secrets, these last hundred years, have been breathed through the grilles of those confessionals, and died with the priest who heard them! How many resolutions have been made, prayers granted, before that Lady statue! How many graces, unfelt, unseen, have been received at those communion rails! A church like this is a great museum of unwritten history; the history that really counts.

And you, the congregation of St Thomas's, are links in that chain of memories. Sound links? Not all the links have held firm. And it is as easy now as it was a hundred years ago to grow discouraged, to think the Catholic faith a small thing compared with the multiplied interests and enthusiasms of our day. But be sure of this—if our blessed Lord turned to you and me with the same question he asked of the twelve, "Would you, too, go away?", we can reply, with more conviction than ever, "Lord, to whom should we go? Thy words are the words of eternal life." A hundred years ago, the world felt sure of itself; a great worship of political freedom had sprung up, which marked the year 1848 with popular risings all over Europe. Men really believed, then, that mankind was to be rid of its shackles, was to come out into an era of universal happiness. This church has stood for a hundred years, and during that time the whole of our optimism has come crashing to the ground. In our time, if you ask, in the popular phrase, "Where do we go from here?", the sages of the world have no answer. They have boxed the compass, from a mood of exaggerated hopes into a mood of exaggerated despairs. But for us, there are no such changes of mood. The thing we live by today is the thing we lived by a hundred years ago. The world's glory passes, the Catholic faith remains; it is, for us, as if Nicholas Wiseman still ruled at Westminster, and Newman still preached, to the deaf ears of London, the words of eternal life.

23

THE BRITISH ASSOCIATION: I[1]

THERE is, surely, an opportunity for some artist—one, perhaps, who is content to follow the more conventional traditions of religious art—to give us a picture of our Lord in an attitude in which I have

[1] This sermon was preached in Dundee Cathedral on 31 August 1947, on the occasion of the meeting of the British Association.

never seen him represented; holding in his hand, and contemplating, one of the lilies of the field. No reason why the lily should be conventional; it was probably some other flower, they tell us; perhaps the narcissus, perhaps even the gladiolus, which grows wild on that favoured soil. "Even Solomon, in all his glory, was not arrayed like one of these"; if our artist were given to imitating the Italian primitives, he might give us a grassy background, at the further end of which you would see, very small, a group representing King Solomon and his court. But the essence of the picture would have to lie in our Lord's expression; a mixture, perhaps, of the creative pride, and the creaturely admiration, which a wild flower could evoke in the meditations of Incarnate God.

You might anticipate that such a text, coinciding with such an occasion, would provoke a sermon on fundamental theology. Something is due to the occasion, when visitors of great scientific eminence honour, and are honoured by, this ancient city, the birthplace of Thomas Dick[1] and the home of James Lindsay.[2] And today's Gospel greets them with one of those very rare utterances in which our Lord seems to put his finger on the doubts, the hesitations, of a later age. "If God so clothes the grasses of the field"—is he not challenging us to find the work of the Creator in his creation; even in what seems the unnecessary upholstery of his creation? Those frail expressions of loveliness, which exist today and must feed the oven tomorrow, does not the very briefness of their career invite us to see them against a background of permanence? Their delicate fashioning, so orderly, so uniform, and yet in its variety so far removed from the mass-produced, does it not plead for the existence of a Mind, infinitely greater if only because more operative than ours? And yet in some sense akin to ours, or how should it speak the same thought-language as ours, diaper our hillsides with a pattern we shall be able to recognize as beautiful? All that context of thought our artist would perhaps want to imply, in his picture of Jesus and the lily.

But of course that is not what our Lord was saying. Be the reason what it may, there is no single utterance of his preserved which is concerned with people who do not believe in God. Always his warnings are addressed to the people who say they believe in God, but do not realize the consequences, the practical consequences, which are involved in such a belief. There was some poor man, perhaps, in our

[1] Thomas Dick (1774-1857): scientist and author of *The Christian Philosopher* (1823) and *The Sidereal Heavens* (1840).
[2] James Bowman Lindsay (1799-1862): electrician and philologist, lecturer on mathematics and the physical sciences at the Watt Institute, Dundee.

Lord's audience, who had been forced to borrow money that day, and left his cloak as a pledge. All very well to be without it under the hot noon; but what of the chill tonight when it will be his only coverlet? The law says, his creditor must let him have it back; but this creditor, perhaps, was not very scrupulous about the law. And as he sits there fretting over his anxieties, our Lord begins to talk about divine Providence. "Is not life itself a greater gift than food, the body than clothing? Will God, who gave you the one, deny you the other? Somehow, he will provide." And then the gladiolus. "See how the wild lilies grow; they do not toil or spin, and yet I tell you that even Solomon in all his glory was not arrayed like one of these." Odd, isn't it, that our Lord should have begun talking about finery? Our Lady didn't often appear, I imagine, except in working dress. But then, the argument is *a fortiori*, all through. The God who gives a wild flower its ball-dress, will he not take care of you, a human creature, you, threatened with the loss of that warmth which you get from your homespun cloak?

Once more, are we to discuss, and before men of science, that most difficult (I think) of all Christian doctrines, the doctrine of Providence? We could hardly say anything valuable about it within the limits of a sermon. I would concentrate, rather, on one particular aspect of it; one turn of language which we are apt to miss when we read the familiar words of the holy Gospel. "Like *one* of these"—our Lord does not see the hillside carpeted with flowers, and compare *that* to Solomon's robe. He takes, at random, one single specimen, one individual flower. "There," he says, "Solomon couldn't beat that." So it is in the parable of the sower; all those multitudinous grains broadcast over the field, but what does it all lead up to? One grain yields a hundredfold, one sixtyfold, one thirtyfold; it is the fate of the individual grain he seems to care about. So, even more expressly, when he takes his argument from the animal creation: "Are not sparrows sold two for a penny? And yet it is impossible for one of them to fall to the ground without your heavenly Father's will." So cheap, you cannot even buy them singly; but God does not see them in pairs. . . . And above all, "If any of you owns a hundred sheep, and has lost one, does he not leave the other ninety-nine in the wilderness, and go after the one? And when he does find it, 'Rejoice with me', he says, 'I have found my sheep, the one that was lost'." Sheep, so much alike that you and I make no difference between the singular and the plural; but to the Good Shepherd there are no "sheep"; there is only this sheep and that.

What does it all mean? Why, surely this—that our Lord saw things through God's eyes. I do not mean to deny that, as Man, he thought humanwise, constructed general ideas for himself as you and I do. No, but he schooled himself to take his heavenly Father's point of view, knowing well where that point of view differed from ours. The divine regard falls on everything singly. It is a weakness of our human minds that we must see things, and even people, in groups, in masses; we are not up to the strain of seeing them individually; Coleridge said, truly enough, that if a man went up to the roof of St Paul's and remembered everything he had seen from it, he would go mad. We select, we generalize, we divide things into classes; lilies, grains of corn, sheep (by which we mean sheeps), sparrows, and so on. But almighty God sees each of them; and how much more evident it is that in this cathedral he doesn't see a mob of people hearing Mass; he sees you and me.

That is why, if you believe in the doctrine of Providence at all, you have got to believe in a Providence which looks after us individually. God sees us individually, and it is impossible that his love should be less all-embracing than his regard. To him, you are not just one flower in a bunch, one grain in a basket, one sparrow in a flight, one sheep in a flock; you are the one he cares about. We (except perhaps when we are in love) find it difficult to think about our fellow creatures except in a general way; masses of men, movements, and tendencies in history, and so on. But to God, each of us is unique, and each of us is the one that matters.

Is it possible that we have found the tail-end of a moral here for the men of science? They, more than anyone else, are in the habit of labelling things, and not only things but people, and generalizing about them, treating them as a class. It is quite right they should; that is their trade. Science is of the general, not of the particular. There is no particular virtue, for the botanist, about this one particular gladiolus; for the ornithologist, about this one particular sparrow. The individual is only a specimen of the group; has interest for science only as an instance. The victim of some obscure disease is, to the doctor who attends him, a *patient*; true enough he is a suffering human being, and everything must be done to alleviate his misfortune. Yes, he is a patient, but he is also a *case*; viewed in the cold light of science, his symptoms are of interest precisely because they are an instance; here they differ from, there they resemble, other cases of the same kind, and out of those resemblances and differences the general body of medical knowledge is being built up. All that is right; all that is as it should be. Only it makes us see danger in one particular cry, which is commonly raised nowadays; that the scientists and the politicians ought to work hand in hand for the future of the race. Well, yes, let them work hand in hand; but not hand in glove. There is a tendency, and we all know it—I am not talking, now, the politics of the moment; the thing has been going on all my lifetime—there is a tendency for the State to assume greater and greater powers over the life of the individual citizen. It is, and is going to be, essentially the debate of our time how much and how far you may rightly sacrifice the freedom of the individual to the interests, real or imagined, of the whole community; and possibly, of the whole community as it will be a hundred years hence. Now, in every country where State-worship gets the upper hand, there is something peculiarly ominous about a conspiracy between the men of action and the men of science. There is the danger that they will start experimenting with human lives, labelling people unfit and disqualifying them from public life, breeding selectively, conditioning, as far as that is possible, the minds and the habits of the young. In plain words, it is slavery; we killed it in Germany, but we have not heard the last of it. And wherever it begins to flourish, there will be a temptation for the men of science to sell their souls.

God forbid that they should so stain their honourable record. We hope rather, and believe that they will use the high position to which their triumphs over nature justly entitle them, to a better end; that they will support everywhere the cause of freedom, among men and among nations. Meanwhile, in a world full of perils and discouragements, let us re-learn the lesson which every generation has to learn, and the next generation always forgets; that we are in God's hands—and what fortune could be better? "All things thou lovest, nor holdest any of thy creatures in abhorrence; hate and create thou couldst not, nor does aught abide save at thy will, whose summoning word holds them in being. They are thine, and thou sparest them; all things that live thou lovest, thou, the Master of them all."

24

THE OXFORD CHAPLAINCY[1]

Rursum aedificabitur platea et muri in angustia temporum.
Street and wall will be built again, though in a time of distress.—Daniel 9. 25.

THE world is never at peace. But, for the most part, those wars which punctuate its annals decide the future of this dynasty or that, of this people or that, a small thing in comparison with eternity. There are moments in history when it seems as if there were something larger at stake, when it seems as if the whole order under which men have learned to live, the whole civilization in which the human mind, so far, has expressed itself, were ready to go under.

So it was, in our own island, a matter of fifteen hundred years ago. You may imagine some remote ancestor of ours watching on the cliffs near Dover, the last dying camp-fire which the Roman legions had left burning to cover the evacuation of the province. He thought of those flames, perhaps, as the beacon-light of a new liberty. In fact, he was contemplating the funeral pyre of a great world-order. All the old landmarks were to be lost, all the tradition that had civilized us was to be buried; laboriously, for several centuries to come, Europe would be engaged in trying to build up, somehow, a new fabric of culture out of the ruins. And Britain, so remote and so defenceless, would experience to the full that time of distress. Religion, the law, the arts, the amenities of life, would have to be learned again as from the beginning.

We have a witness to all that in the story of British architecture. Of the centuries that elapsed between the departure of the Romans and the coming of the Normans, what trace is left, in abiding stone, to recall for us the memory of our past? A church or two like Deerhurst —you can count them on the fingers of one hand; beyond them, nothing. Oh, we were an island of saints, there is no doubt of it; but what visible monument have those saints left behind them? Mention the first half-dozen names that come into your mind, Wilfrid, Cuthbert, Bede, Aidan, Chad, Dunstan, and then tell me where I may find the altar at which any one of them said Mass, the pulpit from which

[1] This sermon was preached at the Old Palace, Oxford, on 23 May 1948, in the presence of the Archbishop of Birmingham and of Fathers Alfonso de Zulueta and Vernon Johnson, former chaplains, and of Mgr Valentine Elwes, the then chaplain to the Catholic undergraduates.

any one of them preached. Mud and wattle, how should their architecture survive? Their churches, even when they began to build in stone, were either destroyed by the invader or overbuilt with the more grandiose edifices of the men who came after them. How they toiled to raise worthy monuments of the religion they lived by! How time has swept away the last vestige of them!

We are here to celebrate the opening of a new temporary chapel.[1] Citizens of a changing world, we read in the very buildings we erect a lesson of impermanence. A time of distress in which we have so many opportunities to build and to rebuild, yet cannot go beyond filling a gap, here and there, with some makeshift substitute! We should do ill not to remember how much it has cost, of labour and enterprise, to build this chapel at all. And it would be a fault in gratitude not to recognize the happy skill which has evoked, from common materials, so stimulating an atmosphere of worship. But when all is said and done, there is sadness mingled with our rejoicing, as there was among the Jews when they saw Zorobabel's temple rise after the Captivity. The chaplaincy has so long been identified with one of the most venerable buildings in venerable Oxford; has the Old Palace defied the centuries in vain? Can its failing energies put forth no fruit more like itself than an extension so functional, so much in the manner of our times? The very stuff of it reminiscent of the air-raid shelter, and of those bad days we are all longing to forget?

Yes, but we are not building for posterity. We are building like those old saints of whom we were speaking just now, for the conditions of an age which promises us no security of living, no leisure for the working out of long-term policies. Heathendom is at the gates, and we must go about our business hand over hand. It is for the ages of quiet reflection to bequeath a graceful legacy in enduring stone; or at least for those ages which have a background of common agreement between men's minds. We are facing—we cannot tell what. All we know is that there are disintegrating forces at work everywhere, unpicking the complacent fabric of our certainties. Man, for the first time in his history, has to reckon with the chance that he may bring down his own planet about his ears. And, short of physical catastrophe, what possibilities of war and of revolution lie half-concealed among the debris of yesterday's Europe! Let it be written of those who planned

[1] After the Second World War when the number of undergraduates was abnormally large, a decision was taken to admit women to the University Chapel in the Old Palace. The new congregation was too large for the chapel built during Mgr Knox's chaplaincy and a large temporary structure was accordingly set up in the garden of the Old Palace, adjoining the former chapel and Newman Room.

this chapel that they lived in a world which had no future. Mankind was going into a tunnel, and should they build you Gothic?

A temporary chapel, if you will have it so; but made for a world in which all is temporary, and for a congregation, besides, which has only a temporary claim to make use of it. If life is transient, Youth is yet more evidently so; Youth is momentary, and all the more ready, for that reason, to follow the mood of the moment. Youth will be always daring, always making experiments; it finds something depressing about last year's model. And this chapel is not like the ordinary parish church, with its register of baptisms, its register of funerals; it is the preserve of Youth. Your chaplain here has many puzzles to solve, many difficulties to contend with; one fear never assails him. He never asks himself: "What will the old people say about it?"—there are no old people. It is fitting that there should be something unconventional, something rather experimental about the material shell which surrounds the worship of the Old Palace; if it were obtrusively reminiscent of Pugin, it would be out of character. We do not want a place for old men to dream their dreams; young men, here, shall have their visions instead. . . . I do not mean, of course, that we want the Old Palace to have a series of temporary chapels, each of them pulled down at the end of twenty years to make room for a new one. Evidently there is a value in continuity. But I think it is genuinely arguable that just at this moment (quite apart from the difficulties of expense and of labour) we are better advised not to commit ourselves to a permanent structure. The times are so changeable, men's thoughts are so fluid, who can tell what style will be in vogue, what artistic ideals will be cherished, twenty years from now? Let those who come after us decide for themselves, when we are laid on the shelf.

Let me be a little personal, a little candid. I cannot pretend that when I myself was chaplain here, the Old Palace was suspected of any exaggerated sympathy with the ardours, the illusions of Youth. It stood here, a gaunt reminder of the past, calculated to chill the aspirations of the visitor, to snub the half-baked modernism of his outlook. My predecessor, Mgr Barnes, God rest him, was fond of describing the difficulties which his correspondents had, when he first took up residence here, in getting his postal address right. "Vey always used to write to me as Monsignor Barnes, Ve Old Place." Well, it remained something of an Old Place even in my time; I found my typewriter had an odd trick of falling into the same error. An old place, where the aesthete of the late twenties must expect to find an atmosphere of cheerful Philistinism flourishing unreproved; representational art, and

bookshelves guiltless of modern poetry; if you wanted to hear about
that kind of thing, you went round to Campion.[1] An old place, where
the near-Left political language of the early thirties found no conspicuous echo; you could air progressive doctrines, but if you wanted
to find a sympathetic hearing, you must look for it in Walton Well
Road.[2] Sixteen hundred and twenty-eight was inscribed legibly over
the door-bell; you had the illusion, in those days, that time had stood
still.

If what I have been saying this morning is, to some extent, a recanta-
tion of all that, I would not be understood to imply that there was no
value in it; that Youth has nothing to learn from the past. The scene
of Pentecost, after all, was the cenacle; all that splendid outpouring
of the divine Spirit had for its background the familiar theatre of past
associations, and of past failures. And I used to think of the Old Chapel
—I mean, the room above Mgr Elwes's room, which was the chapel
when I first came here—as (in its way) a spiritual replica of the cenacle;
a home of memories. After all, it was an Oratory for the Catholic
undergraduates of Oxford; to be a son of the Catholic Church, to be
an alumnus of Oxford, is to be hedged about with memories; it is an
umbilical cord joining you to your past. And when we built the new
chapel—what was then the new chapel—I wanted it to be in some sense
a replica of the old. I did not mean it to be depressingly ecclesiastical.
When Mr Arnold Crush, the architect, brought me a nice set of
Gothic plans, I told him I was sorry, but I didn't want anything which
couldn't be turned into tea-rooms later on. But it was to be a little
chastening, a little sombre; you were not to forget, as you knelt there,
that Oxford and the Catholic Church had got along well enough, these
many centuries past, without you.

All that is still true, and it is still worth saying. But it is one of those
miraculous paradoxes in which the Catholic Church abounds, that if
our religion is always old in its inspiration, in enterprise and adapta-
bility, it is always young. He who said, "The Holy Spirit will bring all
things to your remembrance", said also, "Behold, I make all things
new". I came into the Church when it was still fresh from the condemnation of Modernism; it was common form to say: "See how
utterly old-fashioned the Catholic religion is! How barren, how effete!
Inextricably tied up with the thought-forms of the Middle Ages, with
the privilege-politics of yesterday!" And there has been nothing more
marvellous, I think, in our time, than the way in which the Church

[1] Campion Hall, the Jesuit house in Brewer Street.
[2] The Catholic Workers' College, then in Walton Well Road, now on Boars' Hill.

has risen to challenge the new age. Everywhere new cells of life are developing; everywhere the gnarled trunk is putting forth green shoots. What wonder if the Old Palace takes wings for a new flight?

Only, may this new chapel be a cenacle still! "All these, with one mind, gave themselves up to prayer, with Mary, the Mother of Jesus." Without that, the builder's labour is lost, the watchman guards it in vain.

25

FATHER DOMINIC BARBERI[1]

WE are here to recall, after the lapse of nearly a hundred years, a memory lovable and beloved; the memory of Dominic Barberi, a Discalced Clerk of the most holy Cross and Passion. Charged with the honourable task of interpreting his character to you, I find myself overcome with a kind of embarrassment. The documents of his life are extraordinarily full; there is no lack of material. But there is one secret about it which remains still unanswered; we do not know whether Dominic Barberi was a saint. And the Church insists that we should await her judgment in the matter; that we should not go about calling people saints until she has told us whether they are saints or not. . . .

A hundred years ago—how close the men of his time seem to us, and how remote! Louis XVI was still king of France when he was born, and the battle of Waterloo had not yet been fought when he entered religion; all that sounds as if he belonged to the dead past; to a fancy-dress sort of world you read about in history-books. The notion of England as a dominating factor in world-politics, a new notion then, dazzled his youth. Yet he lived to receive Newman into the Church; Newman, who was still alive when many of us were born. The portrait you see of him was the work of a *Punch* cartoonist; and when he died, he was taken out of a railway carriage to die, just out of Reading. What a span of history his life seems to cover; and yet, what a short life it was! They were not given to us for long, the great evangelists of the early nineteenth century; in the mysterious design of

[1] This sermon was preached in the open air at St Anne's Retreat, Sutton, St Helens, on Sunday, 29 August 1948. The text is taken from an extract published in *The Tablet*, 4 September 1948.

Providence, they used themselves up all too soon in their apostolic labours. Father Gentili died at thirty-nine, Father Faber at forty-nine, Father Dominic at fifty-seven. If they had lived, who knows what might have happened?

It is the shortness of Father Dominic's career which lends a special interest and a special beauty to the record of it; there is a breathless quality about it; the man is working against time, keeping death at bay until his task is accomplished. How often, in our dreams, we have had the nightmare sense of wanting desperately to get somewhere, to get something done, and being fobbed off, again and again, by a hundred ridiculous obstacles and interruptions! There is some important piece of news to be told, some perilous mistakes to be corrected, everything turns on us. And then everything turns against us; journeys seem endless, instruments break in our hands, people play us false, and the attainment of the thing we set out to do seems as remote as ever. So it is when you read the story of Father Dominic; longing to carry the good news to the country of his dreams, longing to correct the tragic mistake of three centuries ago; and as you turn page after page of his biography, you meet nothing but delays and discouragements.

Here is a man who, unless he is labouring under a vulgar delusion, has learned by revelation from almighty God that he is destined to be the new apostle of England. For the first forty years or so of his life he cannot speak any language but his own; he knows nothing of England except what Rome knows of England—and how little that is! A few conversations with one or two over-enthusiastic converts have whetted his appetite for the English mission, but brought him no nearer to the goal of his desires. He is a man of forty-eight when he leaves, for the first time, his native country; even then, only for Belgium, where he is to build up, with very little of local encouragement, a new province of his Order. He has turned fifty, a man doomed to die at fifty-seven, before he crosses the British Channel; with no house to welcome him, no money to carry through his schemes, with companions constantly in bad health, and himself physically the least able of any. He has to contend with the vacillating counsels of ecclesiastical authority; with the double-dyed conservatism of men who are Englishmen and also Catholics; with unfriendly neighbours who jeer at him and assault him; and all the while, as he goes about preaching and giving retreats, he knows that he is not talking English but only babbling a kind of pigeon-English that makes him the laughing-stock of the public. And he has only seven years left him—is it possible, you ask yourself, that for once almighty God has called a man to a special, an arduous mission, and left him to wrestle with circumstances which make it impossible. . . .

We cannot be certain whether Dominic was a saint. But you and I, heaven knows, have plenty to learn even from men who were not saints; generous souls who served Christ in their generation, and left a fragrant memory behind them, although their names are not written over the altar. Saints or no, they lived in a blaze of charity by whose glow you and I can trim our miserable rush-lights. What, then, shall we single out as the characteristic quality of Father Dominic's life? Where all seems so far beyond our compass, the dogged patience of the man, his imperturbable humility, his scrupulous obedience, his high courage, his joyful endurance of suffering, can we detect one emerging strand of holiness which gives the clue to the rest? I think what most impresses you in the story of his life is a kind of splendid simplicity.

Do not mistake me; there is a simplicity which is not a virtue, but a mere condition of the mind. We call a child simple, because it has not yet had enough experience of life to twist its nature or its thoughts. We call a rustic simple, because his business ties him down to a single neighbourhood, and that thinly populated, so that he has never mixed with a great variety of his fellow men. But Dominic was not simple in that sense. True, he joined the Passionists as a lay brother, but it was obvious immediately that he was capable of studying for the priesthood; he became an accomplished and fearless theologian, not at all afraid of meeting the Tractarian pundits on their own ground. He had administrative experience besides, and was a tireless organizer. His stammering attempts to talk English, when he first came over here, made him look ridiculous, and he rejoiced to appear a fool for Christ's sake, but he was no fool in reality. No, the simplicity Dominic had was that of the man who has one overmastering passion in life, and sees everything else in the light of that, and as a means to that; brushes away everything that conflicts with the attainment of his great object, as being irrelevant or worse. That ruthless pursuit of an ideal begets simplicity.

With Dominic, we know what it was. It was the conversion of sinners and misbelievers to the school of Christ; and, if possible, they were to be Englishmen. He bore with infinite patience the objections people raised to his schemes, the obstacles they put in his way, but he could never for a moment understand them. . . . He had the spirit of faith; you could not persuade him that mountains were immovable. To the voice of authority, at home or abroad, he was punctiliously obedient. But what "people said" didn't matter so much. They told him that he didn't understand Englishmen; that he over-rated the possibility of turning England into a Catholic country; you must go about it slowly, and avoid the least danger of arousing prejudice. Probably it was true, to some extent. I daresay Father Dominic didn't really, to the end of his life, understand Englishmen; I think it is almost certain that he over-rated, humanly speaking, the probability of England's returning to the faith. But in a curious kind of way I think it was an advantage that he *did* make these mistakes of judgment. If he had understood people's minds better, if he had envisaged all the difficulties of the task he was undertaking, he might have hesitated, and fumbled, and lost the hour of opportunity. At least, he won his point; he shook us out of our lethargy. Other men, not always by his own methods, carried on his work; and the Catholic body in England became a force you had to reckon with, instead of a defeatist minority that shunned the light.

26

HEROISM[1]

Thou shalt take the atonement money of the children of Israel, and shalt appoint it for the service of the tabernacle of the testimony, that it may be a memorial of them before the Lord, that he may be merciful unto their souls. —Exodus 30. 16.

W E are here to dedicate a memorial. If we are to use words in their scriptural sense, that involves a daring paradox. Wherever you read about a "memorial" in the Old Testament, it means that you are reminding God of something; that we men, so easily forgetful, so soon forgotten, are prompting the memory of a God who never forgets. Human workmanship, of crumbling stone or discoloured bronze, is to challenge the watchful eye of Eternity. A metaphor? Yet where, in our approach to the unseen, do we escape from the influence of metaphor? What we mean is, if he were man, he would forget. And in saying that, we accuse ourselves of forgetfulness.

[1] This sermon was preached at Wimbledon College on 26 September 1948, on the occasion of the Dedication of the War Memorial.

Is it possible? The man who stands by the graveside of one he loved in life tells himself that this mood of aching regret cannot choose but be eternal. It is a thing of the mind, not subject to decay like material things. There can be no quarrels, no misunderstandings now to fray, as between living persons, the cords of affection. This memory, so vivid, so poignant, will be with him forty years hence in unblurred outline, in undiminished intensity. And yet we know that it is otherwise; a merciful Providence has attached to our sorrow a law of diminution. In a few years, perhaps, the wound will have healed; remembering the dead will be an exercise dutifully undertaken, not the solace of his dreams, the purgatory of his waking hours, as it used to be. We are men, and seven times pass over us; there is no tension of the mind which will not, if left to itself, slacken with the years.

So it is with our public memories. "When your children ask you tomorrow, *What mean these stones?*"—oh yes, we try to persuade ourselves that we are only raising a monument for the eyes of posterity. But in truth it is for ourselves, too, that the monument is needed; a knot in the handkerchief to remind us of something we might forget. Just now the mood of regret is so lively in us, so insistent with us; but we want to capture it before it fades. Our schoolfellows—how little effort it takes to recall them in a hundred characteristic settings! We lived so close to them, and in a routine of existence which stamped itself on the mind; "Here it was I first saw him . . . how I can picture him now, leaning out of the window!" And then, we were so gregarious; we lived in droves; the empty place in chapel where your friend sat, and will never sit again, overshadows your own past with a sense of incompleteness. There is a beauty in this sorrow, and we seek to perpetuate it; there is a rightness about this attitude of ours, and we seek to eternalize it. So the appeals are sent out, and contributions are promised and paid, and the memorial takes shape, and is completed. It is like a candle burning before our Lady's statue, continuing the efficacy of our prayer; God will look on it, and remember and have mercy on the souls of Wimbledon men. And for ourselves, it is like a signpost, recalling us to our origins and to the unimaginative companionships of youth.

Meanwhile, there is posterity to be considered. It is posterity that will judge whether the money contributed on such an occasion was well and wisely spent, that will be grateful to us for our foresight, or complain of being saddled with an unwelcome gift. And it is to posterity that we have to transmit a lesson. That is what commemoration, in the modern sense, means. That is, above all, an important reflection when a school is concerned. Boys come here to do their lessons; and it is not only from books, not only from the master's voice droning away at the rostrum, that those lessons are derived. The surroundings in which we grow up, the traditions by which the school lives, are formative influences, not less operative because they are unconsciously imbibed. At school, generation succeeds generation not every forty years, but every five or six years; we are dealing with a vast turnover of humanity, and what we dedicate today is not merely a dumb appeal to almighty God to have mercy on the souls of his loved creatures; it is not merely a reminder, to jog our own treacherous memories when they turn away impatiently from contemplating the past. It is also a monument, designed to inspire a generation yet unborn with some passing thrill of emotion.

We would have them learn to thank God for one of his best gifts to mankind—heroism. Not very important, that they should spell their way laboriously through all the names of all those Wimbledon boys, dead long ago; they will only be names, then, colourless as the names in a telephone directory. Not very important, even, that they should recall the history of those eventful years, 1939-45, and remind themselves what it was their country fought for, their schoolfellows died for. By the time Hitler lies as far back in retrospect as Napoleon is to us, Wimbledon boys will not be moved to lively indignation by the atrocities of Belsen, or catch their breath, as if with a sense of present danger, when they read about the Battle of Britain; all the edges of our present (but even now fading) emotions will be blurred by time. But the fact will remain on record that commonplace English people did, during those years, meet death, accept death, court death, in a hundred grisly forms in jungles and deserts, in the air and on the high seas, when there were safer courses to be pursued, softer options to be had, if only they would have looked round for them. That is heroism.

And I say it is one of God's best gifts to mankind; it is designed to correct, if only a little, our human habit of self-contempt. Even in a world redeemed by grace, how paltry our virtues are, most of them, how shoddy and adulterated our motives! Kindness so calculating, humility so skin-deep, self-control so capricious, piety so mechanical— oh, it is easy for the satirist to make fun of us, and how much there is in modern literature which puts us out of conceit with ourselves! Unfortunately, it is only a step from cynicism to despair; the man who has convinced himself that his fellow creatures are all second-rate is content, as a rule, to be second-rate himself. And then suddenly, just as you have got your picture of human insignificance focused, the moment of danger arrives, and the hero steps out. Quite an ordinary person, just like yourself; he has been to the same school, and had exactly the same advantages; a quiet fellow commonly, who didn't talk much or leave much mark on his company; but he does something that makes your blood run cold to read about it. He comes forward very unobtrusively, no histrionics, no flowery patriotic sentiments; probably he represents himself as having joined the army just through indolence, just through some mistake; he never wanted to, he simply hates the idea of fighting. That is the last sight you have of him; then you come across his name in the paper as the leading spirit in one of those innumerable war-time epics that hardly get into the newspapers at all. Please God, you have the grace to go down on your knees and thank him for his gift of heroism; the new landmark that suddenly comes in sight and shows you that the focus of your picture was all wrong.

Is it out of place, in a sermon, to bestow so much praise on courage —surely, after all, no better than a natural virtue? Well, I suppose we may admire courage, just as we may admire beauty, even when no moral significance attaches to it. We may admire the instinctive courage that bids the lioness fight for her cubs; we may admire the dare-devil courage which enables a schoolboy to undertake some almost impossible climb, for a bet. But courage like that is only the raw-tuned piano, noise without music. The hero is the great pianist stepping to the instrument and waking, all at once, the echoes of which it is capable. Courage becomes *virtus*, man's characteristic variant of it, when a moral purpose comes in to modulate its harmonies.

Whether, in this case or that, it is a natural or a supernatural quality, how should you and I know? To be sure, the Church sets before us certain shining examples of heroism, men and women laying down their lives, unresisting, as martyrs to the Christian faith. That glorious destiny, altogether supernatural in the motive and the circumstances of it, is one in which the Society of Jesus (you might almost say) specializes. To have three of its Old Boys decorated with the Victoria Cross in the course of the two world wars is a record which need hardly surprise us in a Jesuit school; martyrdom is on the syllabus. But martyrdom is for the few; can we doubt that almighty God has crowns of his own, prizes (so to speak) not advertised but nevertheless awarded, for lives immolated with the clean ardour of youth in the cause of an earthly country, and of human freedom?

This at least we can say, we, who watch them from the lower plane of mortality—that the light of faith, which transfigures even our commonplace death-beds, will always gild those heroisms of the battle-field with a splendour of its own. Under the old Law, it seems, the flame which consumed the victims of the altar, jealously guarded, was nevertheless an ordinary flame, kindled and fanned by human effort. But now and again—Elias's ordeal on Mount Carmel is the instance we all remember—there was a direct invasion of the supernatural; fire came down from heaven and consumed the sacrifice. Something of the same quality breathes about the memory of our Catholic dead. Those others, not less noble in their manner of giving, lives in their unfulfilled promise not less to be mourned, yet lack completeness. It was as something guessed at, not as something seen, that the divine hand stretched out to receive their sacrifice.

So great in their fulfilment, so high above us! Yet they were men like ourselves, and, like ourselves, have sins to atone for. May he who made them, and hates nothing that he has made, grant them eternal rest.

27

HOME-COMING[1]

Has he joy of his home-coming, that leans hand on wall, and all at once is bitten by a viper?—Amos 5. 19.

THE England in which we live is a land of increasing security. We can remember, many of us, a time when fully half of our fellow countrymen were haunted by the spectre of the workhouse. They had saved nothing, with their narrow margin of income; or the little savings they had were invested unfortunately, and lost. Economic forces over which they had no control might involve them in a long spell of unemployment; they would fall sick, and lose their jobs, and be unable to find others; they would grow old, and their children would be unable or unwilling to support them. There was no alterna-tive left but to fall back on the charity of the State; and to receive benefits from the State was regarded, in those days, as a disgrace hardly to be mentioned. Nor, it must be confessed, did the conditions of

[1] This sermon was preached at Westminster Cathedral on 24 April 1949, at a Mass offered for the Converts' Aid Society.

public relief do much to efface the stigma of poverty. Within living memory, that shadow has lifted. You may still find poverty, tragic in its incidence upon this or that life, this or that family; but absolute destitution on a large scale will disappear, please God, for ever. A net of security, woven by all the arts of statesmanship so as to be proof against human folly, is being stretched under the anxious passage of our lives. To be without work is not to be without wages. To fall sick is to have all the resources of medicine at your disposal. To grow old is to inherit the rewards of half-forgotten thrift. While England remains safe and solvent, the vast bulk of Englishmen will remain safe and solvent too.

The England in which we live is a land of diminishing freedom. That is inevitable; you cannot have it both ways. If the public purse is to underwrite for us the adventure of living, then our lives, at every turn, must be open to the public scrutiny. We shall have inspectors calling at unwelcome hours to satisfy themselves that the law's requirements are being observed; we shall have to fill in forms, answer elaborate questionnaires which seem to us to be of no importance; we shall queue up at the doors of public offices, and suffer, now from the brusqueness, now from the leisureliness, of public officials. And we are homesick, the older of us, anyhow, for our lost liberties. We grew up in a world where a man could send his children to any school he liked and when they had left school could apprentice them straight away to any job he liked. He could kill and eat the animals on his own farm, and no questions asked; he could travel abroad where he would and as long as he would; if he didn't like his house he could pull it down and build a new one—all that, if he could afford it. Of course, that was a rather important qualification; and perhaps some of us might have realized, more than we did, that our neighbours weren't in a position to afford as much as we could. Still, the theologians will distinguish for you between *libertas a necessitate* and *libertas a coactione*; and it's a plain fact of human nature that people worry less about the pleasures they can't afford than about the pleasures which are forbidden them. More and more we find we've got to have *permits* for doing this and that, appeal to a tribunal before a certain date if we don't want this and that to happen in our back garden; even (a very ominous word) that we are being "directed" to do this and that. What wonder if we write letters to the paper to ask if England is a free country any more?

But there's worse than that. There's a want of liberty about the very air we breathe; the philosophy of our time is responsible for it, questioning, not merely whether we are free *citizens*, but whether we are free *men*. *Does* man shape his own destiny, or does he live at the mercy of blind economic forces which shape his destiny *for* him? We think we know the answer, and then we read in the paper that Great Britain has just signed a trade agreement, running into millions, with a set of gangsters who have set themselves up as the Government in some country of eastern Europe. The responsible Minister apologizes for it in the House of Commons, but explains that we had to do it or starve. And *are* we so certain, *now*, about those blind economic forces? Or again, you have been reading some book about modern psychology; or more probably some novel by an author who has picked up the jargon of modern psychology. And you read of urges and inhibitions produced in our minds by events that happened in childhood, or even before birth, and it makes you wonder whether man is a free agent at all. You know that he *is*, you know that all that is only one side of the medal; and yet, when you next come to examine your conscience, and go back over that sorry record—the little jealousies, the little meannesses, the little outbursts of temper that seem so difficult to account for—the memory of what you read comes back to you, and you are half inclined to treat yourself as a pathological case. Your sense of personal freedom is not *destroyed*, but it labours for breath; did you really *choose* that humiliating sin? Or were you, after all, directed into it by some force stronger than yourself?

What restores our belief in human freedom? The sight of a man making a decision for which conscience is the only motive. Conscience remains superior to all direction, to all controls. Precisely when you extort submission from a man by bullying and browbeating him, you have failed to secure your object, because there was no free consent. Conscience is free.

And what of the man, ordained to the ministry of some non-Catholic body, and now perhaps well on in middle life, who makes such a decision in conscience as can bring him, from any worldly point of view, nothing but disaster? The man who gives up his life's work, that of a sacred and honourable calling, to take what work chance may bring him? Who thereby makes public profession that the opinions he has hitherto expressed were wrong, that the light he has followed was a will-o'-the-wisp, that he has laboured in vain? Who says good-bye to the world he knew, sorrowfully and tenderly enough, only to be answered by cries of protest and ridicule? Who is content that his old comrades-in-arms should look upon him as a traitor, bringing disrepute on their common cause by his desertion? Who is conscious of the distress he is causing to souls that are very dear to him, yet drives the weapon resolutely into his own heart? Who finds himself, perhaps, condemned to undergo this agony of mind at the same moment when he is faced with the loss of his worldly prospects—his wife and children deprived of all the comforts they have been accustomed to, and for his sake? Let the world take heart again; here is a free man. It is not enough that we, we Catholics, should hold out hands to welcome him. He should claim the applause of millions who do not share our faith, yet love the truth. He has risen to the stature of a free man.

A world which has bartered away so much of its freedom, to achieve security! And here is a man who has bartered away security, to achieve freedom. That is the poignant fact; you can and must insure yourself, in our modern society, against accidents over which you have no control; against sickness, against unemployment, against the inevitable encroachments of old age. You cannot insure yourself against the effects of hearing God's call to the soul, and obeying it.

Has he joy of his home-coming, asks the prophet Amos, that leans hand on wall, and all at once is bitten by a viper? To be received as a convert into the Catholic Church is, let none doubt it, a home-coming. When you stood outside, pressing your nose against the window, how strange everything seemed in that lamplit room! The position of our blessed Lady; a barrier, you thought, when she was really a ladder, between you and her divine Son; the principle of authority; how could you know that it commands, not grudging assent, but joyful recognition? The Mass, that looked so dead and mechanical when it was really a storehouse of life; sacramental absolution, the locked door that yields, really, to a touch! Once you are *inside*, you begin to see things as they are, and they become graciously familiar; it is as if you had come into a house seen, and then forgotten, in your dreams. But all that takes time; the home-coming has been like that of a prisoner escaped from the wars; you are bruised and scarred from your long passage through the dark. What if *then*, just when a man leans up against a wall to get back his breath, he must be wounded, in that same hour, by the viper of poverty and neglect?

To your loyalty as Catholics, to your charity as Christians, we appeal for funds to save these men from the consequences of their own heroism. Not a great number of them altogether, but a steady supply; all the more in need of help in days like these, when a clerical salary leaves little margin for saving. Pensioners, let us call them, of an honourable warfare; and their Ministry of Pensions the Converts' Aid Society—no grim Whitehall department, but a charity with a long record of delicate attention to human needs. Security, give them security, the men who let conscience have its way with them, and threw security to the winds. Liberty, let them realize from their first entrance into it that the Catholic Church is the home of liberty, of Christ's followers who have freely received, and freely give.

28

THE ORATORIANS IN LONDON[1]

These occupied themselves continually with the apostles' teaching, their fellowship in the breaking of bread, and the fixed times of prayer.—Acts 2. 42.

WHAT was the immediate effect, upon our Lord's followers, of the Pentecostal gift? Did they immediately set out, staff in hand, alleluia on their lips, to conquer a world? Apparently not. The first thing, at least, was to build up, to consolidate; here was a nucleus of fresh converts to be formed on Christ's model. Day by day they must go to school, with the apostles for their schoolmasters; day by day they must be welded into a supernatural unity, coaugmented by the mysterious virtue of the Holy Eucharist; day by day—more unexpected still—they must observe the prescribed hours of prayer in Herod's temple. Such was the cradling of the Church; difficult to know how long it lasted. Apostolic hearts, bursting with the new wine of the Holy Spirit, must be the prisoners of the cenacle, no less than our blessed Lady herself.

We are here to celebrate the opening of the Oratory in King William Street, Strand, a hundred years ago. And if we want to reconstruct any picture of that event, as it seemed to contemporary opinion, we must dismiss from our minds all the associations of the Brompton Road. Here were a set of wild Popish enthusiasts from Birmingham, who had bought up a disused dancing-hall and turned it into an Oratory overnight—the workmen were still in the church at eleven on the morning when Wiseman was due to preach. Priests walked about the streets in their outlandish habits, to the distress of an Evangelical neighbour, the Commissioner of Woods and Forests;

[1] This sermon was preached at the London Oratory on Whit Monday, 6 June 1949, to commemorate the centenary of the Oratorians in London.

to the distress, it was rumoured, of Father Newman himself. Yet Father Newman himself was called in before long to preach a course of sermons in which he exposed the weaknesses of Anglican theology —so unlike him! It seemed a direct, frontal attack on the religion of Londoners, conceived in the spirit and carried out by the methods of a Nonconformist revival.

Those shock tactics only lasted five years; then the Fathers moved away to Kensington, and the Oratory, instead of seeming an unwelcome gate-crasher, was accepted, became a part of London. From its founder's point of view the old site was better; there was nothing to prevent Faber in King William Street becoming what Spurgeon[1] became a few years later at the Metropolitan Tabernacle, London's favourite preacher, and in an age when men liked listening to sermons. But Father Faber didn't mind about that sort of thing. He knew that the Oratory was not meant for oratory; its pulpit was only meant to be part of a general environment, a general *décor*, in which plain people would feel at home. If the fathers, in his day, had found a permanent site in the middle of London, I suppose their church would be something like what Maiden Lane is—a sudden, welcome retreat just off the Strand, where you can take refuge from the noise and jar of your surroundings; but within those narrow confines there would be no spaciousness, no mystery, no air of challenge to an unbelieving world. It would not be the Oratory we know; unique, irreplaceable, a museum piece in a street of museums.

Let us forget, then, the old Oratory that was for a short time, that might have come to a destiny so different; a token Oratory, a tabernacle in the wilderness, making way for something more solid. Let us think of that more solid thing in Brompton Road. We do well to concentrate our attention on the building first and foremost; the fathers themselves will excuse us, for it is their own habit of mind. Farm Street is the church of the Jesuits, Haverstock Hill the church of the Dominicans, but the Oratory is not the church of the Oratorians. It is not *their church*; they are *its priests*. It is their shell, their native element; they glide to and fro unobtrusively in it, looking like those human figures that were put in old prints to show the height of the building. So they will not find fault with us if we thank God for the Oratory first and the Oratorians afterwards.

I have said that the Oratory became part of London. It is so much a commonplace, a thing we take for granted, that you were not thinking about it till I mentioned it, the dominating position this church holds.

[1] Charles Haddon Spurgeon (1834-92), Baptist preacher.

I have met a taxi-driver who did not know his way to the Athenaeum;
nobody has ever met one who did not know his way to the Oratory.
Site and size of it, in these days of towering architecture, are still
imposing; the present church was built only seventy years back, but
even its predecessor of 1854 must have seemed magnificent then; we
were only just out of the catacombs. How it fills the eye; how instinctively you know, in some crowded omnibus, whether you have
passed the Oratory yet; how the living cross-currents that swirl around
it, when the High Mass is over and the last Mass is beginning, comfort
you with the sense that people still go to church! Is it vulgar to say all
that? Believe me, Father Faber (who never saw this church) would
not have thought so. Think of the tiny structures we were building
in those days, Wiseman's church at Fulham and Manning's church at
Ogle Street, as if we were afraid of scandalizing the Commissioner of
Woods and Forests. Think of the crockets and gargoyles and stencil-
work we spent our money on, for the most part hideous and unnecessary; instead of guessing that London, and the Church, would
grow! And now our priests are killing themselves with duplicating,
and the faithful are exasperated, Sunday after Sunday, by the lack of
elbow-room, and even the rebuilt Oratory is not large enough. Let us
thank God for the gift of faith which made the old Oratorians such
practical men, such realists, taught them, from the first, in those days
of Gothic fervour, to neglect detail and build in wide sweeps of per-
pective, where the eye loses itself in distance, according to the pattern
they had seen on the Seven Hills.

A hundred years ago, a dreadful innovation; today, a recognized
institution—that is the salient fact, I think, about the Oratory; so new
a thing, it has established itself, so foreign a thing, it has acclimatized
itself; it is part of London. We have other churches, to be sure, more
venerable in their associations, whose fabric has endured more winters;
but there is none that impresses the mind with such a sense of continuity. And this sense of continuity depends, not only upon the church
itself, but on something in the life, something in the history, perhaps
even something in the character, of the priests who serve it. Something
in their *life*—the Oratorian does not move about from house to house,
like the active religious; he is the prisoner of his own institute; the
priest who received you into the Church, the priest who married you,
thirty years ago, if he still lives, still lives in the Brompton Road.
Something, too, in their *history*; St Philip left behind him a tradition
rather than a rule, and where you live by tradition you fear the effect
of any change. When I lived as the guest of the Oratorian fathers, just

thirty years ago, I was assured that if you looked carefully about the house you could still find notices that had been pinned up by Father Faber, dead more than half-a-century back. I don't think it was true; my researches, at least, were unsuccessful. But there was a kind of poetical truth in the assertion; time, you felt, had stood still, and the Tractarians were even now a living memory. Something, perhaps, in their *character*; if you are to fit in well with the habits of a community so small, living at such close quarters, you need to be a clubable man; here is no place for doctrinaires and revolutionaries. All that makes for continuity. I do not mean that the Oratory stagnates; it is a hive of industry; but its traditions change slowly, according to the needs of its own nature; they are not imposed on it by the butterfly fashions of the world outside.

The Church does well to try new experiments, not a doubt of it. It is well that she should feel young, young as she felt on the day of Pentecost; it is well that she should come out into the open, and arrest the attention of a world which sets store by publicity. By all means let her spokesmen shout for a hearing in Hyde Park, her guildsmen seek to leaven the Trade Union movement, her cross-bearers make pilgrimage to Walsingham. But always her secret, the spell which she exercises over men's hearts, is her splendid aloofness. They see priests visiting their own sick, rallying their own poor in front of the tabernacle, shriving their own penitents, fortifying men and women after their own rite, under their own laws, for the adventure of matrimony; as if nothing else mattered, as if they had time for nothing else. That the Church should live so near to them, rub shoulders with them, pass them with a smile, and yet remain so aloof—that is what baffles them, what rouses their wistful admiration. "These occupied themselves continually with the apostles' teaching, their fellowship in the breaking of bread, and the fixed times of prayer"; for a hundred years the fathers of the Oratory have done that, and London watched, and wondered, and each day the Lord added to their fellowship others that should be saved.

All these hundred years the same beneficent routine has gone on; the bell of the porteria ringing all day, crowds thronging the altar rails, the shuttle-service of the confessionals; the night prayers with Father Faber's own hymns, the Little Oratory with St Philip's own recipe for the sanctification of souls. All these hundred years the fathers of the Oratory have been at their post; and as each made his last journey to Sydenham a fresh priest has taken his place, ambitious in his turn to bring the great heart of St Philip into the great heart of London; the

old patient attendance to duty, the old gracious courtesy, the old love
of music and of pageantry, have never died out. Few of you have the
same sense of indebtedness to the sons of St Philip as I have; I, who first
learned from their influence what it meant to be a Catholic, what it
meant to be a priest. But from all of you they claim some measure of
gratitude, Londoners like yourselves, Londoners by choice, Londoners
by profession, for the lamp of faith they have kept burning all these
hundreds years. May the prayers of St Philip go with us, and the
Oratory of St Philip renew among us the sacred memory of his life.

29

THE HOLY YEAR[1]

*The Spirit of the Lord is upon me . . . to proclaim a year when men may find
acceptance with the Lord.*—Luke 4. 18.

THAT is not a text which any Christian preacher will take lightly
on his lips. For it is, you will remember, the text our Lord himself
chose when he was asked to preach at Nazareth. But I think it is
important, when the Vicar of Christ speaks to us, to make sure that
we are interpreting his intentions according to the mind of Christ.
His Church, after all these centuries of life, has matured, as living things
do, and men see her with strange eyes. They see her as a tyrant, imposing
her yoke on millions of human souls, with some ulterior motive—
what motive, is not quite clear. They see her as a cunning instrument of
government, making her influence felt, by underground means, in the
distracted diplomacy of our time. They see her as an arrogant teacher,
obstinately upholding certain points of view, not caring about the
truth of them, simply because they are hers. What they do not see
—we do well, at such times, to remind ourselves of it, and to advertise
the world of it—is that the Church exists today for one purpose, the
same purpose for which she has always existed. "The Spirit of the
Lord is upon me; he has anointed me, and sent me out to bid the
prisoners go free, and the blind have sight; to set the oppressed at
liberty, to proclaim a year when man may find acceptance with the
Lord." Behind all the labyrinth of her machinery, behind all her

[1] This sermon was preached at the Church of the Sacred Heart, Westbury-on-Trym,
Bristol, in Advent 1949, after the proclamation of the Holy Year, 1950.

libraries of theology, the Church exists only for one purpose, to go on preaching to mankind her Master's tidings of pardon and renewal.

We live in time, and the ravages of time are all around us. Leave your garden untended, and it will not remain as it was; the weeds will be up before a month is out. How the dust silts up on our shelves, after a year's neglect; how the unanswered letters mount up on our writing-tables, after a week of illness or absence! Left to themselves, things don't stay as they were, they go back; and how easy it is to let that happen, if we are not careful! The days, the months, the years slip by and melt into one another unremarked. For that reason, if we are wise, we address ourselves at certain definite intervals to the task of restoring order. We fix upon some artificial date, New Year's Day, or our birthday, or some anniversary; on that date, whenever it recurs, we will take in hand the business of tidying up. And so it is, not only with outward things but with the affairs of the soul; here too, alas, we are always going back unless, now and again, we pull ourselves together; a retreat, or the beginning of Lent, must be the signal for bringing back order into our lives.

Nations, too, but at longer intervals, because the life of nations is longer, have gone in for a policy of periodic tidying up. The ancient Romans, who were a military people, and for that reason were jealously divided into fixed ranks, found the need of it. Property changed hands, men grew rich or poor, rose to honour or fell into disgrace, and there was a constant danger that these different ranks of society would become gradually merged with one another. Accordingly, every five years, the Romans held a census, which had for one of its chief objects the determining of each man's place in the state. At the end of it, sacrifice was offered for the cleansing of the people; and, once in a hundred years, this sacrifice was performed with special solemnities. Even pagan Rome felt, at long intervals, the need for renewal; even pagan Rome had its holy year, once in a hundred years; and we still possess, among the works of a great Latin poet, the text of a hymn sung upon that occasion. "Now", he wrote, "Faith and Peace and Honour and old-time Modesty come back to us, and long-neglected Fortitude."[1] That was in 17 B.C.; I wonder, was it in that year our blessed Lady was born?

The Jews, profiting by the counsels of a divine Law-giver, knew better still how to defeat the encroachments of time. They were an

[1] Iam Fides et Pax et Honos Pudorque
priscus et neglecta redire Virtus
audet.
Horace, *Carmen Saeculare.*

agricultural people, and, for the most part, men of a restless energy. For six days, therefore, out of seven they were allowed to work; on the seventh day, the sabbath, they must keep holiday. And, every seven years, the land was to have a holiday of its own. For six years they might take the heart out of it as they would; for the whole of the seventh it must lie fallow. But that was not all. They were an agricultural people, and they were meant, in the designs of Providence, to be small-holders. There would be a bad season, or a plague among the cattle, and the small farmer would be obliged to sell to his richer neighbours; gradually, as the years went by, the land passed into the possession of a few rich owners. Worse still, if labour was cheap, and the landlord drove a hard bargain, a penniless man had no resource but to sell his own liberty; gradually, as the years went by, the poorer Israelites became slaves; more than ever, affairs needed tidying up; and for this situation, too, the divine Wisdom found a remedy. Seven of these seven-year periods were allowed to go by, forty-nine years in all, and the fiftieth should be something altogether special, a year of jubilee. In that year, every piece of land went back to its original owner, however short a time the purchaser might have enjoyed its revenues. In that year, every slave went free, however little service his master might have had from him. It was a genuine renewal, a genuine tidying-up; each cycle of fifty years brought things back to the point where they had started.

It was, as we have seen, to this year of renewal that our blessed Lord compared the time of his own coming; Isaias had used the same metaphor, long ago. Jew and Gentile alike, though the Jew in much fuller measure, were prepared for our Lord's coming; the event cast its shadow before it. Our Lord was coming to restore all things exactly as they were, to give us back the inheritance of Paradise that we had lost, to turn our slavery into freedom; that was what the *ingens lustrum*, the "great purifying", of the Romans really meant; that was what the jubilee year of the Jews really meant. And if his birth cast its shadow backwards over the centuries that went before, why shouldn't it cast its shadow forwards over the centuries that have followed since? That is what the Holy Year of the Christians really means. The year 1950 isn't chosen just because it looks a nice round number in the calendar; it is chosen because nineteen hundred and fifty years have elapsed since Jesus Christ was born. That is the event we are trying to recapture in memory, trying to reconstruct in imagination. The message of the Holy Year is the message of Christmas; only this is a special Christmas. When it was first instituted, in the Middle Ages, the Holy Year came only once in a century; we could say of it, as the Romans used to say of their *ingens lustrum*, that it was celebrated by people who had never seen one before and would never see one again. But before long the interval was shortened, and we imitated the fifty-year cycle of the Jews. Then, much later, it was reduced to twenty-five. Mother Church—how she spoils us!

Because the Holy Year is a kind of special Christmas, the Church wants to see as many of her children as possible coming home for their Christmas holiday. It is, or it used to be, when we had larger houses and there was more food going, the custom for all the family to collect and eat its Christmas dinner together. Was it going to be rather uncomfortable? Was it going to be rather embarrassing, because John's wife was hardly on speaking terms with Tom's nephew? All that didn't matter, it was Christmas Day, and you must rally round. So, during the Holy Year, the Church wants you to rally round, if you can get the Government to give you a passport, and your banker to give you some money, and your employer to give you a holiday. Not at Bethlehem; that would be the natural place to meet in, when we want to celebrate the thirty-ninth golden jubilee of our blessed Lord's birth. But Bethlehem is a small place; it was overcrowded when our Lord was born, and I expect it is overcrowded now worse than ever. So we meet at Rome instead, because Rome is the providentially appointed centre of Christendom, if we can and if we would like to. The Church doesn't bind us to go there under pain of mortal sin. No, but she offers us an inducement, in the form of an indulgence; she will make things easier for us when we get to purgatory. "That man", she will say, "may not have been a very good man, but he did *try*; I remember he came out to Rome in 1950."

You see, the Holy Year is essentially a time of indulgence. In the ordinary way, our non-Catholic friends are rather put off by the doctrine of indulgences, not merely because they find it difficult to believe in, but for the much better reason that they think it rather undignified. "Here is your Church", they say, "actually offering you a bribe to go round the Stations of the Cross; why should that be necessary? If you really loved our Lord you would do the Stations of the Cross out of devotion, without expecting any *quid pro quo*." And so, indeed, we ought to; it's only because she knows us so well, idle creatures that we are, that the Church brings in the profit motive at all. But the Holy Year indulgence is something on a higher plane than that; it has a kind of sacramental quality about it. We are going back, in memory, over a bridge of nineteen hundred and fifty years, to the night when Jesus Christ was born; when, as St Paul says, "the kindness of God, our Saviour, dawned on us, his great love for man". The kindness, the indulgence of almighty God; indulgence, that night, was in the air. And if the Church shows us kindness in remitting our purgatory, it isn't anything more and it isn't meant to be anything more than a faint echo, a distant image, of God's kindness when he let us off hell.

"He has sent me out to bid the prisoners go free"; that is the note which Isaias, which our Lord himself caught up from the ceremonies of the Hebrew jubilee; the Church, in her turn, catches up the same note from him, when she publishes a Holy Year. The opening ceremony of it, as you all know, is eloquent of that; on Christmas Eve, the Holy Father will break down a partition of masonry in the wall of St Peter's, thus opening a door which will stand open all the year. A variety of images run through the mind as you contemplate that telling piece of symbolism. You will think, perhaps, of a breach made in the wall of some well-defended city; or you will think of our Lord himself breaking down (as St Paul puts it) the wall that was a barrier between Jew and Gentile, throwing open to a whole world the privileges hitherto reserved for a few. But perhaps the most natural interpretation of that gesture the Supreme Pontiff makes on Christmas Eve is to think of him as tunnelling through the wall of a prison; how often we have read about that, with our hearts beating faster, in stories of escape! Souls freed, we dare to hope, from purgatory, souls here and now reprieved from sentence, that is at once the symbolic meaning, and the quasi-sacramental effect, of the Holy Year. We read in the paper the other day that the republic of Eire means to shorten sentences, to hasten on the release of prisoners in the public jails, in honour of this occasion. Well done, Eire! It was as if she were determined to be the last civilized country left in an unhappy world.

An unhappy world—there are many prisons that will remain unopened, this year; many sentences that will go unremitted. The tragedy of it is that our quarrels run too deep, our principles are too nearly concerned, to allow any facile talk of amnesty. We are contending not, like our ancestors, for territory or for markets, but for a way of life, a philosophy of human values. Amid the janglings of such a debate, how should the message of Christmas come through undisturbed? But, remember, although our public feuds may seem, at present, to open no door for an understanding, you and I, as Christian souls, cannot see the divine treasury of pardon so widely opened without the duty of asking ourselves, Have we forgiven? Nothing is more certain about our Lord's teaching than that God's pardon is conditional on ours; the unmerciful servant forfeits, by one act, his sentence of reprieve; "It is thus that my heavenly Father will deal with you, if brother does not forgive brother with all his heart". I said that the message of the Holy Year was the message of Christmas, and Christmas has ever been regarded as a season of reconciliation; that idea, feebly exploited by the old melodramas till we came to laugh at it, is true nevertheless. When you prepare, this year, for your Christmas communion, think of the Holy Father opening that door in St Peter's, and ask yourself whether there are any shut doors in your own heart. Are there misunderstandings which could be cleared up, if only you would make the first advance on your own side? Are there grudges which could be forgone, if pride did not keep whispering in your ear, "No, one cannot forgive a thing like that"? Is there some estrangement between you and a kinsman or a friend which began (you know it) with a fault of yours, which might yet be healed on both sides if you would only admit it was you who were in the wrong? "The kindness of God our Saviour dawned on us"—he came so far to meet us, and we, to imitate his kindness, have such a little way to go.

A Christmas message, then, and something also of a New Year message. Most of us, as I was saying, do try now and again to take ourselves in hand, to overcome the more glaring faults that betray themselves in our examinations of conscience. And New Year's Day is a favourite time for making this new departure; only, one New Year's Day is so very much like another! The agenda for 1950 will be so painfully like the agenda for 1949! I know; that is where the Holy Year gives us a valuable opportunity. For it is a *holy* year; holy, that is, set apart, marked out from others of its kind; that is what, at the roots of it, the word "holy" means. Nineteen hundred and fifty, then, is a special occasion, bringing a special chance with it. Most of us will not live to see the year 2000; a good many of us will not be here in 1975. Quite possibly, then, this is your last Holy Year; good reason for making New Year's Day a holy New Year's Day. Even if we can't go to Rome and get the indulgence, we can ask our blessed Lord to frame in our hearts that detestation of sin which is one of the conditions for gaining a plenary indulgence; if we can achieve that, we shall not go unrewarded, even without the rod of the penitentiary; it is more blessed, we are told, to give than to receive.

God grant us all a happy Holy Year.

30

THE CENTENARY OF ST MARIE'S[1]

Apostles and prophets are the foundation upon which you were built, and the chief corner-stone of it is Jesus Christ himself. In him the whole fabric is bound together, as it grows into a holy temple, dedicated to the Lord. In him you too are being built in with the rest.—Ephesians 2. 20, 22.

WE are met to praise God for the existence of a human edifice which has stood here, bearing witness to his glory, for a hundred years. So short a span it is, this life of ours, that the work of our own hands can survive us, and become, to its own architects, a monument of eternity. And in how short a time! This church, in which we are gathered, is but a mushroom growth compared with Durham or with York Minster; yet already we contemplate its stones with veneration because it has stood a hundred years. Only a hundred years; and of all the congregation which saw the opening of it in 1850, not one survives to tell us about the sober rejoicing and the ardent hopes which English Catholics felt about it, a hundred years ago.

We can look back, and interpret the meaning of such an occasion, down three separate vistas of experience. This building typifies, in the first instance, the agelong permanence of the Catholic Church; all the more readily because, by a happy accident, the year in which it was raised was the year in which the English Hierarchy was restored. Or again, it records the continued life of a single parish; a hundred years of patient witness borne to the Christian faith, here in the heart of a great city; the role this church has played in the civic life of Sheffield; the silent evidence it has afforded to our fellow citizens that the Catholic Church was not a sinister, alien influence, but a part of themselves. Or, finally, it may make us think of multitudinous obscure lives that were lived in the shadow of this church, and drew from it the sacramental strength that went with them on their journey. How many have been regenerated at that font; how many secrets, never repeated to human ears, have been whispered through the grille of those confessionals; what multitudes have been fed at those altar rails; how many of the faithful departed that bell has rung to their rest! We should do

[1] This sermon was preached at St Marie's, Sheffield, on 3 September 1950, on the occasion of the centenary of the church.

ill to forget them on such an occasion, all the unwritten stories that are commemorated in these stones.

They built this church in the Gothic style; it was the fashion a hundred years ago. And, whatever you say in praise or dispraise of the Gothic, it has this claim at least on the gratitude of Christian people— it rests on the arch, the great pointed arch that is so apt a parable of the whole Christian idea. The arch, after all, is a kind of human miracle; its delicate shafts soaring upwards, and enabled by a feat of engineering to support a weight much heavier than themselves. Even in its older, rounded form, it had appealed to the imagination of some Christian poet, and inspired that beautiful hymn, "*Caelestis urbs Jerusalem*", which we still sing at a dedication feast. The hymn catches up St Paul's metaphor about Christians being built together on the foundation of the apostles and prophets, and sees, in our earthly temples made with hands, an image of that heavenly Jerusalem which is the Christian Church. The Church, militant on earth or triumphant in heaven, it is all one; and you and I are part of its organization, contribute, each of us, to the unity of the whole. We are not isolated units, like pebbles scattered on a beach; we are living stones, each of us occupying an appointed place in the divine scheme of architecture:

> Stones, that full many a stroke have felt,
> The salutary chisel dealt,
> Shaped by the hammer's master-blow,
> Rear the vast fabric from below,
> Or, in the arch's measured sweep,
> Their closely-fitting stations keep.

Shall we consider for a moment how all *that*, all that vision of unity, fits in with the three subjects we mentioned just now; the history of the Church at large, the history of the parish, and the history of those innumerable souls who have lived and worshipped here?

The keystone of an arch; how it explains to us the meaning of authority! Here you have one stone which is larger and heavier than all the rest, and you balance it in the very centre and at the very top of all the rest—surely that will be fatal? Already these other stones are thrusting inwards and downwards; surely this added weight will complete their ruin? But no, it is just the other way about; the keystone corrects the thrust of the others, and keeps them all in their place, by weighing down on them from above. And our Lord Jesus Christ, when he left a Church behind him to be his monument in a world so forgetful as this, would build it enduringly. It was to be for all nations;

national rivalries, national differences of tradition would create strains and stresses, as time went on. It was to be for all sorts of men; allowance, then, had to be made for differences of temperament—some men are ever eager for novelties, some are for sticking to the old ways; there would be a thrust in this direction and in that, which must be counteracted somehow. Our Lord is himself the chief corner-stone of the heavenly building, and he would have a keystone to represent him in his Church on earth. As the keystone is only one stone in the arch, but greater and higher then the rest, so the Pope is only one bishop among the bishops of the world, but greater and higher than the rest, so as to flatten out all the strains and stresses which would otherwise make themselves felt in a Church not yet confirmed in sanctity. In this Jubilee year proclaimed by Pius XII, let today's anniversary carry our minds back to the year 1850, when Pius IX, driven out by the violence of revolutionaries, returned to Rome from Gaeta. And let us thank God once again for the rock of Peter, which, in a world so full of flux and change, still defies the erosion of the centuries.

The same pattern which marks the universal Church—marks, too, the individual diocese. In each diocese, there is one priest who enjoys, as in his own right, the full exercise of priestly powers; the rest exercise them only in dependence on him. He is their overseer, their bishop; once more, he is the keystone of the arch. The bishop in the centre, with his priests arranged round him in a semi-circle—that picture is as old as Christendom. When the apostle John, exiled on the isle of Patmos, was granted a revelation of things present and to come, that was the picture in which the whole of his Apocalypse was framed; he saw almighty God sitting on a throne, with twenty-four elders (or priests; it is the same word) grouped round him. Like the universal Church, every diocese in the universal Church is, when times are normal, an arch with a keystone in the middle. It is a separate, integral part of the Christian commonwealth. But there are times of upheaval and of persecution when the normal structure of things cannot be maintained; the arch must be replaced by scaffolding. Instead of being divided into dioceses, each with a bishop of its own, a country is mapped out into districts, each governed by a personal representative of the Holy See. That happened in England for nearly three hundred years after the Reformation. And then, just when revolutions all over Europe made it look as if Europe might be lost to the faith, Pius IX had the courage to restore in England the privileges we had lost. Of that bold and successful policy let this church stand as a monument. A hundred years ago, it was the newest of the sixty-one churches in the

Yorkshire district. Now, it is one of the oldest among the three hundred and sixty churches in the two dioceses of Leeds and Middlesbrough.

But it is time we came back to ourselves, and said something about this parish in isolation. Think, those of you who have already reached middle age, of some old woman who used to hobble into church, Sunday after Sunday, about the year 1910, when you sat fidgeting there among the schoolchildren. That old woman, perhaps, when she was among the schoolchildren herself, had seen this church opened. Her name swelled the roll of parishioners until the end of the century, and then yours came in to take its place—that is what has been happening all the time; the parish is being built up, from one generation to the next, out of living stones, you and you and you. Most of us, I think, have a strong dislike for a word you often come across in sermons and pious books, the word to "edify". "Such an edifying conversation"— you feel instinctively that it must have been a rather dull conversation; "such edifying behaviour"—you suspect it at once of being hypocritical behaviour. But the word "to edify" only means "to build"; and exactly in so far as we lead Christian lives, you and I, we are edifying other people, we can't help it. We are building up the life of the family, of the club, of the parish, by everything we say or do. "The arch never sleeps", an architect will tell you; meaning that all the time stone is pressing against stone, and what seems to be rest is really only an equilibrium that depends on a balance of strains. It is the same with a parish, or with any collection of human souls; they are affecting one another, interacting on one another, all the time.

"Nor knowest thou what argument thy life to thy neighbour's creed hath lent"[1]—we are not isolated pebbles lying on the beach, we are living stones set in a building, and if one crumbles, it will have an effect on the whole.

One more secret the arch has to tell us; a warning—or is it an encouragement?—for our individual lives. The stones fit into the arch only because the mason has cut them in a certain shape. "Stones that full many a stroke have felt, the salutary chisel dealt, shaped by the hammer's master-blow"—yes, we need that; you and I need that. The Architect who designed this great fabric, the holy Catholic Church, is also the Craftsman who shapes every life until it fits exactly into the niche he has appointed for it. And he shapes it not without the chisel, not without the hammer. I mean, his Providence, which so often entails for us a discipline of suffering. We cannot see why this or that trouble was allowed to befall us, or those who are dear to us; that is not

[1] Ralph Waldo Emerson (1803-82): "Each and All".

wonderful. God does not disclose his design beforehand; we shall see the plans in heaven. But it is all *meant*; there was never yet a slip of the Craftsman's fingers; your niche is there, waiting for you, if you will allow hammer and chisel to do their work.

When a church is consecrated, crosses are built into the wall here and there, to commemorate the fact. But in the heavenly edifice every stone, from our Lady downwards, must bear the mark of the great Artificer; and that mark is always a cross.

May he grant eternal rest to the builders and benefactors of this church, to all who have ministered and all who have worshipped here; and may he bring us all to that Temple where he is perfectly served and wholly manifested, the new Jerusalem, eternal in the heavens.

31

THE CENTENARY OF THE HIERARCHY: I[1]

Mark well how you thrive henceforward, from this twenty-fourth day of the ninth month, when you laid the foundations of the Lord's temple; mark it well. Not yet has the corn ripened, not yet have vine and fig, pomegranate and olive, had time to blossom, but on all these my blessing lies henceforward. —Aggaeus 2.

THE prophet Aggaeus points to the end of the ninth month as the date when the restoration of the temple was taken in hand after the captivity. And the English Hierarchy was restored by the Bull *Universalis Ecclesiae*[2] at the end of the ninth month, a hundred years ago.

For nearly three centuries, England had sat on the stool of penitence. The dwindling remnant of hereditary Catholics were not organized under dioceses, each with its own bishop, its own chapter of canons, after the wont of European Christendom. They were ruled by emissaries from Rome, personally responsible to the Holy See—as if this island had been some newly discovered territory in the Pacific, whose inhabitants were mere beginners in the faith, too barbarous

[1] This sermon was preached at Westminster Cathedral on 1 October 1950, during the Hierarchy Centenary Congress.

[2] The Bull *Universalis Ecclesiae* is dated 29 September 1850; a translation is given in *The English Catholics*, 1850-1950 (Ed. Right Rev. George Beck, A.A.), pp. 107-15.

to be entrusted with the management of their own affairs. So long as the penal laws were in force, that was not wonderful; in a besieged city, constitutional niceties are not observed. It must be confessed, too, that we were not altogether ready for a change; our Catholic fore-fathers were for ever quarrelling among themselves, and noisily. But the penal laws went, and Catholic disabilities went, and still we bore the character of a missionary Church. Then, in 1850, a new Pope, Pius IX of happy memory, decided that we were no longer to be a Crown Colony of the Triple Tiara. Ripe for self-government, we were to achieve dominion status at last.

It was a gracious gesture, but not altogether graciously made, or graciously accepted. It matters little whether we ascribe the sequel to Cardinal Wiseman's habit of flamboyancy, or to the instinct of the British public for getting hold of the wrong end of the stick. As we know, windows were broken, statesmen and churchmen vied with one another in denouncing this act of Roman Catholic aggression. But we are not here to commemorate a storm in a teacup. The Ecclesiastical Titles Bill is only remembered as a constitutional curiosity, because it died at birth. Let us not waste our blushes on the past.

Meanwhile, what had happened? Had so very much happened? We have described the Pope's action as a gesture; was it more than a gesture? After all, the rule of the Vicars Apostolic was Roman only in name; they were English of the English. They worked hard, they governed their districts; few men have been so energetic as Challoner, few so forceful as Milner. Are we certain that if the race of Vicars Apostolic had continued, things would have been very different? Would a Manning, without his title, have been less influential in the Church of his day, a Hinsley without the scarlet, less widely loved? On the other side, we have to remember that the restoration of the Hierarchy was only an instalment. It was only during the present century that the full pattern of parochial life was brought back to England. Why do we look back on the Bull *Universalis Ecclesiae* as a moment so decisive, so great a landmark in our history?

I would suggest, with all submission to wider judgments than my own, that the real significance of the event we celebrate today is to be found, not in the refinements of Canon Law, but in the twists of the human heart. It healed, as nothing else could have healed, an obstinate though ill-defined misunderstanding between the English Catholics and the Papacy. God forbid that we should look back over the past, on such an occasion as this, without acknowledging the debt we owe to some of the leading English families for all they did to preserve the faith in dark times, and the sufferings they underwent in doing it. But you cannot read the history of that struggle which prepared the way for Catholic Emancipation, without realizing that to some of them the Roman allegiance was an ancestral heirloom, rather than a living creed. Even the clergy, that splendid race of which we find the perfect specimen in Dr Lingard, were English to a fault, and distrustful of the "Roman" spirit. Little wonder if pessimistic observers, like Cardinal Acton, feared we might relapse at any moment into the state of our Saxon forefathers under the Heptarchy—the same grudging allegiance, the same narrow conservatism. From that danger, I think, the restoration of the Hierarchy helped to save us.

Am I being guilty of a paradox? You might have supposed that if the English Catholics were half-hearted subjects of the Papacy, that fact was all the more reason why they should be kept under a central control. But that was where Pio Nono showed his greatness; showed his knowledge of human nature, and perhaps of the English nature in particular. If we were distrustful of Rome, it was because we felt that Rome distrusted us; you had only to ride us with a loose rein, and we would answer to a touch. How far that was his conscious calculation, we do not know; there are levels of action at which something higher than mere calculation intervenes. At least it is certain that today no nation is more distinguished than ours by love and loyalty for the person of the Holy Father. That is, after all, only natural; the Englishman finds it easier to be enthusiastic about persons than about ideas, and in a world of republics we remain a monarchy. But the springs of that energy—I doubt if they were ever released till a century ago.

When the rain is over, the colours and the scents of earth have a freshness and a pungency which speak to the mind of renewal. When the storm which broke out over Roman Catholic Aggression had subsided, the same feeling of renewal was in men's hearts. Not least among those fathers who met at Oscott, in 1852, for the first provincial synod of Westminster; it was their mood John Henry Newman interpreted, when he climbed into the pulpit and gave out his text, "The winter is now past, the rain is over and gone, the flowers have appeared in our land"; and when he told them, "The past *has* returned; the dead lives . . . the English Church was, and the English Church was not, and the English Church is again. This is the portent, worthy of a cry. It is the coming in of a second spring; it is a restoration in the moral world, such as that which yearly takes place in the physical." Such power had Newman to grave his words in marble, when you read it you almost catch the magic accents of his voice.

LX

Men say, a wizard to a northern king
At Christmastide such wondrous things did show,
That through one window men beheld the spring,
And through a second saw the summer glow,
And through a third the autumn vines a-row;
And all the while, and in its wonted way,
Piped the drear wind of that December day.

Was Newman such another wizard? Was it merely that his oratory, like Pugin's architecture, had the power to create an illusion; were they living, those fathers of Oscott, in a fool's paradise? "Not yet has the corn ripened, not yet have vine and fig, pomegranate and olive, had time to blossom, but on all these my blessing lies henceforward"— so Aggaeus had prophesied when the foundations of the temple were laid, and it was to such vernal promise that Newman looked forward; was he right?

We know that he was right. His Eminence has reminded us, in his recent pastoral letter, how, since the Hierarchy was restored, the number of Catholics has trebled in a country whose population has grown to little more than twice its former size; how we have six times as many priests, ten times as many schools, four times as many churches now, as then. It has not been a century of effortless progress; there have been disputes, there have been scandals, and every patient forward step has called for sacrifice—today, perhaps, so far as money is concerned, we are called upon to make sacrifices greater than ever. But on the whole this little walled garden of ours, the Catholic Church in England, has fulfilled the promise of its spring; vine and fig, pomegranate and olive have borne their fruit, and we have been enriched, not seldom, by windfalls from next door.

Yes, but it is a garden, a walled garden; and outside? "And all the while, and in its wonted way, Piped the drear wind of that December day"—outside, is the winter past, is the rain over and gone? God forbid that we should criticize the labours of other men, outside our own communion, or seem to make capital out of their embarrassments. Heroic efforts have been made, by men of devoted piety, by men of great learning, to bring England back to God; but would anyone dare to claim that they have succeeded? Just now, in these dark days, there are signs, perhaps, of a hesitation and a return. But is England effectively Christian? And outside this island, matters are worse; there is hardly a theatre of human activity abroad but makes the mind sicken at the contemplation of it; "men's hearts dried up with fear, as they await the troubles that are overtaking the whole world". More and more, it falls upon the English-speaking countries, if it is not too late, to save humanity; more and more, it falls upon the Catholic minorities in those countries to give them a message, to put heart into them. Are we ready for it? Are we equal to the task?

One omen, at least, may encourage us; that, as we celebrate this centenary, the Rosary month of October lies before us. Once again, as at Lepanto, once again, as on the Danube, the Mother of God will be fighting our battles; in her virgin heart, spring is perennial. Christians, to your knees!

32

THE CENTENARY OF THE
HIERARCHY: II[1]

L AST year, down at Exeter, we were celebrating the revolt of the Western men against the new English Prayer Book.[2] It was the last demonstration in favour of the old religion, here in the West, and it was put down in blood by the use of German and Italian mercenaries. Meanwhile, no effort had been spared to secure the permanence of the new order of things. Bristol, then at the height of its greatness, had been made the seat of a Bishopric; so had Gloucester; in both cases out of the spoils of the monasteries. The long struggle between England and Spain helped to make good Protestants of us; sailors from Plymouth and all the little ports of the South coast were making good as merchant adventurers, and something very like pirates. You couldn't divorce religion from nationalism, and Sir Richard Grenville, the hero of the *Revenge*, was known in his own country as a bitter persecutor of Catholics. The West was still a home of loyalties; it was loyal to the Crown in the Civil War; but its sympathies were no longer Catholic; it supported the Duke of Monmouth, it protested against the imprisonment of the Seven Bishops. Glastonbury was forgotten.

Later, the uninspired Anglicanism of the eighteenth century was not good enough for us, and we went Nonconformist. In 1768, when

---

[1] This sermon was preached at the Hierarchy Centenary Rally at Clifton on the Feast of Christ the King, October 1950.
[2] The rising of south-west England in 1549 against the imposition of the first Prayer Book of Edward VI.

John Wesley visited Frome (then, as now, the hub and centre of the
West Country), he found it "a mixture of men of all opinions,
Anabaptists, Quakers, Presbyterians, Arians, Antinomians, Moravians
and what not". Wesley himself made Bristol his headquarters, and
found his best welcome in Cornwall; his preaching annexed the
South-western counties, as that of the Calvinistic Methodists annexed
Wales. Two hundred years after the official religion of the country had
been forced on us, even that had become a back number. In matters of
religion, the West is not easily suited; alone among the cities of the
world, Plymouth has given its name to a special type of Christianity.

Meanwhile, what was happening to the Catholic remnant? The
faith was kept alive; we have a long roll of martyrs, from Cuthbert
Mayne onwards, and we are justly proud of them. But, if we are rich
in martyrs, is it because we sheltered so many priests, or because we
sheltered them so badly? Our part of England was severely policed;
there were Bishops at Exeter, Salisbury, Bath and Wells, Bristol, and
Gloucester; in point of fact too many; Bishops were not slow, as a
rule, to delate recusants. We had a few important Catholic families—
the Arundells at Wardour, the Welds at Lulworth, and after Charles
II's time the Cliffords at Ugbrooke. But we had no such chain of recu-
sant country houses as ran through the Midlands; still less had we the
multitude of small squires and yeoman farmers that kept the faith alive
in Lancashire. Nor were the local magnates friendly to us here, as they
were on the Welsh border.

> Wyndham and Horner, Popham and Thynne,
> When the monks went out, they came in.[1]

Somersetshire fortunes were largely built up on the spoils of Glastonbury, and those who inherited them stood for the new order of things.
By the time Emancipation came, we had one mission at Bristol, others
at Cheltenham, Gloucester, Bath, Salisbury, Wardour, Taunton, and
Lulworth, little else. When you reflect how important the West had
been before the Industrial Revolution, it is a sorry total.

Immediately after the first Emancipation Act, new strength began to
flow into English Catholicism, as a strange by-product of the French
Revolution. Many of our English missions were first put on their feet
by *émigré* French priests who had fled from the Terror; at the same
time, the English Colleges abroad, driven out from the lands which
had sheltered them, came back and took fresh root on English soil.

---

[1] An old local rhyme recorded in Aubrey's *Lives* (I, 279 (A)). These were the four
families to whom the Glastonbury Abbey estate was granted at the Dissolution.

We had our *émigré* priests; Père Grou, one of the greatest of French mystical writers, was chaplain at Lulworth, and the mission at Salisbury was consolidated by the Abbé Bègin. But on the whole, they left little mark; meanwhile, the stream of reimported Catholicism passed us by. The secular colleges settled down in Hertfordshire and Durham, the Jesuits in Lancashire, the Benedictines in Yorkshire and Shropshire. Only the year before Waterloo did we get Downside, and Downside, through no fault of its own, was nearly strangled at birth. The Second Spring had begun, but the barometer of the Western District marked "No change".

Still more important things were happening; the tide of Irish immigration had set in. We talk about the Potato Famine, but it doesn't need a potato famine to make Ireland distressed. Long before 1845 the Irish were on the move, and between the year 1820 and the year 1840 the Catholic population of Liverpool had risen from eighteen thousand to eighty thousand. That was because, in the first place, Liverpool had already a strong Catholic tradition, had already a reasonably large body of Catholic inhabitants. And because, in the second place, the Catholic authorities there saw what was happening, and took measures about it from the first. In the very first years of the century there were already at least six Catholic centres in Liverpool. In Bristol we had one! I think Father Darby must have his tongue in his cheek when he writes: "The number of Catholics was increasing so fast that in 1834 Fr Edgeworth, the Franciscan, bought a site in Clifton, where a temporary church was opened in 1842".[1] On the very eve of the potato famine, we had just built our second church in Bristol; and what had been happening to the Irish immigrants in the meantime? I remember a priest in Plymouth telling me, years ago, that when he made a house-to-house visitation in his parish, he found a whole street of Irish families, and all the people who bore those Irish names were Nonconformists of one kind or another, not through any fault of their own—they didn't even remember that their grandfathers had been Catholics. Little doubt that what was happening in Plymouth was happening in Bristol, which had always (in the nature of things) had a strong connection with Ireland. When the potato famine came in 1845, there would be two churches and about four priests to look after the immigrants; I wonder how many we lost. Once again, we had missed our tide.

Catholicism revived in London through the French *émigrés*; Catholicism revived in the North through the Irish famine; what of the

[1] In the pamphlet *The Diocese of Clifton*, 1850-1950.

Midland counties? The Midlands reaped the full advantage of the Second Spring, of the Oxford conversions. With Wiseman, and Ullathorne, and Newman in Birmingham, with Faber converting whole villages in Staffordshire, with Father Dominic rushing to and fro in his Passionist habit, with Lord Shrewsbury and de Lisle Phillipps working Pugin to death as he built them churches all over the country-side, what wonder if the Midlands felt the impulse of the Second Spring? But not we, down in the West. For two years we had Ulla-thorne as our Vicar Apostolic, then he was sent off to the Midlands.[1] For two years Father Gentili and his splendid Fathers of Charity had the direction of Prior Park, then the Bishop quarrelled with them and they went off to the Midlands. Even the Passionists couldn't maintain themselves at Woodchester; they drew off to Broadway, in such a remote corner of the diocese as to be practically indistinguishable from the Midlands. We had missed our tide again.

When we are saying all this, we mustn't forget that the Western District, and the Clifton diocese after it, will always owe a profound debt of gratitude to the religious orders which have settled here. The West, whatever else it may lack, is rich in rural amenities; and when a Reverend Mother wants to find a nice quiet place for the new novitiate, the first thing she turns to is the map of Somerset. It has been going on steadily from the time of the Napoleonic Wars to the time of the great blitz. I like Father Darby's story of the Benedictine nuns who had their house in Paris searched, because it was thought they were concealing William Pitt, and then came over to Dorset and had their house searched again, because it was thought they were concealing the Emperor Napoleon. What a lot the nuns do for us! And they do it so unobtrusively, we always forget to notice it and to say "thank you" for it. Still, it only meant a school here, an orphanage there, dotted about haphazard, in days when the diocese needed a strong central policy, a uniform plan.

Was it anybody's fault that we so missed our opportunities? It is ungracious to speak evil of the dead; but I cannot help thinking we might have got on better without Bishop Baines.[2] This extraordinary man, our seventh Vicar Apostolic, is remembered with equal lack of enthusiasm at Ampleforth, to which he belonged, and at Downside,

[1] William Ullathorne, o.s.b., was Vicar-Apostolic of the Western District before he was enthroned as first Archbishop of Birmingham on 29 September 1850.

[2] Peter Augustine Baines, Bishop of Siga (1787-1843): Benedictine monk, Prior of Ampleforth; appointed in 1823 Coadjutor to Bishop Collingridge, whom he succeeded as Vicar-Apostolic of the Western District in 1829. He then became secularized, purchased Prior Park as his episcopal residence, adding two wings, one, St Peter's, to serve as a lay college, the other, St Paul's, as an ecclesiastical seminary. He died there 6 July 1843.

where he is buried, as the man who depopulated the one and tried to absorb the other. All the other districts had seminaries; why shouldn't he have one in the West? So he bought Prior Park at Bath, and added two wings to it without ruining its architecture, a feat which is probably unique in the history of English Catholicism. But at the same time he ran up enormous debts, and saddled the district with a white elephant. Its long and troubled history seems to show that nobody can run Prior Park without losing money over it, except the Irish Christian Brothers, who are fortunately in possession of it today. It is difficult not to feel that Bishop Baines, if he had been less enamoured of his own cloudy schemes, and less ready to quarrel with everyone he came across, might have done much more to build up our position here in the West, during the fateful years, 1829-1843, when he administered the district.

And so we get on, perhaps rather later than we should have, to the restoration of the Hierarchy. You will now be expecting me to say that the West, after languishing so long under the Vicars Apostolic, took a new lease of life as soon as it became a diocese with a Bishop of its own. Well, of course, it became two dioceses; Wales had already been separated from us, and at the restoration of the Hierarchy we dropped Plymouth. Or should I say Plymouth dropped us? Anyhow, the counties of Cornwall, Devon and Dorset no longer come into our story, except now and again when they look in to find a new Bishop. The diocese of Clifton—did it at once start on a glorious career in the year 1850; or must we admit that the Bull *Universalis Ecclesiae* had, here in the West, a delayed action? Reading between the lines of Fr Darby's pamphlet, I incline to the latter opinion.

Culturally, indeed, we have a high record. It is not merely that we possess Downside, one of the best-known of Benedictine houses. Even the rest of us are rather a brainy lot. The reform of the calendar, for example—you will remember that that was introduced at Rome in 1582, the year when St Teresa died; that is why we keep her feast on October 15th, although she died on October 4th. Well, just two hundred years later, in the year 1782, England, not to be outdone, determined to follow suit. And one of the astronomers the Government consulted on that occasion was Bishop Laurence York, the Vicar Apostolic of the Western District. It was a priest of the Western District, Father McEnery, who got to work on Kent's Cavern in 1825, and announced, to the derision of the learned world, the immemorial antiquity of man. He proved to be right, and thus completely altered our whole conception of man's emergence on earth—not a bad day's work for a parish priest. And so it was after 1850: your Lordship is probably the only Bishop in the English Hierarchy who has had three predecessors running who were literary men. Bishop Clifford, who governed the diocese from 1857 to 1893, is still remembered for some doubtfully orthodox speculations about the first chapter of Genesis;[1] he also went to the Vatican Council and, I am sorry to say, was on the wrong side about Infallibility. He was succeeded by Bishop Brownlow, an authority on the Catacombs.[2] And *he* made room for that gracious figure many of us remember so well, Bishop Burton,[3] a lover of Latin verse and a friend, as such a man should be, of Leo XIII. Oh, we were all right on culture. But was there much progress in the dull, pastoral work of building up the diocese till the beginning of the present century, when Bishop Burton took over?

Let us take a glance at statistics. There are about a hundred and eighty Mass centres in the diocese at the moment. Of those, only forty are marked in the Directory as dating back beyond the beginning of this century. And of those forty, half are marked as *older* than 1850. It looks as if the first fifty years of the restored Hierarchy only succeeded in doubling our miserable total of twenty Mass centres. In fact, when you go to Mass in the Clifton diocese, the chances are one in nine that you might have been worshipping in the same place a hundred years ago, two in nine that you might have been worshipping in the same place fifty years ago; the remaining seven chances you owe to Bishop Burton and to Bishop Lee.[4]

Or take the statistics of priests working in the diocese. The figures given in the Catholic Encyclopedia, which are those for 1907, show that we had then only a hundred and thirty priests, and of those only fifty were seculars—the rest were religious, who might at any moment be withdrawn to some other part of the country at the will of their superiors. It was not a very impressive total, for a diocese which had been in existence for over half a century. Forty years later, we had two

[1] William Joseph Hugh Clifford (1823-93): consecrated third Bishop of Clifton on 15 February 1857; died 14 August 1893. He proposed the theory (*Dublin Review*, 1881, p. 321) that the story of creation as told in the book of Genesis is not an historical narrative, but a liturgical song, in which the different days of the week are set apart for the praise of the different works of God's creation.

[2] William Robert Brownlow (1830-1901): received into the Church by Cardinal Newman; consecrated fourth Bishop of Clifton 1 May 1894; author of several books on religion, history and archeology; chiefly known for his *Roma Sotterana*, which he wrote with Dr Northcote; he was considered the greatest English authority on the Catacombs of his day; died 9 November 1901.

[3] George Ambrose Burton (1852-1931): classical scholar; consecrated fifth Bishop of Clifton 1 May 1902; died 8 February 1931.

[4] William Lee (1875-1948): consecrated sixth Bishop of Clifton on 26 January 1932; died 21 September 1948.

hundred and fifty priests, nearly twice as many, and of those one hundred and fifteen were seculars, so that their number had more than doubled. It was the twentieth century, not the nineteenth century, that really saw us on the move.

As a matter of fact, if you look into them the figures are much more startling than that; our progress has been a *crescendo*. If you compare the *Catholic Directory* of 1938, just before the war, with the *Catholic Directory* for 1948, you will find that in those ten years the number of Mass centres in the diocese went up from one hundred and twenty-seven to one hundred and eighty, and the number of priests went up from less than two hundred to more than two hundred and fifty. And it was just as well they did, for in those ten years the number of our Catholic baptisms had doubled, and the number of our Catholic marriages had more than doubled. There is no doubt what all that means; it means that British industries are being re-grouped, are being transferred, on the whole, from North to South, and our Catholic population, instead of being concentrated almost entirely in the industrial districts of the North, is overflowing into Cinderella-dioceses like Clifton and Northampton. We are trying to adapt ourselves to a new situation, and at a moment when everything is against us; when you can't build churches because you can't get the permits, when you can't start schools because everybody hates Catholic schools. And I have no doubt the devil is saying to himself, "These people in the West bungled Irish immigration; the Oxford conversions left them unmoved, and when the Hierarchy was restored they went to sleep for fifty years. With any luck, they will miss their tide again."

That we do not intend to miss our tide, this time, is a resolution that deserves to be registered silently, without show of hands, by this magnificent meeting.

33

THE FESTIVAL OF BRITAIN: I[1]

Our home is in heaven.—Philippians 3. 20.

OUR Lord Jesus Christ has left this earth; he has gone to a far country, sundered from us not by so many miles, or by so many light-years, but by those subtle barriers which cut off the invisible

[1] This sermon was broadcast on Ascension Day, 3 May 1951, on the occasion of the opening of the Festival of Britain.

from the visible; barriers so opaque, that the human mind itself, most penetrating of all the instruments we know, cannot reach to the further side of them. Where he is, there (he tells us) his servants shall be; it is their future destination, and even now the centre of their loyalties. He has gone (that is the metaphor he himself used) to claim a kingdom; and therefore St Paul reminds us that we, his servants, have our home in heaven—or rather, if we will do full justice to St Paul's metaphor— have our citizenship; here on earth, all Christians are displaced persons. To this visible world which affords us, in the meanwhile, shelter and companionship, let us ever be grateful, as exiles should. But it is not the country of our dreams.

Has the Christian, then, no earthly citizenship at all; has he no rights, no duties, in connection with the gross soil, English or Irish, French or Belgian soil, that gave him birth? To think like that is to forget, what some Christians are always prone to neglect—that the supernatural does not replace the natural; it perfects and hallows it. Our religion tells us that all men are brothers, that everyone who is in need is our neighbour; it does not therefore abolish the special duties we have to our own family, our own neighbours and friends; it rivets those natural ties into a bond more gracious than ever. And so it is with our civic obligations; the Christian who remembers his heavenly country is a better, not a worse citizen of his heavenly country for that. How do we account for it, this paradox, that a home in heaven is the best school for the disciplines of earth?

Surely there is no real difficulty. That world into which Jesus Christ has ascended is not a world of shadows; it is a world of realities, which casts its shadows on earth. If we do not fall into the error of mistaking shadow for substance, we shall understand heaven better for being like earth, and we shall enjoy earth better for being like heaven. Human love, human beauty, are only the shadow, not the substance. They could not move our natures so deeply, if they had not in them some-thing of the divine; and yet, so imperfect, so fugitive, so unsatisfying, they can only be shadows. Somewhere, beyond the reach of our senses, there must be perfect love, perfect beauty, of which we can form no true idea—meanwhile, these blurred shadows are better than nothing. And because we know that they signify and presage something other than themselves, more real and more enduring, earthly love, earthly beauty, mean not less but more to us; their supernatural background lends an edge to the enjoyment of them which otherwise, in a self-contained world, we could never have known.

And so it is with citizenship. Citizenship is not some extension of the herd instinct which bids the bee work for the hive, the wolf fight for the pack; we must not interpret the higher in terms of the lower. Citizenship, that attitude of the will which inspires a man to make light of his own importance compared with the interests of the group to which he belongs—that, too, is a shadow of heaven reflected on earth. That peace which reigns among the citizens of heaven, that self-forgetfulness which takes delight, not in the happiness of each but in the happiness of all—how should we understand it here? But we may catch the echoes of it, at a time when some great national deliverance or occasion of national rejoicing lifts up our hearts, in spite of ourselves, with a glow of communal sentiment which owes nothing to self. "This is where I belong" is the thought which occurs to our minds; and, if we are trained in the school of Christ, who saw parables everywhere, we shall not stop at that point. "Heaven is where I really belong," we shall add, "and heaven, since it is my true country, must be something even better than this."

Shall we, for that reason, think less of this country of Britain, the foster-mother with whom we were put out to nurse? Rather, we shall love her all the better, because the feeling we have for her is the sacramental expression of that immortal spark in us which longs for heaven. John Bunyan, they say, when he represented heaven to us in the *Pilgrim's Progress* under the image of the Delectable Mountains, was thinking of—what? The Alps? The Peak Country? No, the Bedfordshire hills. Not rising much above six hundred feet, but enough to lift up a man's heart, if he was a Midlander. And so it is with all of us; the sights of home are the stuff out of which we construct—how should we do otherwise?—our picture of heaven. Dare we remember, that when our Blessed Lord was being taken up from the sight of the apostles, he watched, receding from his view, those same hills, the river, the lake, the sea, which his Mother had pointed out to him when they took their walks round Nazareth? He did not feel homesick for them; he knew that heaven was not the loss but the fulfilment of all this. Only I think he loved them; he, their Creator, saw that they were very good.

Sons and subjects of Britain, we shall not be ashamed to admit that among our earthly loyalties Britain comes first. There are signs, in our day, that the barriers which divided the western nations are coming down; faced with a threat not less powerful, not less malignant, than was the threat of Islam in the Middle Ages, we are returning more than ever to medieval notions of European unity. Good Europeans we must needs be, if we are to prosper, nay, if we are to survive. But it is from

our own country that our loyalties will spring; to her that they will
return. "Due meed of punishment the Lord give me, and more than
due, if aught but death part me and thee."

34

THE FESTIVAL OF BRITAIN: II[1]

Others have laboured, and it is their labours you have inherited.—John 4. 38.

THAT interview between our Lord and his apostles from which
my text is taken, like so much else in St John's Gospel, is very
simple on the surface, very perplexing when you try to work it out.
There can be no doubt that our Lord is referring to himself, and
perhaps, out of humility, is associating his forerunner, St John the
Baptist, with himself; these are the "others" who have laboured and
it is their labours the apostles will inherit. *They* have but to reap a
harvest which has already been sown in the hearts of men. Christian
missionaries, in every age, have been quick to acknowledge this
indebtedness. Because the Gospel we preach is a thing not of this world,
we do not expect the triumphs of the Church to be commensurate
with the energy of her earthly representatives. Other factors, beyond
our knowing, have entered into the process; how much, for example,
do we owe it to the efforts of today, or even of yesterday, this con-
solidation of the Catholic position in England which has come about
in our time? If the number of Catholics in the Nottingham diocese
has more than doubled in one generation, how much of that do we
owe to the sufferings and the prayers of the men who went before us?

We do well to think of that; we do well also to remember that we
can expect little reward, in this world or in the next, if we are content
to live on our capital. We in our generation have to pull our weight,
not lie back, passengers in the boat, and allow the impetus of the past
to carry us forward. You are celebrating the Festival of Britain; but
the year draws on, there is autumn in the air, we are concerned to
look round us, and to take stock of our harvest. Forgive me, then, if
I play the part of a skeleton at the feast; if I suggest that these festivities

---

[1] This sermon was preached at St Barnabas' Cathedral, Nottingham, at High Mass on
23 September 1951, in connection with the Festival of Britain.

of 1951, the epilogue to a glorious century of achievement, ought to leave us in a mood of effort and vigilance, not of dull complacency.

Between the wars, a habit set in of laughing at the Victorians. Their clothes, their jokes, their rectitude, their prudery, their art, their insularity, their pretentiousness, their sense of superiority—was there anything to be said for these grandfathers of ours who built the Crystal Palace? Today, we are a little less certain of our judgments; our laughter sounds a little feverish, and we feel, most of us, a kind of wistful nostalgia for the solid things of the past. Oh, to be sure, we live in a better England, so far as comfort and security are concerned. The conditions of labour under which British Industry dazzled the world in the days of the Prince Consort were conditions which would never be tolerated now. But, even there, how much of our social improvement has come down to us, almost automatically, from the political ferment of the nineteenth century! Meanwhile, we are celebrating the centenary, of what? Not so much an event as a frame of mind. A frame of mind in which men felt that the gains of the present were abiding, and looked forward to bright hopes of the future. And we are celebrating the centenary—let us not be ashamed to confess it—with our hearts in our mouths. We begin to see now how much we have been living on capital; how much of the prosperity that is still left was bequeathed to us by the honesty, the good workmanship, the law-abiding instincts of our grandfathers; the men who seemed, till yesterday, so funny!

Other men have laboured, and it is their labours you have inherited —there is no politician, I think, no economist, who doubts that hard work is called for, if the British race is to hold its own at this crisis of its fortunes. The Festival of Britain is not an invitation to rest on our laurels, enjoying the good things which our ancestors have won for us; it is a warning that only thrift and enterprise can maintain what thrift and enterprise have achieved. We have been speaking of material prosperity; you will remind me, quite rightly, that this is a subject for the hustings, not for the pulpit. But it is not only in material well-being that the men of a hundred years ago challenge comparison with ourselves. The salient difference between us, disguise it how you may, is that our grandfathers had, what we have not, a spiritual interpretation of the universe. They lived by a creed; we only live by a code. To be sure, men like Newman, who could read the signs of the times, were already distressed by the state of religion among their fellow countrymen. But Darwin had not yet published the *Origin of Species*;[1] Charles

---

[1] *On the Origin of Species by Means of Natural Selection* was published in 1859.

Bradlaugh had not yet stood for a seat in Parliament;[1] Karl Marx was only a displaced person whom nobody had heard of. The men who went to the Great Exhibition at the Crystal Palace still regarded the wonders of nature as the marvels of God's creation; still regarded the greatness of the British people as a blessing mysteriously sent from heaven, not as a natural consequence of the British way of life. We are still, in many ways, a religious nation. But is the religion we profess vital, is it real to us? Or are we living on capital, here too? Are we repeating, without examining, the religious formulas of yesterday?

All through the latter half of last century, men were prophesying what was going to happen about religion, and getting their prophecies wrong. Some thought that as secular education won the day, and the belief in God was slowly but steadily abandoned, man would lose his moral sense and revert to the animal; in a hundred years' time we should be no better than savages, flying at one another's throats. Others, equally certain that the influence of religion must pass, were confident that it would pass unregretted. Belief in God, belief in a future life, might die out; but the moral sense of the nation, its kindliness, its honesty, its decency, its respect for the marriage law, would not be affected. Why should they? These moral impulses were the fruits of civilization; they did not depend on superstitious sanctions from an imaginary other world!

Both parties were wrong. Both parties forgot our English habit of compromise, our English habit of avoiding direct issues. The urgent debate between the supporters of religion and the supporter of agnosticism, which is so prominent in our literature during the second half of the nineteenth century, dies away and almost disappears during the first half of the twentieth. The ordinary Englishman of today has been brought up in a tradition of benevolent uncertainty about the Christian faith. He has been taught it after a fashion, and it means something to him personally—it may mean a great deal to him personally. But the atmosphere about him is not Christian; the pressure of public opinion, which is so largely responsible for all our actions, has no real relation to the Gospel. Nobody, except a professional beggar, ever appeals to a Christian motive for the performance of some kindly action. Nobody, in criticizing the modern man's conduct or in trying to restrain him, points out that such and such a course of action is contrary to God's will; it is bad form, it is anti-social, it is a mug's game, so one doesn't

---

[1] Charles Bradlaugh (1833-91): free thinker and Republican politician. After being elected M.P. for Northampton in 1880, he refused to take the customary oath on his introduction to the Commons on the ground that he was a professed atheist.

do it. Oh yes, he has a code, and in many respects an uncommonly good one; the pessimists of last century were wrong when they told us we should lapse into mere barbarism.

And yet, were the optimists of last century right, when they told us that it would make no difference? Has it made no difference, this tacit, public abandonment of the creed by which our grandfathers lived? The legal restraints which once safeguarded faithfulness in marriage have all gone. Decency itself is little sought after; how a man likes to behave is his own affair, as long as he doesn't interfere with the convenience of other people. And honesty—we have not said good-bye to honesty, but how much harder a business it seems to be, nowadays, deciding what is honest and what isn't! Are we sure that we are not living on our moral capital, living by the unconscious memory of that creed which our grandfathers held, just as a man who is too old to have any present enjoyment in life lives by the memory of what he enjoyed in the past?

Let us pray God that the younger of us may live to see what the older of us have looked for in vain, these fifty years gone, a national return to God, that we may take up again the burden of belief. And meanwhile, what of ourselves, spoiled children of Providence, Catholics who are renewed day by day at the altar with the food of the strong, who learn—or should learn—from the contemplation of our blessed Lady's perpetual virginity the secret of the Church's perpetual youth? I never come to preach in the Midlands without a certain feeling of sadness—to think of the part which they played at the time of the Second Spring, a hundred years ago, when the Faith seemed to be coming back to England, by a kind of miracle overnight. Imagine what it must have been like to be a Catholic in Nottingham, in the year of the Great Exhibition. Pugin was thought to have said the last word about architecture, and here was this cathedral, Pugin's masterpiece, staring down at the astonished Protestant neighbours. The Fathers of Charity were already installed at Ratcliffe, the Trappists at Mount St Bernard, and over at Garendon Ambrose de Lisle Phillipps was plotting to bring the Passionists in too. In this part of the world, it must have felt as if the conversion of England were just round the corner. Other men have laboured—heavens, how they laboured!— and it is their labours you have inherited. Catholics of Nottingham, what a privilege is yours, and what a responsibility! If you take your faith lightly, who shall pardon it?

Don't let us make any mistake about it; we *are* in danger, we modern Catholics, of living on our capital. Everything is made so easy for us;

our non-Catholic neighbours are so friendly and so tolerant; so many
newspapers and books are produced for our special entertainment, so
many churches and schools compete for our patronage; everything is
laid on, isn't it? What remains, but to sit back and enjoy ourselves?
To be Sunday Catholics, to be passengers in the Barque of Peter? But
that is not the moral, for us, of the Festival of Britain. As Catholics,
no less than as English people, we are concerned to praise famous men
that went before us; and we shall do that best, not by accepting,
passively, the position they bequeathed to us, but by putting our
shoulders to the wheel as they did, leaving some mark of our own on
the page of history, to the glory of almighty God.

35

EARTHLY DWELLINGS[1]

*Once this earthly tent-dwelling of ours has come to an end, God, we are sure,
has a solid building waiting for us, a dwelling not made with hands, that will
last eternally in heaven.*—2 Corinthians 5. 1.

W E are celebrating the feast of our blessed Lady's Motherhood;
and our thoughts wander back to the home at Nazareth, and
what it must have been like to live next door to the Holy Family—
to have neighbours who never quarrelled, never stood on their rights,
never put on airs and thought themselves better than other people,
always minded their own business and never gossiped. How tanta-
lizingly little the Gospels tell us about it, when we all feel that it
would have done us a world of good if they had told us more! Because
we are told so little, I always like to fill out the story by trying to get
side-lights on it from the conversation of our blessed Lord himself. You
see, he was fully Man, and I suppose that the images which he used in
his preaching were, in some part, furnished by memories of the old
days in Galilee. That woman, for example, who had ten pieces of silver,

[1] This sermon was preached on 11 October 1951, at the reopening of the Church of
Our Lady of the Immaculate Conception, Birkenhead, at a Mass offered by the Right
Rev. John Murphy, Bishop of Shrewsbury, in the presence of the Most Rev. Joseph
Masterson, Archbishop of Birmingham. The old church, designed by Pugin, had been
destroyed, together with the schools and presbytery, by a land-mine on the night of 12
March 1941. The parish priest, the Very Rev. Canon John Joseph Tallon, and his domestic
staff were killed in the raid.

and lost one of them, lighting the lamp and sweeping the house and searching carefully till she found it, how naturally all that comes in! They tell us that Jewish women used to have ten silver coins sewed on to their head-dress, to represent the dowry they received when they married. And of course, if the woman in the parable lost even one of those, it would be something like the loss of a wedding-ring. I always wonder if that really did happen, one day, in the home at Nazareth; don't tell me that such a loss could never have befallen our Lady, when today's Gospel has just been telling us how she lost her Son. I wonder whether they all went down on their knees and hunted for it; don't tell me that our Lord couldn't have done that, when he was capable, somehow, of advancing in wisdom with the years. I like to think of our blessed Lady calling in the neighbours round about, and dispensing hospitality to them as best she could; it gives us one more word of hers to meditate over; "Rejoice with me," she says, "I have found that silver piece which I lost."

And I suppose we have a right to think of her as saying something of the kind this morning, this bright October morning when we celebrate the feast of her Motherhood by giving her a present from her children: by giving back to her, all fresh and in apple-pie order, the broken thing that once was hers. Ten years and more it has stood empty, this church that was so crowded with worshippers, has stood silent, this church that was so vocal with prayer. Ten years without the glimmer of a votive candle, or the sound of a Sanctus bell. Such a crown our Lady has, all over the world, of churches dedicated in her honour, ancient shrines like Einsiedeln and Czestochowa, pilgrimage centres like Lourdes and Fatima; and yet, when one jewel is missing from its setting, it catches the eye like a bombed site as you pass along the street; just this one stone was missing, and today we are giving it back to her. Surely we may be allowed to think of her, there in heaven, as calling her friends and neighbours together, just as she would have at Nazareth, and saying, "Rejoice with me, I have got back the church which I had lost". Perhaps she tells them—who knows?—that she always liked that place at Birkenhead; it was built for her by simple Christian folk, and simple Christian folk went there to worship. It was a family sort of place, where people knew one another and helped one another in their difficulties, and didn't forget to go in and say a prayer as they came back from work or from shopping. And somehow when the bomb fell that stilled all that busy exercise of supernatural activity, it was as if a light had gone out on Mersey-side. Rejoice with me, for today the lamp I missed there has been re-lit.

And for you, too, the clergy and the faithful of this parish, it is a day of rejoicing. You, too, have been hunting for coins, with our Lady to help you in the search. Your friends and your neighbours may well rejoice with you heartily on such an achievement as yours. There is, after all, no better way of convincing the world around us that to us religion is something real, than the pertinacity with which we go on building up and developing the external fabric of it in spite of every discouragement. So valiantly you had laboured; a parish that dated from the Crimean war, a church built in eighteen hundred and sixty-two, that stood fifty years before it was clear of debt and could be consecrated; then the great effort for the schools; and at last, just before the war came, Our Lady of the Immaculate Conception had the air of being something permanent in the life of Birkenhead; no more struggles now, you could sit back and rest on your laurels. And in a single night the church you had so loved and so laboured for crashed to the ground; worse than that, the parish priest to whose calls you responded so faithfully, who stood for so much in your history, was taken away from you, buried, like Eleazar Machabaeus, under his own triumph. Well, that was that; it was war-time, and after the war came all the difficulty about permits, all the difficulty about builders' prices— evidently there was nothing to be done just at present. Years hence, perhaps, the laborious task would have to be taken up anew. Were you content to argue like that? No, you set about rebuilding our Lady's church as calmly as if nothing had happened; setbacks like these were all in the day's work; if God had allowed your church to be destroyed, it was so that you could give proof of your faith by building it up again; if God had taken away your pastor, it was so that you might demonstrate your loyalty to his ideals, even when he was no longer at your side. "Master, we have toiled all the night and caught nothing, but at thy word I will let down the net"—so spoke the Prince of the Apostles, and in all her apostolic labours the Church has been faithful to the spirit of that resolution. She will convert a whole nation, and then, overnight, it will be overrun by heathen conquerors, or led away into schism, and she starts building up again, building up again as if nothing had happened. Of that inexhaustible patience you have given us an example, and we are grateful for it; such examples are needed in times like these.

We congratulate you upon having, once more, a parish church. Not that a church is necessary; our fathers worshipped God, acceptably enough, in byres and outhouses, and in our time, owing to the ravages of war, there are many congregations which have to be content with holding services in a parish hall, as you did till yesterday. Nevertheless, the parish church is something more than a convenient roof to keep the rain off our heads when we go to Mass; it is the expression, in architectural terms, of the parish at prayer. It sums up our history for us; we can look round us, and think of all the souls which have been nourished, generation after generation, at the same communion rails, all the stories of guilt which have been whispered and have died away at the same confessionals, all the new recruits in Christ's army who have been regenerated at the same font. We can remember, in Christ, our fellow worshippers who knelt here at our side, and are now separated from us in body, though still united to us with the same links of prayer. It is a kind of sacrament of the parish life; its fabric, so closely knitted together, reminds us of the unity which ought to exist among the Christian family. Are you one of the gossipers? Are you one of the quarrellers? Are you one of the mischief-makers? Then the very stones of this edifice cry out against you, and reproach you with their silent endurance. It is a second home, in which we meet as children of the same Father round a common table. All *that* the parish church is; and we, so wedded by nature to the things of sense, find comfort in its abiding witness to the life of the spirit.

But, when we have said all that, we have not learnt the whole lesson which is taught us by the rebuilt ruins of this, God's sanctuary. That is why I have ventured to take my text from a difficult passage in St Paul's writings, where he looks forward to his own death and speaks of it in terms of the builder's craft. St Paul himself was a builder; but he was a tentmaker, and he thinks of our life here under the image of something less enduring, less substantial, than a fabric of stone. "Once this earthly tent-dwelling of ours has come to an end, God, we are sure, has a solid building waiting for us, a dwelling not made with hands, that will last eternally in heaven." How enduring, how permanent it looked, this church of our Lady, on the twelfth day of March, 1941! "Strange", we reflected, as we looked at it, "that the work of man's own hands should outlast him! We shall pass, and generations of men will pass after us, and still these bricks and stones will be standing here, an enduring memorial of our brief sojourn on earth." And yet the truth was the opposite; only the springing of a trap, somewhere up in the sky, and the whole edifice came tumbling to the ground. All that was really enduring was—what? Three human souls, released in that hour from the body, but eternal, indestructible, the heirs of a dwelling-place in heaven. We had mistaken what was visible for what was solid.

And we are always doing that; sense and sight are so near to us, that we think they are the only things which matter; we wrap ourselves up in material comforts, material advantages, material hopes, as if they must needs be enduring—until some bomb falls to shake us out of our self-complacency. This temple was destroyed, and in ten years we, mortal men, going to work with hod and trowel, have raised it up. And shall we doubt that God has power to raise up the temple of a human body, to make an eternal habitation out of the tent-dwelling of yesterday? Let us thank God for his mercies, let us pray for the souls which were taken from us when this church fell; but let us remember, all the while, that this is but a parable of our human lot. All that is earthly in us must be taken to pieces and then refashioned, as this church was. God grant us all his abiding mercies in eternity.

36

THE TRANSLATION OF FR FABER[1]

May life spring from their bones, where they lie buried.—Ecclesiasticus 46. 14.

DEAR Fathers, dear brothers and sisters in Jesus Christ, we are met on a strange occasion. The bodies of Christian people, that were once the vehicle of the spirit's life, interpreted its thoughts and moods by speech, by gesture, by the play of lines on the face, must not be deposited in the grave without something of solemnity. Body and soul are natural partners, and one day, when this skein of material things is wound off, we shall be body and soul once more. Till then, the body must be laid to rest in its parent earth, the symbol and the earnest of that glorified life which is to be ours, ultimately, in heaven. We meet around the coffin, consecrate it with incense and holy water, the sighs and the tears of Mother Church; then we take our farewells, and leave the outward frame of man's fashioning in the hands of a merciful and loving Creator. There is no more to be said.

And yet, sometimes, the last word has not been said. There are souls so remarkable for the practice of heroic virtues, so distinguished by

---

[1] This sermon was preached at the London Oratory on 16 February 1952, on the occasion of the translation of the remains of Fr Frederick William Faber from Sydenham to St Wilfrid's Chapel. The absolutions were given after the sermon which followed the Mass, not over a catafalque but over the tomb.

THE TRANSLATION OF FR FABER

special proofs of God's favour, that they cannot be simply counted in with the rest; the Church, for all her great caution in such matters, is ready to pledge her word for it that they are saints, reigning here and now in heaven. And when that happens, their bones are left in peace no longer. The piety of the faithful—that same piety which, in the first age, sought protection in Peter's shadow or Paul's handkerchiefs—will have it that there is a virtue and an influence still left even in the mortal remains of such men and women as these. Their bodies must not be left to share the dank churchyard with the rest of us, they must be brought in procession to some crowded church, interred anew in some splendid shrine, so that we may all have the benefit of them. There must be a great High Mass of thanksgiving, and a flowery panegyric in which the virtues of the newly-canonized must be set forth. No longer is it an occasion for tears; we rejoice that one more soul has been added to heaven's citizens. No longer do we say farewell to the dead, and forget about them. The saint is to be a daily influence in our lives; as we kneel before the shrine that contains those precious relics, we shall be mindful of him, we shall be in touch with him, always.

The ceremony at which we are assisting this morning is neither the funeral of a friend, nor the translation of a saint. Or perhaps I ought not to say that; Father Faber's memory *is* the memory of a friend, after all these years—so strong in his legend, so firmly is the life of the Oratory linked with its past. I myself was privileged, more than thirty years back, with the friendship of Father Sebastian Bowden, who talked of old times at the Oratory as if they were a thing of yesterday;[1] it was a legend of the place that if you looked about you carefully in unfrequented passages, you could still find notices on the wall that bore Father Faber's signature. No, it is a friend we have buried here, as it was a friend they buried at Sydenham. Only we are not mourners; mourning is for the memories that are recent. God in his great mercy has set a statute of limitations to our grief; the wound heals, the ache of parting is relieved, and they are replaced by a tender sense of lost companionship. We must not weep, today, over Father Faber's coffin; he himself would tell us, with a touch of acerbity, that we would do better to weep for our sins.

And, on the other side, the remains we have brought here are not the remains of a canonized saint. We may have learned to admire Father Faber's high courage, his unremitting labours, his love for our blessed Lady, his zeal for souls. We may have found in his writings, perhaps, an inspiration hardly less powerful than that which came from

[1] Father Sebastian Bowden, Cong. Orat., died on 26 September 1920.

the writings of the greatest spiritual masters. But still we have no right to use the word "saint" in speaking of one upon whom no solemn judgment has been passed by the Church; there must be no open invocation of him; no honour must be done to his mortal remains beyond that which can be claimed for any faithful Christian. For him, as for any other faithful Christian, we must implore the divine mercy, asking that the stains which his soul has contracted in the course of its earthly passage may be washed away. That is the Church's law, and, were he in heaven thrice over, it is quite certain Father Faber would want us to abide by it.

But, in that case, why are we having a service about it at all? To be sure, there is a kind of poetical thrill to be got out of it, by poetically minded people. There is nothing very poetical about Sydenham, as it is nowadays, and it is somehow more appropriate to think of Father Faber lying here, in the place he loved so, made so lovable, than to connect his memory with some desirable property in the wilderness of South London. Yes, in a way it is a kind of home-coming. But, in hard fact, how are we better off for having the bones of Father Faber here, in the church, since we are not allowed to treat them with any special reverence or to expect any miracle as the result of their presence? His soul is no nearer to us now than it ever was; we cannot pray for it now more effectually than we ever did. Since we cannot say, with confidence, that Father Faber is in heaven, would it not have been best to move his body without any fuss or circumstance, like the body of any other Christian whose soul is in purgatory?

I know. But I wonder whether we don't make the mistake of mapping out the unseen world too confidently, dividing it up too much into water-tight compartments, when you consider how little theology has to tell us about it? I mean, when one of our friends dies, we think of him or her in purgatory; for how long? Well, we go on praying for that soul for the rest of our lives, with a vague idea that our lives will be as long as its purgatory. But if I suggested to you that we should all kneel down and say a *Hail Mary* for the soul of William the Conqueror, your reaction would be: "William the Conqueror? I should think if he ever got to purgatory, he's out by now." Yes, but what do we know about it? And again, we think of purgatory and heaven as two water-tight compartments; you go on in purgatory, a scene of complete darkness and desolation, for months after months, years after years, until at last the decisive *Hail Mary* is said, and all at once, all in a moment, as if a trapdoor had been suddenly released, that soul is in heaven, enjoying the vision of God. Because we don't know that a particular soul is in heaven yet, we behave as if it wasn't; and if we think of heaven we think of it as peopled only by the canonized saints —is purgatory really such a long business? Oughtn't we to think of heaven as peopled already by millions and millions of redeemed souls, uncanonized and unheard of, Tom, Dick and Harry, ransomed by the blood of Jesus Christ?

And if that is so, oughtn't we to think of our Christian dead as a great multitude surrounding us, like the lights of a city when you look across the valley at evening; some brighter, some paler, some nearer, some more distant, but all reflecting, each in its degree, the beauty and the majesty of God? Some will need our prayers more than others; some, more than others, will be able to bestow a blessing on us in return. The canonized saints—yes, by all means let us keep them in a separate category; we know what their state is, there is no guess-work about that. But for those others, cannot we be content to know that they are in God's hands, without being over-curious, whether they belong to the expectant, or to the triumphant Church? Is not heaven, perhaps, purgatory bursting into flower?

Is this unorthodox theology? Lest it should be thought so, let me shelter myself behind an unquestionably orthodox theologian— Father Faber. Many of you have sung, during November devotions at the Oratory, that daring but moving hymn he wrote, which begins: "Oh, it is sweet to think of those that are departed". Now, nobody is going to accuse Father Faber of minimizing the doctrine of purgatory; "In pains beyond all earthly pains, Favourites of Jesus, there they lie" —he is not going to make it comfortable for us. But at the same time, he sees the holy souls as nearer to God than we are, and progressively nearer as the cleansing discipline of purgatory takes its effect. "Yet not as in the days of earthly ties we love them; for they are touched with rays of light that is above them"—the image in his mind is that of snow-clad hills, first one, then another catching the rays of dawn. That, at least, is how I interpret him; he does not, of course, mean to dogmatize about things which have not been revealed to us, but from our point of view it is best, perhaps, to think of our dead as moving all the time closer, closer to God, as they move further and further away from us, from human remembrance.

May we not think, then, of Father Faber himself in those terms? Whether he has already achieved the blessedness of heaven, we cannot be certain; it is God's secret. But we know that his continued existence beyond the grave is a fact, as certain as your existence or mine; we have no reason to think that he has forgotten us, and if he remembers, we may be very sure that he cares, and that he will do his best for us. That we should forget him was never likely; but it will help to present his image to our minds if we reflect that the tortured body which was the partner of that fervent soul rests, now, under the church of the Oratory. This is not, indeed, the church he knew; but it is so much impregnated with his spirit that he might well make the claim made for Christopher Wren in St Paul's, *Si monumentum requiris, circumspice*. He can rest here without disquiet, with the confidence that all around him is as he would have had it, all that is done here is done as he would have done it. Here let him dwell, as a son of St Philip should, among his brethren; and when at last soul and body are reunited, and the reckoning is made, let it be his to boast, with the prophet, "Here stand I, and these children the Lord has given me, a warning from the Lord of hosts to the sons of Israel, a beacon-light in Sion".

37

THE BRIDE OF CHRIST[1]

Hold me close to thy heart, close as locket or bracelet clings; not death itself is so strong as love, not the grave itself cruel as love unrequited; the torch that lights it is a blaze of fire.—Canticles 8. 6.

Vows—what a significant part they have played, what a tragic part, often, they have played in human history! Rash vows, broken vows, vows directed to an evil end and so made dishonourable in the keeping—how much safer, in some ways, the world would be without them! Yet man claims obstinately the right to engage himself, the liberty of signing away his own liberty. For this reason: that the mood of the moment, the mood in which he is carried away out of himself, is sometimes, he feels, the mood in which he is most truly himself, and he does not trust it to last. The mother, kneeling by the bed of her sick child, promises that she will make a pilgrimage to Lourdes if the child recovers; that promise she solemnly registers, puts it in writing, makes it in the presence of witnesses, for fear that later on, when the sense of urgency has evaporated, she might forget what she feels now, thrown

---

[1] This sermon was preached on 5 June 1952, at the Convent of the Visitation, then at Castle Cary, Somerset, at the Final Profession of one of the Community.

back on the mercies of heaven. She may be tempted to change her mind, and she resolves that nothing shall ever make her change her mind; she will see to it, as well as poor human creatures can, that the mood she now experiences shall be eternal.

It is certain that almighty God approves, when there is due occasion for it, this human instinct of binding ourselves. Vows uttered by human lips are the matter of a great sacrament, the sacrament of Holy Matrimony. By a curious paradox, the lover who feels certain that the passion which burns in him is immortal, longs for every opportunity to put that passion on record; as if he feared (alas, too often with good reason) that he might need, one day, the reminder. He will carve a pattern of laced hearts on the trunk of some old tree, destined to outlive him, destined, likely enough, to outlive his love. Holy Church, in the sacrament of Matrimony, overhears those passionate vows of his, and takes him at his word. Man and woman plight themselves to one another, and in doing so, plight themselves to God; the words shyly whispered on earth are graven, irrevocably, on the walls of heaven. For better, for worse, for richer, for poorer, in sickness or in health— no alteration of circumstances can undo the bond.

When we meet to wish man or woman Godspeed as they betake themselves to the life of the cloister, we are not content with a kind of funeral service, we indulge in a sort of holy parody of the wedding service as well. The similarity of the two situations is obvious. In either case, there is a romance; in either case, there is the longing for union; in either case, there is a certain misgiving of the human creature about its own moods, about its own tenacity of purpose. "I feel like this now", bride or nun says to herself; "but what guarantee have I that I shall feel the same in ten, twenty, thirty years' time? I am so changeable; a hundred experiences have warned me to distrust my own sudden enthusiasms. How can I meet him whom I love, look him in the eyes and tell him that I will be true to him always? There is only one thing to be done; I must make the step irrevocable, I must burn my boats. Let me take a vow that I will be true to him, and what is now the bent of my wayward emotions will become, please God, an unalterable determination of the will. Holy Church, administer to me a solemn formula of undertaking, fix my mood for me, and make it eternal."

There are similarities between the two situations; there are also differences. For one thing, Holy Church has a mother's wisdom, and does not allow her children to commit themselves irrevocably until they have tested their dispositions by a long engagement. Far more importantly, the nun does not, like the bride, entrust her happiness into

M

the keeping of a fellow mortal, who may, on his side, prove unworthy of the trust. She knows that, whatever happens, the heavenly Bridegroom will be true to *his* undertaking, there will be no drawing back, no want of considerateness in him. With him there is no change, no swerving from his course; he knows whereof we are made, remembers that we are but dust. You at least, dear Sister, have not made the wrong choice. Yours is a Bridegroom whose beauty can never stale for you, whose nearer familiarity can bring nothing but a fresh revelation of tenderness. There is no half-heartedness, no insincerity about the congratulation with which we call you a happy woman today.

Yes, but the life of a religious, even of an enclosed religious, is not wholly bounded by the spiritual activities proper to her state. She is to live in community, subject to all the petty irritations which are imposed on us when we spend our lives at very close quarters with our fellow creatures. She is to live under obedience, committed to the carrying out of orders which will sometimes seem exacting or unreasonable. In so far as your peace of mind is dependent on the fellow mortals with whom you are in daily contact, there is danger that time and disappointment will rub the bloom off your romance.

We would not trust you, then, over the solemn promise by which you are now engaging yourself, if you had not some talisman to protect you as you set your feet on the road where so many have stumbled. You have such a talisman, and its name is love. "Love", says the *Imitation of Christ*, "makes light all burdens, and bears equably all that is unequal; it is not weighed down by the weight it carries, but makes all that is bitter sweet and dainty to the taste. The lover flies, and runs, and exults; is free, and knows no chain; gives all for all, and has all in all, looking not at the gift given, but above all good at the hand that gives it." We recognize that easily enough as a description of the natural human love that has its seat in the emotions. What we have to remember, often with difficulty, often in times of discouragement and of desolation, is that it is equally true of that supernatural love which has its seat in the will. For a continual strengthening of that supernatural love in your heart we, your well-wishers, invoke the prayers of our Lady and St Jane Frances[1] and your heavenly patrons today.

"All thing shall be well," says Dame Julian of Norwich,[2] "and all manner of thing shall be well." Sometimes, when we make an important decision, we are alarmed by the prospect of unforeseen complications which might occur to make us regret it. That it was the right decision

[1] St Jane Frances de Chantal, foundress of the Order of the Visitation.
[2] Dame Julian of Norwich, *Revelations of Divine Love*.

in general, we are clear; but what if this or that trifling circumstance should arise to endanger our peace of mind? So many vocations are wrecked by little faults of temper, of docility, of humility; are we proof against such dangers? Do not hesitate; all thing shall be well, and all manner of thing shall be well; the details of your life will fit in, if the will is there. God bless you, Sister, and take our prayers with you into his nearer presence; may every year you spend in holy religion be the deepening, and the widening, and the unravelling of a lifelong romance.

38

ST ETHELDREDA'S RESTORED[1]

See where he comes, how he speeds over the mountains, how he spurns the hills!—Canticles 2. 8.

THOSE words are read at the opening of today's epistle. If you refer to their original setting, what picture rises to the mind? A young village girl, carried off from her native home as a recruit for the harem of king Solomon, falls asleep, so it would seem, in the middle of a banquet, with the king himself at her side. And she dreams that her own village lover comes to her, leaping from tussock to tussock on the hill-slopes, to call her back to the scenes she knows. "Winter is over now," he says, "the rain has passed by. At home, the flowers have begun to blossom, pruning-time has come; we can hear the turtle-dove cooing already, there at home. There is green fruit on the fig-trees, the vines in flower are all fragrance; rouse thee, and come." We read only the other day, in the Divine Office, what the pious audacity of St Gregory makes of that picture. The lithe, bronzed figure leaping across the hillside reminds him, you will hardly believe it, of the Incarnation. "When our Lord came to redeem us," he says, "he came, if I may put it in that way, in so many leaps. He leapt from heaven into the womb, from the womb into the manger, from the manger to the cross, from the cross to the tomb, from the tomb back again to heaven." Oh, it is crude, it is *naif*;

---

[1] This sermon was preached at St Etheldreda's, Ely Place, London, on 3 July 1952, when the church, having been fully restored after the bomb damage suffered during the war, was reopened at a solemn High Mass at which Cardinal Griffin, Archbishop of Westminster, presided, and a distinguished company of bishops, clergy, and laymen were present. The Mass was sung by the Right Rev. Thomas Leo Parker, Bishop of Northampton, the successor of the Bishops of Ely to whose London palace this church was once attached.

the taste of the sixth century is not ours. But there is a sense of movement about it which makes all our theologies dull reading by comparison. When our Lord came to redeem us, he did not hesitate and fumble,
as we do, over all the accidents of mortality. He took them in his stride.

And I think that passage in St Gregory's writings is, partly at least,
what the Church has in mind when she tells us to turn up these burning
verses of the Canticles, in honour of our blessed Lady's Visitation. It's
true that there is something in St Luke's narrative which recalls to us
the same sense of brisk motion; "She rose up and went with all haste to
a town of Juda, in the hill country"—just a couple of words in the Greek
to paint in for us the girlish eagerness which makes light of obstacles,
not ashamed to burst in with the breathless announcement, "I've come
to see you". But I think the Church really regards the whole incident
as an incident in the life of our blessed Lord. Our Lord, says St Gregory,
quoting a well-known verse of the Psalms, exults like some great runner
who sees the track before him; the haste is his; even in the womb he
cries out, "There is a baptism I must needs be baptized with, and how
impatient am I for its accomplishment". It is part of the rhythm of the
Incarnation, that prophecy yet unborn should greet its yet unborn
Fulfilment; the great Lover of mankind peers in, like the bridegroom
in the Canticles, through the windows of our prison-house, and bids
us come out to meet the spring.

He does it, says St Gregory, so that we in our turn may be in a hurry;
we are to say to him, once more in the language of the Canticles,
"Draw me after thee where thou wilt; see, we hasten after thee". The
Church, in all ages, has responded to that breathless whisper of his,
imitated the irrepressible bouyancy of his onward march. This is an
extraordinary thing—one of the first impressions you form on becoming a Catholic is that your perspective has lengthened; the events of the
moment have less power to agitate you, because you think, now, not in
terms of the next fifty years, but in terms of the next thousand years.
And yet, all around you, there is a sense of urgency; people, and the
most impressive people, are wanting to get things done at once. It's
always the same, from St Paul trying to see if he can't fit in a visit to
Rome on his way to Spain, to Father Peyton with his Family Rosary
crusade; always same sense of untiring endeavour, the breath of the
mountains and of the spring.

This irrepressible energy which is native to the Church, where will
you find it better illustrated than in the history of a hundred years ago; the
days of Father Dominic, and Father Gentili, and the Oxford converts?
The Second Spring, Newman called it, and it was an apt comparison;

as the buds burst in spite of the cold that still threatens them, in spite of the sheaths that imprison them, so the revival of the faith broke upon England, in spite of influences from the outside that laboured to check it, from inside that thought to discourage it. Men like George Spencer, and Faber, and Pugin, how vast are the ambitions they set before themselves, how they leap over every obstacle in the attainment of them! Among those memorable names there is one which is less remembered than it should be, but must not be forgotten today; the name of Father Lockhart.[1] Of all the Oxford converts, he was the first; and if he is remembered for nothing else, he should be remembered for having provoked one of the greatest passages in English literature. It was of him Newman was speaking when he preached his sermon on the Parting of Friends. It was Father Gentili who received him, and before he had been a Catholic a month, he joined the Fathers of Charity. It would be beyond the needs of the present occasion, to speak of what he did for the Church, or for his Institute. For the present occasion, it is enough to remind ourselves that, but for Father Lockhart, you and I would not be here.

It was only an idea of his, call it a fad of his if you will, that it would impress the public mind with a sense of our continuity, if Catholics could be seen worshipping in a place where Catholics had worshipped before the Reformation. But how right he was! The English mind is the slave of the *fait accompli*; nothing has contributed more successfully to the vogue of Anglicanism than its architectural connection with the past. And here was a pre-Reformation chapel, in the very heart of London, which had escaped the Great Fire and stood there, a graceful relic of the Middle Ages, when all the neighbouring parish churches had been humanized, and somewhat dehumanized by Wren. Father Lockhart, like the giants of his day, took it in his stride; he bought St Etheldreda's. And ever since the 'seventies Catholic Londoners have been able to hear Mass in the chapel where the bishops of Ely said Mass, from the thirteenth century till the Reformation.

We stand on historic ground. The old diocese of Ely was very small; its bishops, as often as not, were men who held important offices in the State. In the house to which this chapel belonged, beyond doubt much of English history has been transacted. It was here, for example, that a royal duke died who perhaps had more to say to our destinies than most of the monarchs who reigned in his period—John of Gaunt. As it

[1] Father William Lockhart (1820-92): follower of J. H. Newman at Oxford; received into the Church, 1843; entered the Rosminian Order, Rome, 1845. His reception into the Church was the immediate cause of Newman resigning from St Mary's.

has been the fate of Father Lockhart to be remembered chiefly by one sermon of Newman's, so it has been the fate of John of Gaunt to be remembered by one speech in Shakespeare.

> This royal throne of kings, this sceptred isle,
> This earth of majesty, this seat of Mars,
> This other Eden, demi-Paradise,
> This fortress, built by nature for herself
> Against infection and the hand of war—[1]

we still quote it; and England remains a sceptred isle, when so many thrones have crumbled. But England is no longer a fortress; the hand of modern war does not grant her immunity. Ten years ago, when London reeled under the German bombardment, Ely Place, that had survived the Great Fire, withstood, but could not escape, the shock.

Let us accept it, then, as a happy omen, expressive of that resilience, that resurgence, which has marked the Catholic Church in all ages, that St Etheldreda's should be re-opened today, on its seven hundredth birthday, for public worship. So little are we, so much at the mercy of our human feelings, that we grieve as at the loss of a friend when something of brick and mortar perishes, because it served to link us with the past. In a world, in a London, where so much is changing, we can rejoice to find the dream of Father Lockhart still true, John of Gaunt's prophecy still justified after a fashion. Here in the heart of the City we shall be able to find our way to yet another of those little London churches which are so full of atmosphere and of intimacy; Moorfields and Maiden Lane and Warwick Street and—Ely Place. It shall be at once a link with the past and a proof of the Church's un- failing energies; here young minds, full of our modern ardours of inquiry, shall graft their new initiatives on the stock of unalterable truth.

And for ourselves—let us take one glance at ourselves; even on such a happy occasion as this, we must not expect to go away from church without a scolding. Don't let us be content to sit open-mouthed in wonder at those giants of yesterday, Father Lockhart and the rest, asking how it was they managed to speed over the mountains, to spurn the hills, in their impetuous apostolate. They were not men of different mould from ourselves; the message they carried with them was the same as ours. The wonder is rather that we, with such examples before us, are content to pick our way gingerly among the cart-tracks, apprehensive of the least stumble. Do let us ask our blessed Lady and

[1] *King Richard II*, Act II, Scene 1.

St John the Baptist to get us back into the atmosphere of the Visitation, its breathless rhythm of movement; to make us expect great things of God, and play our part as if we were certain that God is doing great things for us, instead of always hanging about, whistling for a wind. "This land of such dear souls, this dear, dear land, Dear for her reputation through the world"[1]—if only this reopening of Ely Place might be the omen that she is coming back to her origins, coming back to the faith of Christ!

39

CHRISTIAN CHARITY[2]

There was one heart and soul in all the company of believers.—Acts 4. 32.

WHEN we Christian people get into an argument with Communists, they have one line of attack against us which is not really very difficult to dispose of, but leaves, somehow, a nasty taste in the mouth—it sticks in your mind, as a burr sticks to your coat, when you think you have got rid of it. If there were a Communist here this morning who knew his Bible—fortunately most of them don't—he would point out that when I gave out my text just now I stopped short at a semi-colon. "There was one heart and soul in all the company of believers; none of them called any of his possessions his own, everything was shared in common." There you are, you see (our progressive friend tells us), your Church when it started, when it really remained true to its principles, was a Communist Church; today, its primitive doctrines are taught in Canterbury Cathedral, and nowhere else.[3] As I say, it is not really a difficult argument to dispose of. Plainly it is one thing to join a voluntary society which makes a rule of poverty among its members—what else do you do when you join a religious order?— it is quite another thing to deny, as a philosophical principle, that any private person has any intrinsic right to own productive property. And if you know your Bible you can go further and explain that the Communist experiment was only tried at Jerusalem, and that in

---

[1] *King Richard II*, Act II, Scene 1.
[2] This sermon was preached at the Pro-Cathedral, Clifton, on 3 August 1952, and addressed to the Society of St Vincent de Paul.
[3] A reference to the Communistic teaching of the Very Rev. Hewlett Johnson, Dean of Canterbury since 1931.

Jerusalem it was not altogether a success. Ananias and Sapphira pretending that they had handed over to the apostles more than they really had; the Greek-speaking Christians complaining that the Hebrew-speaking Christians got preferential treatment in the share-out; and finally St Paul sending round the collection plate all over the heathen world, to save the Church at Jerusalem from bankruptcy—nobody can say, human nature being what it is, that the primitive Church was a good advertisement for Communism.

And yet, as I say, when we have scored our point in the debate, we don't feel quite easy about it afterwards. Whether the experiment failed or succeeded, we can't forget that it was, after all, an essentially Christian experiment. And although the churches which sprang up elsewhere did not imitate the mother church of Jerusalem, it is quite plain that the collection for the saints, the relieving of want and distress among Christian neighbours, was a major preoccupation with St Paul; you don't need any very close study of his epistles to tell you that. Whatever be the truth about other Christian institutions, there is one which is quite certainly primitive—the second collection. Indeed, I think that to the outside observer the infant Church must have looked like a carefully run benefit society; see how St Paul lays down, in writing to the Thessalonians, that the man who refuses to work must be left to starve[1]—already we were becoming a magnet for the unemployable. And the Church, in all ages, has continued to hanker after her origins; wherever men and women have founded religious orders, they have gone back to the principle of the common purse, gone back to those first struggles when the Christian community was a tiny sect, that grew up around the apostles, and "Mary and the other women".

Giving alms to the poor had always been an honourable duty among pious Jews; it is so still. But I don't think Christian almsgiving derived its impetus, or at least its whole impetus, from the Jewish tradition; a simpler calculation lay behind it. It dated from those first days, when our Lord still walked on earth, and the apostolic company had a common purpose, with Judas Iscariot for its treasurer; when the would-be convert might be told to go and sell all that he had; when it was possible for a Christian to say without exaggeration, Lord, we have forsaken all things, and followed thee. How much easier it is to realize the sense of mutual obligation in a society while it remains small! The needs of suffering humanity were present to the minds of the first Christians, but there was something else. "Let us practise generosity to all", St Paul writes to the Galatians; "and above all, to those who are

[1] 2 Thess. 3. 10 (Knox translation).

of one family with us in the faith." Of one family with us, that was the point. One family, with a common family budget; how often in the New Testament we hear about the widows, who were a continual charge on the finances of the community! Of course they looked after the widows, just as any family would look after a widowed mother—as they themselves, perhaps, were looking after the widowed Mother of Jesus Christ. So few of them, only just a handful of them, even when the Gospel had begun to spread among the heathen; "the brotherhood you belong to, all over the world",[1] so, in a gracious phrase, St Peter calls it, and love of the brotherhood was a special quality he enjoined on the faithful, over and above the love of mankind. Charity, in those days, didn't mean pulling a long face and getting out your cheque-book and giving some money away. It meant giving practical, concrete expression to the love you felt for a brother of yours; he was hard up, just as you might be hard up some day—of course you shared out with him, what could be more natural? You know, when St Paul uses the word "communion" or "communicate" in his epistles, it has nothing whatever to do with the Blessed Sacrament of the altar. To communicate is to share out your goods with your fellow Christians, and "communion" is this bond of practical fellowship, this blossoming of love between brother and brother.

Well, it didn't last; good things don't last. Christianity conquered the world; and unfortunately that meant that in a sense the world conquered Christianity. We were no longer a set of persecuted fugitives, tied together by our fellowship in a common cause; we were just Tom, Dick and Harry, dragged off to the font in infancy and growing up as Christians of a sort, but not particularly good Christians. The old human instinct of acquisitiveness, of getting on in the world and letting the devil take the hindmost, still asserted itself; we forgot that we were brothers, and charity came to mean something rather different. There were two different brands of people, the rich and the poor; and if you belonged to the rich, it made you feel uncomfortable having so much money—it wouldn't do you any good, you felt, in purgatory. So you gave some of it away, and giving it away was called charity. That's the difference between St Paul and St Vincent de Paul. When St Paul recommended charity to the Christians of his day, he was urging them to give practical demonstration of the love they felt for one another. When St Vincent did the same thing, he was understood to be suggesting that certain rich ladies and gentlemen should begin throwing their money about, for the good of their souls.

[1] I Peter 5. 9 (Knox translation).

The warmth had gone out of charity; and because the warmth had gone out of it, charity itself got a bad name. To live by charity was thought to be a disgrace—what would St Paul have said if you had suggested to him that it was a disgrace to live by charity? We were at cross purposes; we still used the same language, but the whole atmosphere of first-century Christendom was forgotten.

It was the achievement of Frédéric Ozanam that he recalled the atmosphere of first-century Christendom to memory. He lived in those bad years which followed the French Revolution, when it seemed as though religion in France had received its death-blow. And he saw that the Church had allowed the revolutionaries to steal her thunder, when they offered to mankind the blessings of fraternity. Fraternity—was that word to be used as a reproach to Christendom, a word that echoed down the centuries from the lips of St Peter himself? But there was truth in the reproach; Christians had not forgotten the poor, but they had forgotten that the poor were their brothers. And Frédéric Ozanam, in his own words, "went to the poor"; went to them, not as a fine gentleman in a carriage scattering largesse, not as a salaried inspector doling out soup-tickets, but as a friend who wanted to know them better, who would use better knowledge as an excuse for charity, and charity as an excuse for better knowledge. That is the secret he has handed on to later generations of Catholics; to our own generation of Catholics, which finds itself taunted once again, by enemies not less determined than his, with the accusation that religion is a class affair, and has lost its old inspiration of brotherhood. Whatever other weapons the Church may dispense with, as she rearms herself for a new phase of the secular conflict, she cannot do without the Society of St Vincent de Paul. It is our best proof that the Church is unageing.

God bless you, brothers; the secret you have inherited is a simple one. You are to aim at your own personal sanctification; one indispensable means to that end is zeal for the salvation of souls; and one indispensable means to that end is a loving approach to the poorer members of Christ's flock. I think, if you had asked St Paul for his definition of an ordinary Christian, he would have given you no other. Ordinary Christians—that is what you are trying to be; there should be no great temptation to your humility, when you set before yourselves so modest an ambition. And yet, is it a modest ambition? You would hardly think so, when so many Christians, with your example before them, are content to do less for Christ. How far that little candle sheds his beams! Courage, brothers; in a world so dark as this, your light shall shine before men, though it be but a rush-light of charity; and they will see your good works, and glorify your Father who is in heaven.

40

ON DIVINE PROVIDENCE[1]

All things thou lovest, nor holdest any of thy creatures in abhorrence; hate and create thou couldst not, nor does ought abide save at thy will, whose summoning word holds them all in being.—Wisdom 11. 25.

IN earlier times, the providential ordering of creation was regarded, not as a thing which you had to prove, but as itself one of the proofs by which the existence of God could most easily be recognized. If you look, for instance, at Fénelon's splendidly baroque treatise on God and his Attributes, you will find that he argues not (like St Thomas) from the fact of order in creation, but from the evidence it gives of a beneficent purpose. Everything exists, in this created universe, for the sake of man, and how admirably everything has been laid on for his benefit! See how lions and tigers, which might be dangerous to him, breed slowly; how rabbits, which he can eat for supper, breed like rabbits— and so on. Fénelon is not much concerned about the feelings of the rabbits, because he tends to take Descartes' view that animals have no feelings; they are only automata with reflex actions. And on those principles he makes a good case for himself; if the air were a thinner substance, the birds wouldn't be able to fly in it; if it were a thicker substance, the birds wouldn't be able to come down, and so on. It is all quite convincing, and beautifully period.

Why is it so period? What was wrong with the *Grand Siècle*, or what is wrong with our own times, that there should be such a gulf between us? All sorts of influences have gone to modify our point of view. At one end of the scale, we are so impressed nowadays, not to say depressed, by the size of the universe, and by the long perspective of history, that we no longer find it natural to talk as if everything existed

[1] This sermon was preached at St Etheldreda's, Ely Place, London, on 16 November 1952, at the University High Mass.

for the sake of man, in the cheerful fashion of St Ignatius; it feels vaguely snobbish. Not that we find it possible to imagine any other sake for which anything could exist, but there it is. And again the profusion, the multitudinosity of creation no longer affects us as it used to; it all seemed rather splendid, in days when people went about flinging purses of gold to their lackeys; it gives us a slight sense of *malaise* in times when we are chiefly interested in concealing our assets from the Inland Revenue. And at the other end of the scale, we can't help sympathizing with the rabbit, with the individual rabbit; after all, we have spent the most formative years of our life in reading picture books about animals dressed up in trousers. But perhaps what has affected us more than anything else is the whole Darwin business. You can find a very clear parable of that in the story—I must have told it in print before now—of the seminary professor who called attention to the fact that all the trees in the grounds had their leaves growing so high up that the cows just couldn't reach them; which proved, he said, that cows were meant to eat grass, not leaves. But of course all the students knew that the trees had got like that simply because the cows had already eaten all the leaves they *could* reach. Where Fénelon saw the manifest hand of Providence, we see the result of natural selection, or at most of adaptation. To him, it seemed impossible that the fecundity of rabbits was due to blind chance. We simply shrug our shoulders, and conjecture that there must have been hundreds of animals much more palatable than rabbits, which have disappeared in the course of millions of years because they didn't breed fast enough. I don't mean that these considerations upset the scholastic argument from the existence of *order* in nature; they don't. But they do take the sting out of that argument from *design* which suggested that only a loving Father could have produced a universe in which everything was so manifestly laid on for the likes of you and me.

Nowadays, the boot is on the other leg; divine Providence, instead of being an asset to Christian apologetics, is a heavy liability. We've got to believe in it, if we are going to make any sense of our religion at all; neither tradition nor Scripture nor common sense will allow us to doubt it. But the facts, if anything, seem to be against us. However many blessings we have to be thankful for, there is a great deal of evil all around us, physical and moral evil, and we are inclined to wonder why God, being infinitely powerful, infinitely wise, and infinitely good, should have included so much evil in the scheme of things— or, for that matter, any evil at all.

Well, as far as moral evil is concerned, we can just see a glimmer of

light and no more; we could hardly expect to see more. Moral goodness as we know it can only exist under conditions of struggle, and
against a background of evil. We are so shut in with the world of our
own experience, that any other kind of moral goodness is inaccessible
to our imaginations; the goodness of God himself is a thing we have
to receive on faith. Very well, then—if God, in his great wisdom, was
minded to create a universe in which our kind of moral goodness
could operate, it must contain the possibility of evil. Not necessarily the
actuality of evil; in theory, God might have been worshipped to all
eternity by a world of angels and men that was capable of sinning, yet
sinless. What happened—of course, I am talking in very crude terms
and cutting all the corners—was that God created the possibility of
evil and we actualized it.

Once grant that; once grant the intrusion of actual wickedness into
a world which hitherto had known no more than the possibility of
wickedness, and you have to see the whole problem in a new setting.
Man, by sinning, has declared war upon his environment, and in
return it has declared war on him. Can we say that it has declared war
simultaneously on all living creatures—the satellites, as it were, who
take their orders from him? And that that explains why the animals,
too, must suffer? Mr Lewis adopts this view in his book, *The Problem of
Pain*; he got it from Milton, but where Milton got it from is not so
clear. There is no trace of it in the schoolmen; they are content to
avert their eyes from the sufferings of the rabbit and dwell on the
satisfaction afforded to the weasel. Are we to make no comment at all
on *animal* suffering; on a world-order which involves so much pain
and fear in so many guiltless and defenceless lives? Of course, we must
not let sentiment run away with us. No need to go the whole way with
Descartes; but we cannot tell whether the animals feel pain to the same
degree or after the same manner as we do—a man under an anaesthetic
will give heart-rending groans, when he feels nothing. We cannot tell
how much the experience of pain clouds a life which has so little in it
of memory or of anticipation. On balance, for all we know, every
creature would sooner have been born than not. But there is a margin
of mystery for all that. Perhaps there is something in Milton's guess;
perhaps, born into a world that was overshadowed, at its very creation,
by the foreseen event of human guilt, the dumb creatures share with
us, by a strange kind of solidarity, in the expiation we owe. St Paul
seems to hint at something of the kind in the eighth chapter of Romans;
the whole of nature, he says, has been condemned to frustration, groans
in travail all the while, *for the sake of him who so condemned it*; and that,

as St Chrysostom saw, means Adam. But such guesses soon take us out of our depth.

When we speak of *human* suffering, we are on surer ground. The unanimous testimony of the saints and the mystics, from St Paul onwards, makes it clear that at the highest level of spirituality suffering becomes something desirable, if only as making a contribution to that sum of expiation which the human race as a body owes for its size. That contribution, when made in union with the merits of Christ's Passion, is certainly acceptable to God. And may we not guess that there is much suffering in the world besides, endured by those who make no claim to sanctity or even to Christianity, which has something of this same redemptive value? Suffering, I mean, that is inspired by noble motives, suffering that is bravely borne, suffering that is—and how often suffering is!—unselfish. Only in the last resort may we say, of some quite unreclaimable character in difficulties, "Serve him right!"

Some such glimpses we can catch of the pattern which lies behind all our patchwork experience. But these guesses we make are not our reason for believing in divine Providence; it is the other way round—we fall to guessing, because we *know* that there *must* be providence in creation; we do not see that there is. How do we know that there must be? Because God must act like himself, and we know that God is good. How do we know that God is good? Why shouldn't it be the other way round; why shouldn't all the evil in the world be the clue to the problem of existence? There *were* heretics, both in the first centuries and in the Middle Ages, who taught that the world was not created by God, but by some malicious subordinate of his who had got out of control. Long ago, in a book which nobody reads now, I did write an essay in the character of a Modernist clergyman, which was called "Canon Dives' explanation of the existence of Good". And he explained, of course, that without the existence of good there would be no possibility of evil. It worked out right on paper; why is it nonsense? Because whatever else we are uncertain about, we are certain that good is the positive thing, and evil the negative thing, just as light is the positive thing and darkness is the negative thing; evil does not exist in its own right, but only as the privation of good. And because God *is*, God is good and not evil. Somehow, his own character must be reflected, both in his creation of the world and his ordering of it.

His ordering of it—English people, if you talk to them about Providence, don't connect it with creation at all. They mean God arranging history as they would have arranged it themselves. I suppose this habit of mind dates from the Armada; and it outlives, in many of

our fellow countrymen, the rest of their Christian beliefs. When the
R.101, a British airship of the old-fashioned kind, crashed on her trial
cruise with a lot of important people on board, a friend of mine heard
a hospital nurse say, "Now I *know* there isn't any God". If there had
been, you see, he wouldn't have let down the British Raj like that.
Whether this *naif* confidence will outlive the events of our own time,
one cannot be certain. But I think this is certain—we are not meant to
read the riddle of God's dealings with mankind through our own
particular pair of spectacles, eagerly pointing to what *we* think is the
triumph of his cause, what *we* think is the downfall of his enemies.
He will not be constantly interfering, to save us from the consequences
of our own follies. And his plans are long-term plans; the centuries
look very short to him. That is what our Lord meant, I suppose, in his
parables, when he talked of the husbandman who leaves the crop to
come up as it will; of the king who goes into a far country and leaves
his servants to their own devices. The cry of the saints, "How long?",
goes long unanswered; and some of us will find their faith endangered
by that subtle, unexpressed wish we all have to be on the winning side
—the faith isn't always on the winning side. We must be ready, like
the woodman in Stevenson's fable, to go and die with Odin.

But Providence, in this sense, isn't only concerned with the destinies
of nations; it is concerned with you and me. Our Lord tells us that no
sparrow falls to the ground without our heavenly Father's will; every
hair of our heads, he says, is numbered. That picture of an omnipotence which takes every detail into account is something which
baffles the imagination; but we can't doubt that every individual life,
if we only knew it, is worked out on a pattern, and it will be the best
pattern for us if we will only correspond with it; God does underwrite
the business of our souls. Can we go further, and feel confident that he
will underwrite our earthly affairs as well? Can we neglect all human
precautions, and trust Providence to see our plans through, even the
wildest of them? The saints certainly seemed to do that, and a good
many other people—John Wesley, for example—who had a strong
sense of mission. They took risks which no ordinary person would
have taken, and got away with it. But then, we aren't all equally
important to God's purposes. When some lady told Archbishop
Temple—old Archbishop Temple[1]—about an aunt of hers who just
missed a train, and the train had an accident, and didn't he think one
ought to regard that as a special providence, the Archbishop replied,
"You see, I don't know your aunt". No, we mustn't tempt Providence.

[1] Frederick Temple; born 1821, Archbishop of Canterbury 1897-1902.

You do well to abandon yourself, trustingly, to the protection of our blessed Lady or your guardian angel when risks have to be taken; but we mustn't overwork our guardian angels. We must take ordinary precautions, and then tell ourselves, "God will provide".

41

THOMAS WELD'S CHURCH[1]

One day there shall be, none but the Lord knows the length of it, that shall be neither daylight nor dark; but when evening comes, there shall be light. —Zacharias 14. 7.

TODAY, like our brethren all over England, we Catholics of the West are celebrating the martyrdom of St John Fisher and St Thomas More—a Cardinal of the Holy Roman Church, and a great English layman. Here, with a more intimate sense of nearness to the events, we are also celebrating a gesture of faith made two hundred and fifty years later. It was in the year 1786 that a great English layman, Thomas Weld of Lulworth, laid the foundations of the church in which we stand; and perhaps on that occasion, one of the altar-boys would be his eldest son Thomas, a boy of nine years old, who was destined to achieve the purple. From Thomas More to Thomas Weld —what a fascinating interval of Catholic history is bounded by those landmarks! Fifty years of struggle, during which it was not apparent whether the old order would not reassert itself against the new; then a hundred years of intermittent but unrelenting persecution, during which the faith was kept alive by heroic resistance; then—more sad than either—a hundred years of slow decline, during which the Catholic body, no longer persecuted but still disabled and discouraged and shouldered out, dwindles almost to nothing; only kept alive where a handful of country squires, Welds and Petres and Plowdens and Blounts and the rest of them, still practise in secret the medieval rites of long ago. A dull afternoon, you would say, fading into twilight; and under that twilight, Thomas Weld built this church. At Cleobury Mortimer, in Shropshire, you can still make your way into a Catholic

[1] This sermon was preached at St Mary's, Lulworth Castle, on 9 July 1953, when the Apostolic Delegate to Great Britain reconsecrated the high altar of the eighteenth-century church, the first Catholic church to be built in England for public worship after the Reformation. The Bishops of Plymouth and Northampton were present.

place of worship that dates, they say, from 1730; but it nestles at the back of the squire's house, so that you mistake it, and were meant to mistake it, for a dairy or a laundry. Thomas Weld built out in the open; the last despairing gesture, you might conceive, of a doomed and still unemancipated religion. Gossip tells us that his friend, King George the Third, counselled him to make it look like a mausoleum; a mausoleum, perhaps, of the old faith which had been on its death-bed since the days of Thomas More.

It was not to be. Scarcely more than another half-century had elapsed when the Oxford conversions began, and the Church emerged from her twilight into a garish day of publicity. In their enthusiasm for the revival, men became impatient with the unadventurous ambitions, the unassuming behaviour which had characterized Catholics of the older school. You will remember how Newman described those older Catholics in his sermon on the Second Spring, using words which even Newman's tenderness cannot absolve from a hint of reproach: "There, perhaps, an elderly person seen walking in the streets, grave, and solitary, and strange, though noble in bearing, said to be of good family, and a Roman Catholic. An old-fashioned house of gloomy appearance, closed in with high walls, with an iron gate, and yews, and the report attaching to it that Roman Catholics lived there; but who they were, or what was meant by calling them Roman Catholics, no one could tell." So they appeared to Newman in his youth, and their habits had not changed for a hundred years. When the Second Spring came, all that was finished; the Church would now claim a place in the sun, like a bright butterfly that had left behind it the chrysalis of its former self. And, in token of the fact, its architecture and the ornamentation of its churches should go back behind Thomas Weld, even behind Thomas More; we would reconstruct the glories of medieval England, as if the Reformation had never happened. Nothing would serve but a revival of the Gothic; only the soaring arches and the exuberant detail of the fourteenth century would express, sufficiently, the bursting energy of an emancipated Church. First in the Midlands, then all over England, a forest of crockets and pinnacles grew up, to challenge (it was hoped) the dignified appeal of the old parish churches. And even Lulworth, which brooded like an exiled queen over the unhappy memories of persecution, must feel the impact of the new movement. The mausoleum must be brightened up, pulled out here, pinched there, adorned with frescoes and with arched window-frames, to make it look really medieval.

Man's nature is to build, he is *homo faber*, and the draughty securities of Flower's Barrow[1] do not content him. To protect himself against the weather, and against hostile attack, might have been thought sufficient; but no, he has an itch to perpetuate his own memory by raising some edifice of enduring stone which will outlast him; a monument to put some event on record, a great house to be the cradle of his race. And usually what he builds is an expression of the age in which he lives. Usually, not always. Lulworth Castle was built, by a freak of the imagination, in days when artillery had already made castles out of date. But usually the manner of building which dates from a particular age carries with it a genuine echo from the past; we can read in it something of what men felt and thought when it was current—their needs, their moods, their ambitions. And that is perhaps specially true of the eighteenth century. Its literature, its art, and above all, its architecture, seem integrated, all of a piece; all alike have the same character of dignity, of balance, of restraint which we associate with the word "classical". Oh, you may find it cold and unsympathetic; we do not go to the eighteenth century for uproarious amusement or for homely pathos; it calls for admiration, not for ardour. But it is perfect in its kind; you must take it for what it is.

And somehow our English Catholics of the eighteenth century, men like Bishop Challoner and Alban Butler and the rest of them, fit strangely well into the setting of their time. We find a certain rigidity about them, a certain unadventurousness. Not that they were behindhand in spirituality; one of the great masters of devotional literature is the Abbé Grou, who lived an exile at Lulworth and lies buried beneath this church. In piety and mortification they are a reproach, those older Catholics, to ourselves. But somehow there is a difference. They had a true love of our blessed Lady and the saints, but they were critical of exaggerated talk on such subjects and of new-fangled devotions. They were loyal to the Holy See; yet some of the old families—not this family—went to strange lengths in trying to disarm the suspicions of their Protestant fellow countrymen. A little over-cautious, perhaps, a little infected with Jansenist ideas, they are not altogether of our world; they seem colourless and remote. The dignity, the balance, the restraint which characterize eighteenth-century art-forms characterize, too,

[1] This is the local name for an ancient British Camp which is situated on top of a hill overlooking the sea, about a mile south of East Lulworth. It covers about five acres, and the double line of ditches surrounding it is a fairly prominent landmark in the neighbourhood. It is also sometimes called Rings' Hill, but Flower's Barrow appears to be the older name. Bishop Milner wrote an account of this and other barrows in the neighbourhood in the *Gentleman's Magazine* in 1790 (Vol. 60, pp. 897-901). The Bishop was a friend of Thomas Weld, the then owner of Lulworth, and used to stay there frequently.

these eighteenth-century Catholics. And when Thomas Weld built this church, five years before emancipation really began, to be a memorial and a protest, alone of its kind, against the cruel laws which forbade English Catholics to build churches at all, it was inevitable, as it was right, that he should make it a perfect expression of his own art-period, of the tradition then at its height, but so soon to come to an end. We were to see the eighteenth century, and eighteenth-century Catholicism, embalmed in miniature; to assure ourselves that Pugin had no hand in this.

Equally inevitable, perhaps, that seventy years later Thomas Weld's church should be beautified by his descendants. A new taste in church decoration had grown up; good taste or bad taste, we are not called upon to pronounce. They have turned grey now with the smoke of our cities, those neo-Gothic churches which Pugin and his friends flung up so defiantly, to shock their contemporaries and recall them to a memory of the distant past. A fresh change of taste has put us out of humour with them; they are so crowded with detail, so carefully imitative, and time has already found out flaws in their construction. Above all, the decorative schemes in which our great-grandfathers delighted, the brightly stencilled walls, the angular reredoses of stone and marble, the texts in their Gothic lettering, seem restless to the eye, repetitive to the mind. But the spirit which produced them has still power to stir the imagination and evoke in us a sigh of regret. How buoyant were the hopes they cherished, those men of the Second Spring, hopes of an England converted overnight by the spectacle of a medieval world brought to the birth anew! It was a flaming faith that let loose on the world that torrent of antiquarianism; and we, looking back at it in a disillusioned age, must needs be astonished and ashamed by the measure of their achievement.

Inevitable, perhaps, that Lulworth should be beautified; inevitable, but was it right? For here was something unique; the authentic record of a moment in history. St Mary's was built to look as little like a church as possible, because, at the time, those were the only conditions under which it could be built; the neighbours must take it for a rich man's fad, a temple or grotto such as rich men loved to put up in their grounds; that was the very essence of it. To make it look ecclesiastical was worse than a fault in taste, it was a fault in piety. And here, I think, we may criticize the great men of the Catholic revival; they were some-what lacking in piety towards the past. They were impatient with the older school of Catholics, found it difficult to deal with, difficult to move. And they forgot, or tended to forget, that these men had borne the burden and the heat of the day; they had kept the faith, and finished their course; of that, let Lulworth be the memorial.

Today, at least, when the piety of a still later generation has done its best to make Lulworth what it was—not by laborious, word-for-word imitation of the past, but by recovering and re-embodying its spirit—today at least let us be glad to remember those old, eighteenth-century Catholics, and to pronounce their epitaph. Theirs was the task, neither easy nor glorious, of preserving what was left of English Catholicism, in times when persecution was dead, but freedom still tarried, and the love of many had grown cold. A day when it was neither daylight nor dark; and as the agitation for Catholic rights pursued its weary, dispiriting course, they must have said to themselves, "None but the Lord knows the length of it". May we dare to think of those very English forebears of ours in terms of a peculiarly English sport, and say that they were like cricketers with no hope of victory, who play out the innings for a draw? When evening comes, there shall be light, but only the faint glimmers of it were showing when Thomas Weld made his act of faith in the future. On his soul, and the souls of all his kinsfolk that have gone before us, may our Lord have mercy; and raise up still in his family worthy descendants of a great name, to live and fight and suffer in their Master's service.

42

PAGAN AND CHRISTIAN[1]

It is in him that we live and move and have our being; thus, some of your own poets have told us: For indeed, we are his children.—Acts 17. 28.

ST PAUL was a man who always liked to make the best of things. If he wanted to argue with you, he would start by finding common ground somewhere. So it is when he finds himself in a mixed audience of Pharisees and Sadducees; "I am on my trial," he says, "as one who hopes for the resurrection of the dead"—and immediately the Pharisees begin to think he wasn't such a bad fellow after all. Then he is interrogated by King Herod Agrippa; "Well, anyhow," he says to himself,

[1] This sermon was preached at St Etheldreda's, Ely Place, London, on 18 October 1953, at the University High Mass.

"the man is a Jew", and he breaks out: "Dost thou believe the prophets, King Agrippa? I am well assured thou dost believe them." So it is here, when he is standing in the middle of pagan Athens, in full view of the Parthenon. "At least", he says to himself, "these people are humanists. Their idols are figures of men and women; they don't imagine that the world was made by a gigantic boa-constrictor or any nonsense of that sort." And then a quotation comes into his head, remembered from school days, perhaps; a tag from his own fellow countryman, Aratus of Soli. "For indeed, we are God's children"—surely when people have got as far as seeing *that*, it ought to be possible to explain to them how stupid it is to worship gods made in the image of man, instead of the God who made man in his own image!

I don't think you can say that that attitude is typical of Christendom in the first centuries. From the moment when persecution began, it was a head-on collision between Christianity and paganism, and the old gods had a bad press. Even St Augustine, whose roots go so far back into the past, blames himself for having wept over the imaginary sorrows of Queen Dido in the *Aeneid*, instead of lamenting the case of his own sinful soul. It was only when the classics had been more or less lost during the Dark Ages, and were to be found in short supply scattered about in monasteries, that we Christian people first began to feel at home with them. The men of the Middle Ages had an extraordinarily integrated outlook; they could find room for everything in their system, take everything in their stride. The old pagans, Virgil and Aristotle especially, became familiar guides, and almost took rank as honorary Christians. Then comes the sack of Byzantium, and the rediscovery of the classics as a whole by Western Europe; and with that, with the Renaissance, Christendom seems to lose its head rather, and pagan symbols become the natural medium of Christian art; Cherubs are almost indistinguishable from Cupids, and the Blessed Trinity is localized by hymnologists as seated on Mount Olympus. To the great anger of John Ruskin.

With the French Revolution, and the curious reversion to primitive models that succeeded it, the two streams, Christian and classical, that have been flowing so comfortably in a single channel, become sharply divided. Christendom returns to the Gothic; humanism, from Shelley to Swinburne, is the vehicle for a revolt against Christianity, and almost aspires to be its substitute. In our own day, that opposition is less keenly felt, I suppose because Christianity and the classics are both of them optional subjects in the curriculum of the modern mind. Ever since Lowes Dickinson's *Greek View of Life* there has been a thin stream of books by dons trying to represent Greece and Rome, instead of Nazareth, as the true cradle of civilization, but its effect has been negligible. The modern world feels that it can manage to go pagan for itself, without any dons to show it how.

I'm afraid you will have to accept that very rough sketch as covering the history of the matter. You will notice what a see-saw affair it has been; how the Church has sometimes been afraid of Greek gifts, and sometimes has opened her arms to them. And now we must try to get down to the philosophy of the thing. I suppose there are a few of you, a very few, who are old-fashioned enough to have chosen the classics as the subject of your studies at the University; and I suppose it is for their benefit, chiefly, that I have been asked to preach a sermon to you on this unfamiliar topic. With what eyes, then, ought you to be reading the authors of ancient Greece and Rome? Ought you to think of the classical culture and the Christian culture as two things irreconcilably opposed? Such was the view taken, on the whole, in the early centuries by men like Justin Martyr and Athenagoras. Such was the view taken in the nineteenth century by men like Shelley and Swinburne. Or ought you to think of them as somehow dovetailing into one another and even in a sense complementary to one another? That was, perhaps, the implication which underlay the humanist attitude of the Renaissance. I don't mean that people sat down and thought about it and put it to themselves like that. But they were splendidly conscious of a new world of thought from which the ages of faith had been debarred; and they couldn't carve a tomb or write a hymn that didn't betray this slight sense of superiority. Dante and St Thomas had only seen one side of the shield; they were seeing both. Or ought you to think of the classical culture as somehow included within the Christian culture? It was so that the medievals thought of it—again, instinctively. Theirs was a limited world, but all of it was theirs. They knew very little about animals, and most of it wasn't true; but somehow they managed to work the animals into their scheme of things, and derive lessons from them—the lioness, who bore her cubs dead and licked them to life again on the third day, the unicorn who was the test of virginity, and so on. And in the same way they didn't know much about the classics, but the figures they did know were all friendly figures, and when you wrote an epic about hell, as Dante did, there were plenty of them that you left just outside—even poor Ovid—in a fringe-world where they lived *senza spème in disio*,[1] in a hope always unsatisfied.

[1] *Che senza spème vivemo in disio* ('who without hope live in desire'): Dante, *Inferno*, Canto IV, line 43.

Were they right, perhaps, in thinking of these old pagans simply as incomplete people, people who had never grown up?

I know it sounds a disappointing thing to say, but I believe there is truth in all those three points of view. And accordingly we ought to have all three as our book-markers when we read the classics—if the classics are to be, not a subject mugged up for an exam., but a living experience.

The classical genius is not all one thing; it has its moods and its periods. If you will sit down with the Greek Anthology on your lap, and turn idly over its pages, you are dealing with a literary tradition which is spread out over a thousand years. But it is a continuous literary tradition; you never shake your head and say, "That is not really Greek". And it is like a garment of shot silk; your attention will be attracted now by its lights, now by its shadows; as a Christian reader, you will find yourself reacting now in this way, now in that. You come across this, for instance: "All is jest and all is dust and all is nothingness; out of unreasoning stuff all that is, is made". Oh, to be sure, it might almost pass for a Christian sentiment; but it was written by a defender of the old paganism, long after the official world had gone Christian. And I think it sums up a feature of the old paganism which we tend to forget, because it lies under the surface; I mean a great weariness, a spirit of negation. Professing belief in so many gods above and below the earth, your Greek and your Roman, when he had learned to take his culture from the Greek, was at heart an atheist. Again and again, in the epigrams that lie in front of you, you catch the same despairing message, "Death is the end of everything, so nothing matters; the only thing is to go and get drunk". You will remember St Paul's terrible description of what the Ephesians used to be like before they were converted, "strangers to every covenant, with no promise to hope for, with the world about you, and no God". Catch the pagan in that mood, and who would want to be a humanist?

And then suddenly, in those same pages, you come across a couple of lines that bowl you over by the nobility and the simplicity of their sentiments. Take the most famous of all, the epitaph on the three hundred Spartans who died at Thermopylae. "Stranger, if you go to Sparta, tell them how you saw us lying here, in obedience to their orders." There is nothing Christian about it; it might have been written up over the Russians who fell at Stalingrad. And indeed, a Russian epitaph would at least have contained some note of ideology; would have told us that these men died in resisting the tyranny of Nazi Germany. But there is nothing in Simonides' epigram to remind us that the three hundred were resisting the tyranny of barbarian Persia. No, they died obeying orders; theirs was the spirit of the hive; a set of schoolboys, you might say, who didn't run away because it was against the school rules. If they had been Christians, there would have been some reference to immortality, but there is none; there is no suggestion, even, of theism; they are not defending the sanctity of their gods, or even of obeying the laws of their gods; they are simply obeying orders as such. And yet, from the very nakedness of it, the Lacedemonian reticence of it, how splendid it is! And of course it doesn't stand alone; it is of a piece with all those fine gestures we used to read about in our Roman history; how Regulus persuaded the Senate not to ransom himself and his fellow hostages, how Otho committed suicide in order to save Rome from the horrors of civil war. Wasn't it rather special pleading when St Augustine tried to make out that all the virtues of the heathen were really vices? All very well to say that the Christian martyrs had something better to die for; but it is possible to have a special admiration for people who sacrificed their lives with no hope, or a shadowy hope at best, of a blessed immortality. No, I think most of us will be content to leave these and many other acts of heroism, works done apparently without the grace of Christ, in the hands of the God who made us all and hates nothing that he has made. "There shall never be one lost good"—that is all we can feel certain of.

And then our fingers stray through the pages again, and we turn up some epigram that takes our breath away for a different reason; not because it is so characteristically pagan, but because it seems almost Christian. Plato's epitaph, for example, on his dead friend Aster, whose name meant "a star". He wrote, "Once you used to shine, a morning star, among the living; now you shine, an evening star, among the dead". We don't know exactly how much Plato meant, or exactly how much he meant it. But we remember other things he said about the immortality of the soul, and the purgations and punishments that awaited it in a future life—yes, it was like Plato to think of that, although he hadn't read St Paul's great chapter on the Resurrection, which tells us that the heavenly body we shall wear one day differs from our earthly body as star differs from star in glory. . . . And it makes us recall other things Plato wrote; about the just man who would be scourged and go to the stake because the men of his day didn't understand what real justice meant; and about the true shepherd, not the one who is out to make money. And that sets us thinking about all the other odd anticipations of Christian ideas which you find in the pagan world; about the victim king who was slain by his own people, and the sorrowing mother of the Mysteries, and how the earthly Christians put up pictures of Orpheus in the catacombs because Orpheus, in the fable, harrowed hell. And so it goes on to the very eve of the Incarnation, when Virgil wrote his eclogue about the child that should be born, to restore the age of innocence.

When you get *that* angle on your classical studies, you no longer see paganism as an evil thing over which Christianity triumphed, or as a good thing which Christianity has somehow by-passed, but as the raw material of our redeemed nature, Christendom in the making. It is the theme of Mr Hollis's book, *Noble Castle*. The pagan world hunting all the time for the treasure hidden in the field of human history, and always just missing it because they couldn't believe any good thing would come out of Nazareth. Revelation not a desperate drug for humanity at its worst, but a flood lighting of humanity at its best. Those heroes of antiquity seem, like Edith Cavell at her execution, to murmur, "Patriotism is not enough".[1] Read your classics in *that* spirit, and you are like the audience at a Greek play, knowing what was the end of the story when the actors didn't. You will catch a hundred hints of dramatic irony, a hundred overtones of meaning, because you will see the glory that was Greece and the grandeur that was Rome as Act I in the drama of the Incarnation.

43

WESTMINSTER JUBILEE: I[2]

Thou hast set up a standard to rally thy faithful servants.—Psalm 59. 6.

WHEN we let our minds go back over the past, and thank God for the return of some anniversary date—the date upon which this or that institution was set up, this or that fabric of building was completed—we are impressed, as a rule, by the swift flight of time, by the transitoriness of human existence. How they outlive us, the works of our own hands; how they dwarf our human stature, the trees our

---

[1] Edith Cavell: born 4 December 1865; a British nurse who on 12 October 1915 was shot by the Germans for harbouring British soldiers and helping them to escape. In 1919 her body was brought to England and buried in the precincts of Norwich Cathedral.

[2] This sermon was preached at Westminster Cathedral on 6 December 1953, at the inauguration of the week of special services to commemorate the fiftieth anniversary of the opening of the Cathedral for public worship.

grandfathers planted, the stones men piled on one another a couple of centuries back! But today, as we remind ourselves that Westminster Cathedral has been open, these fifty years, for public worship, the emphasis of our thoughts is quite different. Only fifty years ago! There are those of us, not yet altogether laid on the shelf, who can remember London when there was no cathedral at Westminster, when the public ceremonies of the archdiocese still found their focus in Kensington. Only fifty years! Why, these jubilee celebrations of ours are being witnessed by a chaplain of Westminster Cathedral who was already a chaplain when Westminster Cathedral was opened. How it is that within so short a space of years this mushroom growth, this thing of yesterday, has become an integral part of London? In the north, we take Catholicism for granted; you alight from the train at Manchester, say "Holy Name" to the taxi-driver, and "Very good, father," is the expected response. But in London, where we are still so comparatively few, so comparatively insignificant! How is it that we take the words "Westminster Cathedral" so lightly on our lips, confident that nobody will say "You mean Westminster Abbey"?

And this thing has happened, as far as the outside world could see, effortlessly. There has never been any campaign to put the cathedral "on the map". It has not been a great preaching centre, as Farm Street was in the days of Bernard Vaughan. It does not compete with the Oratory as a centre of fashionable weddings. On State occasions, to be sure, it comes into its own, as any cathedral must; but, for the rest of the time, it has nothing to show for itself but a set of parish priests going about their daily work as devotedly, as unobtrusively, as any other set of parish priests; a choir of seculars who sing, with little of circumstance or of parade, the Divine Office. It makes no appeal to our religiosity; its severe, basilica traditions leave little room for meretricious ornament, for cosy corners which encourage devotion to this or that favourite saint. Beauty it has, but it is beauty of proportion, not easily appreciated by the first comer; I still remember looking round it as a schoolboy, when it had little marble to boast of, and wondering what people could see in this great desolate expanse of liver-coloured brick. It has no arts of showmanship; and yet in fifty years it has imposed itself on the public mind; it has become part of London.

What is the secret of the place? Size there is in it, and distance; footfalls come to you muffled by distance; that, perhaps, predisposes us for awe. But there is some further quality about it which I can only call "mystery". I don't say that everybody feels it; I only say that it communicates itself to people who are not, as a rule, particularly conscious of atmospheres. To be sure, other London churches have their sense of mystery, too; especially, I think, the little ones, the old-fashioned ones, Warwick Street and Moorfields and Maiden Lane. All day, that constant shuttle-service of people coming in to say their prayers, hundreds of lonely individuals, each bent on some private errand, each on their knees for some private intention—how it challenges the imagination, with a sense of suppressed drama! But what feeds the sense of wonder in that connection is a human interest in our fellow creatures, total strangers whose lives have thus, for a moment, become foul-hooked with our own. But here, in the cathedral, it is different; the scattered units of humanity visible here and there do not strike us as real people, rather as human figures sketched in to emphasize the vast scale of the building. And we ourselves, how we are dwarfed by our surroundings! We almost forget the intention we came in to pray for, so unimportant do we seem, we and all that belongs to us, on our knees before the majesty of God. It puts us in our place, Westminster Cathedral.

That is when we are inside; and even from the outside, how simple is the symbolism of that aspiring campanile—simple as the mind of the great Cardinal who founded it! Even now, when London has grown so immeasurably taller than it was in his day, it is part of that picture of London which a man forms in his mind's eye. What wonder that it should be in the guide-books! The candid atheist, visiting London for the first time, puts this third among the ecclesiastical buildings in which he ought to have a look-round; only the Abbey and St Paul's take precedence of it. After fifty years! What a shameless upstart it must seem to him, this cathedral of ours, by comparison with two buildings like that; one of them with a history that reaches back into the ages of faith, behind the Norman Conquest, and the other, for centuries, a votive temple for the most prosperous city in the world! And is a late-Victorian experiment in Byzantine to take rank with these?

Those are, perhaps, his first thoughts; that is one way of looking at it, natural, perhaps, to the newcomer. But if he prolongs his stay, and gets to know London and Londoners rather better, a different set of considerations will strike him. The Abbey, sure enough, means a great deal to Londoners when there is a monarch to be crowned in it; but for the rest of the time, how do they mostly think of it? As a show-place, a mausoleum where such and such great men lie buried. And even St Paul's—there is no doubt that Londoners are proud of it; but are they really proud of it as a church, not rather as a monument and almost as a mascot? The modern generation of Englishmen revere the past in a kind of antiquarian spirit; they are always for restoring old customs, for repairing old buildings. But they do not live by the traditions of the past; their outlook is that of a new age, which threatens to travel faster than time. Those old effigies in the Abbey are full of interest; but it is the same kind of interest which attaches to the mummies of the Pharaohs. And if you would gain access to St Paul's, you must pass by the statue of the sovereign in whose reign St Paul's was completed. It is the statue of Queen Anne. And Queen Anne is dead.

Half-consciously, then, our visitor takes the Abbey for a symbol, not of what Englishmen think now, but of what they thought at the time of the Conquest. He takes St Paul's for a symbol, not of what Englishmen think now, but of what they thought at the time of the South Sea Bubble. And Westminster Cathedral remains to him for a symbol of what Englishmen—some Englishmen—thought fifty years ago. Only fifty years; and, to judge by the crowds which frequent it, their mind has not changed. It was part of Bentley's genius, that when he sent in a plan for the new cathedral, he would not design it in Gothic, like Farm Street, to challenge comparison with the Abbey, or in baroque, like the Oratory, to disturb us with memories of St Paul's. He would revert to the Byzantine tradition, ageless, severe, primitive, to our Western minds somewhat outlandish. He would not play up to the Englishman's religious prejudices; there should be no hint of the harvest festival, or of the Pleasant Sunday Afternoon. He would remind Londoners of that thing which lived on in their midst, belonging not to one age or to one latitude, that thing which they were always trying to forget. I can still remember how I found myself, nearly forty years ago, walking through London streets and trying to push away from me the thought of a life's decision which I knew I had to make; and how, down unaccustomed vistas between the buildings, the campanile of Westminster kept on presenting itself to my view, like a warning finger that would not be ignored.

What was it, then, he had done, the great Cardinal who lay in state before that altar fifty years ago, houselling by his requiem the cathedral he did not live to consecrate? For better or worse, he had brought us Catholics out into the open. If the Eucharistic Congress of 1908 had been celebrated in the streets of Brompton or Kensington, it would neither have raised such violent opposition, nor created so profound an impression. And ever since then the public attention has been arrested, at intervals, by some great concourse of Catholic worshippers; never more so, I suppose, than when Bishop Sheen came to preach here last Lent. Even when there is (as we say) nothing special "on", the hum of prayer still haunts about Ashley Gardens; Sunday by Sunday, there is no other place of worship in England which attracts such a crowd of church-goers. People notice it, and are surprised by it, and labour to devise infantile explanations of how it happens—as if it were such an unheard-of thing that a man might want to worship his God one day in the week! But, you see, it is all part of a quiet process that has been going on during these fifty years; the Catholic Church in England has done rather more, in these lean days, than hold its own, and our numbers are beginning to look, by comparison, noticeable. That is why, from time to time, we find ourselves subjected to the peevish comment of our neighbours. It does not, to be sure, take such fantastic forms as it used to. A quarter of a century ago, when some repairs were being executed in this cathedral, the rumour went round that a gang of Spanish workmen had been imported to provide it with a set of torture-chambers which had been left out in the original design. Things have moved since then, but the tittle-tattle goes on. And every Catholic is to some extent a marked man; in the casual contacts of daily life he is bearing witness, or failing to bear witness, to Jesus Christ. We are not long the *gens lucifuga* which passed unnoticed up and down Kensington High Street.

Does that mean that we have to be on our toes all the time, alert for every opportunity of edifying, or not disedifying, our neighbours? That we must look round nervously at our company to see how every chance remark will be taken; that we must arm ourselves with propaganda retorts for every sally of propaganda criticism? I don't think it means that; the point is, not so much that we ought to be better Catholics, but that we ought to be better Christians. That we should be lovers of the truth, fair-minded, ready to believe the best of people, impatient of scandal, considerate towards the unbefriended, generous in our enthusiasms, temperate in our pleasures, discreet in our friendships, that we should have a smile for everybody—in a word, that we should live in the sunlight of that creed which we profess; all that does more for the conversion of England than any amount of mosaics or marble. If only we weren't such an average lot, we Catholics!

Meanwhile, here is our cathedral, our great show-place; the most important and the most frequented, next to Buckfast Abbey, in the kingdom. Because of that, it is not simply ours; we are guardians of it, trustees of it, pledged to make the most of it and the best of it, for the glory of God and the benefit of souls. For the priests, and for all those who have any place in the machinery of it, down to the youngest boy in the choir school, that means a splendid responsibility; it is theirs to be the human interpreters of all this beauty, all this majesty; to make it, not only admired, but loved, by all the multitudinous souls who pass under that doorway. The Divine Office they recite together, the Masses they say, and all their ministrations here—how important that there should be nothing casual, nothing slipshod about them—much more important than if they were attached to some parish church, where everybody knows you and made allowances for you. The music—what a close connection there is, in the minds of English people, between music and religion! But what I am trying to say goes much deeper than that; in a place like Westminster Cathedral, so variously frequented, everything matters; there is a right way and a wrong way of handing a collection-plate. So often you hear people say, "I once went into a Catholic church", and you know what is coming; some tiny piece of unintentional rudeness or brusqueness, and it has been enough to make up this person's mind about the Catholic Church for ever. It is so hard for priests, and for church officials generally, to be always polite, always in a good temper, when they are tired or in a hurry; but it does matter. And in Westminster Cathedral it matters beyond words.

We have spoken of the cathedral as a show-place; God forbid we should think of it as nothing but that. For hundreds of souls, it has a more intimate meaning; it was here that they learnt their first lesson in the Faith, learned to love our blessed Lady and to understand the Mass; it was here that they found strength in the sacraments to face their own problems and achieve their own destiny. Already, after fifty years, how often it has witnessed the hidden triumphs of grace, brought consolation in long-forgotten tragedies! All that patient pastoral work is what almighty God remembers as he looks down on this temple of his; and it will not go unrewarded. To the souls of all who have laboured and worshipped in this church, and of all its benefactors, may he in his mercy grant refreshment, light and peace.

44

THE SHEPHERD OF HIS PEOPLE[1]

Feed my lambs . . . tend my shearlings . . . feed my sheep.—John 21. 15-17.

THE story of the Gospels ends, rather unexpectedly, on a note of repose. Christ, the conqueror of death, still left on earth for a little, but wearing already, under some veil of mortality, that impassible body which will be his for ever, is spending his time—how? Entertaining his disciples to a picnic meal beside the lake of Galilee. And perhaps—it would be natural enough—somewhere on the hillside they can see a shepherd looking after his flock, with all the anxious cares of spring-time upon him. And perhaps St Peter, thrilled by the day's great event, the miraculous draught of fish, watches the man a little contemptuously. What a tame life, to be acting as nursery-maid to those woolly creatures, compared with the fisherman's experience —the handling of the boat, the spreading of the nets, the swarm of silver bodies coming up, with ripples of reluctance, to the surface!

It may well have been on such thoughts that our Lord broke in with that threefold question, "Dost thou love me?", that threefold commission about the tending of his flock. St Peter, the impetuous, the adventurous, the man who has just thrown himself into the sea to greet his Master, is not, after all, being reserved for the work you might have anticipated, pioneer work, breaking new ground, as the spearhead of the Christian army. Only for a little will he be employed in the the tasks that are congenial to him; then, increasingly, he will be caught up in the wheels of administration, as the guiding and controlling influence in the affairs of a universal Church—the prisoner, even in those early days, of the Vatican. When he was young he girded himself and went whither he would; now the fisherman is to turn shepherd.

By hook or by crook, the world has to be won for Christ. And the crook of the shepherd is needed, not less than the hook of the fisherman, if the Church is to hold her own. Above all, when the tide is beginning to turn, when the country which was once a missionary country is now being organized on normal Catholic lines, when there are gains to be consolidated, and a tradition to preserve, the shepherd's

---

[1] This sermon was preached at St Chad's Cathedral, Birmingham, on the occasion of the enthronement of Archbishop Grimshaw as Archbishop of Birmingham, 14 September 1954.

task increases in importance. Think of Birmingham and the Midlands a hundred years ago—what fishermen of souls we had! Newman and Faber and Father Dominic and Father Gentili and the rest of them, how adventurous was their cruising, how brave were their ambitions! But all the time, behind their efforts, a figure less prominent but hardly less significant, the patient genius of Ullathorne was there in the background. Even then, with those small numbers, we had need of shepherding; how much more today!

How close we are to history! I was born on 17 February 1888; and on that date Dr Ilsley[1] became the second Bishop of Birmingham. Today, not unmindful of the blessings God has granted us through his ministry and that of his three successors, Birmingham welcomes her sixth bishop, her fifth archbishop, called away from his nets at Plymouth to these Midland plains where he has four great counties for his shepherding.[2] And we who have come here, in friendship and in homage, must not be content with perfunctory compliments, and conventional expressions of good will. We have come here to pray for a fellow mortal entrusted with a position of terrifying responsibility—that God will be with him, and guide him, and make him achieve the salvation of his own soul in and with and through the flock that is committed to him.

Of terrifying responsibility; more so than in Milner's[3] day, or in Ullathorne's.[4] Partly because the Catholic population of the district has grown beyond proportion larger. The faithful of the archdiocese have three times as many churches to worship in, four times as many priests to minister to them, as they had a hundred years ago. Partly also, because in our day the world has become more centralized, more highly organized; everything has to be referred, nowadays, to headquarters. Inevitably, that has had its effect on the mechanism of our Catholic effort; the diocese, rather than the parish, is the unit, and the bishop is no longer a man who sits there saying "No"; he has to initiate policy, to plan developments. A bishop in our time cannot be content with dogged adherence to a formula; he needs vision and enterprise; rarer gifts.

"Feed my lambs"; the lambs first, the children first. It is a wintry

[1] Dr Edward Ilsley, consecrated Bishop-Auxiliary 4 December 1879; translated to Birmingham 17 September 1888; resigned 15 January 1921; died 1 December 1926.
[2] Dr Grimshaw was consecrated Bishop of Plymouth on 25 July 1947.
[3] John Milner, Bishop of Castabala, consecrated Vicar-Apostolic of the Midland District 22 May 1803; died 19 April 1826, aged seventy-four.
[4] William Bernard Ullathorne, o.s.b.; enthroned as first Bishop of Birmingham 29 September 1850; previously Vicar Apostolic of the Western District; died 21 March 1889.

world our children are born into, a world full of questioning and
disillusionment. They have to be nourished, from the first, with the
gracious certainties of Christian truth, if they are to grow up into a
hardy manhood, proof against the miasma of selfishness and despair.
And it is not as it was in the old days, when the priest would gather the
children of the parish about him, or send them to a dame's school
round the corner, confident that this was all the education they would
get. On the contrary, there is a fierce competition to indoctrinate these
young minds with a wealth of modern ideals, nobly conceived, for the
most part, but not ours. And at the same time, they are distracted by a
jumble of impressions, good, bad and indifferent, which they derive
from the cinema and the wireless programmes. It needs more than a
glib repetition of the Penny Catechism to counteract such influences
as these. Every fresh movement of population in the diocese reminds
the bishop of fresh rises in the cost of building, fresh requirements
made by the educational authorities. "Whence shall we?" he exclaims,
like the apostles before him; "whence shall we provide bread, here in
the desert?"

"Tend my shearlings"; the year-old lambs do not look up to the
shepherd for food, they seek it out for themselves, all too adventurously.
The danger is that they will stray from the fold, climb along the edge
of the precipice. The verb, then, changes; St Peter is no longer commissioned to feed this new category, but to shepherd them. And the
boys and girls who have left school provide their pastors with a fresh
form of embarrassment. Those dangerous years, in which liberty has
been attained, but not discretion! How to cater for the needs of the
adolescent is everywhere a problem; never more so than when they
pursue their education, but in the freer air of a university. This archdiocese, sprawling across the middle of England, embraces at Oxford
the oldest of our university institutions, and in North Staffordshire the
youngest. And its own cathedral city is the home of a vigorous university life; Catholics, like others, share in its advantages; more than
others, they experience its dangers. Birmingham has long been a city
of free enquiry, and it has little tenderness for theology—when I first
lived here, in the nineties, the nascent university excluded that science
by name from its curriculum. Who is to ensure that Catholic students,
exposed to the influence of so many inadequate philosophies, are at
the same time confronted, and effectively, with the eternal truths of
religion? Shall we go to the parish clergy? "Oh, I don't know", they
will say; "you'd better ask his Grace about that." Once more, it is the
responsibility of the diocesan. They say that if you suffer from insomnia

N

it is a good thing to lie in bed and count sheep jumping over a hedge. For some people perhaps it may be; but not, I think, for bishops.

"Feed my sheep"; meanwhile, there is the ordinary, hand-over-hand business of ministering to the needs of the faithful; of shriving them and houselling them and preaching to them, and arranging for the weddings and funerals. Surely the parish priest can be trusted to do *that*? And yet, in reality, is the bishop's responsibility ever more terrifying than when he delegates it? To choose out, for the service of the altar, only the men whose hearts God has touched; to ordain them only when they are ripe for ordination; to post them where they ought to be posted, in a diocese which reaches from the Thames to the Pennines; to watch, without seeming to watch, over their labours; to make friends of them, and learn their difficulties; to make things easy for them in sickness and in old age—is that a light task? And beyond that, the merely administrative part of his work, the bishop has to be a priestly model to his clergy, not by a mere façade of edifying behaviour, but *ex animo*, deep down in the heart. Who can prove himself worthy of such a calling?

It is the custom of Holy Church, when she confers dignities upon her sons, to put them through an interrogation; do they believe this? Are they competent to do that? Will they undertake to do the other? Our Lord's own method was simpler; he only asks St Peter one question, but repeats it three times: "Do you love me?" Only that, it seems, is indispensable. Why then, as we associate ourselves today with his Grace's offering of the Holy Mass, let us put away from our thoughts, as he from his, all these gloomy forebodings of difficulties ahead. Let us ask almighty God, through the prayers of our blessed Lady and Saint Chad and all the patrons of the archdiocese, to make our new Archbishop ever more worthy of the task he has undertaken, by giving him ever more love for Jesus Christ. And the cross which we lay upon him on this feast of Holy Cross will be carried lightly and joyfully, because it is carried in love.

45

THE UNITY OF MANKIND[1]

Do not be disarmed by malice; disarm malice with kindness.—Romans 12.21.

A WEEK ago we were celebrating the moment, full of history, when a Jewish visitor, with a north-country accent, entered Imperial Rome, and looked round for the first time at the monuments of that city in which the long line of his successors was to reign. Today, we have in mind a more familiar picture; that meeting on the road to Damascus by which the first great persecutor of the Church was thrown from his horse, and knocked sensible. No wonder that at such a time our thoughts should be directed towards the historic unity of the Church, and towards that multitude of souls, many of them great lovers of Jesus Christ, who placidly ignore, or angrily reject, the claims of that See which has been the guarantee and the matrix of unity, all down the centuries.

Our modern age, on the strength of rather moderate literary achievements, loves to proclaim itself an age of humanism. The spokesmen of such an age, at a hundred different angles, show themselves more than ever unfriendly to the whole idea of revealed religion. And, more than ever, devout Christians are tempted to grow impatient over those doctrinal differences which separate one denomination from the next, dividing their effort, and discrediting the witness of each. Why should it be impossible to sink these differences, and oppose a common front to the common attack? After all, what are doctrines but an attempt to give intellectual expression to our love of God, our loyalty towards Jesus Christ? And the world, tired of listening to long wrangles between the philosophers, is coming to doubt whether the intellect is a competent judge of the living truth. In matters of religion, especially; how should we express the mystical currents of the supernatural life in a formula? Can we not forget our formulas, and give the lie to a godless world by living, with a visible unity of effort, the Christian life?

The answer is, that you must not think of the godless world as if it lay outside our calculations; as if the many people we know who, conscientiously it seems, reject the whole idea of the supernatural, had no part in the Church Unity Octave. Peter must spread his net wide as

---

[1] This sermon was preached at Westminster Cathedral on 25 January 1955, the Feast of the Conversion of St Paul, during the Church Unity Octave.

humanity; and if he toils vainly all night, he must let down his nets again. We are not satisfied with the prospect of a world divided into two classes—those who have a turn for religion and those who have not. And that is what happens in the long run, if you appeal behind reason to some mystical sense as the basis of religious certitude. With other Christians we have much, thank God, in common. With those multitudes who have had the claim of Christ proposed to them, and rejected it, we have nothing in common except reason, and those natural virtues which reason dictates. If, then, in making terms with the other Christianities, you renounce altogether the intellectual approach, you have cut the ground under your feet. You have broken down the barriers between Christian and Christian, only to break down the bridges between Christians and those outside. St Thomas could reason with Avicenna; Marcel cannot reason with Sartre.

These, too, the unbelievers, are of the family; we and they have a common Father in heaven, have therefore, in idea and in potency, a common father on earth. Many of them have been baptized; the seed of grace never found room to grow, or its growth was stunted for want of fostering, but it is still there, ready to strike. Others, although they may have been born in a Christian country, are technically pagans still; but how many of these, because they were born in a Christian country, and have inherited, with the very air they breathe, something of the Christian tradition, have a common background with us, more than they know, or would acknowledge! "The godless"—they are not some strange race of men, to be met with only at the end of exhausting travels. They are all round us; we rub shoulders with them in the lift; live in the same street, and exchange visits with them. How is it that we think about it so little, pray about it so little, the complete difference between two world-pictures, theirs and ours? Why do we pray so often for the wanderers who are following a false path, so little for those who can find no path at all?

We are to pray, then, on this feast of St Paul's conversion, for those all over the world, but especially for those known to us, who do not accept the Gospel of Christ; do not believe, many of them, in the existence of a divine Power which rules our destinies. With what picture in our minds? First of all, I would say this: let us not be too ready to accuse them, even at the back of our minds, of bad faith. Oh, it is true, the theologians have some hard things to say about the im- possibility of refusing to accept the proofs of the Christian religion, when once you have candidly examined them. But the theologians— it is the way of scientific people—are supposing the existence of an abstract human being, a creature of pure thought, utterly devoid of unconscious prejudices. Was St Paul, when he set out for Damascus, in bad faith? He has only given us one clue to his state of mind; it is when he says before King Agrippa, "I thought it my duty to defy, in many ways, the name of Jesus". I thought it my duty—that is all he has to tell us about it, this man who was ready to proclaim himself, upon another occasion, the chief of sinners. Think of the irreligious people you know well; do you feel certain that they have been guilty of culpable idleness in omitting to consider the claim of the supernatural? Or that having considered it they ran away, through deliberate cowardice, from the thought? And if these were not wholly to blame, what of those others, unknown to you, whom you so readily condemn?

No, I am not trying to defend the atheist. His judgment, like yours and mine, lies in God's hands; it is a small thing that he should be judged by our standards. I am only suggesting that we shall not find it easy to pray for him in that attitude of patience and confidence which is the proper medium of prayer, that we shall not find it easy to disturb the rigid pattern of his thought, if we approach him as a man who has no real intellectual difficulties, who is simply putting up a case against us, out of sheer perversity. And it is very easy to do that. We give our fellow Christians credit for the scruples which make it hard for them to go all the way with us; "this man", we say to ourselves, "has such a dazzling consciousness of our Lord's unique position in the dispensation of grace, that he has no eyes for our blessed Lady, and all that our blessed Lady means to us". Even when there is no bond of common Christianity, we have a vague respect for a man's religion; he is a Buddhist, yes, but he has got hold of something. To have any respect at all for a man's irreligion—that is much harder. And yet he, too, has got hold of something; he believes, as we do, in logical proof; believes, as we do, in historical accuracy; hates, as we do, the very name of superstition. We shall, perhaps, be inclined to resent the tone of these people; there is a cock-sureness about it sometimes, a flippancy which to us seems irreverence. But all that, more than we know, is probably defensive propaganda; is the bravado by which a man tries to bolster up an insecurely held conviction.

And always, if we would be at pains to understand the difficulties of those outside, let us try to see ourselves as they see us. A few months ago, I was giving a retreat for the nuns up at Hampstead; and as I walked round the garden saying my office, I was suddenly interrupted by the voice of a small boy from next door saying, "Please, sir, may we get our ball?" How often, as the youngest of four brothers, I had been fagged to go on these embarrassing missions! And how it would have added to my terrors if I had been met by an old gentleman all covered in red buttons, with his nose buried in a book! For the moment, the years slipped from me, and what I saw at the end of the path was not the small boy, but the old gentleman. I wonder if we practise enough that exchange of personalities? We shall not begin to understand the attitude of the modern unbeliever towards the Church until we realize that he thinks of us as a conspiracy: a conspiracy to set up an unholy Roman Empire over the consciences of an enslaved race. And how often, in the hesitating mind, the imaginary difficulties count for more than the real ones!

What, then, of those countries which seemed, till yesterday, so close to us, now so far off, whole countries in which atheism has become a kind of official religion, to be taught in the schools and sown broadcast by subsidized propaganda? What thoughts are to be in our minds when, at the end of every Low Mass, we kneel down to pray for Russia? Perhaps then we should curb our imaginations, instead of giving rein to them, lest our prayer should be clouded by bitter memories of the past, unhallowed daydreams of the future. Oh, certainly we must pray for the victims of persecution; but, when we pray for Russia, must all our intercessions be earmarked for the con-centration camps? People talk, nowadays, of "co-existence"—the notion that we and the countries behind the Iron Curtain must be content to live in the same world, without having anything to say to one another. That may be the best we can do as a political ideal; but can we be content to think of all those millions of souls, when we fall to our knees, as somehow a different species from ourselves, breathing the same air, yet having no meaning for us, no claim upon us? Rather, I think, we ought to remember them as brothers of ours, deceived at the moment by a lie, but guilty in varying degrees, and those perhaps most needing our prayers, who are guiltiest. "I thought it my duty", says St Paul, and St Augustine reminds us that, as a rule, when we think we are hating an enemy, we are hating a brother without knowing it. Let us ask for all men the mercy we all need, and leave judgment in his hands, who alone can judge, who alone can punish.

46

THE CENTENARY OF SS. MARY AND JOHN[1]

You too must be built up on him, stones that live and breathe, into a spiritual fabric.—1 Peter 2. 5.

WHEN we meet to praise God for the existence of a human edifice which has stood, bearing witness to his glory, for a hundred years, our first thought is that of our own impermanence. So short a span it is, this life of ours, that the work of our own hands can survive us and become to its own architects a monument of eternity. To be sure, a church like this is a mushroom growth compared with the old parish churches which date back behind the Reformation. Yet already we contemplate its stones with awe because it has stood for a hundred years. Only one hundred years and, of all the congregation that saw it opened in 1855, not one remains to tell us about the sober rejoicing and ardent hopes which English Catholics felt about it a hundred years ago. Yet, when I say that, I am conscious of being greeted with a rueful smile by those members of this congregation who can remember the history of the parish over a long period. "A preacher who talks about buildings as permanent", they are saying to themselves, "knows little about the history of St Mary and St John." This church, as we know, has worn down the lives of all its rectors; with huge bills for shoring it up, for repointing it, re-plastering it, re-facing it, substituting new mouldings for the old mouldings which had fallen into decay. Our Catholic predecessors, a hundred years ago, built in faith. But unfortunately that faith was not always justified where builders and contractors were concerned. So much they knew, those architects of the Second Spring, about rood screens and rose windows. So little, it would seem, about strains and stresses and drainage, and they left to us—their successors—not so much a finished product as a fabric perpetually in building, perpetually calling for fresh anxiety on the part of the parish priest, fresh generosity on the part of his congregation. As we meet here and thank God for his mercies in the past, we

[1] This sermon was preached in the presence of Dr Francis Grimshaw, Archbishop of Birmingham, at the Church of SS. Mary and John, Wolverhampton, on 24 April 1955, on the occasion of the centenary of the church.

should be thinking not only of those benefactors who built this church in the first instance, but of all those good Catholic people who have pinched themselves and put themselves about, held bazaars and put money in the second collection from that day to this to keep it in repair and to make it safe for posterity.

All this seems at first sight a rather chastened kind of rejoicing to do duty for a centenary sermon, but I hope you won't think I am speaking in irony if I suggest that all this long record of endeavour and self-sacrifice gives us a truer picture of what the Catholic religion is and stands for than would be reflected in these walls around us if this were Charles Hansom's church, exactly as Charles Hansom built it, a museum piece of early Victorian architecture, unaltered by time. Because that would give us the impression that time stands still, that we live in the past, derive our inspiration from ways of thought and ways of life that are long dead. How annoying it is when our non-Catholic friends talk to us like that and think they are being complimentary! "It must be wonderful", they say, "to go on like that, all the time knowing exactly where you are, right back in the dear old Middle Ages." How hard it is to make them understand that it is just the other way round; that the Catholic Church is alive; always meeting new situations; always putting out fresh shoots of life in the most unexpected directions; that we don't lie back as they imagine and live on our capital. We labour and fight amid constant stresses and strains to keep the faith of Jesus Christ alive in a world which has almost forgotten him.

Here is a church planned, you may say, in the mind of Bishop Milner. Its foundation stone was laid by Archbishop Ullathorne. Cardinal Wiseman preached at its opening. Cardinal Newman was here when the chancel was added, and, at the consecration, one of the sermons was delivered by Father Vincent McNabb. So from generation to generation the torch has been handed on and each generation, as if to attest the fact, has its own contribution to make to the fabric of 1855. The very edifice in which you worship is rich with the scars of conflict. All that is symbolic. It means that the Catholic Church doesn't hold together automatically on some merely mechanical principle. It depends from one generation to the next on a conspiracy of human wills. Our neighbours are so ready to believe that it is otherwise; that Catholics remain Catholics merely by force of habit; because they are too stupid to think of doing anything else; that to be a Catholic involves no strain, no effort of the mind, no combat with temptation. You Catholics of Wolverhampton are Catholics not just because your grandfathers were in 1855, but because you men and women of this generation have kept and keep the Faith. It satisfies the deepest instincts of your nature here and now. "Built up on him, stones that live and breathe into a spiritual fabric." The priests who have preached to you in the name of Jesus Christ have been moulding you, shaping you, all these hundred years to be what you are, to fit in with the pattern of Catholic life and worship to which you belong. To be a Catholic in this country at any rate is not just to stay put and say, "Oh well, I don't know, my people have always been like that". You have to take the strain of it. You have to say, "Yes, I do believe, I do want to save my soul. Here I am, Father—what can I do? I want to help."[1]

They built this church in the Gothic style; it was the fashion a hundred years ago. And, whatever you say in praise or dispraise of the Gothic, it has this claim at least on the gratitude of Christian people—it rests on the arch, the great pointed arch that is so apt a parable of the whole Christian idea. The arch, after all, is a kind of human miracle; its delicate shafts soaring upwards, and enabled by a feat of engineering to support a weight much heavier than themselves. Even in its older, rounded form, it had appealed to the imagination of some Christian poet, and inspired that beautiful hymn, "*Caelestis urbs Jerusalem*", which we still sing at a dedication feast. The hymn catches up St Paul's metaphor about Christians being built together on the foundation of the apostles and prophets, and sees, in our earthly temples made with hands, an image of that heavenly Jerusalem which is the Christian Church. The Church, militant on earth or triumphant in heaven, it is all one; and you and I are part of its organization, contribute, each of us, to the unity of the whole. We are not isolated units, like pebbles scattered on a beach; we are living stones, each of us occupying an appointed place in the divine scheme of architecture:

> Stones, that full many a stroke have felt,
> The salutary chisel dealt,
> Shaped by the hammer's master-blow,
> Rear the vast fabric from below,
> Or, in the arch's measured sweep,
> Their closely-fitting stations keep.

Shall we consider for a moment how all *that*, all that vision of unity, fits in with the three subjects we mentioned just now; the history of the Church at large, the history of the parish, and the history of those innumerable souls who have lived and worshipped here?

[1] The paragraphs that follow are identical with the central portion of the sermon preached on the occasion of the Centenary of St Marie's, Sheffield, as far as "the erosion of the centuries". See *supra*, pp. 292-3.

The keystone of an arch; how it explains to us the meaning of authority! Here you have one stone which is larger and heavier than all the rest, and you balance it in the very centre and at the very top of all the rest—surely that will be fatal? Already these other stones are thrusting inwards and downwards; surely this added weight will complete their ruin? But no, it is just the other way about; the keystone corrects the thrust of the others, and keeps them all in their place, by weighing down on them from above. And our Lord Jesus Christ, when he left a Church behind him to be his monument in a world so forgetful as this, would build it enduringly. It was to be for all nations; national rivalries, national differences of tradition would create strains and stresses, as time went on. It was to be for all sorts of men; allowance, then, had to be made for differences of temperament—some men are ever eager for novelties, some are for sticking to the old ways; there would be a thrust in this direction and in that, which must be counteracted somehow. Our Lord is himself the chief corner-stone of the heavenly building, and he would have a keystone to represent him in his Church on earth. As the keystone is only one stone in the arch, but greater and higher than the rest, so the Pope is only one bishop among the bishops of the world, but greater and higher than the rest, so as to flatten out all the strains and stresses which would otherwise make themselves felt in a Church not yet confirmed in sanctity. Let today's anniversary carry our minds back a little more than a hundred years, to the year 1850, when Pius IX, driven out by the violence of revolutionaries, returned to Rome from Gaeta. And let us thank God once again for the rock of Peter, which, in a world so full of flux and change, still defies the erosion of the centuries.

But always remember, this unity of the Church depends, as I say, on a conspiracy of human wills. A multitude of Christian people each of them determined to keep his or her place; to do his or her duty for the building up of the whole. Think, those of you who have already reached middle age, of some old woman who used to hobble into church, Sunday after Sunday, about the year 1914, when you sat fidgeting there among the schoolchildren. That old woman, perhaps, when she was among the schoolchildren herself, had seen this church opened. Her name swelled the roll of parishioners until the end of the century and then yours came in to take its place. That's what has been happening all the time. This parish is being built up from one generation to the next out of living stones—you and you and you.[1] We are building up the life of the family, of the club, of the parish, of every-

[1] See "The Centenary of St Marie's", p. 294.

thing we say or do. "The arch never sleeps", an architect will tell you —meaning that all the time stone is pressing against stone, and what seems to be rest is really only an equilibrium that depends on a balance of strains. It is the same with a parish, or with any collection of human souls. They are affecting one another, acting on one another, all the time. We are living stones set in a building and if one crumbles or threatens to crumble it would have an effect on the whole.

What sort of influence is yours in the parish? Are you one of the whisperers; one of the tale-bearers who know all the scandal of the district? Are you one of those self-contained people who never find time to do anything for their neighbours; who sit far back in church and don't listen to the notices for fear they might hear of some duty, some appeal they would rather avoid? Are you one of the murmurers who tell everybody how much better the parish was run in the old days? Are you anxious to discuss grievances and fan flames of every quarrel among your neighbours? Then the stones of this church will rise up in witness against you. You were one of the weak points in the architecture of this parish. It is people like you that makes its unity crumble away.

One more secret the arch has to tell us; a warning—or is it an encouragement?—for our individual lives. The stones fit into the arch only because the mason has cut them in a certain shape. "Stones that full many a stroke have felt, the salutary chisel dealt, shaped by the hammer's master-blow"—yes, we need that; you and I need that. The Architect who designed this great fabric, the holy Catholic Church, is also the Craftsman who shapes every life until it fits exactly into the niche he has appointed for it. And he shapes it not without the chisel, not without the hammer. I mean, his Providence, which so often entails for us a discipline of suffering. We cannot see why this or that trouble was allowed to befall us, or those who are dear to us; that is not wonderful. God does not disclose his design beforehand; we shall see the plans in heaven. But it is all *meant*; there was never yet a slip of the Craftsman's fingers; you niche is there, waiting for you, if you will allow hammer and chisel to do their work.[1]

When a church is consecrated, crosses, as you know, are built into the wall here and there to commemorate the fact. But in the heavenly edifice every stone, from our blessed Lady downwards, must bear the mark of the great Artificer—and his mark is always a cross.

May he grant eternal rest to the builders, the benefactors of this

[1] See "The Centenary of St Marie's", p. 295.

church, to all who have ministered and to all who have worshipped
here. May he bring us to that Temple where he is perfectly served
and is wholly manifested—the new Jerusalem—eternal in the heavens.

47

WESTMINSTER JUBILEE: II[1]

*He is like a man that would build a house, who dug, dug deep, and laid his
foundation on rock.—Luke 6. 58.*

IT is only two years ago that we celebrated the golden jubilee of this
cathedral's opening. It seemed so short an interval; only fifty years,
and already it had become part of the enduring fabric of London.
Today, we celebrate a diamond jubilee; it was in 1895 that the foundation-stone of the cathedral was laid. And somehow, that seems to
plunge us back into the past. In 1895 Gladstone was still alive, and
Ruskin, and Huxley, and Millais, and Coventry Patmore—names
which have become part of history. So sharp a line is drawn across our
memories by the death of the great Queen in 1901; what happened
before it, is yesterday; what happened since, today.

Someone else had died between the foundation-stone laying and the
opening: Cardinal Vaughan. We should do ill to forget, on this
occasion, one who was so uniquely the builder of this cathedral.
Between 1865 and 1935 there were only three cardinal archbishops of
Westminster; out of those seventy years he only held the See for
eleven, and from the very shortness of his pontificate he is in danger of
being forgotten. Not in Manchester, where St Bede's and the Rescue
Society are his memorials; not in the foreign missions, where he is still
revered as the founder of Mill Hill. But here, in Westminster, what
mark has he left? Look around you, and be satisfied of his greatness.

Very curiously, for a man drawn from a privileged class in an age of
privilege, he was a most pertinacious and successful beggar. It was,
perhaps, in some measure to humiliate the pride which he recognized
as his chief danger, that he devoted himself, all through his pastoral

---

[1] This sermon was preached at Westminster Cathedral on 29 June, the feast of SS. Peter
and Paul, 1955, at a solemn High Mass, offered to mark the diamond jubilee of the laying
of the foundation stone of the cathedral.

life, to the undignified business of going round hat in hand. But above all, what sustained him in his huge labours for the Church was that he was a man of faith, and a man of prayer. When he was appointed to Westminster, he found nothing here but a heavily mortgaged site. When he died, he left us the structure you see. The piety of the present century has enriched it with marbles and mosaics and much else; but the structure was his.

They dug deep, the Victorians; they dug deep. I do not mean simply that in material things they had a preference for the solid, the durable, which is not ours. I mean that they had a kind of intellectual integrity which would not let them build on insecure foundations of thought; they were not deceived by catch phrases and reach-me-down opinions; there is a conscientiousness about them which lends dignity even to their unbeliefs. Till yesterday, it was the fashion to sneer at them; poor things, they had so little sense of humour. Now, we are not quite certain that the laugh is all on one side, and we write of them, speak of them, still patronizingly but with a certain wistful respect. We have an uncomfortable consciousness that the capital on which we live was of their amassing. And when we look back on the history of the Church in England during the nineteenth century, we recognize —how could we fail to recognize?—the brilliant pioneer activities of Father Dominic, and Father Gentili, and Father Faber, and those others. But we forget the patient spadework which consolidated their achievements in the 'eighties and 'nineties. This cathedral is the climax and the trophy of it. They had dug themselves in.

Plain and severe its columns rise, framing something of the gloom of London in the deep embrasures of their windows; plain and severe is the lesson they preach to us, as we look back on the memory of the great man whose dream they were, still a dream when he awoke into eternity. Humility, and faith, and prayer; in those qualities the foundation was laid, and they must be the echoes which our footsteps arouse as we tread the long-drawn aisles of it.

Humility, not only because it dwarfs us; not only because the sacred ministers, even at the most solemn of functions, look no bigger than ants when you see them up the length of the nave, with the height of the chancel towering above them, to remind us what we men are in the context of eternity. That is true of other great buildings; this one humbles us with more intimate sense of inadequacy, because it is unfinished. For myself, I could never watch the tide of marble slowly creeping up the walls of this cathedral, without being reminded of that other task which remains unfinished, the conversion of England. All these years of endeavour, and what receding perspectives, what bare patches still! It calls for humility in us, because after all nothing under God's grace is going to convert England except integrated Catholic minds and devoted Catholic lives. If the religious map of England remains so patchy, the fault lies with us, patchy Catholics. Humility, then, first; in searching out our motives and seeing ourselves as we really are, we must dig deep.

And then, faith—the spirit of faith that moves mountains. I cannot tell how it is, but I never dip into the biographies of the great men and women who built up the Church in England during the last century without first being amazed at the spirit of faith in which they went about it, and then asking myself why I should be amazed; why should we be any different? The missioners, the founders of religious orders, on how vast a scale they went about it, considering what our numbers were! And we are so prudent in these matters, such realists. How clearly they saw sin for what it is, how instinctively they resented the dishonour done to religion! And we are so broadminded, so ready to make allowances. The spirit of faith—if we would reach down to the bare rock of supernatural conviction, we must dig deep.

And prayer, how it conditioned their outlook, those old-fashioned Catholics of yesterday! To be sure, the tempo of their lives was more leisurely than ours. We cover longer distances, we are more ingenious over our pleasures, we cultivate a wider range of social contacts than they. We have not time to read those long books, listen to those long speeches, that were once fashionable; must we perhaps add, to say those long prayers? Be sure of this—what impresses the multitude of sightseers who go round this cathedral from dawn to dusk is not Bentley's perspective or Gill's stations; it is the sudden reflection, "By Jove, these people do say their prayers!" Am I wrong in thinking that the gracious habit of dropping into a church on your way home from work is growing rarer, in these days when five *Hail Mary's* may cost you your seat on the bus? But it is prayer that does things. Even in ordering the most common affairs of daily life, we must dig deep.

The humility, the faith, the prayer in which Westminster Cathedral was built; if those be ours, God is able of these stones to raise up children to his holy Church.

48

THE GOOD PARISHIONER[1]

You too must be built up on him, stones that live and breathe, into a spiritual fabric.—1 Peter 2. 5.

THIS church, consecrated fifty years ago, has somehow a different flavour from the other churches of mid-London. Even in our over-civilized times, the presence of a river parts and estranges the inhabitants of the same town; build all the bridges you will, the people who live in Chelsea are not neighbours to the people who live in Battersea. There are isolated pockets, contained by the river on one side, which keep something of their own character, refuse to be wholly urbanized. Chelsea, as we all know, is not part of London, but a village rather uncomfortably close to London. The Underground passes it by.

Fitting, then, that this parish should be not quite like other parishes. The priests who have ministered to you within my own memory had a character of their own; Father O'Leary with his explosive views on the political situation in the early 'twenties, and Father Valentin[2] bringing out his little black note-book to ask if you had heard this one—may God rest them and reward them for the work they did here. But indeed, the really characteristic thing about this parish is that it is a parish in a sense in which the other parishes of mid-London are not. Week after week the priests in other churches are conscious of strange voices in the confessional, strange faces at the communion rail; the people at Mass on Sunday are the people who happen to live on the same tube, or happen to be lunching at the restaurant up the street. Here, if I mistake not, you are more of a family party; more than elsewhere, your fellow worshippers are your neighbours; you know who you are sitting next to, and will be able to say, afterwards, what she was wearing—just as we do in a remote country mission. Perhaps I am exaggerating the contrast, but the contrast is there.

And so I think that the parishioners of Holy Redeemer—yes, not just the congregation, but the parishioners of Holy Redeemer—are to be envied, because, unlike your neighbours, you do preserve something of the Christian pattern in your manner of church-going. This church

---

[1] This sermon was preached at the Church of Our Most Holy Redeemer and St Thomas More, Chelsea, on the golden jubilee of its consecration, 26 June 1955.

[2] Fr Barnabas O'Leary, parish priest of the Church of Our Most Holy Redeemer, 1917-33; Fr Philip Valentin, parish priest, 1933-45.

is not, for you, merely the nearest church, as it might be the nearest post-office or the nearest tobacconist, to be applied to in case of emergency, over a wedding or a sick-call; otherwise unvisited, because the times at the Cathedral are really so much more convenient. The tragedy of the church in country places is that the "buses don't run on Sunday mornings"; its tragedy in the towns is that they do. But this is your church; it belongs to you and you belong to it. When I talk of the Christian pattern, I mean this—that ideally the parish priest and his congregation form a single unit of Christendom, a cell with its own life within the life of the larger body. The parish priest is the spiritual father, who regenerates you at the font; the bread-winner who feeds you; he corrects, where it is needed, your faults. And you are brothers and sisters, who meet, week by week, at a common table, bound together at once by human neighbourliness and by a common faith. You are meant to find your salvation not as lonely individuals, lost in a crowd, but as members of a single organism, helping one another, encouraging one another, each making his or her contribution to the life of the whole.

St Paul, of course, is always going on at us about it. And St Peter, good honest man, is not ashamed to borrow a point now and again from St Paul's epistles. He found them hard going sometimes; he tells us as much; but they were useful all the same. And in the passage which I quoted to you just now as my text he picks up a favourite idea of St Paul's—that we Christian people are like the stones of a building, each kept in place by the others and each helping to keep the others in place. Which is surely the right thing to think about when we are commemorating, as we commemorate today, the consecration of a church. After all, why do we make such a fuss about the consecration of our churches; why does the ceremony take such a prodigiously long time? Bricks and mortar, in themselves, don't matter very much; if a church gets blitzed you can always build another. No, but, you see, every Christian church is a sacramental expression of *the* Christian Church; the unity of its structure is symbolic of the unity by which, and in which, Christians ought to live. That is why the hymn at the dedication of a church, the greatest hymn, "*Caelestis urbs Jerusalem,*" is all about the unity of the saints in heaven—*quae celsa de viventibus saxis ad astra tolleris*: the heavenly city is built, as St Peter tells us, of living stones. And of course the unity of the saints in heaven is only the continuation of that unity in which Christian people ought to live on earth. The consecration of this church, fifty years ago, was really the consecration of its worshippers.

Fifty years—it's not really a very long time; but somehow in London (if we may call it London) the buildings change so much, and the people change their addresses so much, that even in that space of time an institution begins to feel venerable. Even in that space of time, how many children have been regenerated at this font, how many a man and woman have plighted their marriage vows here, how often the bell has tolled for a Christian soul gone to its rest!

And if you go beyond that, and think of all the communions—each a separate event—that have been made at these altar rails, all the secrets that have been whispered in these confessionals, you can read here a pageant of history, enacted in the lives of simple folk like you and me. And all the while the personnel of the actors has been changing; one has died and another been born, one has moved and another has come into the parish; a long procession of humanity, in which you, who sit there, have your part. What I want to emphasize more particularly is that we oughtn't to think of all these people, who have used the church during the last fifty years, as lonely units, slinking into church and slinking out again, strangers in a strange world. They were, and are, your fellow parishioners.

What a dreadful word that is, "to edify"! When we hear a book described as an edifying book, we assume without further information, that it is written without style, without humour, without interest. And when we hear that we are going to be introduced to an edifying person, we expect at once that we shall be put off by embarrassing enthusiasms, by forbidding airs of piety. How restive it makes us when St Paul is translated as having written, "Let every one of you please his neighbour unto good, to edification"! But it only means, "Each of us ought to give way to his neighbour, where it serves a good purpose by building up his faith". And that is all edification means, building up; you have got to be a living stone, fitting into your place and helping other people to fit into theirs. We don't do that, commonly, by looking intense and delivering ourselves of pious clichés. "Nor knowest thou what argument thy life to thy neighbour's creed hath lent"—on the whole it is by being natural, and at the same time by being considerate for other people's feelings, that we shall be able to make any contribution towards the good of the society in which we live. But we have a contribution to make, all of us, even if it is only a tiny one. Every stone in the building counts.

As I say, in most London churches we don't know our fellow worshippers even by sight, and our only chance of edifying them is by our behaviour in church. It may be doubted whether we are always successful in this. If you come into church, for example, and take up your position at the extreme edge of the pew, by way of keeping it to yourself: if you look round wearily at everybody who tries to get past, with the air of protesting, "How can I say my prayers with people climbing over me like this?"—if you behave like that (and nearly all Catholics do), you fail to edify. But here, where you see the same faces Sunday after Sunday, find the same dogs and the same babies tied up to the door, you are not just one of a crowd. You belong, whether you like it or not, to a little Catholic world in Chelsea; a microcosm of the universal Church, in which you are meant to find yourself, to which you have duties. Whenever St Paul writes to the Corinthians or the Philippians, urging on them the duty of charity, of forbearance, of courtesy, of minding their own business, he is talking to you, telling you to be a limb of that body, to be a stone in that building, which is the parish of the Holy Redeemer. For that is the normal pattern of Christendom, that the Church universal should be built up of healthy cells, which depend in their turn on the health of the members who belong to them.

May I, then, propose to you very briefly an examination of conscience, by way of making sure that you are just not a good Christian, but a good parishioner? Charity, after all, begins at home. Are you, perhaps, the sort of person who always sits at the extreme back of the church, so that the notices may be inaudible; who never takes a look at the notice-board; who hurries out of church in the middle of the last gospel so as to avoid the embarrassment of meeting his neighbours? That is to be too little of a parishioner. At the same time, it is possible to be too much of a parishioner. I mean, to have such an exaggerated sense of your own importance to the congregation that you are jealous of any infringement of your rights, even if you find somebody installed in what happens to be your favourite seat. Not a flower must be put on the altar, not a light turned off, not a hymnbook returned to its place, without your sanction. Oh, it is all infinitively small; but how cruelly these infinitely small things can disturb the peace of the parish!

There are more serious questions to ask yourself. Are you one of the scandal-mongers, the back-biters? There are few faults that are so often overlooked by the consciences of those who are guilty of them as this, perhaps the most odious. Check yourself the next time it occurs to you to say something disagreeable, and don't say it; ask yourself afterwards what possible good you could have done by saying it. Are you one of the quarrellers, working off your ill temper, which you probably can't help, by taking it out of your neighbours, which you can help? Are you one of the critics, who must be always complaining that things weren't done that way in the late rector's time, or that things aren't done that way at St Mary's? Are you fond of repeating ecclesiastical gossip, of airing mildly unorthodox views, without considering whether you will give scandal to some of your audience; or even, perhaps, half hoping that you will? Oh yes, these are easy habits to slip into, and perhaps we shall not be very harsly judged for it. But you are the person St Paul wrote his epistles to.

How curious it is that we should always be tempted to think of religion in negative terms, when it is all so positive! We have been speaking as if the well-being of a parish like this depended on not doing things. Rather, let us ask Jesus Christ, the chief Corner-stone who binds all in one, to endow this parish abundantly with the gift of his own charity; may you all live as neighbours, and each of you, in his neighbour, see Christ. And when this church celebrates, fifty years hence, the centenary of its consecration, perhaps with daughter churches scattered here and there, to absorb the overflow of its apostle-ship, men will be saying, "This parish was built up out of living stones, men and women linked together by a holy pride in the service of God. That is why it stands for a monument of our Catholic past; that is why it flourished, and grew stronger, and yielded a harvest in eternity."

49

THE BRITISH ASSOCIATION: II[1]

See how the lilies of the field grow: they do not toil or spin: and yet I tell you that even Solomon in all his glory was not arrayed like one of these.— Matthew 6. 28.

This is the second time I have had the honour of preaching before representatives of the British Association, gathered for their annual conference.[2] And on both occasions, when I looked at the Sunday gospel to ask what message I was to deliver, it was this extract

---

[1] This sermon was preached at the Pro-Cathedral, Clifton, on 4 September 1955, at Pontifical High Mass attended by scientists taking part in the meetings of the British Association.

[2] See sermon preached before representatives of the British Association at Dundee, 31 August 1947, p. 261.

from the Sermon on the Mount, in which the frantic struggles of mankind for existence are contrasted with the unhurrying beneficence of almighty God. It seems like a deliberate challenge. Just when we are met to applaud the triumphs of human research, we are reminded that the wisest man of antiquity could not learn how to match the lilies of the field. Just when we are contemplating the possible dangers with which our latest discoveries threaten the future of humanity, and even of the world, that calm voice comes to us from the mountain of the Beatitudes, "Do not fret over tomorrow; leave tomorrow to fret over its own needs; for today, today's troubles are enough".

We are often told, both by the friends of religion and by its enemies, that Christendom has never really learned the meaning of the Sermon on the Mount. "I tell you", our Lord says, "that you should not offer resistance to injury"—how is it, then, that Christian nations are still prepared to settle their differences by the arbitrament of war? "If thy neighbour", our Lord says, "is ready to go to law with thee over thy cloak, let him have thy coat also"—how is it, then, that Christian nations cling with such obstinacy to their territorial possessions, their economic advantages? Let us admit, in ideal at least, the justice of these contentions; but let us point out that they do not go far enough. "Do not lay up treasure for yourselves on earth", our Lord says—how is it, then, that Christian people put their money in the bank? "Do not fret over your life", our Lord says, "how to provide it with food and drink"—how is it, then, that Christian statesmen are hag-ridden by the difficulty of making exports balance with imports?

With these niceties of moral theology we are not concerned today. But, if we read between the lines of the Sermon on the Mount, it is easy to understand why our Lord laid so much stress on the happy-go-lucky finance of the ravens, the unstudied beauty of the lilies. He wanted us to see that man has two ends, a natural and a supernatural end; that this involves him in a twofold struggle, the struggle for existence in this world, and the struggle for eternal life in the world to come. And he wanted us to see that if we were not careful, or rather if we were too careful, we should lose sight of our supernatural end in the pursuit of the natural. The enemy was materialism.

Materialism—when that word is mentioned, you, who are a devotee of the natural sciences, begin to feel uncomfortable. Not that the scientist is to be thought of as a specially worldly person; indeed his reputation is if anything just the opposite. Archimedes is so intent on his studies that he does not notice his country has been captured; Newton makes two holes in his door, a large one for the cat and a small one for the kitten. But the impact of scientific discovery on us others is to make the material world a more comfortable and a more interesting place. For the pure scientist, research is its own reward; he does not want to split the atom, he wants to see whether the atom can be split; he does not want to reach the moon, he wants to find out whether the moon is accessible. But we others are interested in problems, not in theorems, and for the last century or more we have demanded of science that it should produce results. And we have not been disappointed. To put the thing graphically, it took John Wesley a full day to get from Bristol to Crewe; the train does it in something over four hours, and we should expect to do it in less than an hour by air travel. Life lasts longer and is more comfortable, working hours are shorter, disease and pain are more tolerable nowadays than they were two hundred years ago. And we thank God for the conspiracy of human skill and enterprise which has made all this possible.

But, this cushioned existence of ours in the modern world, does it make it easier for us, or harder for us, to live by the spirit of the Sermon on the Mount? At first sight, evidently, easier. We do not tremble for the harvest, saying "What shall we eat?"—we know it is all laid up in cold storage for us, somewhere beyond the seas. We do not feel alarm over the dwindling flocks of sheep, saying, "How shall we find clothing?"—we are dressed from head to foot in mysterious fabrics of whose warp and woof we know nothing. And our statesmen promise us security; a network of pension schemes and insurance policies guarantee us against a fall into destitution. We do not ask how the bill is to be paid; that is the business of the Exchequer. Surely, then, the modern man, relieved of these day-to-day anxieties, is in a better position than his forefathers to take this world's problems in his stride, and devote himself wholly to life's real business, the finding of the kingdom of God.

The argument is a specious one; but alas, experience reminds us that it is false. If only for this reason, that man is a born worrier, and even when he is given, and guaranteed, a sufficiency, he will still worry about getting something more. Luxuries will become a necessity to his table; the needs of decency and warmth will be replaced by the needs of fashion. He will begin to demand, not merely a living but a certain standard of living; and once that demand is made, there is no end to the possibilities of it. But all that lies on the surface; there is a deeper, underlying difficulty which inhibits our modern approach to God. In early days, or among primitive surroundings, man lives close to nature, and is reminded at every turn of his dependence upon the providence of God. In a more elaborate civilization, where a network of human agencies comes between him and his sources of supply, he still admits that dependence, but the thought of it is no longer vivid to him. When the harvest fails, we fall to our knees; when the electric light fails, we ring up the power station. Long ago, God warned his ancient people about the temptation that would come to them when they reached the plenty of the Promised Land, a temptation to forget the hard discipline of their wanderings in the desert. "Never wert thou to flatter thyself that valour of thy own, strength of thy own, had won thee wealth; rather to bethink thyself of the Lord thy God, and the strength he gives thee." And so it is with this promised land into which the discoveries of science have brought us. Man in rude surroundings, fed by his own plough, clothed from his own loom, sharpening his own arrows to defend himself against hostile attack, is quick to realize his own insufficiency, and fall back upon God. In a world of combine harvesters and nylon and guided missiles, the lesson is not so easy to read. Because our promised land flows with pasteurized milk and synthetic honey, we forget where the raw materials came from, and so we are in danger of forgetting who it was that gave them, and what he asks of us.

If we have got into that frame of mind, we must not blame the men of science for it. They did not join in a conspiracy to pamper us, and to spoil the simplicity of our outlook. They only set out, very humbly, to read the book of God's creation; read between the lines of it, and piece together, if they could, something of its marvellous pattern. God has allowed them, in these latter days, to succeed beyond the measure of their hopes; the boundaries of our knowledge have spread in a hundred directions. King Solomon prayed for wisdom, and was granted all that he did not ask for; in wealth, in glory, no king was to compare with him. So it has been with these patient brethren of ours; they sought knowledge, and with knowledge wealth has come to mankind; a general diffusion of wealth unexampled in history. But something else was granted to Solomon—his very name bears witness to it—the gift of peace. And peace has not come to us with this prosperity of ours; neither peace between nations, nor (more importantly) peace of mind in ourselves. The measure of human achievement dazzles and distracts us, like children at their lessons who keep on looking round to see what is happening in the next class. We do not put first things first; our Lord himself has told us how to do that, "Make it your first care to find the kingdom of God, and his approval; and all these things shall be yours without the asking".

The science of the saints—how is it that after all these centuries of Christian teaching it has made so little headway? To find God—no telescope will help you there; you must find God in yourself. To find yourself—no microscope will help you there; humility is the solvent you need. Only by realizing our own insufficiency do we realize what God is to us, what God must be to us, if we are to be anything; and only in that way do we realize what God is to everything, *Rerum Deus tenax vigor*, "the persistent sap of things", lending them their existence.

All that physical science couldn't tell us, because that doesn't lie within its terms of reference—all that we really mean, and the world really means, why we are here in the world and the world is here in us —we learn only in proportion as we make a surrender of ourselves to God. That is why even philosophy is called the *ancilla*, the handmaid, of theology; if we can get that right, then the kingdom of God will be ours, and all things—even the innermost secret of the uttermost star —will be ours without the asking.

50

CHRISTIAN UNITY AND ZEAL[1]

You must be always humble, always gentle; patient, too, in bearing with one another's faults, as charity bids; eager to preserve that unity the Spirit gives you, whose bond is peace.—Ephesians 4. 2-3.

THE word "conversion" has two different meanings; it may signify a change of life, or a change of outlook. When Pascal was converted in 1654, he became an unworldly man, instead of a worldly one. When Newman was converted in 1845, he embraced a true system of Christian philosophy, but the tenour of his life was what it had been before. Which kind of change was it that came over Saul of Tarsus, when a fall from his horse, at the Damascus gate, knocked him sensible? I think, both.

At first sight, you would be inclined to say that it was only a change of outlook. After all, Saul the Pharisee was a conscientious man according to his lights, full of zeal for that law which was the unique religious

[1] This sermon was preached at St Etheldreda's, Ely Place, London, on 25 January, the Feast of the Conversion of St Paul, 1956, at an evening Mass arranged by the University of London Catholic Society to mark the conclusion of the Church Unity Octave.

heritage of his fellow countrymen. No one was more ready, afterwards, to accuse himself of his earlier faults, but if he is the chief of
sinners, the reason is that he used to persecute the Church of Christ—
that and nothing else. Must we not say, then, that his character remained
unmodified after his conversion, like Newman's? That he was a man
passionately devoted to the cause of religious truth as he apprehended
it, Judaism today, Christianity tomorrow? That the same quality which
made him a good persecutor of Christianity made him a good
Christian?

I think that if we say that we do less than justice to the character of
a man who, of all the scriptural writers, has left us the most of himself.
Saul of Tarsus seems to have been a man of one idea, a one-track
thinker, a stranger to pity, visited by no scruples, no afterthoughts.
Whereas Paul the Apostle is a man of the utmost considerateness; he
will maintain his policy just so far as it is needed to secure some
important end, and then, for fear of hurting other people's feelings, will
modify or reverse it. He sees both ways; and therein, I think, lies much
of his greatness.

Take, as one instance of that, his attitude about the law of Moses,
and whether Christians ought to feel bound by it. Here are some
Jewish agitators in Galatia going about telling the Gentile converts,
St Paul's own converts, that if they want to be Christians they ought
to be circumcised, and keep the Mosaic law. Look how St Paul ful-
minates against them: "I would rather they should lose their own
manhood, these authors of your unrest. . . . Who are they, these people
who insist on your being circumcised? They are men, all of them, who
are determined to keep up outward appearances, so that the cross of
Christ may not bring persecution upon them." And when you read
such things, you are inclined to shake your head and say, "Ah, the
old Paul! The same as ever, only now he thinks the law of Moses is a
trap to ensnare men's consciences, whereas he used to tell us the law
of Moses was the only thing that mattered!"

Yes, I know; and now let me switch you over from Galatia to
Corinth. Here are the Gentile converts, his converts again, telling one
another it's all nonsense about not eating meat that has been offered
to false gods. (I suppose it was remaindered and sold in the market next
day, so that you got it at a reduction.) "The Jews can't, of course,"
these people told one another, "because it's against their law; but that's
got nothing to do with us. We know better than that; a false god is
nothing; so meat that has been offered to a false god hasn't been
offered to anything. Christ has called us to liberty; don't you remember

Paul telling us so? *I am free to do what I will*; that was his slogan." And so on. Now, as a matter of fact, when the apostles met at Jerusalem to discuss the whole matter, they had laid it down that everybody, Jew or Gentile, had got to respect the law of Moses by abstaining from defiled meat. And St Paul could have referred them to that decision; but no, he gives them his own sentiments instead. "Each of you ought to study the well-being of others, not his own. . . . If someone says to you, This has been used in idolatrous worship, then for the sake of your informant you must refuse to eat; it is a matter of conscience—his conscience, I mean, not yours. . . . If a mouthful of food is an occasion of sin to my brother, I will abstain from flesh meat perpetually, rather than be the occasion of my brother's sin." St Paul is taking up arms, you see, on the other side of the controversy. He knows that it takes all sorts, Jew and Gentile, to make a Church, and somehow we have all got to stick together.

It takes all sorts to make a Church—as we know, it is the main tragedy of Christendom that people won't see that. Always there will be Christian people, good Christians for the most part, who want to strike out and try new experiments. The Gospel of Christ isn't just a tradition which is meant to lie dormant through the ages; it has life in it, has explosive material in it. Always, whether inside the Church or among the other denominations, there will be a party which wants to try new experiments, and another party which hangs back and says, "Yes, but is it true to tradition? Is it true to the spirit of Christ?" Outside the Church, that generally means a schism; look how hard John Wesley laboured to keep his followers within the bounds of the Establishment, and yet the grass had scarcely grown over his tomb before Wesleyanism became one among the sects! Inside the Church, what commonly results is the loss of splendid initiatives. Think what the history of China might have been, if the Jesuits there, long ago, had not been hampered in their work, to satisfy the scruples of Jansenism! Always the same melancholy pattern; Christian zeal a threat to Christian unity; Christian unity a drag on Christian zeal!

That's why I say that I think much of St Paul's greatness lies in this quality of restraint, of prudence, of consideration for other people's feelings. Always you will find him eager to go back to headquarters and see the other apostles and make sure that he is not getting out of step; Titus must be circumcised, Timothy must be circumcised, just for the fear of possible scandal; never, despite all his missionary zeal, will St Paul build on another man's foundation—that is, if you put it into coarse modern English, poach on another man's preserves; he will keep the Jewish feasts, take Jewish vows, to make it clear that he, Paul, champion of the Gentiles as he is, does not mean to show any personal disrespect to the traditions of his fathers. I don't think all that came natural to him; by nature, as we were saying, he was a fire-brand, a bull in a china-shop. The other apostles will have seen that, and been afraid of the consequences; that is why, when he came back to Jerusalem after his conversion, they spirited him away to Tarsus—just as the Franciscans, centuries later, deported St Ignatius from the Holy Land; they thought he would be too much of a good thing. No, it wasn't St Paul's nature; it was his supernature, imposed on him as the result of his conversion; by the grace of God he was what he was. The charity of Christ constrained him.

Charity—that, for St Paul, was everything; in little or in large it was the cement which tied together the whole edifice of Christendom; the nervous system which protected the organic unity of the mystical body. No wonder, then, that when our minds turn, as they do during the Church Unity Octave, to the divisions of Christendom, we should look to St Paul for aid. He has finished his course on earth; there is still a work he has to do in heaven. By a strange irony he, with that other great champion of Christian unity, St Augustine, has been honoured time out of mind, has been quoted in season and out of season, by the defenders of the Reformation. We pray, then, that they may read him with fresh eyes; that they may become, as the years go on, more Pauline. But at the same time we have a petition to make for ourselves; that in all our love for the Church and our ambition for the spread of Christian truth we may be living models, not only of St Paul's zeal, but of St Paul's charity. The great courtesy, the great considerateness which was given to him at his conversion—we can never have too much of this, never examine our consciences too carefully about this.

Meanwhile, let us remember that when we pray for the unity of Christendom we are not only praying for those who are now separated from us, that they may be restored to the fullness of Christian fellowship. We are praying also for unity among ourselves; that we may be spared, in our day, those shocks and strains inside the Church which have so often given rise to scandal and unhappiness, sometimes to lapses from the faith. We live in times of great activity among the rank and file of Catholic people. That watchword given us by the late Holy Father, "to renew all things in Christ", has stirred our imaginations; it is like St Paul telling the Corinthians, "I am free to do what I will". Catholics have entered into new political and social groupings;

have explored new by-ways of philosophy; have cultivated new art-forms, new idioms, in literature; there are movements among us to get this and that done, to go back to older models of worship, or to restore the vernacular liturgy; and there are strictly spiritual movements, like the Legion of Mary, which encourage a lay apostolate. All such departures are capable of setting up stresses and strains within the Catholic body, at present hardly foreseen; may lead to excesses and to conflicts with ecclesiastical authority. That danger we must bear in mind, when we ask our Lord, at the breaking of the Host, to grant peace and unity to his Church.

Charity, they say, begins at home; and that spirit of charity which St Paul saw as the bond of Christian fellowship begins with you and me; begins in the diocese, in the parish, at the club, round the tea-table. It is a force which you and I, in our small way, can generate or fail to generate; in moments of careless gossip, when we malign, and criticize, and complain; in petty struggles for unimportant posts of leadership, in cabals and whispering campaigns. Talk, always, as you would talk if St Paul was in the room. "You must be always humble, always gentle; patient, too, in bearing with one another's faults, as charity bids; eager to preserve that unity the Spirit gives you, whose bond is peace." That is the language of a man who was aflame with zeal, and who felt deeply; "Does anyone feel a scruple? I share it. Is anyone's conscience hurt? I am ablaze with indignation." The same Paul underneath, who had once been Saul of Tarsus; but named now, the wolf turned into the lamb, because the love of Christ constrained him.

51

WHAT BISHOPS ARE FOR[1]

Aram was the father of Aminadab, Aminadab of Naasson, Naasson of Salmon.—Matthew 1. 4.

A SOMEWHAT uninspiring text, you will complain, taken from a somewhat uninspiring gospel. Here are we, gathered in this cathedral town, so beautifully named after our Lady's well; it is our Lady's birthday, and we are giving her a birthday present by presenting

---

[1] This sermon was preached at Motherwell Cathedral on 8 September, the Nativity of our Lady, 1955, on the occasion of the Enthronement of Monsignor J. D. Scanlan as Bishop of Motherwell.

a bishop to her vacant See. And as we listen to the deacon's chant, proclaiming the words of life, what rewards us? Forty-odd names from the Old Testament, mostly people we have never heard of. Could not the liturgy have issued a more resonant challenge to our devotion?

That is only a surface view. If we stand back from the picture, forget the details, and try to capture the general effect, we shall see what a gracious effect it is; this dull genealogy bears witness that our Lord was truly Man. All very well for St John to start his gospel, "At the beginning of time the Word already was"; but if that had been the whole truth there would have been no Incarnation, and no redemption. No, St Matthew insists, when our Lord came to earth, he came as a member of a human family; when he died on the cross, he "slept with his fathers" —Abraham, Isaac and Jacob waited there, beyond the grave, to welcome him. Not that St Matthew is laying any stress on mere physical descent; as we know, the list ends with our Lord's foster-father, and there is reason to think that some of the other names given are not those of father and son, except by adoption. No, but the same care and protection which St Joseph gave to our blessed Lord, the same instinct of fatherhood, had built up all those earlier generations, right back to Abraham—right back, St Luke points out, to Adam, who knew no father but almighty God.

And now let us notice another consideration which arises out of this prosaic list of names. I mean, its continuity. This genealogical table runs right across the expanse of human history, like a majestic river that nourishes, and is nourished by, the plain. And just as such a river will pass through alternations of scenery, now between frowning hills and now across flat, marshy levels, so this most important pedigree in all history has its ups and downs, its alternations. From Juda down to Jesse, the persons mentioned are quite unimportant; no great warriors here, as far as we know, no judges who directed the counsels of a people. Then, with David, the family suddenly attains royal status, and right down to the time of the Captivity they are rulers, influencing for good or ill the lives of their fellow countrymen. After the Captivity, there is a fresh change in its fortunes; it comes down in the world, by gradual stages perhaps, and when the hour of destiny strikes, how is it represented? By a working man who makes chairs and tables for the people of Nazareth. But always, among all these vicissitudes, the stream flows continuously.

And there is a third point to notice, before we finish our meditation on these opening verses of St Matthew. The unimportant people get their mention quite as much as the important ones. David and Solomon and Zorobabel, they are all just items in the catalogue, there is no thumb-nail biography to tell us who they were and what they did. They stand side by side with Aram and Aminadab and Naasson and Salmon, mere nobodies as far as history is concerned. As if almighty God were determined to show that it didn't matter for his purposes whether the people he chose to be our Lord's ancestors were men of fine natural abilities, men of commanding personality, or not. He didn't always choose the eldest son; Jacob and Juda weren't eldest sons, David and Solomon weren't eldest sons. God's choice is not the world's choice: he picks on just anybody, and makes him into the kind of instrument he wants him to be. Aram and Aminadab and Naasson and Salmon—yes, they will do. "By arms, by force, nothing canst thou; my spirit is all, says the Lord of hosts."

Have I forgotten that we are enthroning a bishop? Am I just giving you the beginning of a course of meditations on the New Testament? No, all that I've been saying has a relevance and an importance of its own, if we are to understand what bishops are like, and what bishops are for. In this country, the name of "bishop" is suspect; our non-Catholic neighbours here are singularly wedded to an alternative form of Church government. We must be clear, then, and accurate in explainto them exactly where we stand. May we just take those three points in reverse order, the three points I have been mentioning about our Lord's ancestors, and see how they apply to the office of the episcopate? "By arms, by force, nothing canst thou; my spirit is all, says the Lord of hosts"; a bishop is and will be what God makes of him; that and nothing else. He is, above all, a link in a chain; he is part of the universal episcopate, and part, therefore, of the Church's continuity. And he is our father in God.

The instinct which lies behind the Presbyterian protest is an understandable one. Can it be right, in a religious context, to set a mortal man head and shoulders above his fellows, in a position which demands, not mere loyalty, not mere compliance, but obedience in the name of religion? Is not this to court the dangers of pride, of avarice, of petty tyranny? And indeed, in times when the episcopal office carried with it great revenues, or a high position in affairs of state, there was some reason to fear that it would fall into the hands of the ambitious schemer. But as things are, our safeguard lies in the very nature of the case. How could a man of any imagination covet the spiritualities of such an office, when he reflects on the dreadful responsibilities they entail? To bind and loose; to give an example to the faithful; to choose out men for the ministry; to appoint the right man to the right mission; to discipline the offender; to correct the erring—how should any man think to do this by the exercise of his own gifts, by the light of his own judgment? Will he not rather say, with King Solomon, "Lord, what am I? No better than a little child, that has no skill to find its way back and forth. And here am I, thy servant, lost among the thousands of the people thou hast chosen"? By his own strength he can do nothing; what is left but to pray, and ask us, his brethren, to pray, that God will make him the kind of bishop God wants him to be?

But we haven't said enough about the meaning of this occasion, when we have spoken of the bishop's relations to his flock. He is in relation, too, with all the bishops of the world, bearing witness, as one of their number, to the tradition which has been handed down to us by the apostles. Just as the continuity of our Lord's ancestry guarantees his humanity to us, so the continuity of the episcopate, linking us with the past, guarantees to us the inviolable deposit of Catholic truth. Through times of prosperity and times of persecution, that stream of witness has flowed on, and it unites us not only with the past but with the future. When the Council of the Vatican was suspended in 1870, there was no diocese of Motherwell to be represented there. But if and when it is summoned to reassemble, the bishop of this diocese will take his place with the rest, and bear testimony to the faith which has been handed down, across the centuries, to the people of Lanark. So that the appointment of a new bishop is not merely an occasion for thinking about our own corner of Christendom, our own churches, our own schools. We ought to be renewing our loyalty to the Holy Father; we ought to be remembering those bishops in many parts of the world who are maligned, and persecuted, and imprisoned for the faith. And we greet his Lordship not only as our ruler, but as our representative in the counsels of the universal Church.

But above all we greet him as our Father in God. That advantage at least we must be permitted to claim for the episcopal system of government; when you are dealing with a personal ruler, he can be fond of you, and you can be fond of him. No such exchange of sentiments is possible when you are dealing with a synod or with a committee. And a bishop, because he is privileged to enter into such personal relations with his flock, has an opportunity which, in these bureaucratic days, is granted to few of us. He will be remembered on earth, and judged in heaven, not so much by his administrative competence, not so much by his judicial prudence, as by the eyes that kindled at his coming, the hearts that were lightened at his passing by. There is, to be sure, a kind of geniality of manner which can be assumed at will, a gift of posing well in front of the camera—that is not what we are speaking of. We are speaking of a real affection that comes from, and is felt by, the heart. It is an auspicious circumstance that your new bishop, in coming to you, comes home; it is easier for a man to make friends where he belongs. But even a genuine natural benevolence is not enough; life makes such a drain on us, we cannot be sure that our good dispositions will last. No, the fatherliness which is the true characteristic of a bishop can only come from him, after whom all fatherhood in heaven and earth is named. We must ask him for the abundant gift of his spirit, if the task of our new bishop is to be, not a round of office routine, but a perpetual romance.

And so we wish him many happy returns of our Lady's birthday; may her gracious influence linger always, as her name lingers, in the diocese of Motherwell.

52

SHREWSBURY CATHEDRAL[1]

Not unremembered, Lord, not unrewarded be these services done to thy people.—Nehemias 5. 19.

WHEN you find yourself in one of our great English towns, asking the way to the Catholic cathedral, the answer is not always easily forthcoming. "The Roman Catholic cathedral?" says the benevolent stranger, knitting his brows, as if to imply that the cathedral of any other denomination would be less of a problem; less remote, less secluded. That does not happen in Shrewsbury. There are certain townscapes (if I may so call them) scattered up and down England —not many of them—that catch the eye with a sense of beauty, and remain fixed in the memory, so that they recur to the mind whenever you hear the place mentioned. Such, for example, is the view of Durham across the valley, such is the hill on which Lincoln stands. In the same way, the word "Shrewsbury" recalls a definite picture to the mind of anyone who has lived here; that of the town walls rising from the river, and the roofs massed behind them. At one point, just where

[1] This sermon was preached at Shrewsbury on 30 October 1956, on the occasion of the centenary of the opening of the cathedral.

it was needed, just where an artist would demand it, the line of them is broken by an ecclesiastical building perched, after the Italian fashion, on the very edge of the slope. "What is that?" the visitor asks instinctively; and this time there is no hesitation. "That? Oh, that is the Roman Catholic cathedral."

Such pictures are, perhaps, more firmly impressed on the memory if they are associated, for you, with some intimate spiritual experience. It was when I was living just across the Severn that I first conceived those doubts which brought me into the Church.[1] And always, on the further bank of the river, the cathedral church of Our Lady Help of Christians stood like an obstinate question-mark. How was I to decide whether it was a beacon-light, or will-o'-the-wisp?

When an architect views such a building, shored up on the slopes of an almost precipitous hill, his comment will probably be, "Most of the money must have gone underground". I dare say it did; if so, let it stand to us for a parable of the very thing we are here to commemorate this morning—the patient striving of men now forgotten, who were content that their work should go underground, so far as human memory was concerned; they built for the glory of God, not for the praise of men. When I say that, I am not thinking of the innumerable benefactors whose shillings and pennies have gone to the building of this, as of all our English churches, though we should do ill to forget them today. I am thinking rather of certain influential Catholics who lived and died a century ago or thereabouts, the leaders in that movement which is known to historians of art as the Gothic Revival, but to us, in Newman's phrase, as the Second Spring. Men well known in their own day, but now—memories are so short, and times move so quickly—almost forgotten.

I will mention only two, both laymen: Ambrose de Lisle Phillipps and John, Earl of Shrewsbury. It was, for the most part, their faith and their munificence which drew a cordon of spacious neo-Gothic buildings right across the northern Midlands—Nottingham Cathedral, Mount St Bernard Abbey, Oscott, St Chad's, Birmingham, and the rest. I half expect you to interrupt me there, with the complaint that I have left out Shrewsbury cathedral. Was not that built by Pugin, with the Earl of Shrewsbury for its founder? No, Pugin died in 1852, and the cathedral was built by his son; the Earl died in the same year, and his heir, its chief benefactor, died two months before it was opened. It is the last, late flowering of a thing so remote from us that

[1] Mgr Knox taught at Shrewsbury School during the First World War. See Evelyn Waugh, *The Life of Ronald Knox*, pp. 143-150.

it is beginning to have a kind of period value, Pugin's Gothic. And it is the abiding monument of that great generation of Catholics whose faith and liberality put the Church back on the map a hundred years ago; men whose lives were a model and a challenge to posterity.

A hundred years ago—how long it seems! The sermon at the cathedral opening was preached by Cardinal Wiseman, to us almost a legendary figure. A man of my own age who was present on that occasion—Provost Weedall, for example, from Oscott—dated back behind the French Revolution. The whole Catholic population of the Shrewsbury diocese only amounted to twenty thousand souls, for the most part scattered in rural areas; the great development of Birkenhead was only just beginning, and it was hardly more than a dozen years since "Crewe" had been the name of a farmhouse. If you or I could be carried back, by a stroke of the magician's wand, a century back into the past, what should we be feeling about the ceremony itself, and our fellow worshippers? We should feel as if we were looking round not merely at a different age, but at a different world.

We say that; and yet we know, as we say it, that we are in a sense allowing imagination to cheat us. We pin-point a particular date in the past, and contrast it with our own, as if nothing had been happening in between. But history is not a series of discrete moments, it is a continuous stream; our past belongs to us, and we to it; patient years of human foresight and human endeavour have made us what we are. The Shrewsbury diocese is a very different thing from what it was in the time of our grandfathers. I suppose there are four priests in it for every priest there was then; four churches in it for every church there was then; and the Catholic body, instead of being one in fifty, is much nearer being one in ten of the population. All that is due to a multitude of causes, but we must not think of it as an automatic process, to be accounted for by natural and economic developments. It has meant, all through these hundred years, the patient work of human beings; of priests, secular and regular; of the nuns, nagging at us with their unobtrusive persistence; of schoolmasters and scoutmasters, and Brothers of St Vincent de Paul. The setting up of a new diocese is not the act of a moment, done and finished with once for all. It is the beginning of a new chapter in religious history, a continuous process which has lasted to our time and will last beyond us. Of that process, you are a part, formed by, and to some extent forming in your turn, its traditions.

And the centre of all this activity is, must be, your cathedral church; the cathedral church is the hub and the hearth of the diocese. It is a

O

sacrament in stone, symbolizing for us and guaranteeing to us that unity of structure which every see of Christendom enjoys, and enjoys in its own right. We are accustomed to think of the unity of the Church as depending on the Papacy, and so in a sense it must, because there has got to be somebody who can make policy decisions at top level. But the essential unity of the Church is that of a body, of which each cell is a diocese, and the nucleus around which that cell coheres is the bishop, or, if you will, his cathedral. Bishop and cathedral are complementary, belong to one another, just as a man's home belongs to him and yet, in a sense, he belongs to his home. The Church loves to derive her symbolism from the common things of life; she seizes on the essentials of the picture and makes them her own. How well we know what it is to go round and see a friend, to recognize that he is at home because his hat and his stick are in the hall, and then go in to find him sitting in his favourite chair! The hat, the stick, the chair— the mitre, the pastoral staff, the throne, the bishop is at home in his cathedral, he is in his element there. He and it form two sides, as it were, of one medal, which teaches us how we are to enjoy and to realize the indestructible unity of a Christian diocese; this is our Father, here is our home.

We men are only passengers through the world, and the work of our own hands outlives us. Bishop after bishop fulfils the task allotted to him, and goes to his reward; the cathedral lasts on. Of that, we have little need to be reminded; because, for nearly all of us, the memory of one man haunts about this place, and will not be denied admission to our thoughts. During forty years out of those hundred years of which we have been speaking, the mention of this building registered itself in the mind as that of Canon Moriarty's church, or that of Bishop Moriarty's cathedral. This is not the occasion to recall, even if that were necessary, the gracious qualities of the man. But his still fragrant memory does help us bridge the gap, to overleap the barrier of a hundred years. He knew and loved every stone of this edifice; his lore was of this countryside, his memories were of this diocese. He could tell you how, as a young student, he had seen the great Lord Acton come as a guest to the speech-day at Oscott—his first appearance at any Catholic occasion since Infallibility was defined in 1870. And he was himself the nephew of Bishop Allen, who ruled this diocese at the turn of the century; Bishop Allen, who may well have been here as an altar-boy when the cathedral was opened. We thank God today for the work of all your Lordship's predecessors, and for his not least who came last, so vivid a memory, and so endearing.

Meanwhile, we must not allow the celebration of a centenary to rivet our attention wholly on the past. Such is the agility of the human mind, that we can pin-point for ourselves another date in history, the year 2056. In that year, if all goes well, men still unborn will be gathering here, in the cathedral church of Our Lady Help of Christians, to give thanks for its two-hundredth birthday. We, and our way of life, will seem as strange to them as our grandfathers and their way of life seem to us now. But what will they be saying of our achievements? The prophet Samuel, when he raised a monument in enduring stone to commemorate a great victory over the Philistines, made public acknowledgment of it in the words, "Hitherto the Lord has helped us". Hitherto—his prophetic heart knew that there were battles still to be fought, ground still to be gained, vantage-points still to be consolidated. And it must not be said of us, a hundred years hence, that we were content to rest on our laurels, and live on our capital. May God bless the work of this diocese, and this cathedral parish, and make priests and people in time to come worthy of the faith and patience that went before us.

53

THE ROAD TO DAMASCUS[1]

Amen, Amen I say to thee, when thou wast younger thou didst gird thyself and didst walk whither thou wouldst. But when thou shalt be old, thou shalt stretch forth thy hands, and another shall gird thee, and lead thee whither thou wouldst not.—John 21. 18.

THESE words, the Evangelist tells us, our Lord spoke to St Peter "signifying by what death he should glorify God". He, who in the impetuosity of youth had run out to meet martyrdom, "Lord, I will go with thee to prison and to death", was to find martyrdom, after all, but at a time, and in circumstances, not of his own choosing. God wants even the sacrifices we make for him to be made in his way, not in ours. That is the plan with which he most commonly deals with us, his creatures; it was not only to St Peter, not only for the guidance of

[1] This sermon (undated) was preached at the Church of the Holy Apostles, Pimlico, London, at the annual meeting of the Converts' Aid Society, on the feast of the Commemoration of St Paul.

those who covet the crown of martyrdom, that the words were spoken. We shall not do wrong, then, I think, in applying them to the career of others; surely not in applying them to the career of that great colleague of St Peter, whose commemoration we celebrate today. "When thou wast younger thou didst gird thyself and didst walk whither thou wouldst, but when thou shalt be old another shall gird thee and lead thee whither thou wouldst not"—might it not have been said of St Paul, signifying not only by what death but by what life he was to glorify God?

Think of St Paul as he was in his young days, as he was when he girded himself to set out on that fateful journey to Damascus. How superbly the cocksureness of his youth takes all his prejudices for granted! Does it ever occur to him to wonder whether, after all, these Christians may be in the right? I don't think so. In the wrong? Of course the Christians are in the wrong! He will hardly stop to argue with you, so impatient is he to be off on his errand, one foot ready in the stirrup. Why, they have spoken contemptuously of the Law of Moses, the Law that has made the Jewish people what it is. They have suggested that it is actually possible to worship God elsewhere than in the Temple—the dear old Temple, with all its historic associations, with its beautiful, orderly round of services, with its unique position as the centre and rallying point of all that is best in the national life. They have even been known to fraternize freely with the Gentiles, these impossible Gentiles, who eat pork, who don't wash, who have never been through the healthy discipline of a sound rabbinical education, people of no class whatever, and not even of a Semitic type! They never make any converts among the upper classes, or even if they do, what good comes of it? Think of poor old Ananias, who joined them only the other day! They have all their goods in common, which means that they have no proper admiration for that sturdy spirit of commercial enterprise which has so distinguished the Jewish race all over the world. For the most part they're not Jews at all, they are Galileans, who speak with a brogue and are for ever getting into trouble with the police. In the wrong? Of course they're in the wrong! They are disloyal, un-Jewish, a menace to the national life. They want stamping out, that's what it is, d'you hear? Stamping out!

I am not suggesting that the prejudices of youth are always wrong —how could it be so? I am suggesting that they are in themselves a little hasty, a little unreflective. They are not, when all is said and done, a complete guide to right action. But they are all the light young Saul follows, Saul in the pride of his vigorous manhood and his Tarsus degree. Don't believe it, when people tell you that he was already wavering in his allegiance to his Jewish faith when he set out on that journey, that his conscience was already aroused, and only needed the touch of a divine inspiration to complete a conversion already begun. There's not a word of that in his apologia: "And I indeed did formerly think that I ought to do many things contrary to the name of Jesus of Nazareth . . . and many of the saints did I shut up in prison; and being yet more mad against them, I did persecute them even to foreign cities." Does that sound like a man half-convinced? No, when he fell from his horse on the Damascus road, the whole direction of his thought boxed the compass. He was trepanned by divine grace; he came on board the Ark of Christ like a sailor who has been shanghaied in the slums of a sea-port. Another had girded him, and led him whither he would not.

We do not know to what extent St Paul's worldly position was damaged by his conversion to the Christian faith. One of the most acute of Protestant critics has suggested that in all probability he was cut off without a penny by a rich family, and that his own writings bear traces of that experience. I do not suppose it would have been easy to recognize the proud young horseman on the Damascus road in the insignificant evangelist at Corinth who passed as the foreman of Aquila and Priscilla, tent-makers, waiting, when trade was bad, for the arrival of fresh charitable relief from the Church at Philippi. But this at least is certain, that from the day of his conversion, St Paul was never his own master, was constantly being headed off by the divine Providence and made to alter or cancel his plans in defiance of his own wishes. What more natural, than that the convert should preach to his fellow countrymen? "Get thee hence," says our Lord, "for I will send thee far off to the Gentiles." He goes obediently: he wants to preach the Word in Asia, but "they were forbidden by the Holy Ghost"; in Bithynia, but "the spirit of Jesus suffered them not". "We would have come unto you," he writes to the Thessalonians, "I, Paul indeed, once and again, but Satan hath hindered us." And to the Romans, "I was hindered very much from coming to you, and have been kept away till now". St Paul did get to Rome in the end, but he reached it under a military escort, in chains! "When thou shalt be old, another shall gird thee, and lead thee whither thou wouldst not."

Yes, when St Paul first learned to obey the voice of duty, his life became a slavery to duty thenceforward. Only he does not call it a slavery; he calls it "the glorious liberty of the sons of God". There is only one slavery really, as the great convert knew; and that is to disobey the voice of your own conscience. This evangelist, constantly at the beck and call of divine command and human circumstances, is the same man who said to himself, years before, "How about a trip to Damascus? I ought to find good hunting there." Only all that lies far behind him now.

May I be permitted to recall the fact that the text on which I am preaching today is the same passage from which I took my text on the last occasion when I preached at a Protestant service? May I even be permitted to quote what I said then? I was speaking, as the occasion demanded, about the parting of friends. "Divisions, sharper than the sword of earthly jealousies, differences, wider in their estrangement than mere geographical distance, may drift us and them apart; all the comfortable certainties of familiar surroundings we may be called upon to renounce. The past, with its memories, will not be a home to which fancy can return, but a distant harbour at which we have touched, now faded beyond the horizon. To be ready to give up all, houses, and brothers, and sisters, and father, and mother, and lands—that is what it means, to follow Christ."

So much of bitterness even those may feel, to whom the call of grace comes early in life, when they find themselves threatened with severance from the past. And what of those whom this same imperious mandate of conscience finds already well on in years, already hardened into fixed habits of life, fixed grooves of thought? How difficult for them to settle down into a world whose ideas and values are so largely strange to them, to make fresh acquaintances, to allow for new angles and new prejudices among those whose Faith they share! "It is good for a man", says the prophet, "when he hath borne the yoke from his youth"—there are rigidities about the Catholic point of view, matter-of-factnesses about the Catholic atmosphere, to which a mind already formed does not easily accommodate itself. And when a man in middle life, whose tastes and daily occupations have accustomed him to a different outlook, when, above all, a minister of religion, with all the fads and foibles of his caste, makes his submission to the Catholic Church, then the exchange of allegiance is not effected without some laceration of the mind. We are all a little like fish out of water when we are landed in Peter's net.

It is not a light burden, then, at the best of times, that is undertaken by these later labourers in the vineyard of Christ. And now, what if they find themselves, in those same difficult moments, faced with the loss of all worldly prospects, and even worldly means? Those who, perhaps from childhood upwards, have never had any other ambition than that of serving God in the ministry; who have never, in consequence, learned the arts or cultivated the opportunities which would open to them, now in middle life, the doors of any other profession? Marriage or other ties which they cannot avoid make it impossible for them to aspire to the priesthood. They have children dependent on them, to be fed, to be educated; and the unselfish care with which they have provided for these hitherto has left no margin for saving. Their relations are Protestants who disapprove too deeply of their religious departure to help in financing it; or they are too proud to apply for relief to those who might read them a lecture on the folly of their conduct. With all that before them, how many are there whose hearts failed them a little when conscience made itself heard? How many, alas, whose hearts still fail them, so that the voice of conscience is muffled? "When thou shalt be old, another shall gird thee, and lead thee whither thou wouldst not."

Oh, I could harass your imagination with pictures of what some natures may have to undergo, sensitive natures, accustomed to a position which enabled them to enjoy certain comforts, and to hold their heads high. But would you wait to hear harassing details before answering such an appeal? Common sense reveals the necessities of the situation; common humanity demands that they should be met. Only one institution exists which can meet them with that tact and discrimination which undeserved and unexpected poverty demands; it is that institution which appeals to you. Have we done so much, you and I, for the conversion of England, that we can look with unconcerned eyes at the destitution of such converts? Have we gone so far towards winning back our Lady her dowry, that we can grudge some little dowry to these novices of the Catholic Church? God forgive us if we cannot emulate the spirit of St Barnabas, when he raises up among us so often the spirit of St Paul!

54

THE MISFORTUNES OF OUR NEIGHBOUR[1]

Thy neighbour as thyself.—Matthew 19. 19.

I WANT to give you two pictures from the Bible, one from the Old Testament and one from the New Testament, to illustrate what it means, loving your neighbour as yourself.

When the patriarch Joseph had been sold into Egypt, he was thrown into prison under an unjust charge preferred against him by his master's wife. And in that prison he had distinguished company, the chief butler and the chief baker of King Pharaoh, both of whom had offended their royal master. Each of them had a dream on the same night; and Joseph, who was inspired with a divine gift for the interpretation of dreams, offered to read the riddle for each of them. To the chief baker he gave a message of despair. "After three days Pharaoh will take thy head from thee, and hang thee on a cross." To the chief butler he announced good news: "After three days Pharaoh will remember thy service, and will restore thee to thy former place". And then he adds, "Only remember me, when it shall be well with thee; and do me this kindness, to put Pharaoh in mind to take me out of this prison".

It fell out as Joseph had said. Almighty God, who had sent the dreams for that very purpose, did not allow his servant to err in the interpretation of them. The chief baker hung on his cross; the chief butler was restored to favour and to his office. But the chief butler, adds the sacred narrative, when things prospered with him, forgot his interpreter. So slight is the value of human gratitude. We all love the bearer of good news; we feel as if he had himself effected the deliverance we hoped for, instead of being merely the first man to announce it. And no doubt at that moment the chief butler was ready to promise anything, if once he were set free from his dungeon. To be sure, if he really regained his master's favour, he would not forget —how could he?—the fellow prisoner who had languished there with him. Sympathy is quickly bred between companions in misery: the participation of suffering makes us feel the misfortunes of our neighbour

[1] This sermon was probably preached in aid of the Catholic Prisoners' Aid Society.

almost as if they were our own. Of course, if he can be of the least use, if he can bring any influence to bear, he will be ready to do it; that is only to be expected between friends.

But—the expected day comes, with what different feelings had they counted the hours to it! And the chief baker is hurried off, with all the grim circumstances of an execution; the chief butler, still professing his unalterable sympathy, takes leave of Joseph, and breathes the pure air of heaven once more. Once more he stands at the king's side, and hands him the cup he is to drink from. There is a story about one of the kings of Persia, which tells us that he ordered his cup-bearer to remind him, whenever he drank, of his resolve to take vengeance upon a country which had offended him. Perhaps it was so with King Pharaoh; perhaps it was part of the cup-bearer's office, to act as the royal remembrancer. At least, he was a privileged official; at least he was in a position to secure the king's attention when he was in benevolent mood. And I daresay the first night this chief butler quite forgot about Joseph in the excitement of his restoration; and the second night he meant to say something about it, but was accidentally prevented; and the third night he thought it would be better to wait a little; and still Joseph languishes in his dungeon, hoping to hear, every time the door opens, that his friend's intercession has availed for him, but still no tidings come through. And, as time goes on, the chief butler's procrastination develops into genuine forgetfulness; he does not think of Joseph at all, or if he does, it is only as a distant memory; "a man I used to know once", so he describes him, tactfully suppressing the circumstances in which they met. Now and again he reminds himself, "I really must do something about that poor fellow". But, in these days of his prosperity, the fellow feeling which united him to his fellow prisoner has disappeared. Only remember me, when it shall be well with thee—alas, the very motive that should encourage our human pity to remember, encourages our human ingratitude to forget!

The patriarch Joseph foreshadows to us in many ways the Passion of our blessed Lord. Joseph was hated by his brethren because he had dreamed that he was one day to be their master; our Lord was hated by the Jews because he made himself the Son of God. Joseph was sold by his brother Juda for twenty pieces of silver; for thirty pieces of silver our Lord was betrayed by Judas, his favourite apostle, his familiar friend. The crime of Joseph's brethren was a fortunate one, because it led him to a position of high office in Egypt, so that he was able to assist them when they were perishing of famine. The crime of the Jews in crucifying our Lord is described by the Church's liturgy, in a daring paradox, as *felix culpa*, a happy transgression; through it he entered into his rest, as our Patron and our Representative. And, even in detail, there are curious resemblances between the two histories, nowhere more curious than in the matter we are concerned with.

I suppose that when our Lord was awaiting his sentence from the Roman governor, he had for his companions two thieves; one innocent captive with two guilty ones, just as Joseph was. Three prisoners, with the shadow of crucifixion hanging over them; only this time it fell not upon one of them but upon all three. Yes, the sentence of bodily death awaits them all that day, but something else lies beyond. After three days—what is to become of them after three days? Once more, the fortunes of the two guilty men are to be very different; they will be judged by a tribunal higher than that of any earthly monarch; one will be exalted to the glories of heaven, the other (so far as our human guesses serve to guide us) will be delivered over to the eternal punishment his sins have merited. But this time the positions are reversed; it is Joseph who must ask a favour of Pharaoh's butler, it is our Lord who will grant a favour to the penitent thief. "Only remember me, when it shall be well with thee"—it is the innocent man addressing the guilty. "Lord, remember me when thou shalt come into thy kingdom" —it is the worthless criminal addressing incarnate Innocence.

And he? He hangs there, with all the weight of a world's tragedy upon his shoulders, our sins the nails that fasten him, our sorrows his crown. Yet he has time, even then, for this one penitent; will suffer this one distraction to interfere with the perfect prayer in which he offers his death to the eternal Father. "Amen I say to thee; this day thou shalt be with me in Paradise." This day—there is no procrastination here. Joseph had to wait in his dungeon whilst, from day to day, his former friend and fellow prisoner put off the opportunity of coming to his rescue—it was only an accidental reminder that made him do his duty at last. Not such is the exercise of the divine Mercy; "this day", it is marked by promptitude; the reprieve, once pronounced, takes effect as from now. "With me"—this is no impersonal act of charity. What the chief butler offered to do, and failed to do, was only to speak a word in Pharaoh's ear which, if Pharaoh remembered it, might or might not set in motion the machinery for Joseph's release. It is not thus that our Lord offers his assistance; no, he will take the penitent thief by the hand, lead him, as his escort, into the joys that are prepared for him; "with me"—the divine Mercy is marked by a personal interest. "In Paradise"—that was not what the penitent thief asked for; he did not dare ask for so much. He only believed, in the face of all human probability, that his innocent fellow sufferer would triumph in the end over the conspiracy of evil that oppressed him; and he hoped, in that hour, to find whatever relief was possible from whatever pains he might be suffering. He wins, in return for that request, not some mitigation of purgatorial pains, but a plenary indulgence; he is to be translated from a felon's gibbet to the splendours of a heavenly immortality. So Joseph came out of his prison to be a king's counsellor and the governor of a great kingdom; but this through his own deserts, not through any recommendation from the forgetful patron who had at last befriended him. Not such is the charity of the Crucified; "in Paradise", he promises the poor thief a royal dignity, and imparts to him, in doing so, the merits his sordid life had never won; "in Paradise" —this is no grudging recognition, but a divinely multiplied recompense.

See, then, the contrast—human gratitude, for all the obligations which prescribe it, so late in its effects, so distant in its methods, so grudging in its results; divine Mercy, freely exercised without any antecedent merit, so prompt in its operation, so personal in its influence, so rich in its fulfilment! But then, you see, our blessed Lord loved his neighbour as himself—his neighbour, though it were the neighbourhood of cross to cross. He loved him as himself—how else could he love him? What could God find to love in us, except his own image, marred by our sins and buried under a thousand imperfections, yet his image still? To all outward appearance, this penitent was no doubt unpromising enough, his face marked with greed, brutality, and cunning, his speech rough and coarse, the very accents in which he appealed for mercy infected, through force of habit, with the false whine of the beggar, and yet—there was something left beneath it all. There was a faith, and a humility, and a penitence, that bore witness to the image of God surviving yet in that poor, broken creature; and that image of God called, from the cross, to the perfect Image of God hanging there, too, crucified, and the Saviour of the world looked in mercy, and loved his neighbour as himself.

Dear brothers and sisters in Jesus Christ, the Church Militant is divided into two classes, the sinners who are in gaol and the sinners who are out of it. And your fellow sinners who, by transgressing against human justice, have received sentence of imprisonment from an earthly tribunal, call upon you, who must one day stand with them before a divine Judge, and perhaps share with them the expiatory sufferings of purgatory, to give them what assistance you can. Only remember us, they say, when it is well with you; they do not ask for their freedom, only for help, when their time has been served, to set them up afresh in life and to win them space for the amendment of their ways. It is easy to go away from church impressed by a sermon, and to do nothing about it afterwards. When things prosper with us, it is wonderful how faint, how evanescent, is the appeal of human misery; the chief butler was no worse than the rest of us when he forgot Joseph and left him in prison. But I have tried to set before you a higher example, the charity of a crucified Saviour who redeemed us all when we lay under sentence of eternal death. In the name of that example, I call upon you to remember your brethren in prison, loving them as yourselves, and assisting them, as you yourselves would hope to be assisted, with a promptitude, a personal interest, and a super-abundance of charity that shall be worthy of our Master's cause.

IV

PANEGYRICS

FATHER HENRY HARRINGTON[1]

I FEEL a difficulty in saying anything about Father Harrington today which needs saying.[2] You, amongst whom he had come so lately, had no time to make his acquaintance properly or to appreciate him as he deserved; you, who have come from a distance to do honour to such a memory, knew him too well, I think, to need any reminder of our common loss. Yet I should be sorry not to make this tribute of piety over his mortal remains. We were ordained together, he and I, the only priests of our ordination; since then, even when separated, we have remembered one another each October on our day of anniversary;[3] we have looked forward to our common jubilee, and wondered, in the circumstances, which of us was to sing the Mass. From the time when he came back from Cambridge to St Edmund's till the time when I left St Edmund's for Oxford, we were always closely associated in those varied ties, not the less intimate because they are trivial, which a community life begets. And now he who was so close a companion of memory has passed beyond human call, and we, before we commit his soul to the Creator's mercy, must indulge, for a moment, our human instinct of regret.

If we dared question the decrees of Providence—but, please God, both faith and experience make us too wise to question them—we might well have wondered why he was not left among us for a work which he, more than most of us seculars, seemed qualified to do. I mean the task, very necessary and by no means yet accomplished, of showing history to our fellow countrymen in a true light. This past decade has taken, if you come to think of it, a heavy toll of Catholic scholarship, especially where history is concerned. We have lost Bishop

[1] This panegyric was preached at the funeral of Father Henry Harrington, at St Alban's Church, North Finchley, London, on 4 November 1929.

[2] Fr Henry Harrington: born 1892 and educated at Stonyhurst; he taught at St Edmund's from 1922 until September 1929, when he was transferred to the staff of the Catholic grammar school which had been opened by Cardinal Francis Bourne in Finchley the previous June.

[3] Fr Henry Harrington and Mgr Knox were ordained priests at St Edmund's on 5 October 1919.

Ward,[1] we have lost Canon Burton,[2] we have lost Monsignor Mann;[3] we have lost more recently Cardinal Gasquet.[4] It is time that a fresh generation of Catholic historians should be picking up the mantle they have dropped; and among those who seemed qualified for such a vocation, Fr Harrington, if the leisure and opportunity had been granted him, might surely have taken no inconsiderable place. It was not merely that he had knowledge; knowledge is easily come by; but he had, if I am not mistaken, that spirit of candour which is essential to the historian; the capacity for seeing through facts, in the spirit of the scholar, not merely seeing round them, in the spirit of the controversialist. I think his essay in the recently published volume about the English martyrs is eloquent testimony of that gift.[5] We might have hoped that it was reserved for him to do in our own day something of what Lingard did in the early part of last century to restore the Catholic perspective in history. *Dis aliter visum*; he has been taken from us without any considerable literary work to his credit. I am happy to think that, through my eager recommendation, he was selected to write a contribution about the history of the Church in the new edition of the *Encyclopaedia Britannica*; some taste of his gifts will remain fixed there, though in a humble setting. But in the main his influence will be the transitory influence of the teacher; here and there men will say, "I know this, for he taught me; I appreciate this, because he opened my eyes to it". But the influence of the teacher is restricted to a few; and of those few, only a minority, at the best, do justice to the pains he took over them.

Let us forget, then, what might have been; let us think rather of our human contact with him, while this circle surrounds him, the circle which his death has brought together, which his death will separate. What we all felt, I suppose, when the news of his death was announced to us, we who had known him at St Edmund's, his colleagues, and the students he knew so well how to treat as colleagues, was that a whole well of genial companionship would henceforward

[1] The Right Rev. Bernard Ward, D.D.: third son of W. G. Ward and first Bishop of Brentwood; author of *The History of St Edmund's College* (1893) and *St Edmund of Canterbury* (1903). He died 20 January 1920.
[2] The Very Rev. Canon Edwin Burton. His best known work is the two-volume *Life and Times of Bishop Challoner*; he edited with Fr J. H. Pollen, S.J., *The Lives of the English Martyrs*. He died on 13 December 1925.
[3] Mgr H. K. Mann: born 1859; headmaster of St Cuthbert's Grammar School, Newcastle-upon-Tyne, 1890–1917; Rector of the Beda College, 1917; died 1 August 1928. His best-known work is the history of the medieval Papacy in several volumes, entitled *Lives of the Popes in the Middle Ages*.
[4] Cardinal Gasquet: born 1846; created Cardinal 1914; died 4 April 1929.
[5] "The Climax of the Persecution, the Week of 1585" in *The English Martyrs* (Cambridge Summer School Papers, 1928).

be stopped for us; that a vivid personality, whose lot had been inter-twined with ours, would no longer share with us the gracious pleasures of memory. He had the art of friendship; he would squander, over the difficulties of a pupil, over the character of a student who was (he thought) too little understood, treasures of care and conscientiousness which he never gave to his own health or to his own ambitions. He had the art, too, of companionship; he enriched the routine of college life with his quick gift of humorous vision and his sudden, whole-hearted appreciations. Many of us still remember the evening when he came into the common room after a play which he had organized, and wearied us with his repeated exclamation, "Those are good boys". And he had that rare humility which enjoys, which is the first to enjoy, a joke against itself. If you rallied him, he would always defend him-self; "No, you're wrong there", would be his correction of every criticism, but not until he had had his laugh out at his own expense. I have known people irritated with him; I have never known anybody who could harbour a grudge against him. He was too frank, too natural, too unselfconscious, for that.

Strange, and perhaps humiliating, that our memories of the lately dead should be so much preoccupied with the little tricks of personality, the jokes, the prejudices, the poses of the living man we knew; that they should reach so little to the inner heart of him, to the secret springs of character and of motive which God alone sees, which alone God judges. More especially, when a friend has been taken from us with little warning, in the full tide of life, with ambitions still young and hopes still unrealized. The very human weaknesses of such a character, the untidinesses, the violences, the conversational egotisms, endear his memory to us by bringing him closer to ourselves—what of that just though merciful scrutiny which his soul has already undergone before the Father of all spirits? We are Christians; we do not pick out virtues in the deceased before we can feel secure about his eternal destiny; enough for us that he kept the faith, believed and hoped in that Saviour but for whom all human virtues must be squandered in vain. No, it is not that; but we would like to distil, if we could, some essential fragrance from the character of the departed which should inform our gratitude for his friendship and inspire, a little, our own lives from his memory. Let me suggest, then, to the friends who knew him, that we knew, in Father Harrington, a character whose essential background was a certain grand simplicity—the simplicity of a boy, behind all those talents, all that matured faculty of discrimination. He had not the health or the natural temper which inspires careless lightheartedness;

he felt too deeply, perhaps was by temper too critical, to be a mere optimist or a mere enthusiast. But when I find myself envying him, I find myself envying him the simplicity of heart which made him so generous a critic of others, so ready a critic of himself.

I do not speak to strangers; you have understood my efforts to make him live in the memory; if you have disagreed with them, you have found in them the material to make a better estimate for yourselves. Let us leave him, then, in the hands of God; only praying that the faults of his earthly conversation, for which, perhaps, some measure of responsibility lies on our own souls, may be speedily and mercifully forgiven him; and that we, for whom the memories of our priesthood are so charged with the recollection of his friendship, may be true to the faith in which he died, and may be found worthy of that vision for which he lives. May his soul, and the souls of all the faithful departed, through the mercy of God, rest in peace.

2

G. K. CHESTERTON[1]

Blessed are they that saw thee and were honoured with thy friendship. For we live only in our life, but after death our name shall not be such.— Ecclesiasticus 48. 11.

THE man whom we laid to rest the other day in the cemetery at Beaconsfield was one of the very greatest men of his time. If posterity neglects him, it will pronounce judgment not upon him, but upon itself. He will almost certainly be remembered as a great and solitary figure in literature, an artist in words and ideas with an astonishing fecundity of imaginative vision. He will almost certainly be remembered as a prophet in an age of false prophets. He warned us in spacious times that human liberties were threatened, and today human liberties are in debate. He warned us in times of prosperity against the perils of industrialism, and industrialism is labouring for breath. He warned us, when imperialism was a fashion, that nationalism was a force not easily destroyed; today nationalism is the shadow over men's hearts.

Whether he was a great author, whether he was a true prophet, does

---

[1] This panegyric was preached at the Requiem Mass of Gilbert Keith Chesterton at Westminster Cathedral on 27 June 1936.

not concern him now—he lies deaf to the world's praise and secure from its catastrophes—nor does it concern us here. We are met, as Christians, to say farewell in our own fashion to a fellow Christian who has outstripped us in the race for eternity. The most important thing about Chesterton, he would have been the first to say it, the most distinctive quality in Chesterton was a quality which he shared with some three hundred million of his fellow men. He was a Catholic. The public discovered him in the early years of the century. It was not till twenty years later that he discovered himself. There is a legend told of his absent-mindedness that he once telegraphed home the words, "Am in Liverpool; where ought I to be?" And it took him fourteen years after the publication of his book *Orthodoxy* to find out that he ought to be in Rome.

I hope I do not wrong such a man in preaching his panegyric, when I confine myself to considering the position which belongs to him as a religious force; what Catholicism meant to him, and what he meant to Catholicism. In the case of a meaner man we should be content to celebrate his domestic virtues, his inconspicuous acts of charity. But Chesterton moved, though with the personal simplicity of a child, in a world of apocalyptic images; he saw his religion everywhere; it mattered furiously to him. What he did is in God's hands; what he was is a matter of gracious recollection to his friends; it is the effect he made on the world that claims the world's attention and its gratitude.

I would speak first of the influence which Chesterton's earlier works had, on young men for the most part and on Protestants. And it is the only claim I have to stand here, in the place of older and closer friends, that at the time when his earlier works were published, I was myself a young man and a Protestant. I think it is true to say that the generation which grew up between the turn of the century and the Great War had a tendency all the time to react in favour of religious orthodoxy. The triumph of evolutionary materialism had seemed complete; the faith of Englishmen was laid out for burial, with'the cynics, the pessimists, the positivists driving the last nails in its coffin. There was a reaction of which we should hear more if the events which began with 1914 had not decimated it and left its less characteristic specimens to represent it. I do not wish to discount the influence of other religious leaders, Anglicans like Scott Holland or Catholics like Hugh Benson. But the spearhead of that reaction was a man so plainly on the side of the angels that you did not stop to inquire whether he were an Anglican or a Catholic, G. K. Chesterton. The brilliance of his work, the wideness of his appeal set the fashion in favour of a religious attitude which the fashion of an earlier age had derided. He was conscious, himself, of the change of atmosphere when he wrote the introduction to his book, *The Man Who Was Thursday*. It is an extraordinary book, written as if the publisher had commissioned him to write something rather like the *Pilgrim's Progress* in the style of the *Pickwick Papers*. And the poem which introduces it is a song not of triumph but of release from tension in the middle of a conflict.

> But we were young; we lived to see God break their bitter charms—
> God and the good Republic came riding back in arms;
> We have seen the city of Mansoul even as it rocked, relieved—
> Blessed are they that have not seen, but, being blind, believed.

The direct effect of that reaction in stemming the tide of religious liberalism has been in great part obliterated by the war. Its indirect effect, in producing conversions to the Catholic faith, made itself felt only during the war, when the annual figure of conversions went up from eight thousand to ten and from ten to twelve, where it has remained ever since. Meanwhile the prophet, who had acted as a sign-post for us, remained himself outside the Church, content to fight a lonely battle for the philosophy he could see was right but could not see was ours. What changed him then four years after the Armistice? What was the new momentum which lent impetus to his thought, so that he no longer believed, being blind, but saw? I never knew yet a convert who could give a precise answer to that question. To give a precise answer we should have to understand, as we shall never understand it here, the economy of God's grace. We can only say that if it were possible to deserve the grace of conversion, Chesterton had deserved it for years as no other man did; and, if he had to wait so long for it, there is hope in that for many a waiting soul, perhaps for some waiting soul here, which still cannot see the end of its despairs.

Meanwhile what had happened was, to Chesterton himself, admirably clear. He had the artist's eye which could suddenly see in some quite familiar object a new value; he had the poet's intuition which could suddenly detect, in the tritest of phrases, a wealth of new meanings and of possibilities. The most salient quality, I think, of his writing is this gift of illuminating the ordinary, of finding in something trivial a type of the eternal. In the first of his books which really made a name for him, *The Napoleon of Notting Hill*, the story opens at a moment when a Government clerk, walking behind two friends in town coats, suddenly sees the buttons on their coats as two eyes, the slit underneath as a nose line; he has a vision of his two friends as two dragons walking backwards away from him. There is a law (he says in that connection) written in the darkest of the books of life, and it is this: If you look at a thing nine hundred and ninety-nine times, you are perfectly safe; if you look at it the thousandth time, you are in frightful danger of seeing it for the first time. That was all that happened when Chesterton was converted. He had looked for the thousandth time at the Catholic faith and for the first time he saw it. Nothing in the Church was new to him, and yet everything was new to him; he was like the man in his own story who had wandered round the world in order to see, with fresh eyes, his own home. That it was his home, neither friend nor foe had doubted; men did not even dare to whisper to him the old pathetic lie that converts are unhappy. Whether his work as a Catholic has been as influential as the work which he did when he was only a defender of Catholics, is a question hard to resolve. He was no longer the latest fashion; he had reached the age at which most men have had their say; his health had begun to decline, and he was overworked, partly through our fault. Nor, I think, will the world ever give a just hearing to one who has labelled himself a Catholic. But this I will say, that, if every other line he wrote should disappear from circulation, Catholic posterity would still owe him an imperishable debt of gratitude, so long as a copy of *The Everlasting Man* enriched its libraries. This I will say, that whenever I ask an inquirer whether he has read any Catholic books his answer regularly begins, "I've read some Chesterton, of course".

"We live only in our life and after death our name shall not be such"; few men of our time could refuse that epitaph to Gilbert Chesterton. Meanwhile, "blessed are they that saw him and were honoured by his friendship"; they found in him a living example of charity, of chivalry, of unbelievable humility which will remain with them, perhaps, as a more effective document of Catholic verity than any word even he wrote. But the familiar voice, with its high chuckle of amusement, will reach us no longer; he, whose belief in immortality was so publicly influential, can give us no whisper of reassurance, now that he knows. Only we know what we would say if he heard the suggestion that nothing remains of him beyond what was interred at Beaconsfield.

> The sages have a hundred maps to give;
>   They trace their crawling cosmos like a tree;
> They rattle reason out through many a sieve
>   That stores the sand and lets the gold go free.
> And all these things are less than dust to me
>   Because my name is Lazarus and I live.

3

ABBOT EDMUND MATTHEWS, O.S.B.[1]

If you have ten thousand schoolmasters in Christ, yet not many fathers.—
1 Corinthians 4. 15.

WE have come to bury, in the corner of earth which Abbot Matthews loved so well, that perishable part of him for which he cared so little.[2] His health, to which for years he had been a hard master, had begun to show, in these last few months, visible traces of decline; the lines about his mouth had altered, and he spoke to you with the feverish utterance of a man who is fighting down some inward enemy. A week ago he consented, grudgingly enough, to take a month's rest after Easter; you wondered how or where he would find it, a man who seemed to have no home but Ampleforth, to find no recreation but in his work. The things that are impossible with men are possible with God. Father Abbot sang the Mass of Maundy Thursday, in commemoration of his Master's farewell to earth; watched that evening at the hour when his Master watched; and next morning, at the hour when his Master was judged, went from us to his judgment. He has redeemed his promise; and heaven, we dare to hope, has given him the rest which earth denied him, that sabbath of Eastertide which has no term to its fruition.

The world will remember him as a great schoolmaster, and it is fitting that he should be so remembered. If I were speaking to strangers, if a visible monument were needed to convince the mind of his achievement, it would be enough to indicate the plan of the buildings which surround us; to isolate the little cluster of roofs that was Ampleforth when he came back from Oxford at the beginning of the century, and to show the stages by which, since then, his inspiration has altered the face of this valley. We have watched it grow, year by year, that

---

[1] This panegyric was preached at the Requiem Mass for Abbot Matthews at Ampleforth Abbey on Easter Tuesday, 1939.

[2] Abbot Edmund Matthews entered Ampleforth as a thirteen-year-old boy in 1884 and received the monastic habit four and a half years later. He went to Oxford and was the first English Benedictine monk to take his degree there since Abbot John Feckenham in 1556. He was Headmaster of Ampleforth from 1903 until 1924, when he was elected Abbot. He died early in the morning on Good Friday, 1939.

panorama of masonry which stretches from the Junior School to the new houses, clinging to the terraced slope as if it were the symbol of one man's tenacity of purpose. All this interference with the build of nature had to pass his scrutiny before the sabbath day came, and he was at rest.

The material increase is only a crude expression of the change which has passed over the abbey during those years. A generation ago, the stranger passing through Gilling would look up and say, "What's that?" Today, the reflection occurs to him without difficulty, "That must be Ampleforth". It is no part of my purpose to record how the school has grown in fame and in importance; we are here to praise the dead, not to flatter the living, and a school becomes great, not by one man's initiative but by a conspiracy of service. For all that, the world is justified in calling him a great schoolmaster, the world which knows nothing of him except that he was the headmaster of a great school. Somehow, under God's providence, his patient work, his unobtrusive personality, started Ampleforth on its cycle of achievement; and when you chose him to succeed the holy abbot[1] under whom he had served, he must have contemplated almost with stupefaction the thing which had grown up between his hands. Thenceforth it was for his wisdom to regulate the development which his energy had originated; a task perhaps not less hard, certainly not less responsible. That responsibility, with perfect command over his failing strength, he shouldered to the end.

Well, a great schoolmaster—is that all it means, to be a great schoolmaster? To have built and planned, to have organized a multitude of details successfully? Rather, it means to be skilled in the most difficult of the arts, which has human lives for its incalculable material. To be a living paradox, taking a personal interest in every boy without ever showing a preference, forming the character of the young without stunting its natural growth, unbending without losing their esteem, punishing them without forfeiting their affection. Abbot Matthews had the gift of being severe; he was capable, if I may use the expression, of flattening out the delinquent by merely telling him what he thought of him, in those quiet, measured tones that somehow probed into you like a knife. There was no blustering or shouting, no unfair use of irony; a searching beam of disappointed benevolence penetrated you and showed you to yourself. Yet he was such a man as everywhere to be loved; boys who worked under him may have been more conscious, at the time, of respect; but they found afterwards it was their

[1] Abbot Oswald Smith, elected first Abbot of Ampleforth in 1900. He died in November 1924.

love he had claimed and had elicited; a great schoolmaster, with that sure touch which belongs only to greatness. To many of you, who went to school under him, his influence has become a part of your lives; he inspired you, he loved you, and he is gone.

Have we yet pierced to the inner greatness of the man who lies here? Forgive me the foolishness of the question; we who were privileged to know him know that he was something more than a great schoolmaster; he was a great abbot. I do not mean merely—though we should do ill to forget it, and he more than any man would rebuke us if we forgot it—that Ampleforth is a monastery first and a school afterwards. I mean that the rule of a religious community is a more delicate thing, depends upon a subtler bond of association than the government of a school. And perhaps especially the rule of a Benedictine community. The Society of Jesus is military in its inspiration; the mendicant orders breathe an air of political democracy; the Benedictine spirit dares to imitate an institution which is older and more intimate, the institution of the family. The abbot is a father among his children. And St Paul tells us that though we may have many schoolmasters, we must not expect to have many fathers. He who lies here was a father: a great father in God.

At first sight, it would be tempting to suppose that a father's rule differs from that of a schoolmaster in being milder and more indulgent; no severity, no stern looks, only gentleness here. But we must be on our guard against representing fatherhood as it is conceived by a modern and, on the whole, an ill-regulated age. The modern father despairs of exercising authority because he is unable to inspire respect. Such an example would quickly breed relaxation in a religious community; to rebuke faults, to refuse unreasonable requests, is part of a superior's duty. And Abbot Matthews did not need to alter his nature when he became an abbot instead of a schoolmaster; he retained something of his awe-inspiring quality. A shy man, he did not shrink from the duty of correction; a kindly man, he did not yield readily to the suggestion of the first-comer. He saw the danger that increasing preoccupation with the school, and the dissipation of forces which school organization demanded, might have a weakening effect on community life and community discipline; perhaps we shall never know how much we owe it to him that Ampleforth remains, in the true sense, a home of monks. Did any of his brethren feel that, here and here, the yoke of discipline bore too hard on him? The voice of self-pity was silenced, when he reflected that there was one member of the community to whom no indulgence was ever granted, for whom no allowance was ever made, for whom no labours were too exacting —and that was the Abbot himself.

He was a great abbot because he was a good monk. Into that inmost fastness of all we may not penetrate. "You are dead", the Easter-day epistle reminds us, "and your life is hidden with Christ in God."[1] I do not think Abbot Matthews ever forgot, in the most worldly surroundings, that he had renounced the world. You heard him making an after-dinner speech; it would begin on the note set for him by others, but in a minute or two, without any airs of pietism, without any effect of embarrassment, he would be talking in dead earnest of the things that were near his heart. You were in conversation with him; his face was lit up with that smile of his that was like a sunny day in winter; then for a moment you were detained in conversation with somebody else; and you looked back to find the same face drawn and tense, the eyes looking into distance, its common expression when in repose. And you saw, in that play of light and shadow, that this was a man whose thoughts were never far away from God. We shall not see it again; he has passed beyond our world of light and shadow; may the face of Jesus Christ show gay and gentle to him. You must turn, with heavy hearts, to elect another in his place. Reverend fathers, God send you a father like him.

So we leave him in his Creator's hands, of whom all paternity in heaven and earth is named, our father in God, our father now with God. His body will be with his brethren, in the place he loved so well and left so seldom; that is but fitting; so far as earthly gifts were concerned, he received from Ampleforth all he had, gave to Ampleforth all he had; we would not separate his name from hers. Those heavenly graces which he received from God, as surely he gave back to God; the soul knows larger horizons. Yet, where he rests with God, if any thoughts of his still turn towards earth, surely they will turn towards this place and dwell like a benediction over this place; *haec requies mea in saeculum saeculi; hic habitabo, quoniam elegi eam.* May the prayers of our blessed Lady and St Edmund and the saints of his order win him, now and hereafter, refreshment, light and peace.

---

[1] Colossians 3. 3.

4

HILAIRE BELLOC[1]

Up, then, gird thee like a man, and speak out all the message I give thee. Meet them undaunted, and they shall have no power to daunt thee. Strong I mean to make thee this day as fortified city, or pillar of iron, or wall of bronze, to meet king, prince, priest of Juda and common folk all the country through.
—Jeremias I. 17-18.

THE other day, in a curiously moving country church at West Grinstead, we laid to rest, not without the tears of memory, an old and tired man. It was a funeral of circumstance; the Mass was Pontifical, the habits of many religious orders graced the sanctuary, and schoolboys' voices lent an intolerable beauty to the *Dies Irae*. But in essence it was a country affair; some of Hilaire Belloc's friends had met to see his body lowered into the grave—there, in Sussex earth; there, beside the wife he had so long mourned; there, with the house he had lived in for forty years, till it became "like a bear's fur" to him, only a few miles away. Today, as if humouring that other side of him, which loved stateliness and the just proportion of well-ordered things, we gather with muffled footfalls among the echoing vaults of a great cathedral—we, lesser men, who have lived so long under the shadow of his championship, to remind ourselves what it is we have lost, and to do him honour.

We ask foolishly what such a man would have wished to hear said in his praise if he were alive; perhaps still more foolishly, what he is wishing to hear, if the dead know so much, care so much, about transitory things. It was a question that exercised him greatly, especially at the end of his life; the appetite for fame was, he said, at once the most irrational and the strongest of all appetites; of fame itself he told us, "It is but a savour and an air". For his friend Chesterton he prophesied enduring fame only on condition that the cause for which they both did battle should ultimately triumph, and England should return to a happier way of living. Whether that was right, may be a matter of dispute; but I think it gives us a clue to Belloc's own feeling about such matters. What he cared for was not the good word of posterity taken in the gross, but the praise of Christendom.

[1] This panegyric was preached at the Requiem Mass for Hilaire Belloc at Westminster Cathedral on 5 August 1953.

Only such praise concerns *us*, here before his catafalque. Let others remember him—have no fear, he will be remembered—as a great master of English prose, that virile, nervous English prose which he shares with men like Sterne and Cobbett; or as a satirist to be mentioned in the same breath as Swift and Molière; or as a historian who had the rare quality of making the past live. For us, these are but the trappings of his greatness. Here was a man that interpreted divine things for us, under homely images and in our common speech. He was a prophet

When I say that, I do not mean to suggest that he had any special skill in forecasting future events; he made mistakes there, like the rest of us. I mean he was such a man as saw what he took to be the evils of our time in a clear light, and with a steady hatred; that he found, or thought he had found, a common root in them, and traced them back, with what light God gave him, to their origins in history. In this, he resembled a great man whom he was proud to claim as his master, Father Vincent McNabb, of the Order of Preachers. Father Vincent, who has left us so little record of his splendid gifts, was an inspiration to all that brilliant circle of Catholics among whom Belloc moved; men like John Phillimore, the professor of humanities at Glasgow, and Maurice Baring, whose novels we shall read again. But only two accepted from him the mantle of prophecy, Belloc and Chesterton. And of these, Belloc had the double portion; he was a prophet by destiny and by temperament.

A prophet, by derivation, is one who speaks out. He must not wrap up his meaning; he must not expect success. "To brazen-faced folk and hard-hearted thy errand is, and still from the Lord God a message thou must deliver, hear they, or deny thee a hearing; rebels all, at least they shall know that they have had a prophet in their midst." There is the double tragedy of the prophet; he must speak out, so that he makes men dislike him, and he must be content to believe that he is making no impression whatever. Such is the complaint of Jeremias: "An ill day when thou, my mother, didst bring me into the world! A world where all for me is strife, all is hostility; neither creditor I nor debtor to any man, yet they curse my name." He would be rid, if he could, of the prophet's burden; and there were moods, at least, in which Belloc would indulge in the same complaint. Even when he wrote *The Path to Rome*, he was conscious of the strain; "We are perpetually thrust into minorities, and the world almost begins to talk a strange language. . . . And this is hard when a man has loved common views, and is happy only with his fellows." And in his tribute to

Chesterton, one of his last works, you will find him exclaiming, half
in envy, half in reprobation, at the man who took part in so much
controversy, yet never made an enemy; "without wounding and
killing", he said, "there is no battle". With Chesterton, as with
Johnson's friend who tried to be a philosopher, "cheerfulness was
always breaking in"; Belloc's destiny was conflict, and he did not love
it. He was "a prophet lost in the hills":

> I challenged, and I kept the faith;
> The bleeding path alone I trod.

Why must he always be different, not thinking the thoughts of common men?

A sad life? You would not venture to assert it; as a young man, he
would sing in chorus, and ride, and sail the seas; nor did he lose, to the
end, the pleasures of old memory and of tried friendship. But he was
melancholy by temperament; the undercurrents of his mind were sad,
and his face never looked happy in repose. And because this melancholy
was fed, at all times, by a sense of intellectual loneliness, he stood,
mentally, a confessor to the faith that was in him. Many, who shared
that faith, would not go all the way with him in following out its
implications: Was the story of the Reformation really so simple as he
made it out to be? Were financial interests so powerful, were modern
politics so corrupt, in real life as in *Emmanuel Burden*? But his vision was
prophetic, and therefore integral. If you could not trace every link in
the chain of historical causation, still you could not doubt the logical
sequence of events; it was no mere accident that the world which
accepted the Reformation drifted, after a few centuries, into being the
world we know. If we had lost good fellowship and good craftsmanship and a hundred other things which the natural side of him regretted,
it was, it must be, a nemesis traceable to the loss of certain other things,
which the supernatural side of him regretted inconsolably.

Does the prophet do good? No such promise is made him when he
sets out with his message. His task is to deliver that message to the men
of his time, whether they hear or refuse him a hearing. It may be, the
stark language he talks to them, the unconventional gestures by which
he tries to thrust it home, will produce a reaction, and wed them all the
more firmly to their old ways of thought. There are one or two terrible
passages in the Old Testament which almost seem to imply that the
prophet is sent out, not to inspire repentance, but to redouble the guilt
of his unbelieving audience. What is important, it seems, is that they
should know they have had a prophet in their midst. Must that be the

epitaph we pronounce today over a man so widely read, so greatly loved? That the violence of his protest defeated itself, and left England less kindly disposed than ever to a propaganda so crude, so exaggerated?

To be sure, he was prophet rather than apostle; he did not, as we say, "make converts".

Indeed, I can still remember the agitation of Maurice Baring when Chesterton first showed signs of becoming a Catholic; "Don't tell Hilary", he said, "he'd ruin everything."

You do not often hear it said of Belloc, as you hear it said of Chesterton, "I owe my conversion to him". But the influence of a prophet is not to be measured by its impact on a single mind here and there; it exercises a kind of hydraulic pressure on the thought of his age. And when the day of wrath comes, and that book is brought out, written once for all, which contains all the material for a world's judgment, we shall perhaps see more of what Belloc was and did; how even his most irresponsible satire acted as a solvent force, to pierce the hard rind of self-satisfaction which, more than anything, kept Victorian England away from the Church; how the very overtones of his unostentatious piety brought back to us memories of the faith, and of the Mass, and of our blessed Lady, to which English ears had grown unaccustomed.

Have I represented him as a figure of marble? No one who knew him, no one who has read the more intimate of his writings, can picture him otherwise than as a man essentially human, twinkling with fun, rippling with vitality. Even as we commit his soul into the hands of his Creator, with those severely impersonal prayers the Church dictates to us, we are haunted by a thousand human memories of him, recall a hundred endearing characteristics of him—his undisguised admiration for lesser men than himself, the punctilious care with which he would bestow charity on a beggar, his rather stiff courtesy to strangers, his fondness for company and good cheer. Human? God knows he was human. For human frailties, may he receive the pardon he always desired. For the wideness of his human sympathies, may he find reward.

And yet, you who loved Hilaire Belloc, you who read him, and found inspiration in the reading, do not imagine that he would be satisfied if we wrote for him the epitaph, "This man endeared himself to his fellows". He was a prophet; men thought him a fanatic, and he has written his own epitaph, I think, in a poem of that name. A fanatic, he says, is one who keeps his word—not merely this or that casual promise, but

That great word which every man
Gave God before his life began:
It was a sacred word, he said,
Which comforted the pathless dead,
And made God smile when it was shown
Unforfeited before the Throne.

He has given an undertaking (that, surely, is the sense) that he will be
true to himself, that he will carry out faithfully the mission God gave
him to perform, that he will challenge the men of his age with his own
characteristic protest. Unforfeited—no human flattery, no love of ease,
no weariness of conflict, shall make him retract the pledge he has given.
"I have fought the good fight, I have finished the race, I have redeemed
my pledge"—that is what Hilaire Belloc would wish us to say of him,
and there are few of whom it could be said so truly.

May his soul, and the souls of all the faithful departed, through the
mercy of God, rest in peace.

5

FATHER PAUL NEVILL, O.S.B.[1]

*What, do we need letters of recommendation to you, or from you, as some
others do? Why, you yourselves are the letter we carry about with us, written
in our hearts, for all to recognize and to read.*—2 Corinthians 3. 1-2.

IN the first age of the Church, when there was danger of half-
instructed Christians confusing the minds of the faithful by preaching
another gospel than that which the apostles had received, a missionary
travelling from one preaching centre to another carried with him letters
of recommendation, to prove that he was in good faith. And St Paul,
defending himself from a charge of inconstancy which his friends at
Corinth were half prepared to believe, suddenly pulls himself up (as his
wont is) and says, "What! Can it really be necessary for me to build
up my reputation like this, when I am writing to you? Must I court
your good opinion like a stranger, when you are my own children in
Jesus Christ? Why, you yourselves are my letter of introduction; only,
my message to you was not written with paper and ink; it was, or
should be, engraved on your hearts." But at this point St Paul, who

---

[1] This panegyric was preached at the Requiem Mass for Father Paul Nevill at the London
Oratory on 1 February 1954.

always got his metaphors mixed, puts it the wrong way round, and says, "You are written on my heart", instead of "I am written on your hearts"—which was what he meant. Never mind, it all comes to the same thing. What it means is that St Paul, the author of all those epistles which have been read and studied and argued over for nineteen centuries, wasn't really proud of his performances with paper and ink. What he was proud of was a little group of souls at Corinth, on whom the image of Christ had been stamped through his ministry. They were his credentials, they were the sign-manual of his apostleship.

When it was last my melancholy privilege to preach before a friend's catafalque, trying to interpret something of his quality, and weigh the measure of our loss, it was a writer of history whose name is known throughout the civilized world; and the congregation which filled the cathedral was, I suppose, a cross-section of London. Today, we are once again mourning a historian, but one whose vocation, and perhaps his tastes, opened up to him a quite different way of externalizing the message that was in him. And that, not merely by teaching history, though he was an exact and a stimulating teacher. For thirty years of unremitting devotion he laboured to stamp his Master's image on each boy—not on all the boys, on each boy—who passed through Ampleforth. That was his epistle in life, that is his testament in death. I suppose I am talking to many who enjoyed that privilege; thinking little of it at the time, because boys don't think much, but seeing more clearly, now in retrospect, what it meant. Is it intrusive of me if I labour the moral of my text? You are his epistle; his influence is graven in your hearts; and do not doubt that, like the Apostle of the Gentiles, he carried you, and carries you, in his.

Not that the school, or the boys in the school—that was the extra-ordinary thing—absorbed all his energies. We others, who knew Ampleforth only as guests, knew Father Paul as a friend who always had leisure for you, always welcomed you as if you were the person he had looked forward to seeing. That welcome of his, how we valued it! Curiously, in this respect I bracket him in my mind with another Benedictine of the English obedience who died barely a week before him, Abbot Hicks of Downside. So often I have enjoyed the hospitality of our two great monasteries; and neither, now, can be quite the same again. Only a few days ago I was discussing recent changes in the staff with a great friend of Ampleforth, who said: "Of course, there's always Father Paul". But alas, in this unsatisfying world there is never always anybody. On the feast of St Paul's conversion he sat in his room, his breviary at his side, as if he had just put it down. Perhaps some remembered phrase from the epistles was among his last earthly thoughts. "This is what we look for in choosing a steward; we must find one who is trustworthy. Yet for myself, I make little account of your scrutiny, or of any human audit-day"—did his mind travel back over that long pageant of speech-days in which he had stood, so deprecatingly, before the storm of our applause? And so, imitating closely the example of that great Abbot who had been his predecessor, he died suddenly and in harness, left us as unostentatiously as he had ruled us, all those thirty years. Ampleforth, please God, will remain what he made it; but we shall miss the air of gracious preoccupation that went with Father Paul.

"What he made it"; when I have said that, have I said too much? Nobody who has watched the splendid curve of Ampleforth's development can doubt of one thing about it; it has been done by team-work. But that very fact, that he could work with and through a set of loyal colleagues without any cost to his sense of responsibility or their sense of independence, was a fresh flowering of greatness. There are, in a general way, two kinds of great administrators: those who have an uncanny mastery of detail, and those who know how to delegate responsibility to their lieutenants. Father Paul defied all the probabilities by being both at once. His grasp of detail was staggering; you could not talk to him about any boy in the school, or any Old Boy, or any parent for that matter, without discovering that he knew them, and knew all the relevant facts about them. He had everybody pigeon-holed. And yet, at Ampleforth more than at most schools, you are conscious that each house does reflect, in some undefinable way, the influence of the house-master. Devolution was a reality, because Father Paul trusted his staff, and they trusted him.

Was he, then, a martinet, a totalitarian genius determined to force every boy who came to Ampleforth into a single mould? Was it by methods of a moral drill-sergeant that he achieved, in these thirty years, such impressive results? That is the idea many people have of Catholic education; and such methods are not in accord, obviously, with the spirit of our times. Well, if there is anybody in this church who did not know Father Paul, let me tell him that to us, who knew Father Paul, such a notion of him is laughable. One of my earliest memories of Ampleforth is standing talking to Father Paul watching a football match; and just in front of us was a small boy who, for no earthly reason, was grinding his heel into the muddy ground and making an ugly brown hole. All that I had ever known of school-masters convinced me that it was only a matter of time before a stentorian "Stop doing that, boy!" put an end to the performance. It never came. I realized, with a shock, that the misdemeanour of destroying the grass on the touch-line did not rank high in the new headmaster's scale of priorities. Always he rode you with a light rein; what left his stamp on you was not a code of rules, but daily contact with a man whose life was an example of living.

The same qualities which made such a conscious and such a profound impression upon outside observers who came across him, and above all in that world of schoolmasters and educationalists which is so critical, yet found in Father Paul nothing to criticize—those same qualities were impressing themselves on you, quite unperceived, from the mere fact of daily intimacy; the influence of the man was getting in under your skin, although you would have scorned to admit it. A man full of natural dignity, yet utterly free from affectation, retaining, for all his great experience of life, the massive simplicity of the cloister; not charitable merely in his judgments, but always generous in his appreciation of other people's good qualities; an enthusiast without illusions, a stern moralist without harshness of censure, and, above all, as a religious should be, a man of exact observance and living faith. Such a man has gone from us; and, let me repeat it, you are the epistle he has left behind him, for all to recognize and to read. What you make of life, what mark you leave on the world, will be the measure of Father Paul's success.

Only, let me repeat it, he makes little of our scrutiny, or of any human audit-day. To his own Master he stands or falls; may that Master's face shine on his, gentle and welcoming, as his did on ours. For him, as for all men, encompassed as we are by frailties, we must ask God's mercy. Only, ever since the feast of St Paul's conversion, the words of St Paul's hymn have been forcing themselves on my memory, applied, in his own measure, to the friend we have lost:

> Paul, 'tis the end; the task is done,
> The good fight fought, the course well run;
> Enter the heavenly rest, and wear
> The righteous crown that waits thee there.
> Still yearns thy love, remembering yet
> Those that thou didst in Christ beget,
> Sons of the travail of thy soul
> Whose tears would keep thee from the goal.
> Yet be content; thy Lord and theirs
> Justly for them and thee prepares;
> The hour is come; heaven calls its own;
> Amidst the judges take thy throne.

6

CARDINAL GRIFFIN[1]

I DO not find it easy to write dispassionately about Cardinal Griffin. When you find, in your immediate superior, a man who gives you nothing but encouragement, and is always ready to fight your battles, you do not easily write of such a man except in terms of mere eulogy. And such a superior I had in Cardinal Griffin.

Should his career be written down as triumph, or as tragedy? They were strangely blended in it. When Cardinal Hinsley died, we looked about, instinctively, for some great figure, of the same rugged impressiveness, to take up the mantle he had dropped. And who was Bishop Griffin? He had worked hard in Birmingham, administered an orphanage with conspicuous success. But here was a man of insignificant stature, with a twinkling eye and a merry laugh, a stranger to dignity. Would he do? Wiseman's scholarship, Manning's statesmanship, Vaughan's social charm, Bourne's dogged resolution, Hinsley's splendid warmth of charity—would they be reflected in this cheerful stranger from Birmingham?

As usual, we were wrong and Rome was right. Two years after the appointment, the dictators had fallen, a Labour Government was in power, and we had entered the Age of the Common Man. We did not, after all, need an outstanding figure at Archbishop's House. We needed an official, patient in negotiation, quick to take decisions, business-like. Those years at the orphanage were not wasted; the new archbishop had learned how to deal with, and how to get on with, the not-quite-top levels in Whitehall. He was, above all, a representative churchman, none the worse for having worked his own way to the front, without any advantage of birth or influence.

This is not to suggest that he was a mediocrity. His early elevation to the Sacred College discovered in him a capacity for leadership on the international scale; for a brief period of years, Westminster counted, as perhaps never before, on the European and the imperial scene.

Those years were cut short by the heart trouble which made of him, at the end of his life, a tragic and heroic invalid. No man was ever more determined to burn himself to the socket; but the devoted care of those around him defeated, in some measure, his resolution. It

[1] Cardinal Griffin died on 20 August 1956. This appreciation was published in *The Sunday Times* on 26 August following.

was his heroism that he did so much, his tragedy that he could do so little. You detected a certain listlessness in his public appearances; he found it difficult to concentrate, for long, over the problems that still had to be submitted to him.

His death seems like a determined dash through the net of watchfulness that surrounded him.

Bishop Wand[1] has written his true epitaph in summing him up as a good Christian. He lived, always, very close to the supernatural.

I have often given a retreat meditation about "consolations" in prayer; if we had to do without them (I argued) we must not suppose that the divine goodness had deserted us; if we experience them, we must not imagine that we were the victims of a delusion.

Many people have thanked me for the first half of my thesis: only one for the second. It was Bernard Griffin.

[1] Bishop of London, 1945-55.

Index

Manning, Cardinal, 136, 240, 283, 296, 418

Margaret Clitherow, Bd, 130

Margaret Mary, St, 66

Marriage, *see* Matrimony

Martin, Gregory, 147

Martyrs, Apostles as, 5-6; English, 14; 103-154 *passim*, 170, 181, 246, 300, 400; Jewish, 114; relics of, 5, 109-110; saints as, 10; seed of Church, 201, 230; virgins as, 6; witnesses to truth, 250, 344

Mary, Blessed Virgin, Our Lady: Birthday, 379, 383; carpenter's wife at Nazareth, 150, 263, 307, 312-313; at Cenacle, 269, 281; chivalry and, 67, 213; devotion to, 208, 239, 252, 274, 280, 317, 338, 350, 354, 359, 413; early Church and, 235, 328-329; England as Dowry, 170, 198, 212, 391; of Fatima, 313; humility of, 33; Immaculate Conception, 83-90, 241; Immaculate Heart, 113; of Lourdes, 83-84, 86-90, 313, 320; and month of May, 108, 113-114; Mother of Christ, 38, 40-41, 150, 190, 200, 312-313; prayers invoked, 14, 19, 29, 99, 160, 175, 181, 186, 223, 322, 335; Queen of Peace, 19, 144; Reformation and, 124, 133, 162, 413; Rosary, 299; Saints and, 44, 56, 65, 121; suffering and, 295; virgins as handmaids, 60; Virginity of, 7, 175, 311; Visitation, 324, 326-327; of Walsingham, 162, 284

Mary I, Queen, 133, 137

Mass, Holy, and converts, 280, 350, 413; and English martyrs, 105, 124, 132-133, 143, 153; and priesthood, 228-229; renewal of Calvary, 206; and Saints, 53, 58, 266; and vernacular hymns, 76

Mathathias, and sons of, 62-63, 65

Materialism, 86, 176, 372-374, 403

Matrimony, 9, 25, 35, 41, 54, 107, 170, 180, 216, 284, 310-311, 321; mixed marriages, 8, 168-169

Matthew, St, Gospel of:
1.4: 379-380
5.13: 34, 71
6.28: 371-372
8.24: 79
13.52: 47
18.3: 95
19.19: 392

Matthews, Abbot Edmund, 406-409, 416

Maundy Thursday, 225

Mayne, *see* Cuthbert Mayne

Middle Ages, 11, 22, 63, 67, 72, 75, 91, 113, 117-118, 120, 213, 269, 287, 307, 325, 334, 341-342, 360

Milner, Bishop, 296, 352, 360

Motherwell, Diocese of, 379, 382-383

Modernism, 178, 180, 269, 334

Mohammedanism, 48, 55, 63, 213, 307

Monasteries, 32, 341; dissolution of, 153; monastic reform, 31-32

Mortification, 44, 60; of Saints, 113, 145

Moses, 14, 43, 61, 83-87, 89-90, 103, 166, 187-188, 190-191; Mosaic Law, 62, 114, 201, 203, 227, 277, 376-377, 388

Mount St Bernard Abbey, 311, 384

Myers, Archbishop, 45

Nazareth, 285, 307, 312-313, 380

Nehemias, Book of, 5: 383

Nevill, Fr Paul, 414-417

Newman, Cardinal John Henry, 74-75, 126, 136-139, 174, 234, 236-253, 259, 261, 270, 282, 297-298, 302, 309, 325-326, 337, 352, 360, 375-376, 384

Noe, 103

Nonconformists, 35, 177, 192, 193-196, 282, 299-300, 381

Nottingham, Diocese of, 308, 311, 384

Numbers, Book of, 12.3: 43

Oates, Titus, 153, 173

Old Testament, 60-61, 79, 90, 103, 273, 380, 392, 412 (*see also Bible references*)

Oliver Plunkett, Bd, 104, 165

Oratory, Congregation of (Oratorians), 63, 70, 73-74, 75-78, 237-238, 246, 248, 253, 259-260, 281-285, 317-320; Brompton Oratory, London, 207-209, 237, 251, 259, 261, 281-285, 317-320, 346, 348; Birmingham Oratory, 207, 237, 240, 246; Oratory School, 237

Orthodox Church, 177, 192, 194-199

Oscott, 297-298, 384-386

Oswald, St, 26

Oxford, University of, Catholic conversions and Second Spring in, 75, 136-137, 168, 236-241, 244, 251, 302, 324-325, 337; Chaplaincy, 267-270; martyrs of, 125-131, 138; religious Orders in, Benedictines, 255, Dominicans, 255, Franciscans, 157-160, Jesuits, 254-257, 269; Tractarian Movement, 137, 236-238, 241, 244, 251, 284

Ozanam, Frédéric, 233-234, 330

Paganism, 48, 73, 188, 190, 286-287, 356; pagan culture and Christianity, 341-345

Papacy, 5, 22, 34, 59, 73, 82, 110, 115-116, 124, 136, 158, 195, 198, 213, 293, 295, 351, 362, 286; and English Catholics, 296-297, 338; Infallibility of, 178, 386; Vatican Council, 178, 382

Paschal Baylon, St, 84

Passionists, 270-272, 302, 311

Patrick, St, 10

Paul, St, conversion of, 182-186, 188, 243, 355-358, 375-379, 388-391, 415, 417;